AF840833

Copyright Page

Data in Plain Sight

Finding, Classifying, and Protecting Sensitive Data Before AI Exposes It

Published by Heather Case-Hall.

Author: Heather Case-Hall
Book Title: *Data in Plain Sight*
Subtitle: *Finding, Classifying, and Protecting Sensitive Data Before AI Exposes It*

First Edition, 2026

ISBN: 979-8-9962638-0-6 (paperback)

ISBN: 979-8-9962638-1-3 (kindle)

ISBN: 979-8-9962638-3-7 (hardback)

Imprint: Heather Case-Hall

Printed in the United States of America

A Note on AI Assistance

This book was written with the assistance of ChatGPT, which feels appropriate for a book about protecting data before AI exposes it. I saw a need for a practical guide on DSPM, data security, and AI-era risk, and I used AI the same way many professionals do: as a brainstorming partner, editor, organizer, and occasionally a very patient writing assistant.

The thoughts, experience, judgment, and opinions are mine. AI helped make them clearer, cleaner, and less likely to wander off into a 47-page tangent. Any mistakes are mine too, because apparently even with AI, humans are still accountable.

Disclaimer and Release of Liability

The information in this book is provided for educational and informational purposes only. While every effort has been made to ensure the accuracy and usefulness of the material, the author and publisher make no warranties, express or implied, regarding the completeness, accuracy, reliability, or suitability of the information for any particular purpose.

This book does not constitute legal, regulatory, compliance, cybersecurity, financial, or professional advice. Readers are responsible for evaluating their own circumstances and should consult qualified professionals before making decisions based on the content of this book.

Cybersecurity tools, technologies, threats, laws, regulations, and industry practices change frequently. The examples, recommendations, exercises, templates, and scenarios included in this book may not apply to every environment or situation.

By using the information in this book, the reader agrees that the author, publisher, contributors, and associated parties shall not be held liable for any loss, damage, claim, security incident, business interruption, data loss, regulatory consequence, or other outcome arising directly or indirectly from the use or misuse of the information provided.

Any references to products, vendors, frameworks, organizations, or third-party materials are provided for illustrative purposes only and do not imply endorsement unless expressly stated.

Dedication

To my husband and children,

Thank you for your love, patience, encouragement, and belief in me through every chapter of my life and career. You have been my foundation, my motivation, and my reminder of what truly matters. This book exists because of the strength, support, and grace you have given me along the way.

To Bertrum Carroll,

My mentor, my friend, and the best boss I ever had.

Thank you for seeing something in me before I fully knew how to see it in myself. You gave me room to grow, permission to lead, and steady encouragement at a time when I was still learning to trust my own voice. You showed me that leadership can be strong and kind, and that good leaders protect people, develop people, and make room for them to become more than they believed they could be.

So much of who I am as a leader, mentor, and security professional carries your fingerprints. Thank you for believing in me, advocating for me, and taking the time to read and advise on the content of this book.

To Rory Townley,

Thank you for the conversations that helped shape the way this book thinks about data, knowledge, mission, and memory. Your perspective on data leadership and knowledge management helped me see more clearly that data is not only something organizations store or secure. It is the record of how people work, what they know, what they build, and what they leave behind for others to understand.

Your insight helped strengthen the heart of this book: that data security is not only about tools and controls. It is about stewardship, context, trust, and the responsibility to protect what matters before it is lost, misused, or exposed.

To my Myriad360 team,

Thank you for being part of this journey. Your collaboration, insight, curiosity, and commitment to solving meaningful security challenges continue to inspire me. Working alongside people who care deeply about customers, innovation, and doing the right thing has made this work even more meaningful.

This book is dedicated to the people who have supported, challenged, encouraged, and believed in me.

With gratitude,

Heather

Contents

Preface: A Practical Field Guide for Data Security in the AI Era

Data has become one of the most valuable assets an organization owns, and one of the hardest to protect well. It lives in cloud platforms, SaaS applications, databases, collaboration tools, data lakes, developer repositories, backups, endpoints, and AI systems. It is copied, moved, enriched, shared, analyzed, retained, forgotten, rediscovered, and often exposed in ways no single team fully understands.

That is the problem this book is meant to help solve.

This book is for security, privacy, data, risk, compliance, and technology leaders who need to build a practical data security program for the AI era. It is written for people who are responsible for reducing risk, enabling the business, supporting compliance, and making better decisions about how sensitive and business critical data is discovered, classified, governed, protected, monitored, and eventually retired.

You do not need to be a data scientist, attorney, cloud architect, or product specialist to use this book. You do need to care about one very important question:

How do we turn data visibility into measurable risk reduction and safer business use of data?

That question sits at the center of every chapter.

This book is not a vendor comparison guide. It is not a legal manual. It is not a substitute for privacy counsel, regulatory *interpretation*, or a formal compliance assessment. It is also not a purely technical implementation guide filled with product specific configuration steps. Technology matters, but tools alone do not create a data security program. A strong program also requires ownership, governance, operating models, policy decisions, risk prioritization, reporting, and business alignment.

Think of this book as a field guide. It is meant to help you understand the landscape, ask better questions, evaluate capabilities more clearly, and build a program that moves beyond dashboards and discovery reports. The goal is not just to know where sensitive data exists. The goal is to act on that knowledge in a repeatable, defensible, and measurable way.

How to Use This Book

This book can be read from beginning to end, but it is also designed for readers who need to jump directly into a problem they are facing.

If you are building a strategy, start with the early chapters on data security program foundations, business drivers, risk appetite, and governance. If you are evaluating tools, focus on the sections covering capability requirements, buying considerations, architecture, integrations, and operational fit. If you are implementing a program, spend time with the chapters on discovery, classification, access analysis, remediation workflows, operating models, and reporting.

If your priority is AI risk, look for the sections on data readiness, sensitive data exposure, model access, unstructured data, shadow data, and safe AI enablement. If you are modernizing or replacing DLP, pay close attention to the differences between prevention, posture management, access intelligence, and response. If you need to report progress to executives or the board, use the sections on metrics, maturity, risk reduction, and business aligned storytelling.

The chapters are connected, but they are not rigid. A mature organization may use this book to refine governance and measurement. A smaller or less mature organization may use it to establish a baseline and decide what to do first. A highly regulated organization may focus on defensibility, audit readiness, and control validation. A fast growing company may focus on practical guardrails that protect sensitive data without slowing the business down.

For CISOs and Security Leaders

This book is designed to help security leaders move data security from a tool conversation to an enterprise risk conversation. A CISO can use this book to define the business case for DSPM, align security with privacy and data governance, evaluate vendor capabilities, prioritize remediation, measure risk reduction, and report progress to executives and the board.

The central leadership question is not whether the organization owns a DSPM tool. The question is whether the organization can continuously answer: Where is sensitive data, who can access it, how is it exposed, whether its use is approved, who owns the risk, and whether risk is going down.

Definitions Used Throughout This Book

To avoid confusion, this book uses the following terms consistently:

Data Security Posture Management, or DSPM:
A set of capabilities and practices used to discover, classify, assess, prioritize, and reduce risk to sensitive and business critical data across cloud, SaaS, databases, data stores, and other environments. DSPM focuses on understanding where data lives, who or what can access it, how it is exposed, and what risks should be remediated.

Data Detection and Response, or DDR:
The monitoring and response layer of data security. DDR focuses on detecting risky or suspicious activity involving data, such as unusual access, movement, exposure, misuse, or potential exfiltration, and helping teams respond quickly.

Data Loss Prevention, or DLP:
Controls designed to prevent sensitive data from leaving approved locations or being shared in unauthorized ways. DLP is often associated with email, endpoints, web traffic, cloud applications, and content inspection. In this book, DLP is treated as one part of a broader data security program, not the entire program.

Data governance:
The policies, roles, responsibilities, decision rights, and processes used to manage data responsibly. Governance defines who owns data, how it should be handled, how policies are enforced, and how exceptions are managed.

Data cataloging:
The process of creating an inventory of data assets, often with metadata about location, ownership, schema, lineage, usage, and business context. Data catalogs are commonly used by data, analytics, and governance teams. They may overlap with security needs, but they are not the same as a data security platform.

Privacy tooling:
Technology used to support privacy operations such as data subject rights, consent management, privacy impact assessments, records of processing, retention workflows, and regulatory obligations. Privacy tooling is closely related to data security, but its purpose and primary users are often different.

This book will return to these distinctions often because many organizations blur these categories. That confusion can lead to poor buying decisions, unclear ownership, weak implementation, and unrealistic expectations.

The central idea is simple: visibility is only the beginning. The real value comes from what happens next. A successful data security program turns discovery into governance, governance into action, action into measurable risk reduction, and risk reduction into safer innovation. That is the work ahead.

Chapter 1: Why Data Security Changed

For years, most organizations believed they understood data security because they understood where their systems were.

The customer database lived in one place. The file shares lived somewhere else. Email had retention rules. Backups had recovery points. Security teams monitored the network. IT patched the servers. Privacy teams wrote notices and policies. Legal reviewed contracts. Audit tested controls.

It was never perfect, but it had shape.

Data security was treated as a technical discipline: encrypt the database, restrict access, monitor the network, back up the systems, and prepare for an incident. Privacy regulations pushed organizations to document how data was collected, stored, shared, retained, and deleted. Cybersecurity regulations pushed companies to harden systems and prove they could recover from disruption. Ransomware made executives pay attention because it threatened business continuity, revenue, and reputation.

Then the shape changed.

Artificial intelligence shifted the center of gravity.

The issue was no longer only whether data was protected. The issue became whether the organization could control how data was discovered, copied, summarized, interpreted, combined, inferred from, exposed, retained, reused, and trusted.

That is why data security feels different now.

AI does not simply access data the way traditional applications do. It consumes context. It searches across repositories. It summarizes information, generates new content, connects data from multiple sources, and creates outputs that can look authoritative even when the underlying data is stale, overexposed, incomplete, or misunderstood.

A spreadsheet, contract, customer record, support ticket, source-code repository, email thread, or data lake table can move from a controlled business system into a model, vector database, SaaS copilot, prompt log, third-party API, or autonomous workflow. Once that happens, the old questions about where the database is hosted or whether a server is patched are no longer enough.

The new question is harder:

Can the organization govern the data wherever it goes, however it is used, and whatever it becomes?

That question sits at the center of this book.

1.1 The Old Data-Security Model

The old model of data security was built around containment.

Data was assumed to live in systems owned or approved by the company. Security teams protected networks, endpoints, databases, applications, cloud accounts, and identity platforms. Privacy teams tracked personal information, consent, deletion requests, and regulatory obligations. Infrastructure teams managed backups and disaster recovery. Legal teams reviewed contracts. Audit teams tested controls.

The model was imperfect, but it had boundaries.

A customer database sat in a data center or cloud platform. A file share had permissions. A SaaS platform had an administrator. A data warehouse had roles. A backup system had recovery points. A vendor contract had security language. A breach had an investigation path.

That world still exists, but it is no longer the whole story.

A generative AI assistant may search across documents, messages, tickets, and knowledge bases. A retrieval-augmented generation system may convert enterprise content into embeddings and store them in a vector database. A developer may use production data to test an AI feature. A sales team may upload customer call transcripts into an AI note-taking service. A business unit may connect a copilot to shared drives that were never cleaned up.

A model may not "store" the original document in the traditional sense, but it may still produce sensitive output based on that document. A user may not download a file, but they may ask an AI assistant to summarize its contents. A third-party tool may not look like a database, but it may retain prompts, logs, outputs, metadata, or derived content.

The security issue is no longer only unauthorized access.

It is also authorized overexposure.

That is the heart of the change. Many AI-related data risks do not begin because a hacker broke in. They begin because an approved user, approved integration, approved workflow, or approved AI feature has access to data that should not be available for that purpose.

1.2 Regulations Were Warning Us All Along

AI did not make data security important.

It made weak data security harder to hide.

For years, privacy and cybersecurity regulations were already pointing organizations toward the same basic discipline: know what data you have, protect it based on risk, limit unnecessary collection and access, delete it when required, retain it when legally necessary, recover it after disruption, oversee third parties, and prove that controls are working.

The problem was not that the rules were silent. The problem was that many organizations treated them as compliance paperwork instead of operational requirements.

A privacy notice could be published while old personal data remained scattered across file shares. A retention schedule could exist while no one knew which SaaS platforms contained regulated data. A vendor questionnaire could be completed without anyone understanding what data actually moved to the vendor. A backup plan could be documented without a clear view of which data mattered most to restore first.

AI exposes the weakness in that model.

A company cannot honor deletion rights if it cannot find personal data. It cannot apply minimization if every copilot can index broad repositories. It cannot govern third-party AI use if sensitive data is flowing into prompts, logs, embeddings, or model-evaluation datasets. It cannot prove appropriate security if the evidence lives in disconnected tools and undocumented workflows.

GDPR warned organizations about security, deletion, minimization, and data protection by design. NYDFS emphasized encryption, asset inventories, secure disposal, third-party risk, and recovery. CCPA and CPRA strengthened deletion rights, reasonable security expectations, and downstream obligations for service providers and contractors. HIPAA required safeguards for electronic protected health information. GLBA and the FTC Safeguards Rule connected customer information protection to governance, vendor oversight, and board reporting. SEC cybersecurity disclosure rules elevated cyber risk, material incidents, and board oversight into investor-facing obligations. The EU AI Act connected AI governance directly to data governance and cybersecurity for high-risk AI systems.

Different laws. Different industries. Different enforcement models.

Same direction of travel.

Organizations are increasingly expected to know where sensitive data exists, how it is protected, who can access it, why it is retained, how it moves, who processes it, whether it can be deleted, whether it can be restored, and whether the organization can prove its answers.

AI makes those expectations more urgent because AI changes the speed and scale of data use.

A privacy team may have spent years building a process for data subject requests, only to discover that personal information now exists in prompt logs, AI-generated summaries, embeddings, SaaS exports, and collaboration tools that were never part of the original data map. A security team may have encrypted databases and hardened cloud accounts, only to find that users are pasting regulated data into AI tools because the approved process feels too slow. A legal team may have negotiated vendor terms, only to learn that an AI-enabled feature was activated inside a platform the business already used.

The rules did not suddenly change overnight.

The operating environment did.

1.3 Ransomware Made Data a Boardroom Problem

Before AI dominated the conversation, ransomware forced executives and boards to care about data in a different way.

A ransomware event does not begin as an abstract security issue. It becomes practical very quickly. Can employees work? Can customers be served? Can orders be processed? Can patients be treated? Can payroll run? Can the company invoice? Can the business recover before money, trust, and patience run out?

That is why ransomware changed the tone of data security.

It made availability real.

Backups stopped being a quiet infrastructure topic. Recovery time became a business question. Leaders who had never asked about data dependencies suddenly wanted to know which systems mattered most, which data had to come back first, and whether recovery plans had ever been tested under pressure.

Verizon's 2025 Data Breach Investigations Report found that ransomware was present in 44% of breaches, an increase from the previous year, and that third-party involvement in breaches had doubled to 30%. The same report highlighted vulnerability exploitation and credential abuse as major initial access vectors.

Those findings reinforce what many security leaders already feel: disruption rarely stays inside one technical lane. A single incident can involve infrastructure, identity, third parties, cloud platforms, backups, business continuity, legal exposure, customer trust, and executive accountability.

NYDFS's business continuity and disaster recovery requirements reflect this same shift. The regulation expects covered entities to maintain written plans for incident response, business continuity, and disaster recovery, including recovery from backups and identification of essential data, facilities, infrastructure, services, and personnel.

Ransomware made organizations care about whether data could be recovered.

AI makes organizations care about whether data should have been exposed, indexed, copied, inferred from, or used in the first place.

Both concerns matter.

One asks whether the business can get its data back.

The other asks whether the data should have been available to that user, system, model, vendor, or workflow at all.

1.4 AI Changed the Risk Model

AI changes data security because it changes the way data is used.

Traditional applications usually perform defined transactions. A user logs into a system, opens a record, runs a report, updates a field, exports a file, or sends a message. Security teams can monitor many of those actions because the workflows, systems, and movement patterns are relatively predictable.

AI systems operate differently.

They consume context. They search across repositories. They summarize information. They generate new content. They combine data from multiple sources. They automate decisions or workflows. They may rely on prompts, embeddings, retrieval systems, plugins, agents, APIs, vector databases, and model outputs. In the process, they often create new copies or derived forms of sensitive information in places the original data owner never expected.

That is why AI turns old data problems into urgent enterprise risks.

A forgotten file share is no longer just a messy permission issue. It may become source material for a copilot. A stale customer export is no longer just a retention problem. It may be uploaded into an AI analytics tool. An overprivileged user is no longer just an access-control concern. That user may now ask an AI system to summarize, extract, correlate, or combine information at massive scale. A third-party SaaS platform is no longer only a vendor-risk consideration. It may become an AI processing environment capable of storing prompts, generating derived outputs, or retaining sensitive context.

AI also changes human behavior inside the organization.

Employees are under pressure to move faster, collaborate broadly, and adopt productivity tools that promise to save time. When approved workflows feel too restrictive, too slow, or too difficult, users often look for another path. Sometimes that path is an unsanctioned SaaS platform. Sometimes it is a browser-based AI tool. Sometimes it is a personal device. Sometimes it is a feature quietly added to a tool the organization already approved.

In many organizations, shadow AI adoption is not driven primarily by malicious intent. It is driven by convenience, speed, workflow friction, and the belief that the business cannot wait for governance to catch up.

This creates an uncomfortable reality for modern security programs:

Controls that are technically secure but operationally unusable often fail because users route around them.

Effective data security programs must balance governance with usability. Security teams are no longer only protecting systems from attackers. They are also designing workflows that users will realistically follow under pressure.

Research and industry guidance point in the same direction. The OWASP Top 10 for Large Language Model Applications identifies risks directly tied to data security, including prompt injection, sensitive information disclosure, supply-chain vulnerabilities, insecure output handling, and training data poisoning. IBM's 2025 Cost of a Data Breach research points to a growing AI governance gap and emphasizes foundational controls such as data discovery, classification, access control, encryption, and key management. The World Economic Forum has also observed that AI increases the attack surface, that data fuels AI, and that cybersecurity must be embedded throughout the AI lifecycle rather than added after deployment.

The message is consistent.

AI does not create the need for data security.

It exposes the weakness of data-security programs that were never designed for AI-speed data use.

1.5 The Core Change: From Securing Systems to Governing Data

The most important shift is architectural.

For decades, security programs were organized around systems: endpoints, servers, applications, networks, databases, cloud accounts, and identities. Those controls still matter. They are not going away. But AI forces organizations to focus on the data itself.

A modern data-security program has to know what sensitive data exists, where it lives, who can access it, why that access exists, whether the data is encrypted, whether it can be deleted, how long it should be retained, whether AI can use it, whether that use is appropriate, and whether the organization can prove the answer.

These are not abstract governance questions anymore.

They determine whether AI can be deployed safely. They determine whether privacy rights can be honored. They determine whether a breach can be scoped. They determine whether legal hold can be applied correctly. They determine whether a board can rely on management's statements about risk. They determine whether a customer, regulator, auditor, or business partner will believe the organization's story after something goes wrong.

This is why Data Security Posture Management has become so important. DSPM reflects a broader movement from infrastructure-centric control to data-centric control. The goal is not merely to secure the database. The goal is to continuously discover sensitive data, classify it, understand exposure, map access, identify risky movement, enforce policy, and remediate weaknesses.

AI turns DSPM from a useful capability into a foundational requirement.

1.6 Why Traditional Controls Are No Longer Enough by Themselves

Traditional security controls still matter. Encryption, access control, DLP, vendor risk management, backup, disaster recovery, privacy notices, retention schedules, and policy frameworks are all necessary.

They are just not enough by themselves.

Encryption is essential, but it does not determine whether a user should be allowed to send regulated data to an AI tool. Access control is essential, but it does not determine whether a copilot should index every file a user can technically open. Data loss prevention is useful, but many DLP programs struggle to understand context, lineage, purpose, model behavior, embeddings, or AI-generated outputs.

Vendor risk management is necessary, but a questionnaire alone does not show what sensitive data is actually being transmitted, stored, logged, retained, or used for model improvement. Backup and disaster recovery are critical, but they do not solve overexposure, oversharing, unlawful retention, or improper AI use. Privacy notices and policies matter, but they do not, by themselves, discover forgotten datasets, stale exports, shadow AI workflows, or excessive entitlements.

I have been in conversations where a customer could explain the firewall rules, the backup architecture, the identity provider, and the cloud tenant, but no one could confidently explain what sensitive data was inside a collaboration platform.

Everyone knew the system.

No one knew the data.

That is the gap.

This is not an argument against traditional controls. It is an argument that traditional controls must be connected to live data intelligence. AI requires organizations to understand data in context, including sensitivity, ownership, location, access, purpose, lineage, retention, regulatory obligations, third-party exposure, and AI usage.

Without that context, organizations may have controls in place but still lack the visibility needed to govern how sensitive data is used, shared, retained, and exposed in AI-enabled environments.

1.7 The New Board-Level Concern

Data security has become a board-level issue because the business risk has changed.

Ransomware can stop operations. Data breaches can create legal, regulatory, contractual, and reputational consequences. AI misuse can expose trade secrets, personal data, regulated records, confidential strategy, source code, customer information, or privileged communications. What was once viewed as a technical control issue now has direct consequences for business continuity, market trust, regulatory exposure, investor confidence, and executive accountability.

The regulatory environment has also expanded. Privacy, cybersecurity, financial services, healthcare, and AI regulations increasingly expect organizations to show governance, documentation, risk assessment, access control, encryption, minimization, deletion, resilience, and third-party oversight. SEC cybersecurity disclosure rules further connect cybersecurity risk management and governance to public-company disclosure obligations.

At the same time, AI adoption is no longer limited to the security team or the data science team. It is being used across sales, marketing, finance, HR, engineering, legal, customer support, analytics, and operations. As a result, data-security decisions are often being made implicitly by users and business units far outside traditional security review.

Boards do not need to understand every technical detail of embeddings, prompts, APIs, model tuning, or vector databases.

They do need to understand whether management knows what sensitive data the organization has, whether that data is properly governed, whether AI systems can access it, whether third parties can use it, whether deletion and retention obligations can be met, and whether the organization can provide evidence.

That is where data sovereignty becomes especially important.

Historically, data sovereignty was treated primarily as a legal, privacy, or cloud-hosting concern. Organizations focused on where data was stored, which jurisdiction applied, and whether cross-border transfer requirements were satisfied.

AI changes that conversation.

In the AI era, sovereignty is not only about where data resides. It is also about where data is processed, indexed, embedded, retrieved, logged, enriched, inferred from, and used to generate decisions or outputs. A company may keep its primary database in an approved region while still allowing sensitive data to flow into prompts, vector stores, SaaS copilots, model-evaluation datasets, support logs, or third-party AI services outside the expected governance boundary.

That makes data sovereignty a strategic AI risk.

If the organization cannot explain which data is available to AI systems, where that data is processed, what jurisdictions apply, which vendors handle it, and whether derived AI artifacts can be retained or deleted, then the AI strategy is being built on an unstable foundation.

1.8 What Changed Inside the Organization

AI has moved data security from a specialist function to an enterprise responsibility.

Security teams still own many controls, but they cannot solve the problem alone. Privacy teams understand lawful basis, consent, deletion, minimization, and regulatory rights. Legal teams understand privilege, contracts, litigation holds, and regulatory exposure. Data teams understand pipelines, warehouses, lakes, quality, and lineage. IT teams understand identity, SaaS, endpoints, and collaboration tools. Business units understand how data is actually used. Boards and executives own risk appetite.

AI forces all of these groups into the same conversation.

The new data-security operating model has to bring together ownership, access, approved use, third-party processing, encryption, exposure, retention, legal hold, regulatory category, business criticality, recovery, monitoring, and evidence. Those topics used to live in separate parts of the organization. AI connects them because AI uses data across organizational boundaries.

That is why the old handoff model breaks down.

Security cannot simply tell the business to classify everything. Privacy cannot simply assume personal data is inside known systems. Legal cannot manage retention without knowing where copies exist. IT cannot secure data it does not understand. Data teams cannot make information useful if security and privacy requirements are bolted on afterward. Business teams cannot safely adopt AI if they do not understand the sensitivity and ownership of the data being connected.

The work has become shared.

That does not mean every team owns everything. It means every team has a piece of the answer.

AI turned latent data problems into active business risk.

1.9 The New Data-Security Principles

The organizations that succeed in the AI era will treat data security as a continuous discipline, not a one-time project.

The first principle is continuous discovery. You cannot secure data you cannot find. Discovery must include structured data, unstructured data, SaaS platforms, cloud storage, data lakes, collaboration tools, endpoints, backups, logs, and AI-connected repositories.

The second principle is classification with context. Labels such as "confidential" or "restricted" are helpful only when they reflect real meaning. Classification should consider regulatory category, business sensitivity, ownership, age, location, exposure, access, purpose, and AI usage.

The third principle is exposure reduction before AI amplification. Overpermissioned data becomes more dangerous when AI can search, summarize, and combine it. Access reviews, least privilege, data segmentation, and purpose-based controls are now AI-readiness requirements.

The fourth principle is governed data movement. Sensitive data should not move into prompts, embeddings, AI logs, third-party platforms, test environments, or training datasets without policy, approval, monitoring, and contractual control.

The fifth principle is lifecycle discipline. Organizations must be able to retain what they are required to retain, delete what they are required to delete, recover what they need to recover, and explain what happened to the data along the way. AI copies, derivatives, logs, and summaries make this harder, not optional.

These principles are not separate from the business. They are how the business earns the right to use data safely.

CISO Takeaway

A CISO cannot govern AI safely without governing the data AI can access.

The security program must move beyond protecting systems and toward continuous understanding of data: where it lives, who can access it, how it is exposed, whether it is approved for use, what obligations apply, and whether risk is going down.

Key Takeaways

Data security did not become important because of AI. Privacy, cybersecurity, financial services, healthcare, and AI regulations had already been pointing organizations toward better data governance for years.

Ransomware made data availability a boardroom issue because it threatened business continuity and recovery.

AI made data exposure a boardroom issue because it changed how data is accessed, copied, summarized, inferred from, reused, and exposed.

Traditional controls still matter, but they are not enough without live data intelligence and business context.

The old model asked whether the organization could protect the systems that stored data.

The new model asks whether the organization can govern data wherever it goes, however it is used, and whatever it becomes.

That is a much harder question.

It is also the question every organization now has to answer.

Chapter 2: Data as Mission, Memory, and Risk

Data has always mattered, but most organizations do not always treat it that way.

For a long time, data was treated as something that lived inside something else. It lived inside an application, a database, a file share, an email system, a ticketing platform, a cloud bucket, a backup repository, or a business workflow. The system had a name. The system had an owner. The system had an administrator. The system had a budget, a support model, and sometimes even a disaster recovery plan.

The data inside that system was often treated as secondary.

If the application was running, the business assumed the data was available. If the database was encrypted, security assumed the data was protected. If the file share had permissions, IT assumed access was controlled. If the platform was backed up, leadership assumed the organization could recover.

Each of those assumptions contains some truth, but none of them are complete.

A system can be available while the data inside it is unmanaged. A database can be encrypted while access is excessive. A SaaS platform can be approved while its contents are unknown. A ticketing system can be operational while quietly collecting sensitive employee, customer, legal, or financial information no one intended to store there. A collaboration site can be backed up and still contain stale content that should have been archived, deleted, restricted, or excluded from AI.

That is the shift this chapter is about.

Modern organizations can no longer afford to think only in terms of systems. Systems still matter. They must be secured, patched, monitored, recovered, and governed. But data has become the thing that drives decisions, feeds automation, trains AI, proves compliance, supports operations, preserves history, and creates risk.

The system still matters.

But the data has become the mission.

2.1 The System View

IT teams are often asked to keep the organization running under conditions that are more complicated than most people appreciate. They support users, maintain platforms, manage identity, troubleshoot access, migrate systems, restore services, respond to outages, patch vulnerabilities, support projects, and explain why something broke before the business has fully described what happened.

Because of that, IT naturally sees the world through systems. There is an email system, a collaboration system, a customer system, a financial system, a ticketing system, a cloud environment, a backup platform, and a collection of applications that all need to function. This view is necessary. No organization can operate if its systems are unreliable.

But a system view has limits.

Most organizations can produce a reasonable inventory of their major platforms. They know where Microsoft 365 is. They know where Salesforce is. They know where ServiceNow is. They know which cloud providers they use. They know where the data warehouse lives. They know which backup platform protects critical systems.

What they often cannot produce is a reliable inventory of the sensitive, regulated, business-critical, stale, duplicated, overexposed, or AI-accessible data inside those platforms.

That gap is where modern data risk lives.

It becomes visible after a breach, an audit, a privacy request, a cloud migration, an AI rollout, or a leadership change. Suddenly the organization is not being asked whether the platform exists. It is being asked what was in it, who could access it, whether that access was appropriate, how long the data had been there, whether it should have been retained, and whether anyone can prove the answer.

That is a very different problem from keeping a system online.

2.2 Data Is Evidence of Work

One of the reasons data is hard to govern is that it rarely looks important at the moment it is created.

A user exports a report because the official dashboard does not answer the question quickly enough. A manager builds a spreadsheet because the workflow is too slow. A team creates a SharePoint folder because it is easier than requesting a new application. Someone uploads an attachment into a service ticket because that is the fastest way to get help. A training video is recorded during a system rollout and forgotten after the project closes. A process document is saved in a folder with a name that makes perfect sense to the person who created it and makes no sense to anyone else.

Years later, those artifacts become part of the organization's memory. The spreadsheet explains a decision no one remembers making. The folder reveals how a process worked, not how the policy said it worked. The ticket attachment shows what data customers were sending into support. The training video captures knowledge that never made it into formal documentation. What looked like clutter becomes evidence.

Data is not just content.

It is evidence of work.

It represents decisions, habits, shortcuts, obligations, mistakes, institutional memory, and human effort. It tells the story of what people were trying to accomplish with the tools they had at the time.

That is why old or messy data should not be dismissed too quickly. Some of it is clutter. Some of it is risk. Some of them are the only remaining record of how the organization actually works. A mature data security program must learn the difference.

2.3 The Memory Problem

Every organization has a memory problem.

People leave. Leaders rotate. Teams reorganize. Systems are replaced. Projects are renamed. Platforms are migrated. Custom tools are retired. Business processes evolve. What was once obvious becomes mysterious.

A process may have been created ten years ago by someone who understood the mission, the users, the constraints, and the reason the system was designed a certain way. That person leaves, but the process remains. The next person inherits the workflow but not the story. They learn enough to keep it moving, then add their own workaround. Over time, the process becomes a stack of decisions made by people who are no longer there.

The data remains, but the context fades.

That fading context is one of the most overlooked risks in cybersecurity and data governance. When an organization no longer understands why data exists, it struggles to decide how to protect it. It does not know whether the data is still accurate. It does not know whether it is still needed. It does not know who should own it. It does not know whether access is appropriate. It does not know whether the data can be deleted, archived, migrated, shared, or connected to AI.

This is where knowledge management becomes more than documentation.

Knowledge management is the discipline of turning what people know into something the organization can use, preserve, protect, and improve. It captures the tacit knowledge that sits in people's heads and turns it into explicit knowledge that can be transferred, challenged, refined, and governed.

That matters deeply for data security.

A scan can tell you that sensitive data exists in a repository. It may even tell you what type of sensitive data it found. But it cannot always tell you why the data is there, whether it still matters, whether it is the authoritative copy, whether it supports a critical process, or whether deleting it would break something important.

For that, you need people.

You need the assistant who knows how approvals really move. You need the administrator who knows which shared drive everyone uses even though the official process says otherwise. You need the analyst who knows which report is trusted and which one is outdated. You need the person who has been quietly holding the process together for years.

Data security is technical, but it is also historical.

It depends on memory.

2.4 A Conversation That Changed the Frame

This chapter grew out of a conversation with my friend and mentee, Rory Townley, whose work in data leadership and knowledge management helped me think differently about the relationship between data, systems, people, and mission.

We were talking about data security, but the conversation quickly moved beyond cybersecurity tools. Rory described data operations as the foundation, information management as the systems layer, and knowledge management as the discipline that turns what people know into something the organization can use. That framing stayed with me because it explains a gap I have seen across many organizations.

Security teams often protect the environment. IT teams often keep the systems running. Data teams often manage pipelines, warehouses, quality, and analytics. Privacy and legal teams interpret obligations. Business teams know how work actually gets done. But the data itself crosses all of those boundaries.

No single team sees the whole picture.

Rory used the language of mission, but the lesson applies to any organization. Data is not just the material left behind by business systems. It is the memory of the organization. It is the record of what people built, decided, repaired, approved, changed, rejected, and learned.

When that memory is unmanaged, organizations repeat mistakes. They rebuild what already existed. They lose context during staff transitions. They migrate data without understanding it. They preserve what should have been destroyed and destroy what should have been preserved. They connect AI to repositories that were never ready for AI.

The result is not just inefficiency.

It is risk.

2.5 The Lifecycle We Pretend Not to See

Most organizations are better at starting things than ending them.

They launch new tools, create new repositories, build new workflows, migrate to new platforms, and announce new initiatives. Starting feels productive. It has energy. It has funding. It has executive attention. It has a project plan.

Ending things is harder.

Retiring old systems, cleaning up old data, closing stale workspaces, removing unnecessary access, deleting outdated content, and documenting what should happen next rarely receives the same attention. The organization moves on, but the data stays behind.

Over time, the organization ends up with an estate of both value and liability. Some records still carry operational, legal, historical, or business importance. Some contain sensitive information that should be restricted. Some are outdated but useful for training or context. Some are redundant copies that increase exposure without adding value. Some should have been destroyed years ago.

The risk is not that old data exists.

The risk is that no one can reliably tell which category it belongs to.

That is how data becomes an archaeological record of past business decisions. Layer by layer, the organization accumulates old exports, retired project folders, duplicated reports, archived emails, unused Teams sites, stale SharePoint libraries, forgotten databases, abandoned applications, and backups of things no one has looked at in years.

Some of that data should be preserved. Some should be modernized. Some should be restricted. Some should be defensibly destroyed. Some should be excluded from AI. Some should be moved carefully because it still carries value.

The problem is that many organizations do not know which is which.

They keep everything because deletion feels risky. They move everything because migration timelines are tight. They restrict nothing because access cleanup is politically hard. They classify nothing because the work feels overwhelming. They connect AI because the business wants speed.

Then they wonder why data security feels impossible.

Data has a lifecycle whether the organization manages it or not. It is created, used, shared, copied, modified, stored, archived, rediscovered, and eventually retired or abandoned. When that lifecycle is unmanaged, risk grows quietly. By the time the organization notices, the problem is no longer a single repository or system. It is years of accumulated decisions that were never revisited.

A good data security program does not pretend this lifecycle can be avoided.

It brings the lifecycle into the operating model.

2.6 Data as a Strategic Asset

The Department of Defense Data Strategy provides a useful way to think about data, even outside a military context. This book does not use the DoD Data Strategy as a requirement for commercial organizations. It uses it as a practical reference model because it explains something every organization now needs to understand.

Data must be usable and protected at the same time.

The DoD strategy frames data as a strategic asset and describes a data-centric organization as one that can use data at speed and scale for operational advantage and increased efficiency. That language was written for the defense mission, but the business lesson is broader. Every modern organization is trying to move faster, make better decisions, reduce waste, improve resilience, and use data more intelligently.

The private sector may describe the mission differently, but the pressure is the same. Leaders want data that can support action before the moment has passed.

That is why this framework belongs in a business conversation about data security.

Most companies already have data everywhere. They have customer data, employee data, financial data, operational data, product data, contracts, tickets, emails, recordings, reports, source code, chat messages, knowledge articles, logs, backups, analytics outputs, and AI-generated content. The problem is not that data is missing. The problem is that much of it is not managed in a way that makes it dependable, secure, or ready for reuse.

The DoD framework helps explain why.

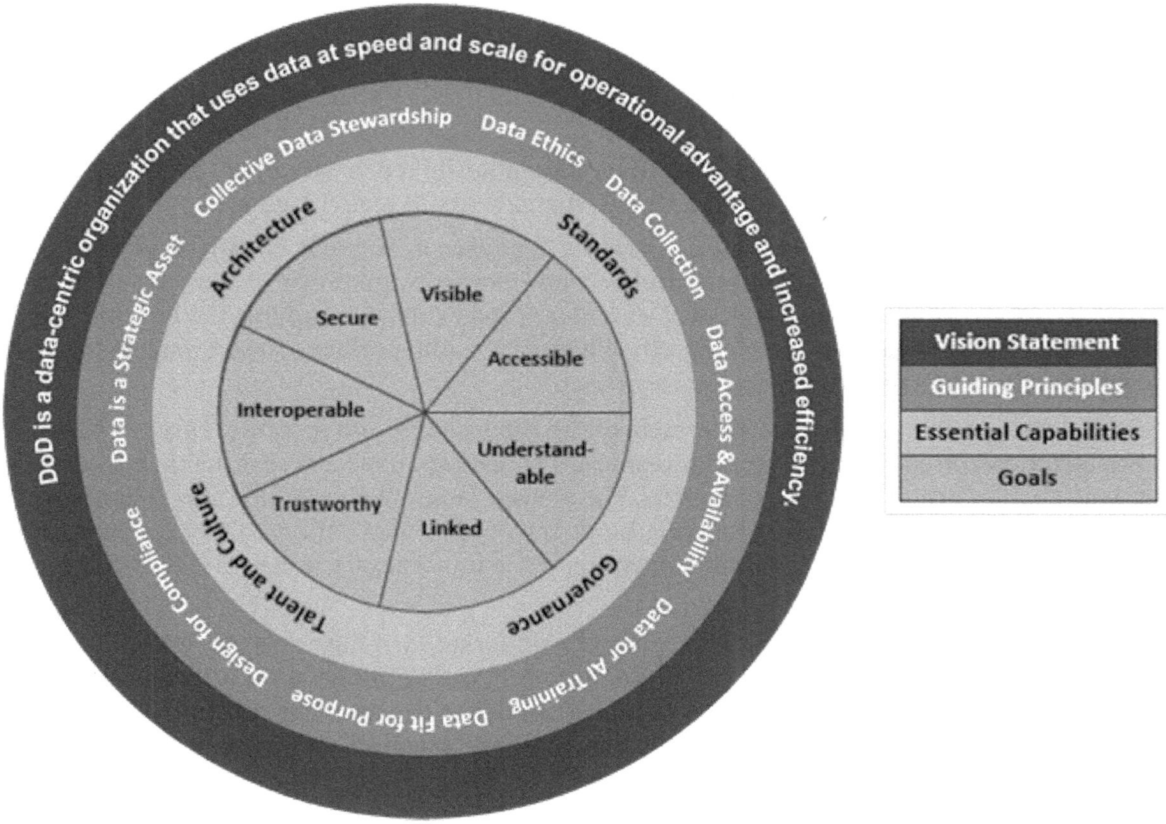

Figure 1: DoD Data Strategy Framework. The VAULTIS goals provide a practical lens for helping organizations understand whether data is ready to be found, used, trusted, shared, protected, and governed at scale.

At the outside of the model is the outcome: a data-centric organization that uses data at speed and scale. Inside that are the principles that must surround data before it can become useful at scale. Data has to be treated as a strategic asset, not as exhaust from business systems. It has to be stewarded collectively because no single team understands every business, legal, technical, security, and operational meaning attached to it. It has to be governed ethically, collected with care, made available to authorized users, prepared for AI, fit for purpose, and designed for compliance from the beginning.

That is a very different conversation from simply asking whether a database is encrypted or whether a file share has permissions.

For a company, adopting the spirit of this strategy means accepting that data security is not only about locking information down. It is about making data safe enough to use. A business cannot become more intelligent if its data is invisible, inaccessible, confusing, disconnected, untrusted, trapped in isolated systems, or insecure. At the same time, a business cannot safely innovate if every repository is broadly available, poorly classified, over-permissioned, and connected to AI without ownership or review.

The center of the model, VAULTIS, gives organizations a practical way to understand this balance.

2.7 The VAULTIS Lens

VAULTIS stands for visible, accessible, understandable, linked, trustworthy, interoperable, and secure. It is useful because it describes data maturity in plain language.

Data must be visible before anyone can protect it, govern it, delete it, classify it, or use it. Invisible data is the most dangerous kind because it creates unknown risk. It may sit in an old SharePoint site, an abandoned project folder, a SaaS export, a support ticket, a backup, or a cloud bucket no one remembers. When a breach, audit, privacy request, migration, or AI rollout occurs, invisible data becomes a crisis.

Once data is visible, it has to be accessible to the right people and systems. This is where organizations often struggle. Security teams are trained to restrict access, while business teams need information to move quickly. The answer is not to choose one side. The answer is governed access. Data should be available to the people, applications, analytics platforms, and AI systems that have a legitimate purpose, while unnecessary access is reduced before it becomes exposure.

Accessibility is not enough if the data cannot be understood. A file, table, or report may be technically available, but still useless or dangerous if no one knows what it means, where it came from, whether it is current, or whether it applies to the decision in front of them. This is why metadata, classification, ownership, lineage, and business context matter. Data without context becomes a guessing game.

Linked data is where the organization begins to see relationships. A customer record connects to a contract, a support ticket, a payment history, a privacy request, a data retention rule, and perhaps an AI use case. A security finding connects to a data owner, an identity group, a business process, and a remediation workflow. When data is linked, the organization can move beyond isolated facts and begin to understand impact.

Trustworthy data is the point where leadership can depend on the answer. This is especially important in AI-enabled environments. AI can summarize, combine, and present information confidently, even when the underlying data is stale, duplicated, biased, incomplete, or wrong. Trustworthy data requires quality, accuracy, freshness, lineage, and accountability. Without those, faster decisions may simply become faster mistakes.

Interoperable data allows the organization to move information across systems without losing meaning. This is where many modernization efforts fail. A company may migrate data from one platform to another, but if the structure, labels, ownership, and context do not move with it, the organization has not modernized the data. It has only changed its location. Interoperability is what allows data to travel safely across cloud, SaaS, analytics, security, privacy, governance, and AI environments.

Secure data completes the model, but it does not sit apart from the others. Security is woven through every stage. Data cannot be securely accessible if access is not governed. It cannot be securely linked if relationships expose sensitive information to the wrong audience. It cannot be securely used for AI if classification, retention, consent, ownership, and purpose are unclear.

Security is not the final lock placed on data after innovation happens.

Security is the condition that allows data to be used with confidence.

2.8 Where Legacy Controls Fit

The VAULTIS model helps explain why older security controls still matter, but also why they are not enough by themselves.

Legacy security tools were built to protect known systems, known data types, known users, and known movement patterns. DLP, CASB, database security, and CSPM all remain important controls. They each solve part of the data security problem. The issue is that they were not designed to continuously answer the full data security question across the entire lifecycle of the data.

Traditional DLP tools protect data primarily through policies, patterns, regular expressions, fingerprinting, dictionaries, and monitored channels such as email, web uploads, removable media, and cloud storage. CASB platforms help govern sanctioned and unsanctioned cloud application usage. Database security tools monitor, encrypt, mask, or control known databases. CSPM tools identify risky cloud configurations and compliance drift.

Each tool has value.

But each tool also depends on assumptions that are often incomplete.

DLP assumes the organization knows which data patterns matter and which channels must be watched. CASB assumes the relevant cloud applications and user behaviors are visible enough to govern. Database security assumes the sensitive data is still in known databases and protected by the right database-level controls. CSPM assumes that cloud configuration risk can be understood without always knowing the sensitivity, ownership, and business context of the data inside the resource.

That assumption is often wrong.

In practice, organizations rarely have a complete handle on all the data that matters to users, customers, executives, regulators, auditors, and business partners. Sensitive data may exist in production databases, analytics warehouses, SaaS platforms, backups, developer environments, logs, exports, spreadsheets, collaboration platforms, support tickets, and AI prompts. Once data is copied, transformed, uploaded, exported, embedded, summarized, or moved into a new environment, legacy controls may lose context.

I have seen this firsthand with tools such as Forcepoint, Symantec DLP, and Cisco Umbrella. These products can be valuable. They can enforce policy, inspect traffic, reduce certain kinds of leakage, and help security teams control known channels. But they are not a substitute for continuous data discovery, classification, entitlement analysis, exposure mapping, and risk prioritization.

A DLP rule may block a Social Security number from leaving through email. That is useful. But the same data may already have been copied into a cloud warehouse, exported into a spreadsheet, uploaded into a SaaS workflow, pasted into a ticket, synced to a collaboration space, or entered into a generative AI prompt. The DLP control may have worked exactly as designed and still not answer the more important question: where else does this data live, who can reach it, and what risk does it create now?

That is the difference between controlling a channel and understanding data posture.

2.9 When the Data Leaves the Expected Path

The problem has become more urgent because exfiltration is no longer limited to traditional channels such as email, browsers, removable media, and cloud storage.

In many organizations, data exposure now happens through ordinary productivity workflows. A user pastes code into an AI tool to debug it. A sales team uploads customer call transcripts into an AI note-taking application. A project manager uses a generative AI assistant to summarize a confidential strategy document. A developer sends logs to an external service without realizing the logs contain customer identifiers. A business unit adopts an AI-enabled SaaS feature that was never reviewed as an AI tool because it arrived quietly inside an application users already trusted.

The user may not be trying to steal data.

The user may be trying to work faster.

That is why this problem is so difficult. Traditional data loss language often assumes a clear line between approved work and unauthorized movement. AI blurs that line. Sensitive data can leave the organization because an employee is trying to improve productivity, not because the employee intends harm.

Samsung became an early public example of this risk when employees reportedly entered sensitive semiconductor source code, equipment-related code, and meeting content into ChatGPT. Samsung later restricted employee use of generative AI tools and limited prompt size. More recently, research cited by Axios from Harmonic Security found sensitive corporate data in more than four percent of generative AI prompts and more than twenty percent of uploaded files across a sample of AI and AI-enabled SaaS applications.

These examples show that data loss has expanded beyond classic exfiltration.

It now includes everyday use.

2.10 What Breaches Teach About Legacy Control Gaps

Major breaches and investigations show the same pattern from different angles. Organizations do not usually fail because one tool was missing. They fail because sensitive data was copied, over-permissioned, insufficiently monitored, poorly governed, or exposed through approved systems and identities.

The Desjardins breach is a useful example because it was not a simple perimeter failure. A malicious employee exfiltrated personal information over a period of at least twenty-six months, affecting close to 9.7 million individuals. The investigation found that personal information had been transferred from a credit data warehouse into user folders and shared drives, and then copied from the shared drive onto a work computer and USB keys. The lesson is not merely that insider threats exist. The deeper lesson is that data copied out of controlled systems into ordinary working locations can create risk that DLP, access control, and retention practices may not catch if they are incomplete, poorly tuned, or not monitored in context.

Capital One illustrates a different failure pattern. The company disclosed that a cloud incident affected approximately 100 million individuals in the United States and approximately 6 million in Canada. The OCC later assessed an $80 million civil money penalty, citing failures in risk assessment processes before migrating significant IT operations to the public cloud and failure to correct deficiencies in a timely manner. The lesson for this chapter is that cloud security cannot be reduced to migration success or platform adoption. A cloud resource may be part of a modern architecture and still carry data risk if risk assessment, least privilege, monitoring, and data-aware controls do not mature with the environment.

Equifax shows why database security cannot rely only on perimeter controls or application-layer assumptions. The GAO reported that attackers accessed personal information of at least 145.5 million individuals. Equifax's investigation identified major factors related to identification, detection, database access segmentation, and data governance. In practical terms, the breach showed that sensitive data must be discovered, segmented, governed, and monitored continuously. A database is not protected simply because it is inside an enterprise environment.

Marriott and Starwood show how data risk can survive through acquisitions, integrations, and long detection windows. The FTC alleged that Marriott and Starwood experienced multiple breaches affecting hundreds of millions of consumers. One Starwood breach went undetected for years and included access to hundreds of millions of guest records, including millions of unencrypted passport numbers. The FTC cited failures involving access controls, firewall controls, network segmentation, patching, logging, monitoring, and multifactor authentication. The lesson is that encryption and database controls are not enough if organizations do not know where sensitive fields exist, whether they are consistently protected, how long they are retained, and who can access them.

The Snowflake customer-targeting campaign shows the modern SaaS and cloud data warehouse problem. Mandiant reported that threat actor UNC5537 used stolen customer credentials to access Snowflake customer environments, with incidents traced to compromised customer credentials rather than a breach of Snowflake's enterprise environment. In one described case, the compromised account did not have MFA enabled. The actor used valid access to reach customer data and exfiltrate it. This is exactly where CASB and SaaS governance controls can struggle when activity occurs through sanctioned platforms and legitimate credentials. The organization needs identity context, MFA, network restrictions, data access monitoring, and abnormal data movement detection tied to the sensitivity of the data being accessed.

Each incident is different.

The pattern is not.

Sensitive data rarely stays neatly inside the control boundary where the organization first protected it. It moves into shared drives, cloud environments, SaaS platforms, warehouses, exports, unmanaged copies, and user workflows. Attackers and insiders do not always need to break the system if they can use valid access, weak monitoring, excessive permissions, stale credentials, or poorly governed copies.

This is why legacy tools are necessary but incomplete.

2.11 The Limits of Each Legacy Control

DLP can inspect and block data movement through known channels, but it often depends on predefined patterns and policies. It may miss sensitive data that has been copied into unmanaged repositories, transformed into new formats, stored in SaaS applications, or shared through AI tools. A DLP tool may understand the content pattern but not the business context, ownership, lineage, or downstream copy.

CASB can help govern cloud application usage, but it may not understand the full sensitivity of data inside every SaaS platform, data warehouse, collaboration tool, or AI-enabled workflow. CASB also struggles when users or attackers operate through approved applications using valid credentials. From the application's perspective, the activity may look like normal use. From the data's perspective, it may be exposure.

Database security can protect known databases through access controls, monitoring, masking, encryption, and activity analytics. Those controls matter. But many breaches show that attackers do not always need to break the database. They may abuse excessive privileges, weak segmentation, stale credentials, poorly monitored exports, unencrypted fields, or downstream copies of regulated data. The database may be secured while the data has already escaped into a less controlled environment.

CSPM can identify risky cloud configurations, but cloud posture is not the same as data posture. A storage bucket, database, or analytics workspace may be technically compliant from a configuration perspective while still containing highly sensitive data accessible to too many identities. CSPM can tell an organization that a cloud resource is misconfigured. DSPM helps explain why that misconfiguration matters by showing what sensitive data is exposed, who can reach it, and how severe the business risk is.

The common weakness across these tools is that they often protect locations, channels, systems, or configurations rather than the full lifecycle of the data itself.

Modern data security requires continuous visibility across structured data, unstructured data, SaaS, cloud storage, data warehouses, developer environments, backups, logs, collaboration tools, and AI workflows.

That is the gap DSPM is designed to help close.

2.12 Why VAULTIS Belongs in a Company Data Security Program

The value of VAULTIS is not that companies should copy government language or adopt military doctrine. The value is that it gives leaders a way to talk about data without immediately collapsing into tool categories.

Most organizations do not struggle because they lack tools. They struggle because they lack a shared model for what good data should look like.

A data catalog may help with inventory and metadata. A DSPM platform may help with discovery, classification, access exposure, and risk prioritization. A DLP tool may help prevent certain types of sharing or exfiltration. An identity platform may control who can authenticate and what groups they belong to. A privacy platform may help track obligations, assessments, requests, and retention requirements.

All of those tools matter. But tools do not automatically create a data-centric organization.

VAULTIS helps explain the larger goal. Data should be visible enough to find, accessible enough to use, understandable enough to interpret, linked enough to create context, trustworthy enough to support decisions, interoperable enough to move safely, and secure enough to protect the organization.

That is the bridge between data strategy and data security.

A company that adopts this model is not simply trying to buy better software. It is trying to change how the organization thinks about data. It is moving from passive accumulation to active stewardship. It is moving from system ownership to data ownership. It is moving from "we have the platform" to "we understand what the platform contains." It is moving from "the user had access" to "the access was appropriate for the purpose." It is moving from "AI can search it" to "AI should be allowed to use it."

That is a much more mature conversation.

2.13 Why "Just Move It" Is Not a Strategy

Modernization often begins with good intentions.

A legacy file share needs to move to SharePoint. An old intranet needs to be rebuilt. A ticketing system needs to move to the cloud. Reports need to move into a business intelligence platform. Collaboration needs to shift to a new enterprise tool. A knowledge base needs to become searchable. A repository needs to be connected to AI.

On paper, this is progress.

In practice, it can become a very efficient way to move old risk into new places.

If an organization migrates data without understanding it, the new platform inherits the old problems. Overexposed files remain overexposed. Stale data remains stale. Sensitive content remains unlabeled. Business ownership remains unclear. Retention problems follow the data. Duplicate copies multiply. The new system may even make the risk worse because the data becomes easier to search, easier to share, easier to index, and easier for AI to summarize.

A migration is often treated as a technical success when the data lands in the new platform and users can access it. But that is only part of the story. If the organization moved stale, overexposed, unclassified, redundant, or ownerless data into a more searchable and AI-ready environment, it did not modernize the data.

It modernized the risk.

Migration should be one of the best opportunities an organization has to improve data security. It is a natural moment to decide what should move, what should be archived, what should be destroyed, what should be restricted, what should be labeled, and what should never be exposed to AI.

Too often, those decisions are skipped because the migration is treated as a technical project instead of a data governance event.

The better migration question is not simply whether the data can be moved.

The better question is what risk is being carried forward.

2.14 AI Did Not Create the Problem

It removed the hiding places.

Before AI, poor data hygiene could survive because finding information still required effort. A user had to know where to look, what to search for, which folder mattered, what the file might be called, or who to ask. Overexposed data was still risky, but friction limited the blast radius. A user might technically have access to too much, but they had to work to find it.

AI changes that.

A copilot, chatbot, agent, or enterprise search tool can make messy data feel organized. It can summarize content users did not know existed. It can connect dots across repositories. It can produce confident answers from stale documents. It can surface sensitive information from old files, tickets, chats, and knowledge articles. It can make over-permissioned data available through a conversational interface that feels harmless.

That is why permission-aware AI is not enough by itself.

If the permissions are wrong, AI will honor the wrong permissions. If stale data is accessible, AI may use stale data. If sensitive content is unlabeled, AI may not know it requires special handling. If a repository has no owner, there may be no one to approve whether it should be connected to AI in the first place.

AI readiness begins with data readiness.

An organization should be cautious about connecting AI to repositories it does not understand. The risk is not only that AI will expose secrets. The risk is that AI will make unmanaged data useful before it is governed.

That sounds like innovation. It can also become exposure.

2.15 Security Must Follow the Data

Security programs have historically followed systems, networks, users, devices, and applications. That still matters. But modern data security must also follow the data itself.

Data does not stay politely inside one system. It moves from a database into a report, from a report into a spreadsheet, from a spreadsheet into an email, from an email into a ticket, from a ticket into a knowledge article, from a knowledge article into a search index, and from that index into an AI-generated answer.

Each step changes the risk.

The original database may have strong access control, but the exported spreadsheet may not. The official report may be reviewed, but the copy in someone's folder may be forgotten. The ticketing platform may be approved, but the attachment inside the ticket may contain information that belongs somewhere else. The AI search experience may be permission-aware, but the permissions may reflect years of convenience rather than true need.

This is why data security has to connect discovery, classification, access, ownership, retention, privacy, legal obligations, monitoring, and remediation. None of those disciplines can stand alone anymore.

DSPM is useful because it helps reveal where sensitive data lives, how it is exposed, and who can access it. But DSPM is not the entire answer. It gives the organization visibility and context. The program still has to decide what to do.

A tool can discover risk.

People have to own it.

2.16 How DSPM Gives Legacy Controls Better Context

DSPM does not replace DLP, CASB, database security, CSPM, IAM, privacy platforms, data catalogs, or cloud security tools.

It gives those tools better context.

DSPM identifies sensitive data, maps where it lives, analyzes access and exposure, detects risky copies, prioritizes the highest-risk findings, and helps security teams focus controls where they matter most. It helps explain not only that something is misconfigured, but what sensitive data is at risk because of the misconfiguration. It helps show not only that a user has access, but whether that access creates meaningful risk because of the data involved. It helps prioritize not simply by severity score, but by sensitivity, exposure, identity, business impact, and remediation path.

That context matters because security teams are already overwhelmed. They do not need another dashboard full of findings that no one owns. They need a way to decide what matters first.

DLP becomes more effective when it is informed by where sensitive data actually lives and how it moves. CASB becomes more useful when cloud application risk is connected to the sensitivity of the data being accessed or shared. Database security becomes stronger when sensitive fields, access patterns, and downstream copies are understood. CSPM becomes more actionable when cloud misconfigurations are prioritized based on exposed data, not only configuration drift.

Legacy tools enforce controls at known points.

DSPM helps explain where those controls should be focused and why the risk matters.

That is the difference between having security tools and having a data security posture.

2.17 The Human Layer of Data

The human layer is where many data security programs succeed or fail.

People create the data. People name the folders. People build the spreadsheets. People decide where to save the export. People grant access because someone is in a hurry. People resist labels because labels feel like friction. People keep old files because they are afraid to delete the wrong thing. People build shadow processes because the official process does not work well enough.

This does not mean users are the enemy. Most users are trying to get their work done with the tools and incentives in front of them.

That is why data security cannot be designed only from a policy document or architecture diagram. It has to account for how people actually work.

If a new classification requirement feels like meaningless extra work, users will resent it. If a retention policy threatens files they care about without explaining why, users will fight it. If a security control breaks a process the team depends on, they will find another way. If AI governance is too slow, business teams may route around it with unsanctioned tools.

The answer is not to give up on controls.

The answer is to explain the purpose and design the process with enough empathy that people can follow it.

A sensitivity label is not just a dropdown. It is a way to protect work someone created. A retention rule is not just a compliance requirement. It is a way to reduce risk while preserving what matters. An access review is not just an audit task. It is a chance to confirm that the right people still need the right data for the right reasons. A data owner is not just a name in a spreadsheet. It is the person or function accountable for understanding the purpose and risk of the data.

Data security becomes real when people can see how it protects the work, not just the system.

2.18 From Hoarding to Stewardship

Many organizations are data hoarders because hoarding feels safer than deciding.

Storage is cheap. Deletion is scary. Ownership is unclear. Legal requirements are confusing. Business teams do not want to lose history. IT does not want to be blamed for removing something important. Security does not always know what can be safely destroyed. Privacy may want less data retained, while legal may need some data preserved.

So the organization keeps everything.

At first, this feels cautious. Over time, it becomes dangerous.

The more data an organization keeps, the more it must protect. The more copies it creates, the harder it is to know which version is authoritative. The longer stale data remains accessible, the more likely it is to be misused, exposed, or pulled into an AI system. The more old repositories remain active, the more access paths must be managed.

Stewardship is the alternative to hoarding.

Stewardship replaces passive retention with intentional decisions. It establishes why the data exists, who needs it, how long it should remain available, what would happen if it were exposed, and what harm could come from deleting it too soon. It also forces a modern question that older governance programs did not have to answer clearly enough: whether the data is appropriate for AI use.

Stewardship does not mean deleting everything. It means making decisions with context. Some data should be preserved because it has operational, legal, historical, or business value. Some data should be restricted because it is sensitive. Some data should be transformed because the old format is no longer usable. Some data should be archived because it is no longer active but still required. Some data should be destroyed because keeping it creates more risk than value.

Those decisions are not always easy, but avoiding them does not remove the risk.

It only delays the moment when the organization must answer for it.

2.19 What Leaders Need to Understand

Leaders do not need to know every table, folder, bucket, or permission group in the environment.

They do need to understand that data security has become an enterprise capability.

Breach response depends on knowing what data was exposed. Privacy operations depend on knowing where personal data exists. AI readiness depends on knowing what content a model, copilot, connector, or agent can access. Risk reduction depends on ownership, context, and evidence. Without those pieces, data security remains a technical activity instead of a leadership discipline.

This is why data security belongs in leadership conversations.

It connects cybersecurity, privacy, legal, IT, data governance, operations, compliance, resilience, and AI strategy. Each group sees a different part of the problem. Security sees exposure. Privacy sees obligations. Legal sees liability. IT sees systems. Data teams see quality and lineage. Business teams see operational use. AI teams see possibility.

The data sits in the middle of all of them.

A mature program brings those perspectives together instead of letting each team solve only its piece.

2.20 What Good Looks Like

A mature organization does not have perfect data.

No organization does.

A mature organization has a defensible understanding of its most important data. It knows where sensitive and business-critical information lives, which repositories are ready for AI, and which ones need cleanup first. It has a practical ownership model and a classification approach that supports decisions instead of creating labels for their own sake. It treats migration, retention, access review, and AI enablement as connected parts of the same lifecycle. It includes the people closest to the work because they often understand the data better than the formal system record does.

Most importantly, it can tell a credible story.

It can explain what data matters, why it matters, who can access it, what controls protect it, what risks remain, and what the organization is doing to reduce those risks over time.

That story is what boards, regulators, auditors, customers, executives, and internal teams increasingly need to hear.

Not a perfect story.

A credible one.

CISO Takeaway

A CISO cannot govern AI, reduce data exposure, modernize DLP, or make DSPM operational without understanding data as more than content inside systems. Data is mission, memory, and risk. It must be visible enough to find, accessible enough to use, understandable enough to trust, linked enough to create context, interoperable enough to move safely, and secure enough to protect.

DLP, CASB, database security, and CSPM are still necessary controls. They are not obsolete. They are incomplete when used alone because they do not continuously provide discovery, classification, access analysis, exposure mapping, and risk prioritization across the full data lifecycle.

Key Takeaways

Data security begins when an organization stops treating data as a byproduct of systems and starts treating it as a mission-critical resource.

Technology teams keep systems running. Security teams reduce exposure. Governance teams define accountability. Business teams understand purpose. AI teams want to unlock value. Data crosses all of those boundaries, which is why no single team can govern it alone.

Legacy tools are necessary, but they are not sufficient. DLP, CASB, database security, and CSPM can enforce controls at known points, but they do not continuously answer the core data security question: where sensitive data lives, who can access it, how it is exposed, and what risk should be fixed first.

This is why DSPM matters. DSPM does not replace legacy controls; it gives them better context. It helps security teams understand where sensitive data lives, who can access it, how it is exposed, which copies are risky, and which remediation actions matter most.

The future of cybersecurity, privacy, governance, and AI readiness depends on whether organizations can see their data clearly enough to protect it, use it, and trust it.

The data was always there.

The question is whether the organization is finally ready to understand it.

Chapter 3: What DSPM Is and What It Is Not

The first mistake many organizations make with DSPM is believing they bought a solution when they really bought visibility.

That visibility may be powerful. It may be exactly what the organization needed. It may reveal sensitive data in places no one expected, show risky access paths, uncover stale data, identify overexposed repositories, and give security teams their first real look at the data estate.

But visibility is not the same as ownership.

A DSPM platform can show the organization where sensitive data lives. It can identify who has access to it. It can reveal whether data is overexposed, duplicated, stale, misclassified, or stored in risky locations. It can alert security teams when data moves outside approved boundaries. It can integrate with ticketing systems, SIEM platforms, SOAR tools, DLP, IAM, cloud security controls, and other parts of the security ecosystem.

That is valuable.

But the tool cannot decide what the company values. It cannot assign business ownership by itself. It cannot determine risk appetite. It cannot settle disagreements between security, privacy, legal, IT, data teams, and the business. It cannot decide whether a dataset should be deleted, retained, restricted, archived, labeled, moved, or excluded from AI.

That responsibility belongs to the organization.

DSPM stands for Data Security Posture Management. In the market, it is often described as a technology category. In practice, it only works well when the platform is wrapped in governance, ownership, decision rights, remediation workflows, business participation, and measurable risk reduction.

This is the difference between buying a DSPM tool and building a DSPM program.

3.1 The First Mistake: Buying Visibility and Expecting Ownership

The story often starts with a strong business case.

The organization knows it has sensitive data in too many places. Security leaders are worried about AI access, cloud storage, SaaS exposure, excessive permissions, and the limits of legacy DLP. Privacy teams are worried about deletion, retention, data subject requests, and regulated data that may exist outside known systems. Executives want better answers. The board wants a clearer view of data risk.

The company buys a DSPM platform.

At first, the deployment feels like progress. The tool starts scanning. The dashboard begins to populate. Sensitive data appears across cloud storage, SaaS platforms, databases, file shares, collaboration tools, developer environments, and old repositories no one has reviewed in years.

For a moment, the organization finally sees what had been hiding in plain sight.

Then the second wave hits.

The tool found sensitive data in a department folder, but no one knows whether the data still matters. It found customer information in a shared drive, but the business owner left two reorganizations ago. It found regulated data in a SaaS workflow, but the team using it insists the process will break if access is restricted. It found stale exports, but legal wants retention reviewed before anything is deleted. It found excessive access, but IT does not know who should approve the change. It found risky AI-accessible content, but the AI governance process is still being defined.

The tool did its job.

The organization was not ready to do its part.

That is how a DSPM deployment becomes an expensive dashboard instead of a risk-reduction program. The technology discovers risk, but no one owns the decision. The platform identifies sensitive data, but the business has not agreed on what should happen next. Alerts are created, but response expectations are unclear. Automation is possible, but governance has not determined when automation is appropriate. Posture is measured, but leadership has not defined what healthy posture looks like.

Technology can expose the problem.

Governance decides what the organization will do about it.

3.2 What DSPM Actually Does

DSPM helps organizations understand and reduce risk to sensitive and business-critical data.

At its most practical level, DSPM helps answer several connected questions. Where is sensitive data? What type of data is it? Who or what can access it? Is that access appropriate? Is the data exposed, duplicated, stale, or stored in a risky location? Has it moved somewhere it should not be? Which findings matter most? Who needs to act? Has the risk actually been reduced?

Those questions are simple to ask and hard to answer at scale.

Sensitive data does not stay politely inside one database. It spreads through cloud storage, SaaS applications, collaboration tools, data lakes, warehouses, backups, endpoints, logs, developer environments, tickets, spreadsheets, and AI workflows. It is copied, exported, transformed, shared, retained, forgotten, and rediscovered. It may be structured in a database table or buried in an old PDF. It may be in a sanctioned business application or sitting in a folder created for a project that ended years ago.

A DSPM platform helps bring that scattered picture into view.

It can discover and classify sensitive data. It can map access and exposure. It can identify risky combinations, such as regulated data in an overexposed repository or sensitive files accessible to external users. It can help prioritize findings based on sensitivity, access, exposure, business context, and risk. It can create tickets, notify owners, support remediation, and feed other tools with better data intelligence.

This is why DSPM matters.

It gives the organization a way to move from guessing to knowing.

But knowing is only the beginning.

3.3 What DSPM Cannot Do for You

DSPM is powerful, but it is not magic.

It will not decide what the company values. It will not make a reluctant business unit own a data store. It will not define acceptable risk for the board. It will not settle every disagreement between privacy, legal, security, IT, and operations. It will not create a security culture by itself. It will not make users care about classification, retention, or approved use unless the organization explains why those things matter.

A DSPM platform can show that sensitive data is exposed to too many people. It cannot decide whether the data is still needed for the business process.

It can show that regulated data exists in an unexpected location. It cannot determine whether legal hold, retention, or contractual obligations apply without input from the right stakeholders.

It can show that a repository is AI-accessible. It cannot decide whether that data is appropriate for AI use.

It can show that a data store lacks an owner. It cannot force the business to accept accountability unless leadership supports the program.

That is why DSPM must be treated as a program, not only as a product.

A DSPM tool provides visibility, intelligence, automation, and control. The organization provides ownership, authority, priorities, judgment, and accountability.

Without the organization's part, even the best DSPM tool will struggle to deliver lasting value.

3.4 The DSPM Maturity Curve

Most DSPM programs mature through the same uncomfortable path.

They begin with the excitement of discovery. They move into the visibility of dashboards. They struggle through the operational reality of workflow. They mature through governance. Only then do they become a measurable risk capability.

Each stage adds value, but each stage also reveals the next gap.

A scanner finds sensitive data, but it does not create ownership. A dashboard shows risk, but it does not guarantee action. A workflow engine routes remediation, but it still needs policy and decision rights. A governance program creates accountability, but it must be measured to prove value. A mature DSPM capability connects discovery, visibility, action, governance, and measurable risk reduction into one operating model.

This maturity curve matters because many organizations mistake one stage for the whole program.

They buy a scanner and expect accountability.

They build a dashboard and expect remediation.

They automate tickets and expect governance.

They create a steering committee and expect measurable risk reduction.

DSPM reaches its full potential only when the organization connects all of those pieces.

Stage 1: Scanner — The First Honest Inventory

Most organizations first meet DSPM as a scanner.

This is the honeymoon phase.

The tool begins to find sensitive data that used to be hidden across file shares, SaaS tools, databases, cloud storage, developer environments, collaboration platforms, and old repositories. For many teams, this is the first honest inventory they have ever had. The findings may be uncomfortable, but they are useful.

The organization can finally see that sensitive data is not where everyone assumed it was.

It may find customer records in shared folders, employee information in old spreadsheets, secrets in developer repositories, regulated data in cloud storage, financial records in collaboration tools, and confidential documents in spaces with broad access. The first scan often confirms what security leaders suspected but could not prove: sensitive data has spread farther than the organization's governance model.

This stage answers the first basic question: where is sensitive data?

That question matters. No organization can govern data it cannot find.

But scanning alone is not enough.

The first inventory often creates as much anxiety as clarity. A scan may produce thousands of findings. Some are critical. Some are duplicates. Some are false positives. Some are technically accurate but low risk. Some are tied to business processes the security team does not understand. Some require privacy review. Some require legal input. Some require the business to decide whether the data still has value.

The scanner gives the organization visibility.

It does not decide what happens next.

At this stage, DSPM is useful, but limited. The organization has found risk, but it has not yet created accountability.

Stage 2: Dashboard — Visibility Without Ownership

The next stage is the dashboard.

The organization begins to aggregate findings, visualize exposure, and report on risk. Security teams can see where sensitive data is concentrated, which systems contain regulated data, which users have access, which data stores are overexposed, and where risk is increasing.

This is where the program starts to feel more real.

Dashboards help teams see patterns. They can show that one department has more sensitive data exposure than others. They can reveal that a collaboration platform contains more regulated data than expected. They can show that external sharing is concentrated in a few business units. They can help security leaders explain data risk to executives in a way that is more concrete than a generic risk statement.

A good dashboard can change the conversation.

But dashboards can also create a false sense of progress.

A chart showing overexposed sensitive data does not remove access. A heatmap showing risky repositories does not assign business ownership. A trend line showing stale data does not decide what can be deleted. A report showing regulated data in an unapproved location does not tell the business how to fix the process that put it there.

The risk is visible, but visibility is not action.

This is where many DSPM deployments stall. The security team can show the problem, but the organization has not agreed on who owns the data, who approves remediation, who handles exceptions, how fast teams must respond, or what level of risk leadership is willing to accept.

At this stage, DSPM is informative, but still reactive.

The organization can see more clearly, but it has not yet learned how to move.

Stage 3: Workflow Engine — Findings Become Work

The third stage begins when findings become work.

The organization starts connecting DSPM findings to action. Tickets are created. Data owners are notified. Security teams define remediation steps. IT teams remove access or change configurations. Privacy teams review regulated data. Legal weighs in on retention, deletion, and legal hold. Integrations with ITSM, SIEM, SOAR, DLP, IAM, cloud security platforms, and collaboration tools begin to operationalize response.

This stage answers a practical question: who needs to do what, and by when?

This is where DSPM starts to move from visibility to execution.

A workflow engine can assign tasks, track status, escalate overdue items, and help teams coordinate response. It can support actions such as removing excessive access, relocating sensitive data, deleting stale data, applying labels, adjusting permissions, triggering DLP policies, or opening investigations.

This is progress.

It is also where the organization learns that workflow without decision rights can become noise.

A ticket routed to the wrong owner will sit. A remediation request sent to a business unit with no context will be ignored. A deletion task without legal or privacy review may be blocked. An access change without business input may disrupt operations. An automation rule without policy support may create more fear than efficiency.

Workflow makes the program operational, but it does not replace governance.

At this stage, DSPM begins to feel useful because findings are no longer trapped in a dashboard. They are moving into the systems where work gets done. But if the organization has not defined decision rights, workflows can become inconsistent. One business unit may remediate aggressively while another ignores tickets. One team may approve exceptions casually while another escalates every issue. Automation may be enabled in some areas and blocked in others because there is no common policy.

At this stage, DSPM is operational, but not yet fully governed.

Stage 4: Governance Program — The Business Joins the Program

The fourth stage is the turning point.

DSPM becomes sustainable when the business joins the program.

At this stage, the organization has moved beyond tool deployment and workflow routing. It has defined policies, roles, responsibilities, escalation paths, exception processes, and success criteria. Data owners understand their responsibilities. Business units participate in risk decisions. Legal, compliance, and privacy teams help define requirements. Security teams have authority to act. Executives understand the risk-reduction strategy.

The question changes again.

The organization is no longer asking only where sensitive data is or who needs to fix a ticket. It is asking how sensitive data risk should be governed across the enterprise.

That is a business question.

The governance program defines what good looks like. It determines which data types matter most. It defines acceptable and unacceptable exposure. It establishes remediation timelines. It creates exception handling. It sets standards for automation. It aligns DSPM findings with regulatory obligations, business priorities, and risk tolerance.

This is where the tool becomes part of an operating model.

The platform still matters. It provides intelligence, visibility, prioritization, and evidence. But the operating model determines whether the intelligence becomes action. Governance turns DSPM from a security project into an enterprise capability.

At this stage, DSPM is governed, accountable, and repeatable.

Stage 5: Measurable Risk Capability — Proving Risk Is Going Down

The highest stage is not discovery.

It is not reporting.

It is not ticketing.

It is measurable risk reduction.

At this stage, the organization is not just finding sensitive data or managing remediation tasks. It is measuring whether data risk is actually going down. Leadership can see trends over time. The board can understand how data exposure relates to operational, regulatory, financial, and reputational risk. Security and business teams can evaluate whether controls are working and whether remediation efforts are improving the organization's posture.

This is where DSPM becomes part of enterprise risk management.

The platform provides intelligence. The workflows drive action. The governance model creates accountability. The metrics prove whether the program is working.

Measurable outcomes may include reduced overexposure of sensitive data, fewer stale sensitive records, faster remediation of high-risk findings, more critical data stores with assigned business owners, broader coverage of approved classification and handling rules, and clearer executive reporting tied to business impact.

At this stage, the organization can tell a credible story.

It can show where it started, what risk it found, what actions were taken, what remains unresolved, and whether exposure is trending down. That story matters because executives and boards do not need another dashboard full of disconnected findings. They need evidence that the program is reducing meaningful risk.

This is the difference between having a DSPM tool and having a mature DSPM capability.

3.5 Quick Reference: The DSPM Maturity Curve

The maturity curve can be summarized this way:

Maturity Stage	Primary Focus	Main Question	Limitation If Used Alone
Scanner	Discovery	Where is sensitive data?	Finds risk but does not assign ownership.
Dashboard	Visibility	What does data risk look like?	Shows risk but may not drive action.
Workflow Engine	Operational response	Who needs to do what?	Routes work but may lack consistent governance.

Governance Program	Accountability	How do we govern data risk?	Requires sustained business participation.
Measurable Risk Capability	Business risk reduction	Are we reducing risk?	Requires mature metrics, ownership, and executive alignment.

This table is useful as a reference, but it should not be mistaken for a checklist that can be completed once and forgotten. Organizations often move through these stages unevenly. A company may have strong dashboards but weak ownership. It may have workflows but inconsistent policy. It may have governance in one business unit and chaos in another.

The goal is not to make every part of the organization equally mature overnight.

The goal is to keep moving from visibility toward action, from action toward governance, and from governance toward measurable risk reduction.

3.6 From Tool Deployment to Risk Reduction

DSPM is most effective when technology and governance work together.

The platform provides visibility, intelligence, automation, and control. The organization provides ownership, authority, priorities, and accountability. One without the other is incomplete.

A DSPM tool can discover the data.

The organization must govern it.

A scanner can find sensitive data, but it does not create ownership. A dashboard can show risk, but it does not guarantee action. A workflow engine can route remediation, but it still needs policy and decision rights. A governance program can create accountability, but it must be measured to prove value.

This is why DSPM should be treated as an enterprise data security program, not simply a security tool deployment.

The business must be involved from the beginning. Data owners must understand their responsibilities. Executives must support the risk-reduction strategy. Users must be educated. Security teams must have authority to act. Compliance and privacy teams must help define requirements. The board must understand how data risk connects to operational, regulatory, financial, and reputational exposure.

DSPM is powerful, but it is not magic.

It does not replace governance, policy, data ownership, executive accountability, or security culture. It makes the truth more visible. It helps the organization see where sensitive data lives, how it is exposed, who can access it, and where action is needed.

But the organization still has to decide what it is willing to do about that truth.

With the right program around it, DSPM becomes more than a discovery engine. It becomes a strategic capability for reducing data risk across the enterprise.

CISO Takeaway

DSPM begins as visibility, but it only becomes valuable when the organization turns visibility into ownership, action, governance, and measurable risk reduction.

A CISO should not measure DSPM success only by how much sensitive data the platform finds. The better measure is whether the organization can assign ownership, remediate exposure, reduce unnecessary access, improve classification, support privacy and legal obligations, and prove that data risk is going down.

Key Takeaways

DSPM is not just a tool. DSPM is a program.

The tool can discover the data. The organization must govern it.

A scanner finds sensitive data, but it does not create ownership.

A dashboard shows risk, but it does not guarantee action.

A workflow engine routes remediation, but it still needs policy and decision rights.

A governance program creates accountability across security, privacy, compliance, IT, and the business.

A mature DSPM capability measures whether data risk is actually being reduced.

DSPM reaches its full potential when discovery, visibility, action, governance, and measurable risk reduction work together as one operating model.

Chapter 4: Build the Program Before the Purchase

A DSPM program does not begin with a scan. It begins with business agreement.

Before an organization buys a DSPM platform, connects repositories, classifies data, or opens remediation tickets, it must answer a more important question:

What business outcome are we trying to achieve by securing and informing the organization about its data?

Many DSPM conversations start too far downstream. Vendor guidance often describes a data security lifecycle or product operating model: discover, classify, govern, protect, control, monitor, respond, and destroy. That lifecycle is useful, but it is not the same thing as a business program.

For example, Cyera's "Building a Modern Data Security Program" article frames the program through an eight-stage lifecycle beginning with discovery and classification, then moving through governance, protection, monitoring, response, and destruction. That is helpful operational language, but it does not define the business charter, ownership model, funding model, stakeholder commitments, risk prioritization method, or success criteria required before a tool is deployed.

A true DSPM program is not a tool rollout. It is an enterprise operating model for answering, governing, and acting on questions such as:

- *Who owns our critical data?*
- *Where does critical data live?*
- *Who has access to it?*
- *Is it exposed, copied, over-retained, or being used in ways the business did not approve?*
- *Which risks matter most?*
- *Who is accountable for remediation?*
- *What evidence proves the risk was reduced?*

NIST Cybersecurity Framework 2.0 reinforces this program-first mindset. Its Govern function states that cybersecurity risk management strategy, expectations, and policy should be established, communicated, and monitored. It also emphasizes cross-organizational input, clear roles and responsibilities, legal, regulatory, and contractual obligations, and continuous oversight.

That is the purpose of this chapter: to help the organization build the DSPM program before purchasing the DSPM platform.

4.1 Why the Program Comes First

A DSPM platform can discover sensitive data, classify it, identify exposure, detect excessive access, and generate findings. Those capabilities are valuable only if the organization is ready to make decisions and take action.

Without a program, DSPM often becomes a visibility exercise. The tool finds risk, but the business does not reduce risk.

A program-first approach ensures that the organization defines:

- The business purpose for DSPM
- The data risks that matter most
- The stakeholders who must participate
- The owners who will make decisions
- The remediation lanes that will receive findings
- The metrics that will prove progress
- The procurement requirements the tool must satisfy

The message to leadership should be direct:

We are not buying a scanner. We are building a data security program that uses technology to identify, prioritize, assign, remediate, and report data risk.

The tool should answer the program's questions. The program should not be shaped by the tool's dashboard.

4.2 Build Company-Wide Buy-In

The first business requirement for a DSPM program is company-wide buy-in.

Buy-in does not mean every department agrees that data security is important in theory. It means the organization agrees to participate in a program that will expose uncomfortable truths about data ownership, access, duplication, retention, sharing, and remediation accountability.

A DSPM program will reveal data that no one owns, data copied into unmanaged locations, sensitive data sitting in development environments, excessive access, external sharing, orphaned repositories, stale data, shadow analytics, and business processes that bypass policy.

Without executive and cross-functional buy-in, the DSPM platform may produce dashboards, but the business will not produce risk reduction.

Company-wide buy-in should establish agreement on seven points:

1. Data risk is business risk, not only a security issue.
2. Critical data requires defined ownership.
3. Not all sensitive data has equal business impact.
4. Regulatory obligations are important, but actual risk determines priority.
5. Engineering and business teams must participate in remediation.
6. Dashboards are not success; measurable risk reduction is success.

7. A DSPM tool should be selected only after the program defines what it needs the tool to do.

Use **Template 1: Data Security Program Charter** and **Template 2: Executive Summary** at the end of this chapter to document the business agreement and leadership message.

4.3 Define Business Objectives Before Tool Objectives

A common DSPM failure pattern is confusing tool objectives with business objectives.

A tool objective describes what the platform can do.

A business objective describes what the organization must accomplish.

The difference matters because a DSPM tool can successfully scan, classify, and generate findings while the organization still fails to reduce material risk.

Business Objective	Tool Objective
Reduce exposure of critical customer, employee, financial, and intellectual property data across priority environments.	Connect the DSPM platform to cloud storage, databases, SaaS applications, and data warehouses.
Establish ownership and accountability for critical data domains.	Display data stores, owners, and sensitivity labels in a dashboard.
Prioritize remediation based on business impact, exposure, access, regulatory obligation, and exploitability.	Generate findings for sensitive data, excessive permissions, public exposure, and policy violations.
Provide executives with reliable data risk reporting and remediation progress.	Produce reports, charts, and executive dashboards.
Reduce unapproved data duplication and over-retention.	Identify duplicate, stale, or abandoned sensitive data.
Improve regulatory evidence and audit readiness.	Map findings to frameworks, regulations, and policies.
Prevent "scan everything, fix nothing."	Run broad discovery scans across enterprise repositories.

A tool objective becomes valuable only when it supports a business decision, business control, or business outcome.

The program should be able to state:

We need DSPM capabilities because they help us reduce specific data risks, support defined owners, produce evidence, and improve executive decision-making.

Use **Template 3: Goals & Objectives** to convert business outcomes into measurable program objectives before evaluating vendors.

4.4 Identify Stakeholders and Decision Rights

A DSPM program crosses multiple authority boundaries. Security may sponsor the program, but security cannot own every data decision, business process, legal obligation, privacy requirement, engineering fix, or risk acceptance.

The program must identify stakeholders before purchase because those stakeholders determine requirements, scope, remediation workflows, and success criteria.

Data owners are key stakeholders because they understand the business purpose, sensitivity, usage, retention needs, and acceptable risk for the data. Data subjects are also affected parties, especially from a privacy and regulatory perspective, but they are usually represented through privacy, legal, compliance, or governance teams rather than participating directly in DSPM operations.

Stakeholder	Program Role	Key Decisions
CISO / Security Leadership	Executive sponsor or co-sponsor of the data security program.	Risk strategy, funding, escalation, control expectations, security reporting.
Chief Data Officer / Data Governance	Defines enterprise data ownership, data domains, metadata expectations, and data governance alignment.	Data ownership model, data stewardship, data quality, catalog integration.
Legal	Interprets legal obligations, litigation risk, contractual duties, privilege, discovery, and breach notification requirements.	Legal risk thresholds, contractual requirements, evidence preservation, notification triggers.
Privacy	Defines privacy risk, personal data handling expectations, retention, lawful use, DPIA/PIA alignment, and data subject rights impact.	Privacy risk prioritization, personal data handling, retention and minimization expectations.
Engineering / Platform Teams	Own technical remediation, integration, deployment patterns, infrastructure, data pipelines, and SDLC changes.	Remediation feasibility, automation, access control changes, infrastructure fixes.
Business Data Owners	Own business decisions about the value, use, criticality, and acceptable risk of data.	Criticality decisions, risk acceptance, remediation priority, business impact.
CIO / IT Operations	Owns enterprise systems, SaaS platforms, endpoint repositories, identity integration, and operational support.	System onboarding, identity controls, service ownership, operational change windows.
Risk & Compliance	Aligns findings to enterprise risk management, control frameworks, audit evidence, and regulatory reporting.	Risk register entries, control evidence, audit readiness, compliance mapping.
Internal Audit	Provides independent validation of program design, control operation, and evidence sufficiency.	Audit criteria, control testing, governance maturity validation.

Procurement / Third-Party Risk	Ensures DSPM requirements apply to vendors, suppliers, integrations, and external data processors.	Vendor requirements, contract clauses, supplier data access, due diligence.
SecOps / Incident Response	Uses DSPM context during investigations and response.	Escalation thresholds, incident classification, detection and response integration.

A DSPM program should not proceed to tool selection until these stakeholders agree on decision rights.

At minimum, decision rights should be documented for:

- Program scope
- Critical data tiers
- Risk severity model
- Risk acceptance
- Regulatory interpretation
- Technical remediation approach
- Tool selection
- Budget approval

Use the decision rights section in **Template 1: Data Security Program Charter** and the RACI in **Template 5: Program Design** to capture these agreements.

4.5 Build the Business Case Before the Purchase

A DSPM program needs a business case before it needs a product comparison.

This does not mean every organization needs a complex financial model before starting. It means the organization should be able to explain why the program exists, what risk it reduces, what business outcomes it supports, and why the investment matters now.

Too many DSPM efforts begin with a vendor demo. The dashboard looks impressive. The findings look urgent. The proof of concept produces a long list of sensitive data, excessive access, stale repositories, public exposure, or unowned data stores. Then the project stalls because no one has translated the findings into business value.

A strong business case connects DSPM to measurable business outcomes.

The business case should answer:

Business Question	Why It Matters
What business problems are we solving?	Prevents the program from becoming a tool-led discovery exercise.
What data risk is creating business exposure?	Connects technical findings to privacy, security, regulatory, operational, and reputational impact.
Which business units are affected?	Shows that DSPM is an enterprise issue, not only a security project.

What happens if we do nothing?	Defines the cost of inaction, including breach exposure, audit findings, AI misuse, regulatory risk, and operational inefficiency.
What outcomes will justify investment?	Creates a measurable definition of success before the tool is purchased.
Who owns the risk after it is discovered?	Prevents the security team from becoming the default owner of every data problem.
What evidence will prove progress?	Aligns the program to reporting, audit readiness, and executive oversight.

The strongest DSPM business cases usually include several value drivers.

First, DSPM reduces breach and exposure risk by identifying sensitive data that is overexposed, misclassified, stale, unencrypted, unowned, or accessible to too many users, applications, service accounts, vendors, or AI systems.

Second, DSPM improves regulatory readiness by helping the organization prove where regulated data exists, who can access it, how it is protected, whether it is retained appropriately, and whether remediation activity is tracked.

Third, DSPM supports AI readiness by identifying which sensitive repositories could be indexed, retrieved, summarized, embedded, copied, or exposed by AI tools. This is increasingly important because many AI failures are not caused by malicious use. They are caused by approved tools having access to data that should not have been available for that purpose.

Fourth, DSPM improves operational efficiency by reducing manual discovery work, accelerating data owner identification, prioritizing remediation, and providing evidence for audits, privacy requests, access reviews, and executive reporting.

Fifth, DSPM improves decision-making by helping leadership understand which risks matter most. The goal is not to fix every finding at once. The goal is to identify the risks that create the greatest business exposure and move those risks through an agreed decision process.

A simple business-case statement may look like this:

The organization needs a DSPM program to reduce business risk created by unknown, overexposed, unowned, stale, regulated, and AI-accessible sensitive data. The program will improve visibility, assign ownership, prioritize remediation, support privacy and regulatory obligations, reduce AI data exposure, and provide measurable evidence of risk reduction to executives and the board.

The business case should be approved before the organization enters final vendor selection. Without it, the buying process can drift toward feature comparisons instead of business outcomes.

The goal is not to buy the tool with the most features.

The goal is to fund the operating model that will reduce data risk.

4.6 Formal Risk Acceptance

Not every DSPM finding can be remediated immediately. Some risks require business context. Some require budget. Some require architectural change. Some require legal review. Some exist because the business has chosen speed, access, collaboration, or operational continuity over tighter control.

That is normal.

What is not acceptable is allowing risk to remain open indefinitely because no one made a decision.

A mature DSPM program needs formal risk acceptance language so that unresolved findings are documented, owned, reviewed, and time-bound. Risk acceptance should not be a quiet escape hatch for hard remediation work. It should be a deliberate business decision made by the appropriate owner with visibility to security, privacy, legal, compliance, and leadership when needed.

Risk acceptance should be required when:

- Sensitive data remains exposed beyond the approved policy.
- Excessive access cannot be remediated within the required SLA.
- A repository containing regulated or confidential data does not have an assigned business owner.
- A business unit requests an exception to classification, retention, deletion, access, encryption, or sharing requirements.
- AI systems require access to data that creates privacy, regulatory, contractual, or confidentiality concerns.
- Remediation would disrupt critical business operations.
- A compensating control is being used instead of the preferred control.
- A legacy system cannot meet current data security requirements.

Risk acceptance must include:

Required Element	Description
Risk description	Clear statement of the data risk being accepted.
Affected data	Type, sensitivity, location, and business context of the data.
Business owner	Named individual accountable for accepting the risk.
Technical owner	Individual or team responsible for maintaining related controls.
Reason for acceptance	Business rationale for not remediating immediately.
Compensating controls	Controls that reduce likelihood or impact while the risk remains open.
Expiration date	Date when the exception must be reviewed or closed.
Review cadence	Frequency of reassessment.
Approval authority	Person or committee authorized to accept the risk.

Escalation trigger	Conditions that require leadership review or immediate remediation.
Evidence location	Where the decision, approval, and supporting evidence are stored.

Sample Risk Acceptance Language

The following language can be adapted for DSPM program charters, policy exceptions, governance workflows, or executive decision records.

The business owner acknowledges that the identified data security risk has been reviewed and is being formally accepted for a limited period. The accepted risk involves sensitive or business-critical data that remains exposed, accessible, retained, shared, or otherwise handled outside the organization's preferred control standard.

The business owner confirms that the risk has been evaluated in partnership with security and, where applicable, privacy, legal, compliance, data governance, and technology stakeholders. The decision to accept this risk is based on documented business need, operational constraint, technical limitation, or approved exception.

This acceptance does not remove accountability for the risk. The business owner remains responsible for ensuring that compensating controls are maintained, the risk is reviewed on the approved cadence, and remediation is completed by the agreed expiration date unless the risk is renewed through the formal exception process.

Risk acceptance must be time-bound, evidence-based, and subject to escalation if the risk increases, the data sensitivity changes, access expands, regulatory obligations change, AI access is introduced, or compensating controls fail.

Sample Risk Acceptance Record

Field	Example
Risk ID	DSPM-RA-001
Risk Title	Excessive access to restricted customer data in legacy collaboration site
Business Owner	VP, Customer Operations
Technical Owner	Collaboration Platform Administrator
Data Type	Customer records, support notes, account identifiers
Sensitivity	Restricted
Risk Description	Restricted customer data is accessible to all members of a legacy department group, including users without current business need.
Reason for Acceptance	Immediate access removal may disrupt open customer support workflows during system migration.
Compensating Controls	Monitoring enabled, export restrictions applied, access review scheduled, no AI indexing permitted.
Expiration Date	90 days from approval

Review Cadence	Monthly
Approval Authority	Data Security Steering Committee
Escalation Trigger	Public exposure, external sharing, AI indexing, evidence of bulk download, or missed review date
Final Disposition	Remediate, renew, transfer, or close

The most important rule is simple: risk acceptance is not risk avoidance.

If the organization chooses not to fix a known data risk immediately, that decision must be visible, owned, justified, and reviewed.

4.7 Data Security Steering Committee Decision Table

A DSPM program needs a decision body. Without one, the security team may discover risk but lack the authority to resolve business disputes, approve exceptions, prioritize remediation, or enforce ownership.

The steering committee does not need to be large. It does need to include the functions that influence data risk. At minimum, this usually includes security, IT, privacy, legal, compliance, data governance, and business leadership. In smaller organizations, the same person may represent more than one function.

The committee's role is not to review every finding. That would create delay and frustration. Its role is to make decisions that require cross-functional authority.

The steering committee should decide:

Decision Area	Decision Needed	Recommended Owner	Required Participants	Output
Program scope	*Which environments, data types, and repositories are in scope first?*	Security leader	IT, data, privacy, business owner	Approved DSPM scope
Critical data definition	*Which data types are considered restricted, regulated, confidential, or business critical?*	Data governance or privacy leader	Security, legal, compliance, business owners	Critical data standard
Risk prioritization	*Which findings must be remediated first?*	Security leader	Privacy, legal, IT, business owners	Prioritized remediation queue
Ownership disputes	*Who owns a data store, repository, or remediation obligation?*	Business executive sponsor	Security, IT, data governance	Ownership decision record
Remediation SLA	*How quickly must different risk levels be addressed?*	Security leader	IT, compliance, business owners	Remediation SLA standard
Risk acceptance	*Who may accept unresolved data risk, and for how long?*	Risk or compliance leader	Security, legal, business owner	Risk acceptance record
AI access	*Which data may be indexed, retrieved, embedded, or used by AI systems?*	AI governance lead or security leader	Legal, privacy, data, business owners	AI data access decision
Exceptions	*Which policy exceptions are allowed, denied, or escalated?*	Steering committee chair	Security, legal, compliance, owner of affected data	Exception decision
Automation	*Which remediation actions may be automated?*	Security and IT leaders	Business owner, legal, privacy	Automation approval matrix
Reporting	*What metrics should be reported to executives and the board?*	Security leader	Risk, compliance, privacy, executive sponsor	Executive scorecard
Tool selection	*Which DSPM capabilities are mandatory before purchase?*	Security leader	IT, procurement, privacy, data governance	Minimum capability requirements
Funding	*What budget, staffing, or managed service support is needed?*	Executive sponsor	Security, finance, IT	Approved investment plan

The steering committee should operate with a simple cadence.

Cadence	Purpose
Weekly during initial deployment	Resolve scope, ownership, and early remediation blockers.
Biweekly during stabilization	Review priority findings, exceptions, risk acceptance, and implementation progress.
Monthly during steady state	Review metrics, trends, aging risks, business unit performance, and executive reporting.
Quarterly for executive review	Review risk reduction, AI readiness, regulatory alignment, funding needs, and unresolved decisions.

A steering committee should not become a place where findings go to die. It should remove friction, make decisions, assign accountability, and keep the program moving.

The committee should be judged by the quality and speed of its decisions, not the number of meetings it holds.

4.8 Minimum Viable Operating Model for Smaller Organizations

Not every organization can launch a full enterprise DSPM program on day one.

Smaller organizations may not have separate security, privacy, legal, compliance, data governance, IAM, cloud, and platform teams. One person may own several functions. Budget may be limited. Tooling may be immature. Documentation may be incomplete. Data ownership may be informal. Remediation may depend on a small number of administrators who are already overloaded.

That does not mean smaller organizations should delay data security.

It means they need a minimum viable operating model.

A minimum viable operating model gives the organization enough structure to make decisions, reduce risk, and avoid buying technology it cannot operationalize. The goal is not to create bureaucracy. The goal is to define the smallest set of roles, processes, decisions, and metrics needed to turn DSPM findings into action.

Minimum Roles

Role	Responsibility
Executive sponsor	Approves the program, removes blockers, and accepts business risk when needed.
Security owner	Owns the DSPM process, risk prioritization, reporting, and coordination.
IT/platform owner	Supports access changes, configuration updates, integrations, and remediation.

Data/business owner	Confirms data value, business need, retention requirements, and acceptable use.
Privacy/legal advisor	Reviews regulated data, deletion, retention, contractual, and AI-use concerns. This may be internal counsel, outside counsel, or a part-time advisor.

In a small organization, these roles may be combined. The important point is that the responsibilities must still exist.

Minimum Processes

A smaller organization should define five basic DSPM processes before or during tool deployment.

Process	Minimum Requirement
Discovery intake	Decide which systems and repositories will be scanned first.
Data classification	Define a simple classification model, such as Public, Internal, Confidential, Restricted.
Risk prioritization	Rank findings by sensitivity, exposure, access, business criticality, and regulatory impact.
Remediation workflow	Assign findings to an owner, track status, and define due dates.
Exception and risk acceptance	Document when a risk is accepted, why, by whom, and until when.

These do not need to be complex. A spreadsheet, ticketing queue, shared decision log, and monthly review meeting may be enough at the beginning. What matters is that the process exists and is followed consistently.

Minimum Decision Rights

Decision	Who Must Decide
What data matters most?	Executive sponsor with security and business input
What gets scanned first?	Security owner and IT/platform owner
Who owns each critical repository?	Business owner or executive sponsor
What must be remediated immediately?	Security owner with business owner input
What can be accepted temporarily?	Business owner with executive or risk approval
What data can be exposed to AI tools?	Executive sponsor with security, privacy, and legal input
What metrics will be reported?	Security owner and executive sponsor

Minimum Metrics

Smaller organizations should avoid reporting too many metrics early. The first scorecard should be simple and outcome-focused.

Metric	Why It Matters
Percentage of critical repositories scanned	Shows visibility progress.
Number of restricted data findings	Establishes the sensitive data baseline.
Number of high-risk exposures	Shows immediate risk.
Percentage of findings with assigned owners	Measures accountability.
Number of overdue remediation items	Shows operational follow-through.
Number of accepted risks with expiration dates	Shows whether risk decisions are controlled.
Number of AI-accessible sensitive repositories	Measures AI readiness and exposure.

Minimum Operating Cadence

Meeting	Frequency	Purpose
DSPM working session	Weekly during first 30 to 60 days	Review findings, assign owners, clear blockers.
Risk review	Monthly	Review high-risk findings, accepted risks, overdue items, and policy exceptions.
Executive update	Quarterly	Report progress, unresolved risks, investment needs, and AI readiness.

Minimum Documentation

At minimum, smaller organizations should maintain:

- DSPM program charter
- Critical data definition
- Repository scan list
- Data owner list
- Risk prioritization rules
- Remediation tracker
- Risk acceptance log
- AI data access decision log
- Executive scorecard

This is enough to begin.

The organization can mature later by adding formal steering committees, richer data governance, automated workflows, integrated ticketing, DLP tuning, SIEM/SOAR integrations, privacy workflow automation, and board-level reporting.

The minimum viable operating model should be practical, not perfect.

A small organization that consistently reviews findings, assigns owners, documents exceptions, and remediates the highest-risk exposure is more mature than a large organization with a powerful DSPM platform and no operating discipline.

4.9 Map Regulatory Drivers to Actual Risk

Regulations matter, but they are not the same as risk.

Regulatory drivers help the organization understand which obligations may apply. Actual risk shows where harm is most likely, most severe, or least governed.

A weak DSPM business case says:

> We need DSPM because we have GDPR, HIPAA, PCI, GLBA, SOX, CCPA, or contractual obligations.

A stronger DSPM business case says:

> We need DSPM because critical data subject to regulatory, contractual, operational, and business obligations is overexposed, over-retained, duplicated, unowned, or accessible by too many identities across environments we cannot currently govern.

This distinction is important. The purpose of DSPM is not simply to prove that regulated data exists. Most organizations already know it exists. The real value comes from proving where that data creates unacceptable exposure, governance gaps, or business risk.

Data sovereignty should be evaluated the same way, especially in the context of AI. It is not enough to say, "We have EU data," "We have customer data," or "We use approved cloud regions." The organization must understand whether that data is being accessed by AI tools, copied into AI workspaces, indexed into retrieval systems, stored in prompt logs, transferred to vendors, or used in model development.

A sovereignty risk exists when the organization cannot prove where regulated, customer, employee, or confidential data is processed, or whether AI use changes the jurisdictional, contractual, retention, or deletion obligations attached to that data.

NIST SP 800-53 supports this risk-based approach by describing security and privacy controls as flexible and customizable within an organization-wide risk management process. Those controls should be derived from mission and business needs, laws, regulations, policies, standards, and guidelines.

Regulatory Driver	Actual Data Risk
GDPR / CCPA / privacy laws	Customer personal data is copied into analytics, development, and collaboration environments without clear retention or access controls.
HIPAA	PHI exists outside approved systems in spreadsheets, exports, support attachments, or shared drives.
PCI DSS	Cardholder data appears in logs, data lakes, testing environments, or unapproved databases.
GLBA / financial regulations	Consumer financial data is accessible to excessive internal users or third-party processors.

SOX	Financial reporting data is stored in uncontrolled repositories without integrity or access governance.
Contractual confidentiality	Customer confidential data is shared externally or retained after contract termination.
Data sovereignty / residency obligations	Sensitive or regulated data is processed, indexed, logged, or made available to AI systems in jurisdictions, vendor environments, or cloud regions that were not approved for that data use.
AI governance	Sensitive or regulated data is available to AI tools, model training pipelines, or copilots without approved use controls.

The goal is not to prove that sensitive data exists. The goal is to prove that the organization understands where critical data creates unacceptable risk and has a process to reduce that risk.

Use **Template 9: Regulatory-to-Risk Mapping** to connect obligations to actual data risk scenarios.

4.10 Define Critical Data

A DSPM program must define critical data before scanning at scale.

Sensitive data is broad. Critical data is prioritized.

Not all personal data, financial data, intellectual property, credentials, contracts, logs, or customer records create the same level of business risk. A single customer email address in a controlled CRM system does not carry the same risk as a bulk export of customer identity data stored in an unmanaged bucket with external access.

Working Definition

Critical data is data that would create unacceptable business, legal, financial, operational, privacy, security, reputational, or strategic impact if it were exposed, altered, deleted, misused, over-retained, or made unavailable.

Criticality should be determined by business impact, not merely by sensitivity label.

Critical Data Tiering Model

Tier	Category	Description	Examples
Tier 0	Crown Jewel Data	Data whose compromise could create material, existential, regulatory, or strategic business impact.	Bulk customer identity data, core intellectual property, payment data at scale, regulated health or financial records, production secrets, merger/acquisition data.
Tier 1	Highly Sensitive / Regulated Data	Data subject to significant legal, regulatory, contractual, or business confidentiality obligations.	PII, PHI, PCI, GLBA data, employee HR data, legal matter data, source code, credentials.

Tier 2	Sensitive Business Data	Data that could harm the business if exposed but may not trigger the highest regulatory or material impact.	Internal financial plans, pricing models, customer lists, product roadmaps, operational reports.
Tier 3	Internal Data	Data intended for internal use with limited harm if exposed.	Internal procedures, non-sensitive project documents, general business communications.
Tier 4	Public Data	Data approved for public release.	Published marketing materials, public documentation, press releases.

Criticality Risk Amplifiers

A DSPM program should elevate priority when sensitive data has one or more risk amplifiers.

Risk Amplifier	Why It Matters
Large volume	Bulk exposure increases regulatory, notification, and reputational impact.
External exposure	Public links, external sharing, third-party access, or internet-facing repositories increase likelihood.
Excessive privileges	Broad access increases misuse, insider threat, and accidental exposure risk.
Privileged identities	Admin, service account, contractor, and machine identity access can increase blast radius.
Unknown owner	No accountable party means findings will not be remediated.
Unapproved location	Data outside approved systems may bypass logging, retention, DLP, and access controls.
Production data in non-production	Development and test environments often have weaker controls.
Stale or abandoned data	Old data creates risk without business value.
AI/tool ingestion	Sensitive data available to AI systems may create new use, disclosure, and retention risks.
Contractual restriction	Customer, partner, or supplier contracts may impose stricter handling obligations.

Use **Template 10: Critical Data Decision Record** to document criticality decisions before broad scanning begins.

4.11 Build the Labeling and Tagging Strategy

Once data has been discovered and classified, the next architectural step is to make those classifications operational. Labels and tags provide the metadata that DSPM platforms, cloud controls, data catalogs, DLP tools, IAM systems, SIEM workflows, and compliance processes use to apply the right controls to the right data.

NIST describes data classification as a way to characterize data assets using persistent labels so those assets can be managed properly. NIST also emphasizes that classification helps organizations apply cybersecurity and privacy protection requirements to data at scale, including use cases such as secure data sharing, compliance monitoring, zero trust architecture, and large language models.

In DSPM, labels and tags should not be treated as cosmetic metadata. They should drive security decisions.

A strong labeling and tagging strategy helps answer:

- *Who owns this data?*
- *What type of data is it?*
- *How sensitive is it?*
- *What would happen if it were exposed, changed, deleted, or misused?*
- *Where is it allowed to live?*
- *Who is allowed to access it?*
- *What controls should apply?*
- *Which workflows should be triggered?*

NIST Foundation for Labels and Tags

NIST guidance provides several concepts that translate well into DSPM architecture.

First, FIPS 199 establishes the idea of categorizing information and systems based on the potential impact to confidentiality, integrity, and availability if the information or system is compromised. The impact values are typically expressed as low, moderate, or high.

Second, NIST SP 800-60 provides a methodology for mapping information types to security categories and impact levels. This is useful for DSPM because different types of data create different levels of business, privacy, regulatory, and operational risk.

Third, NIST SP 800-53 Rev. 5 includes the concept of security and privacy attributes in control AC-16. These attributes can be associated with information in storage, in process, or in transmission, and retained with the information to support policy enforcement. This aligns closely with the way DSPM platforms use labels, tags, and metadata to drive automated controls.

For DSPM architects, the practical lesson is this:

Labels and tags should represent risk, ownership, business context, and control requirements in a way that both humans and systems can understand.

Labels vs. Tags vs. Attributes

The terms label, tag, and attribute are often used interchangeably, but they are not always the same thing.

Term	Meaning	Example	Typical Use
Label	A classification or designation applied to data.	Confidential, Restricted, Regulated	Communicates sensitivity and handling expectations.
Tag	A metadata value attached to an asset or resource.	owner=finance, environment=prod	Supports inventory, filtering, automation, and ownership.
Attribute	A security, privacy, or business property associated with data.	impact=high, residency=EU, PII=true	Supports policy decisions and access control.

In a DSPM program, these should work together. A file, table, bucket, database, or SaaS object may have a sensitivity label, multiple data type tags, an owner tag, a residency attribute, and an impact rating.

Asset	Labels	Tags	Attributes
Customer database	Restricted	PII, Customer Data, Production	confidentiality=high, owner=sales, region=US
HR payroll export	Restricted	PII, HR, Payroll	confidentiality=high, retention=7 years
Marketing brochure	Public	Marketing, Approved Content	external_share=true
Developer test bucket	Confidential	Source Code, Non-Production	owner=engineering, environment=dev

Recommended DSPM Label and Tag Model

A DSPM labeling model should be simple enough for business users to understand and structured enough for security tools to enforce. The goal is not to create the most complex taxonomy. The goal is to create a practical control language for data security.

Category	Required	Example Values	Purpose
Sensitivity	Yes	Public, Internal, Confidential, Restricted	Establishes baseline handling requirements.
Data Type	Yes	PII, PHI, PCI, Credentials, Source Code, Financial Data	Identifies the kind of data present.
Impact Level	Yes	Low, Moderate, High	Aligns to NIST-style impact thinking.
Business Owner	Yes	HR, Finance, Legal, Engineering, Sales	Establishes accountability.
Technical Owner	Recommended	CloudOps, DBA Team, App Team	Identifies who can remediate issues.

Environment	Yes	Production, Development, Test, Backup	Identifies operational context.
Regulatory Scope	Conditional	GDPR, HIPAA, PCI DSS, CCPA, CJIS	Maps data to compliance requirements.
Data Residency	Conditional	US, EU, UK, Canada	Supports sovereignty and location-based controls.
Handling Rule	Yes	Encrypt, Restrict Sharing, Retain, Quarantine, Review	Converts classification into action.

Sensitivity Labels

Sensitivity labels should describe how carefully the organization must protect the data. These labels should be easy to explain, consistently applied, and mapped to specific handling requirements.

Sensitivity Label	Description	Example Data	Baseline Handling
Public	Approved for public release.	Published marketing material, public job postings.	External sharing allowed.
Internal	Business data not intended for public release.	Internal process documents, non-sensitive project notes.	Limit to workforce or approved partners.
Confidential	Sensitive business or customer data that could cause harm if exposed.	Customer lists, contracts, internal financial reports.	Restrict access, monitor sharing, encrypt where appropriate.
Restricted	Highly sensitive, regulated, privileged, or high-impact data.	SSNs, credentials, payment data, legal holds, sensitive HR data.	Strong access control, encryption, monitoring, approval-based sharing.

A useful rule for architects:

Sensitivity labels should describe the required level of protection, not just the type of data discovered.

For example, "PII" is not a complete sensitivity label by itself. PII describes the data type. The sensitivity depends on context, volume, identifiability, exposure, jurisdiction, and potential impact.

Scenario	Data Type	Sensitivity
One employee name in a meeting note	PII	Internal
A full employee export with SSNs and bank account numbers	PII	Restricted
Customer email list in a CRM export	PII	Confidential
Public executive bio on the company website	PII	Public

Impact Labels

NIST's categorization model is useful because it forces the organization to think about consequences. In DSPM, impact labels help prioritize remediation and determine how aggressively controls should be applied.

Impact Label	Meaning	Example
Low	Limited adverse effect if exposed, changed, or unavailable.	Public or low-risk internal reference data.
Moderate	Serious adverse effect if exposed, changed, or unavailable.	Customer records, contracts, business financials.
High	Severe or catastrophic adverse effect if exposed, changed, or unavailable.	Credentials, regulated health data, payment data, sensitive legal data.

Impact should consider confidentiality, integrity, and availability.

Impact Dimension	DSPM Question
Confidentiality	*What happens if this data is disclosed to the wrong person?*
Integrity	*What happens if this data is changed without authorization?*
Availability	*What happens if this data is unavailable when needed?*

For many DSPM use cases, confidentiality gets the most attention, but integrity and availability should not be ignored. A data set used for fraud decisions, patient care, financial reporting, or security automation may carry high integrity impact even if the data is not the most confidential asset.

Tagging Strategy

Tags add operational context to labels. Labels explain sensitivity and handling. Tags explain ownership, location, environment, business process, and technical context.

Tag Type	Example Format	Why It Matters
Owner Tag	owner=finance	Routes findings and approvals.
Technical Owner Tag	tech_owner=data-platform	Supports remediation.
Environment Tag	environment=production	Separates production risk from test data risk.
Application Tag	app=claims-processing	Links data to business systems.
Business Process Tag	process=payroll	Supports impact and compliance analysis.
Region Tag	region=eu	Supports residency and sovereignty controls.
Retention Tag	retention=7-years	Supports lifecycle management.

Regulatory Tag	regulation=PCI	Supports audit and reporting.
Exception Tag	exception=approved-until-2026-09-30	Prevents permanent unmanaged exceptions.

Tags should be standardized. Free-form tagging creates duplicates, inconsistent values, and reporting problems.

Avoid inconsistent formats such as:

- owner=Finance
- Owner=finance
- business_owner=FIN
- department=Accounting
- data-owner=finops

Use a controlled format instead:

- owner=finance
- technical_owner=cloudops
- environment=production
- region=us
- regulation=pci

Label and Tag Governance

A labeling strategy needs governance or it will decay over time. DSPM architects should define who can create labels, who can modify them, and how exceptions are handled.

Governance Question	Recommended Decision
Who owns the label taxonomy?	Security, privacy, governance, and data office jointly.
Who approves new labels?	Data governance council or security architecture board.
Who can change labels on sensitive assets?	Data owner with security review.
How are false positives corrected?	Documented review and tuning workflow.
How are exceptions tracked?	Exception tag with owner and expiration date.
How often are labels reviewed?	Continuously for high-risk data, periodically for lower-risk data.
How are labels audited?	DSPM reporting, SIEM events, data catalog history, and policy logs.

Label Persistence

NIST's discussion of persistent labels is important for DSPM. A label is most useful when it remains associated with the data as the data moves or changes.

DSPM architects should consider how labels persist across:

- Cloud object storage
- Databases and data warehouses

- SaaS repositories
- File shares
- Data pipelines
- Backups
- Exports
- Third-party transfers
- AI and analytics platforms
- Development and test environments

Some platforms support embedded labels or metadata. Others only support external catalog entries. In many real environments, the label may not literally travel inside the file or record. Instead, the DSPM platform maintains the association through asset ID, path, table name, object metadata, schema, hash, catalog reference, or cloud resource tag.

That distinction matters. If the label association breaks when data moves, the organization may lose visibility and control.

Policy Mapping

Every important label or tag should map to an action. Otherwise, the organization may be collecting metadata without reducing risk.

Label or Tag	Policy Action
Restricted	Require encryption, least privilege, monitoring, and owner approval for sharing.
PII	Apply privacy review, access monitoring, and jurisdiction checks.
PCI	Validate segmentation, access, encryption, and retention controls.
Credentials	Alert security, rotate secrets, remove from exposed locations.
Production	Prioritize remediation over comparable non-production findings.
EU Region	Enforce residency and cross-border transfer controls.
Public	Allow external sharing only when approved for public release.
No Owner	Generate governance finding and route to data stewardship queue.

DSPM Workflow Example

Step	DSPM Action	Label or Tag Output
1	Discover S3 bucket containing customer exports.	asset_type=object_storage
2	Detect names, emails, phone numbers, and account IDs.	data_type=PII
3	Identify production source system.	environment=production
4	Determine business owner from CMDB or cloud tags.	owner=sales

5	Identify external sharing exposure.	exposure=external
6	Assign sensitivity and impact.	sensitivity=confidential, confidentiality_impact=moderate
7	Trigger policy workflow.	restrict_sharing, notify_owner, open_ticket
8	Validate remediation.	status=remediated

This is where labels and tags become valuable. They turn raw discovery results into control decisions.

Common Labeling and Tagging Pitfalls

Pitfall	Why It Creates Risk	Better Approach
Too many labels	Users and tools apply labels inconsistently.	Start with a small, controlled taxonomy.
Labels without enforcement	Classification does not reduce risk.	Map labels to access, encryption, sharing, and monitoring controls.
Manual-only labeling	Coverage becomes incomplete and stale.	Use DSPM automation with data owner validation.
No ownership tag	Findings have nowhere to go.	Require business and technical owner tags.
Treating all PII the same	Context and impact vary widely.	Combine data type, sensitivity, volume, exposure, and jurisdiction.
Static labels	Data changes over time.	Reassess labels continuously.
Free-form tags	Reporting becomes unreliable.	Use approved keys and values.
Permanent exceptions	Risk becomes invisible.	Require exception owner, reason, and expiration date.
Tool-specific taxonomy only	Labels do not translate across platforms.	Define an enterprise taxonomy and map tool-specific values to it.

Architect Guidance

When designing a DSPM labeling and tagging strategy, architects should avoid building the taxonomy around one tool. Instead, define the enterprise model first, then map individual platforms to that model.

A good model should be:

- **Understandable:** Business users and data owners can interpret the labels.
- **Enforceable:** Security tools can take action based on the labels and tags.
- **Persistent:** Labels remain associated with the data across movement, copies, and lifecycle changes where technically possible.
- **Auditable:** The organization can explain who applied a label, when it was applied, why it was applied, and what action resulted.

- **Risk-based:** Labels reflect potential business, security, privacy, legal, and operational impact.
- **Interoperable:** Labels and tags can be used across DSPM, DLP, IAM, cloud security, data catalog, SIEM, SOAR, GRC, and ticketing workflows.

Use **Template 11: Enterprise Label Standard** and **Template 12: Sample Labeling Rules** to convert classification decisions into operational metadata.

4.12 Establish Ownership and Accountability

DSPM findings fail when no one owns the data, no one owns the system, or no one owns the risk.

The program must distinguish between different types of ownership.

Role	Accountability
Executive Sponsor	Funds and champions the program. Removes blockers. Escalates unresolved risk.
Program Owner	Owns program execution, roadmap, governance cadence, reporting, and outcomes.
Data Owner	Accountable for business use, criticality, access expectations, and risk decisions for a data domain.
Data Steward	Maintains metadata, quality, classification, and operational governance for a data domain.
System Owner	Owns the application, database, SaaS platform, storage environment, or data platform where data resides.
Control Owner	Owns the operation of a specific control, such as access review, encryption, logging, retention, or DLP.
Remediation Owner	Performs or coordinates the technical fix.
Risk Owner	Accepts, mitigates, transfers, or escalates residual risk.
Evidence Owner	Produces proof that remediation or control operation occurred.

A simple rule should be adopted:

No finding should be reported as actionable unless it has an owner, severity, remediation path, due date, and risk decision.

Ownership must be established before tickets are generated. Otherwise, the DSPM program becomes a finding factory instead of a risk reduction program.

4.13 Avoid the "Scan Everything, Fix Nothing" Trap

Risk acceptance should not be treated as a quiet workaround for unresolved findings. Accepted risk should have a named business owner, documented rationale, expiration date, compensating controls, review cadence, and escalation path. If the accepted risk involves regulated data, external exposure, privileged access, AI access, or material business impact, it should be visible to the appropriate governance body.

One of the most common DSPM failures is scanning too broadly before the organization is ready to act.

The result is predictable:

- The tool finds thousands or millions of issues.
- Dashboards look impressive.
- Engineering teams are overwhelmed.
- Data owners dispute findings.
- Tickets are ignored.
- Security cannot prove risk reduction.
- Executives lose confidence.

This is the **scan everything, fix nothing** trap.

A DSPM program should establish guardrails before the first scan.

Guardrail	Purpose
Define the first risk themes before scanning.	Example: public exposure of Tier 0/Tier 1 data, excessive privileged access, sensitive data in non-production.
Limit the first wave to priority environments.	Start with crown-jewel data domains or high-risk repositories.
Define severity rules in advance.	Avoid treating every sensitive data match as equal.
Assign owners before generating tickets.	Findings without owners create noise.
Create remediation SLAs.	Critical and high-risk findings require time-bound action.
Define exception and risk acceptance workflows.	Some findings cannot be fixed immediately and require formal decisions.
Validate findings before executive reporting.	False positives damage trust.
Report risk reduction, not finding volume.	The goal is fewer material exposures, not more dashboard entries.

Suggested DSPM Severity Model

Severity	Criteria	Example SLA
Critical	Tier 0 or Tier 1 data with public exposure, external access, privileged overexposure, active misuse, or regulatory breach potential.	7 to 15 days
High	Critical or regulated data with excessive internal access, unapproved location, weak controls, or unknown owner.	30 days
Medium	Sensitive data with control gaps but limited exposure or compensating controls.	60 to 90 days

Low	Internal data hygiene issue, low-risk duplicate, or policy improvement opportunity.	Backlog / planned remediation
Accepted Risk	Business-approved exception with documented rationale, expiration, and compensating controls.	Review by expiration date

A strong operating principle is:

No scan without a remediation lane. No finding without an owner. No dashboard without a decision.

Use **Template 5: Program Design** and **Template 6: Implementation Plan** to define operating workflows before deployment.

4.14 Define Success Before the Tool Is Deployed

Before a single DSPM tool is deployed, the organization should already have evidence that a program exists.

Success before tool deployment means the organization has completed the business foundation.

Program Element	Success Indicator
Executive sponsorship	CISO, CDO, Legal, Privacy, Engineering, and business leadership agree to the program purpose.
Program charter	Approved charter defines mission, scope, authority, governance, and success criteria.
Stakeholder model	Named stakeholders and decision rights are documented.
Critical data definition	Critical data tiers and risk amplifiers are approved.
Ownership model	Data owner, system owner, control owner, remediation owner, and risk owner roles are defined.
Regulatory-to-risk mapping	Regulatory drivers are mapped to actual data risk scenarios.
Initial scope	First-wave data domains, platforms, and risk themes are selected.
Remediation workflow	Ticketing, SLA, validation, escalation, and exception processes are defined.
Metrics	KPIs and KRIs are agreed before dashboards are built.
Procurement requirements	Tool requirements are derived from program needs, not vendor demos.
Budget and staffing	Funding, staffing, and operating cadence are approved.
Governance cadence	Steering committee, working group, and reporting schedule are established.

NIST Privacy Framework also supports using profiles to inform buying decisions by generating prioritized privacy requirements, evaluating partners, making trade-offs, and addressing residual risk. This is directly applicable to DSPM: define the program requirements first, then use them to evaluate technology.

Use **Template 4: Market & Needs Analysis**, **Template 7: Budget & Resources**, and **Template 8: Evaluation & Growth Strategy** to prepare for procurement and long-term program maturity.

How DSPM Programs Fail

- Tool purchased without operating model
- No data owners
- Findings routed to teams without authority
- Security owns risk that belongs to the business
- No severity model
- No remediation SLAs
- No executive sponsor
- No exception process
- No integration into IAM, DLP, ticketing, GRC, privacy, or SIEM
- Dashboards report activity instead of risk reduction
- AI initiatives outrun data governance

4.15 Business Objective Document Set

The business objectives for a DSPM program should be captured in a formal document set before tool purchase.

At minimum, the organization should create:

1. Data Security Program Charter
2. Executive Summary
3. Goals & Objectives
4. Market & Needs Analysis
5. Program Design
6. Implementation Plan
7. Budget & Resources
8. Evaluation & Growth Strategy

These artifacts help leadership, security, data governance, privacy, legal, engineering, risk, and business owners agree on what the program is designed to accomplish before the organization evaluates or purchases a DSPM platform.

A DSPM business case should not be built only around tool capability. It should be built around measurable risk reduction. The investment should connect to reduced sensitive data exposure, faster remediation, better AI readiness, improved audit evidence, reduced DLP noise, stronger privacy operations, lower breach impact, and fewer unmanaged repositories containing regulated or business-critical data.

4.16 Templates

The templates in this section are designed to help turn the concepts in this chapter into practical program artifacts. They provide a starting point for documenting the DSPM program charter, executive alignment, business objectives, stakeholder needs, operating model, implementation plan, budget, growth strategy, regulatory risk mapping, critical data decisions, and labeling standards.

The templates in this chapter are original working templates created for this book from field experience. They are not legal, regulatory, or vendor forms. Organizations should adapt them to their own governance model, obligations, and counsel-approved requirements

These templates should be completed before tool selection whenever possible. They help ensure that the organization understands what it is trying to accomplish, who must participate, which data matters most, how risk will be prioritized, and what evidence will be used to prove progress. They are not meant to be static documents. As the DSPM program matures, they should be reviewed, updated, and used to guide governance decisions, vendor evaluation, remediation workflows, and executive reporting.

Template 1: Data Security Program Charter

Document Control

Field	Entry
Program Name	Enterprise Data Security Posture Management Program
Version	v1.0
Date	Date
Prepared By	Name / Role
Executive Sponsor	Name / Role
Program Owner	Name / Role
Approvers	CISO, CDO, Legal, Privacy, Engineering, CIO, Risk, Business Sponsors

1. Program Name

Example: Enterprise Data Security and DSPM Program

2. Purpose and Background

This program exists to establish an enterprise operating model for identifying, prioritizing, governing, remediating, and reporting risk associated with critical data across the organization.

The organization currently faces increasing data risk due to:

- Cloud adoption
- SaaS growth
- Data lake / warehouse expansion
- AI and analytics use
- Regulatory obligations
- Third-party data sharing
- Data duplication
- Excessive access
- Unclear data ownership
- Retention and minimization gaps

This program will ensure that data security decisions are business-aligned, risk-based, owner-accountable, and measurable.

3. Program Mission

The mission of the Data Security Program is to protect critical business data by establishing clear ownership, visibility, prioritization, remediation, governance, and reporting across the enterprise.

4. Program Objectives

Objective	Description	Target Outcome
Identify critical data	Define and locate Tier 0 and Tier 1 data across priority environments.	Critical data inventory established.
Establish ownership	Assign accountable data owners, system owners, and remediation owners.	Findings are routed to accountable owners.
Prioritize risk	Rank findings based on business impact, exposure, access, regulation, and likelihood.	High-risk issues are addressed first.
Reduce exposure	Remediate public exposure, excessive access, unapproved locations, and stale data.	Measurable reduction in material data exposure.
Improve governance	Align security, privacy, legal, data governance, and engineering workflows.	Cross-functional operating model established.
Support compliance	Produce evidence for regulatory, contractual, audit, and board reporting.	Improved audit readiness and evidence quality.
Enable safe innovation	Support secure data use for analytics, AI, product, and business operations.	Business can use data with defined guardrails.

5. Guiding Principles

The program will operate according to the following principles:

- Business-first: Data security priorities will be based on business impact.
- Risk-tiered: Not all sensitive data will be treated equally.
- Owner-accountable: Every material finding must have an accountable owner.
- Remediation-ready: The program will not scan broadly without defined remediation workflows.
- Evidence-driven: Success will be measured through risk reduction and control evidence.
- Privacy and legal aligned: Regulatory and contractual obligations will be mapped to actual risk.
- Technology-enabled, not technology-led: Tools will support a program; they will not define it.

6. Scope

In Scope:

- Production cloud data stores
- Data warehouses and lakes
- SaaS repositories
- Collaboration platforms
- Databases containing Tier 0 or Tier 1 data
- Critical business data domains
- Data access and exposure risks
- Data retention and duplication risks
- AI data usage risks

Out of Scope:

- Systems not included in Phase 1
- Archived systems without active risk
- Public data repositories
- Low-risk internal repositories
- Systems pending ownership validation

7. Critical Data Definition

The program defines critical data as:

Data that would create unacceptable business, legal, financial, operational, privacy, security, reputational, or strategic impact if exposed, altered, deleted, misused, over-retained, or made unavailable.

Tier	Description
Tier 0	Crown jewel data
Tier 1	Highly sensitive or regulated data
Tier 2	Sensitive business data
Tier 3	Internal data
Tier 4	Public data

8. Governance and Roles

Role	Name / Function	Responsibility
Executive Sponsor		Funding, executive support, escalation.
Program Owner		Program execution and reporting.
Security Lead		Security requirements and risk prioritization.
Data Governance Lead		Data ownership and stewardship.
Privacy Lead		Privacy obligations and privacy risk.

Legal Lead		Legal, contractual, breach, and privilege considerations.
Engineering Lead		Technical remediation and implementation.
Risk / Compliance Lead		Control mapping and audit evidence.
Business Data Owners		Criticality, risk decisions, remediation prioritization.

9. Decision Rights

Decision	Decision Owner
Program scope	Steering Committee
Critical data tiers	Data Governance + Security + Business Owners
Risk severity model	Security + Risk + Privacy + Legal
Risk acceptance	Business Risk Owner
Regulatory interpretation	Legal / Privacy
Technical remediation method	Engineering / System Owner
Tool selection	Steering Committee + Procurement
Budget approval	Executive Sponsor

10. Timeline and Milestones

Milestone	Target Date	Owner
Charter approved		Executive Sponsor
Stakeholder council established		Program Owner
Critical data standard approved		CDO / CISO
Regulatory-to-risk mapping completed		Legal / Privacy / Risk
Phase 1 scope selected		Steering Committee
Remediation workflow approved		Security / Engineering
DSPM requirements finalized		Program Owner
Vendor evaluation completed		Procurement / Steering Committee
Phase 1 deployment begins		Engineering / Security

11. Budget Overview

Category	Estimated Cost	Notes
Program staffing	$	Program manager, architect, analysts, data governance support.
DSPM platform	$	Licensing, deployment, support.
Integrations	$	SIEM, SOAR, ticketing, IAM, data catalog, cloud, SaaS.
Professional services	$	Implementation or advisory support.
Training and change management	$	Stakeholder education and operating procedures.
Contingency	$	Unexpected integration or remediation support.

12. Risks and Mitigation

Risk	Impact	Mitigation
Lack of business ownership	Findings remain unresolved.	Assign owners before scanning.
Tool-first implementation	Program becomes dashboard-only.	Approve charter and operating model first.
Too many findings	Teams are overwhelmed.	Use phased scope and severity model.
Engineering resistance	Remediation slows.	Involve engineering in design and SLAs.
Regulatory ambiguity	Misaligned priorities.	Legal and Privacy approve obligations mapping.
Poor data quality	Incorrect owners or classifications.	Validate metadata and integrate with data governance.

13. Success Criteria

The program will be considered successful when:

- Critical data domains are defined and approved.
- Priority data stores are inventoried.
- Material findings have named owners.
- Critical and high-risk remediation SLAs are operating.
- Executive reporting shows risk reduction.
- Regulatory and audit evidence can be produced.
- Tool requirements are mapped to approved business objectives.

14. Approval

Approver	Role	Signature	Date
Name	CISO		
Name	CDO		
Name	Legal		
Name	Privacy		
Name	Engineering		
Name	Risk / Compliance		

Template 2: Executive Summary

Purpose: This executive summary provides a concise, leadership-level explanation of why the DSPM program exists, what business risk it addresses, what outcomes it will deliver, and what decisions are required.

Field	Entry
Program Name	Enterprise Data Security and DSPM Program
Executive Sponsor	Name / Role
Program Owner	Name / Role

Business Problem

The organization's data footprint has expanded across cloud platforms, SaaS applications, databases, data lakes, collaboration tools, analytics environments, and emerging AI use cases. Current processes do not provide sufficient enterprise-wide visibility into where critical data resides, who owns it, who has access to it, where it is exposed, how long it is retained, or whether it is being used in approved ways.

This creates business risk in the form of regulatory exposure, breach impact, excessive access, unmanaged data duplication, contractual risk, privacy risk, intellectual property exposure, and reduced executive confidence in data security posture.

Program Purpose

The purpose of this program is to establish a business-led, risk-based data security operating model that enables the organization to identify, prioritize, remediate, govern, and report risk to critical data.

Why Now

This program is needed now because:

- Cloud and SaaS data growth has increased.
- AI and analytics use has expanded.
- Regulatory obligations have increased.
- Data ownership is inconsistent.
- Security lacks reliable visibility into critical data risk.
- Audit, compliance, or board reporting expectations have increased.
- Recent incidents or near-misses revealed data exposure gaps.

Strategic Outcomes

Outcome	Business Value
Critical data visibility	The organization can identify where high-value and regulated data resides.
Ownership and accountability	Findings are assigned to business and technical owners.
Risk-based prioritization	Teams focus on the highest-impact risks first.

Reduced exposure	Public, external, excessive, and inappropriate access are reduced.
Regulatory support	Evidence is available for audits, compliance reviews, and privacy obligations.
Safer data use	Business teams can use data for analytics and AI with defined guardrails.

Initial Scope

- Top critical data domains
- Priority cloud platforms
- Selected SaaS repositories
- Data warehouses or lakes
- Public exposure and excessive access
- Production data in non-production environments
- Unapproved AI or analytics use

Investment Request

The program requests approval for:

- Program resources
- Stakeholder participation
- DSPM tool evaluation
- Implementation support
- Engineering remediation capacity
- Governance cadence

Decisions Required

Leadership is asked to approve:

1. The program charter.
2. The executive sponsor and program owner.
3. The stakeholder council.
4. The definition of critical data.
5. The first-wave program scope.
6. The budget and resource model.
7. The DSPM tool evaluation criteria.

Executive Summary Statement

The Enterprise Data Security and DSPM Program will establish a risk-based operating model to identify, govern, remediate, and report risk to critical data across cloud, SaaS, data, and analytics environments. The program will focus first on the organization's highest-value and highest-risk data, including regulated personal data, customer data, financial data, intellectual property, credentials, and business-critical datasets. Success will be measured by ownership coverage, reduction of material exposure, remediation of critical findings, improved audit evidence, and executive visibility into data risk.

Template 3: Goals & Objectives

Purpose: This document defines the measurable goals and objectives of the DSPM program. Objectives should be SMART: specific, measurable, achievable, relevant, and time-bound.

Goals & Objectives Template

Goal	Business Rationale	SMART Objective	Key Results	Owner	Timeline
Identify critical data	The organization cannot protect what it cannot locate.	Identify and validate Tier 0 and Tier 1 data across Phase 1 platforms within 90 days.	X% of Phase 1 repositories scanned; Y critical data domains validated.		
Establish data ownership	Findings cannot be remediated without accountable owners.	Assign business and technical owners to X% of critical data stores within 120 days.	Owner coverage; unresolved ownership gaps.		
Reduce material exposure	Exposed critical data creates breach and regulatory risk.	Remediate X% of critical findings involving public or external exposure within SLA.	Critical findings closed; exposure reduction trend.		
Improve access governance	Excessive access increases insider and compromise risk.	Reduce excessive access to Tier 0 and Tier 1 data by X% within Y months.	Access removed; privileged access reviewed.		
Reduce stale data risk	Retained data without business value creates unnecessary liability.	Identify and disposition X% of stale Tier 1 data in Phase 1 environments within Y months.	Data deleted, archived, or exception-approved.		
Support compliance evidence	Audit evidence is inconsistent and manual.	Produce repeatable evidence reports for regulations/frameworks by date.	Reports produced; audit acceptance.		
Operationalize remediation	Findings must move through a managed workflow.	Implement DSPM triage, assignment, remediation, validation, and exception workflow within 90 days.	SLA adherence; closure rate; exception rate.		

Objective Detail Template

Field	Entry
Objective Name	Name
Objective Statement	What will be accomplished
Business Outcome	Why it matters
Baseline	Current state
Target	Desired measurable state
Metric	How success will be measured
Data Source	DSPM, IAM, CMDB, ticketing, data catalog, SIEM, audit report
Owner	Accountable owner
Contributors	Supporting teams
Start Date	Date
Target Date	Date
Dependencies	Systems, teams, approvals, integrations
Risks	Risks to achievement
Acceptance Criteria	What proves completion

Template 4: Market & Needs Analysis

Purpose: For a DSPM program, "market and needs analysis" should not only mean external vendor market research. It should also mean understanding the internal enterprise environment, stakeholder needs, current capability gaps, regulatory pressures, and business demand for data security.

1. Purpose

The purpose of this analysis is to determine the organization's need for a DSPM program and supporting technology by evaluating business drivers, stakeholder requirements, current-state gaps, regulatory obligations, data risk scenarios, and available market capabilities.

2. Business Environment

Area	Current State	Impact on DSPM Need
Cloud adoption		
SaaS usage		
Data warehouse / lake usage		
AI and analytics		
Third-party sharing		
Regulatory footprint		
Data governance maturity		
Security tooling maturity		

3. Stakeholder Needs

Stakeholder	Need	Current Gap	Required Capability
CISO	Executive visibility into critical data risk.	Data risk reporting is incomplete or manual.	Risk dashboard, severity model, remediation reporting.
CDO	Data ownership and governance alignment.	Data stores lack owners or metadata.	Owner mapping, catalog integration, data domain tagging.
Legal	Evidence of contractual and legal data handling.	Data location and sharing are difficult to prove.	Regulatory mapping, evidence reporting.
Privacy	Visibility into personal data use, location, retention, and exposure.	Personal data exists outside approved workflows.	Classification, retention insight, privacy risk reporting.
Engineering	Actionable, prioritized remediation guidance.	Findings are noisy or lack context.	Ticketing, APIs, severity, remediation workflow.

Audit / Compliance	Repeatable evidence.	Manual evidence collection.	Control mapping and exportable reports.
Business Owners	Understanding of risk to their data domains.	Data risk is technical and unclear.	Business-facing reports and risk decisions.

4. Current Capability Assessment

Capability	Current State	Target State	Gap
Data discovery			
Classification			
Data ownership			
Access analysis			
Exposure detection			
Retention / stale data			
Remediation workflow			
Compliance evidence			
AI data governance			
Executive reporting			

5. External Market Capability Review

Capability Area	Required?	Notes
Cloud data discovery	Yes/No	AWS, Azure, GCP storage and databases.
SaaS discovery	Yes/No	M365, Google Workspace, Salesforce, ServiceNow, etc.
Data warehouse support	Yes/No	Snowflake, Databricks, BigQuery, Redshift, Synapse.
Structured and unstructured classification	Yes/No	Databases, files, documents, objects.
Identity and access analysis	Yes/No	Users, groups, roles, service accounts, machine identities.
Exposure analysis	Yes/No	Public, external, cross-account, third-party sharing.
Data lineage / movement	Yes/No	Movement between systems and copies.
Remediation workflows	Yes/No	Ticketing, ownership, SLA, validation.
Policy engine	Yes/No	Custom policies based on business rules.
Compliance mapping	Yes/No	Evidence for regulatory and audit requirements.
API and integrations	Yes/No	SIEM, SOAR, IAM, CMDB, data catalog, GRC.
AI data risk visibility	Yes/No	Sensitive data accessible to AI tools or pipelines.

6. Prioritization Matrix

Need	Business Impact	Urgency	Feasibility	Priority
Identify Tier 0/Tier 1 data	High	High	Medium	Critical
Reduce public exposure	High	High	High	Critical
Assign data owners	High	Medium	Medium	High
Integrate with ticketing	Medium	High	High	High
Automate retention workflows	Medium	Medium	Low	Medium
Expand to all SaaS platforms	Medium	Medium	Medium	Medium

7. Recommendation

Based on the analysis, the organization should proceed with a DSPM program that first focuses on:

- Critical data domains
- High-risk environments
- Exposure and access risks
- Ownership and remediation workflow
- Compliance evidence
- Vendor evaluation based on program-defined requirements

Template 5: Program Design

Purpose: The Program Design document defines how the DSPM program will operate. It translates the charter into workstreams, processes, roles, workflows, and control expectations.

1. Program Operating Model

The DSPM program will operate as a cross-functional governance and remediation program involving Security, Data Governance, Privacy, Legal, Engineering, Risk, Compliance, IT, and Business Data Owners.

2. Program Workstreams

Workstream	Purpose	Owner
Governance and Steering	Provide oversight, decisions, escalation, and executive reporting.	
Critical Data Definition	Define critical data tiers, data domains, and risk amplifiers.	
Discovery and Classification	Identify where critical and sensitive data resides.	
Ownership Mapping	Assign business, technical, and remediation owners.	
Access and Exposure Risk	Identify excessive access, public exposure, third-party sharing, and privileged access.	
Remediation Operations	Triage, assign, remediate, validate, and close findings.	
Regulatory and Evidence Mapping	Align findings and controls to obligations and audit evidence.	
Metrics and Reporting	Produce KPIs, KRIs, executive reporting, and board-level summaries.	
Change Management and Training	Educate stakeholders and drive adoption.	

3. DSPM Operating Workflow

Step	Description	Owner
1. Scope	Select approved data domains, platforms, and risk scenarios.	Steering Committee
2. Discover	Identify data stores and sensitive data.	Security / Platform Team
3. Classify	Categorize data by type, sensitivity, and criticality.	Security / Data Governance
4. Enrich	Add owner, business process, system, identity, regulatory, and risk context.	Program Team
5. Prioritize	Apply severity model and risk scoring.	Security / Risk
6. Triage	Validate findings and remove noise.	Security / Data Owner

7. Assign	Route findings to remediation owners.	Program Team
8. Remediate	Fix access, exposure, duplication, retention, or policy violations.	Engineering / System Owner
9. Validate	Confirm risk reduction.	Security / Control Owner
10. Report	Report status, trends, exceptions, and residual risk.	Program Owner

4. RACI Template

Activity	Executive Sponsor / Steering Committee	CISO	CTO	CDO	Legal	Privacy	Engineering	Directors / Sr. Managers	Data Owner	Risk / Compliance
Approve program charter	A	R/C	C	C	C	C	C	C	C	C
Define critical data	C	C	C	A	C	C	C	R	R	C
Define severity model	C	A	C	C	C	C	C	R	C	R
Approve first-wave scope	A	R	C	R	C	C	R	R	C	C
Validate regulatory obligations	C	C	C	C	A	A	I	C	C	R
Remediate findings	I	C	C	I	I	C	A/R	R	R	C
Accept residual risk	C	C	C	C	C	C	C	C	A	C
Report executive metrics	A	R	C	C	C	C	C	R	C	R

R = Responsible
A = Accountable
C = Consulted
I = Informed

5. Policy and Standard Alignment

The program should align to:

- Data classification standard
- Access control policy
- Data retention policy
- Encryption standard
- Cloud security standard
- Third-party data sharing policy
- Incident response plan
- Privacy policy
- AI governance policy
- Acceptable use policy

6. Tool Requirements Derived from Program Design

Program Requirement	DSPM Capability Needed
Identify critical data across priority platforms.	Discovery and classification across cloud, SaaS, databases, and data warehouses.
Map findings to owners.	CMDB, data catalog, IAM, and ownership integration.
Prioritize based on exposure and access.	Risk scoring using sensitivity, exposure, identity, and business context.
Support remediation.	Ticketing, workflow, SLA, validation, and exception handling.
Provide executive reporting.	Dashboards, trend reporting, evidence exports.
Support compliance.	Regulatory mapping and control evidence.
Govern AI data risk.	Visibility into sensitive data accessible to AI platforms or pipelines.

Template 6: Implementation Plan

Purpose: The Implementation Plan defines how the DSPM program will be launched, phased, staffed, governed, and measured.

Phase 0: Program Mobilization

Activity	Owner	Target Date	Exit Criteria
Approve charter	Executive Sponsor		Signed charter
Establish steering committee	Program Owner		Members named
Define critical data tiers	CDO / CISO		Approved standard
Define severity model	Security / Risk		Approved scoring
Define remediation workflow	Security / Engineering		Workflow approved
Select Phase 1 scope	Steering Committee		Scope documented

Phase 1: Baseline and Discovery

Activity	Owner	Target Date	Exit Criteria
Connect priority environments	Engineering / Security		Approved systems connected
Discover data stores	Security		Inventory created
Classify sensitive data	Security / Data Governance		Classification results validated
Map owners	Data Governance / IT		Owner coverage reported
Identify initial findings	Security		Findings triaged

Phase 2: Prioritization and Remediation

Activity	Owner	Target Date	Exit Criteria
Apply severity model	Security / Risk		Prioritized findings
Validate critical findings	Security / Data Owners		False positives removed
Assign remediation tickets	Program Team		Tickets routed to owners
Remediate critical exposure	Engineering / System Owners		Validated closure
Document exceptions	Risk Owners		Approved risk acceptance

Phase 3: Governance and Reporting

Activity	Owner	Target Date	Exit Criteria
Launch executive dashboard	Program Owner		Dashboard approved
Establish monthly reporting	Program Owner		First report delivered
Produce compliance evidence	Risk / Compliance		Evidence accepted
Review SLA performance	Steering Committee		SLA metrics reviewed
Update risk register	Risk / Compliance		Risks documented

Phase 4: Scale and Optimize

Activity	Owner	Target Date	Exit Criteria
Expand to additional platforms	Security / Engineering		New scope approved
Automate remediation workflows	Engineering		Automation deployed
Integrate with additional tools	Security Architecture		Integrations operating
Mature AI data governance	Privacy / Security / AI Governance		AI data risk reporting
Conduct maturity assessment	Internal Audit / Risk		Maturity score reported

30/60/90-Day Launch Plan

Timeframe	Focus	Deliverables
First 30 Days	Alignment	Charter, stakeholders, critical data definition, initial scope.
Days 31–60	Design	Severity model, workflow, RACI, tool requirements, vendor evaluation.
Days 61–90	Initial Execution	Phase 1 onboarding, baseline discovery, validated findings, first remediation sprint.

Template 7: Budget & Resources

Purpose: The Budget & Resources document defines the people, funding, tools, implementation support, and operational capacity required to run the DSPM program.

Budget Template

Budget Category	Description	Estimated Cost	Owner
Program Management	Program owner, project manager, governance support.	$	
Security Architecture	DSPM architecture, integrations, severity model, control alignment.	$	
Data Governance Support	Data ownership, stewardship, catalog alignment.	$	
Privacy / Legal Support	Regulatory mapping, privacy risk, contractual obligations.	$	
Engineering Support	Integration, remediation, automation, platform changes.	$	
DSPM Platform	Licensing, support, storage, usage-based costs.	$	
Integrations	Ticketing, IAM, SIEM, SOAR, CMDB, data catalog, GRC.	$	
Implementation Services	Vendor or third-party support.	$	
Training	Stakeholder training, engineering training, owner enablement.	$	
Contingency	Unplanned remediation, integration, or advisory needs.	$	

Resource Plan Template

Role	FTE / Allocation	Responsibilities
Executive Sponsor	X%	Sponsorship, escalation, funding.
Program Owner	X FTE	Program execution and reporting.
DSPM Architect	X FTE	Technical architecture and requirements.
Security Analyst	X FTE	Finding validation and triage.
Data Governance Lead	X%	Ownership and data domain mapping.
Privacy Lead	X%	Privacy risk and personal data requirements.
Legal Counsel	X%	Legal and contractual interpretation.
Engineering Lead	X%	Integration and remediation coordination.
Platform Engineers	X FTE	Technical fixes and automation.
Risk / Compliance Analyst	X%	Evidence, control mapping, risk register.
Business Data Owners	X%	Criticality decisions and risk acceptance.

Business Value / Benefit Model

Benefit	Measurement
Reduced breach impact	Reduction in exposed critical data stores.
Reduced regulatory risk	Improved evidence and control coverage.
Reduced remediation noise	Percentage of findings prioritized by severity and owner.
Improved data ownership	Percentage of critical repositories with accountable owners.
Reduced excessive access	Access reduction to Tier 0/Tier 1 data.
Reduced stale data liability	Volume or percentage of stale sensitive data disposed.
Improved executive visibility	Monthly reporting adopted by steering committee.
Improved audit readiness	Evidence produced on demand.

Template 8: Evaluation & Growth Strategy

Purpose: The Evaluation & Growth Strategy defines how the DSPM program will measure effectiveness, mature over time, and expand beyond initial deployment.

Evaluation Metrics

Evaluation Area	Metric	Frequency	Owner
Critical data visibility	% of Tier 0/Tier 1 data domains inventoried.	Monthly	Program Owner
Ownership coverage	% of critical data stores with assigned business and technical owners.	Monthly	Data Governance
Exposure reduction	Number of critical public/external exposure findings open vs. closed.	Monthly	Security
Access risk reduction	% reduction in excessive access to critical data.	Monthly	IAM / Security
Remediation performance	SLA adherence by severity.	Monthly	Program Owner
Exception management	Number of accepted risks, expired exceptions, and overdue reviews.	Monthly	Risk
Compliance evidence	Evidence completeness for selected obligations.	Quarterly	Compliance
Data minimization	Volume of stale sensitive data deleted, archived, or approved.	Quarterly	Data Governance
Program maturity	Maturity score by workstream.	Semiannual	Steering Committee
Business adoption	Stakeholder participation and remediation completion.	Quarterly	Program Owner

Growth Strategy

Stage 1: Foundation

Focus areas:

- Critical data definition
- Ownership model
- Initial scope
- Severity model
- Remediation workflow
- Executive reporting

Success criteria:

- Charter approved
- Owners assigned
- Initial critical findings remediated
- Steering committee operating

Stage 2: Expansion

Focus areas:

- Additional cloud platforms
- Additional SaaS repositories
- Data warehouses and lakes
- Broader business units
- Compliance reporting

Success criteria:

- Increased coverage
- Repeatable onboarding
- More complete ownership
- Improved evidence quality

Stage 3: Automation

Focus areas:

- Automated ticketing
- Access remediation
- Policy enforcement
- Integration with IAM, SIEM, SOAR, CMDB, GRC, and data catalog

Success criteria:

- Reduced manual triage
- Faster remediation
- Improved SLA performance
- Reduced repeated findings

Stage 4: Optimization

Focus areas:

- Predictive risk scoring
- AI data governance
- Data minimization automation
- Business risk dashboards
- Continuous control monitoring

Success criteria:

- Risk trends improve
- Executive reporting matures
- Residual risk is actively governed
- DSPM becomes part of enterprise data risk management

Quarterly Program Review Template

Review Area	Questions
Scope	*Are we focused on the right data domains and platforms?*
Risk	*Which risks increased, decreased, or changed?*
Remediation	*Are critical findings being closed within SLA?*
Ownership	*Where do ownership gaps remain?*
Controls	*Which controls are working or failing?*
Exceptions	*Which accepted risks are expiring or increasing?*
Compliance	*What evidence was produced? What gaps remain?*
Tool Performance	*Is the platform supporting program requirements?*
Resourcing	*Are teams properly staffed to remediate findings?*
Next Quarter	*What should be expanded, paused, automated, or improved?*

Template 9: Regulatory-to-Risk Mapping

Field	**Description**
Regulatory / Contractual Driver	*Which law, regulation, contract, policy, or standard applies?*
Data Type	*What data is involved?* PII, PHI, PCI, credentials, financial data, IP, source code, legal data, etc.
Business Process	*Which business process creates, uses, stores, or shares the data?*
Data Location	*Where does the data live?* Cloud, SaaS, database, data lake, endpoint, collaboration tool, backup, AI platform.
Risk Scenario	*What could go wrong?* Exposure, misuse, unauthorized access, breach, retention violation, regulatory failure, IP theft.
Business Impact	*What happens to the business if the scenario occurs?*
Likelihood Factors	Exposure, access level, identity type, control gaps, known incidents, data volume, external sharing.
Existing Controls	*What controls already exist*? IAM, DLP, encryption, retention, logging, approval workflows.
Control Gaps	*What is missing or ineffective?*
Risk Priority	Critical, High, Medium, Low.
Risk Owner	*Who is accountable for accepting or reducing the risk?*
Remediation Owner	*Who performs the fix?*
Evidence Required	*What proof is needed for audit, governance, or executive reporting?*

Template 10: Critical Data Decision Record

Field	Entry
Data Domain	Customer, Employee, Product, Financial, Legal, Health, Payment, etc.
Data Owner	Named accountable business owner
Data Steward	Operational data governance contact
System / Platform Owner	Technology owner
Data Description	What the data is and how it is used
Criticality Tier	Tier 0, Tier 1, Tier 2, Tier 3, Tier 4
Sensitivity Types	PII, PHI, PCI, IP, credentials, confidential, regulated, etc.
Business Impact if Exposed	Describe impact
Business Impact if Altered	Describe impact
Business Impact if Unavailable	Describe impact
Regulatory / Contractual Drivers	Applicable obligations
Approved Locations	Systems where this data may reside
Prohibited Locations	Systems where this data must not reside
Approved Access Groups	Roles or groups allowed access
Retention Requirement	Retention period and deletion expectations
Risk Acceptance Authority	Who may accept residual risk
Review Frequency	Quarterly, semiannual, annual

Template 11: Enterprise Label Standard

Field	Required	Allowed Values	Example
sensitivity	Yes	public, internal, confidential, restricted	restricted
data_type	Yes	PII, PHI, PCI, credentials, source_code, financial, legal, intellectual_property	PII
confidentiality_impact	Yes	low, moderate, high	high
integrity_impact	Recommended	low, moderate, high	moderate
availability_impact	Recommended	low, moderate, high	low
business_owner	Yes	Approved business owner list	HR
technical_owner	Recommended	Approved technical team list	data-platform
environment	Yes	production, development, test, backup, archive	production
region	Conditional	Approved region list	EU
regulation	Conditional	GDPR, HIPAA, PCI-DSS, CCPA, CJIS, SOX	GDPR
retention	Conditional	Approved retention schedule	7-years
handling	Yes	encrypt, restrict_share, monitor, quarantine, review	encrypt

Template 12: Sample Labeling Rules

Condition	Labels and Tags	Required Action
Data contains payment card numbers	data_type=PCI, sensitivity=restricted, confidentiality_impact=high	Encrypt, restrict access, validate PCI control coverage.
Data contains SSNs or government IDs	data_type=PII, sensitivity=restricted, confidentiality_impact=high	Block public exposure, require owner review.
Data contains customer emails and account IDs	data_type=PII, sensitivity=confidential, confidentiality_impact=moderate	Monitor access, restrict external sharing.
Data contains credentials or secrets	data_type=credentials, sensitivity=restricted, confidentiality_impact=high	Alert security, rotate secrets, remove exposure.
Data is public marketing content	sensitivity=public, confidentiality_impact=low	Allow external sharing if approved.
Production data appears in development	environment=development, production_data=true, sensitivity=restricted	Open remediation ticket, remove or mask data.
Sensitive data has no owner	owner=missing	Create governance finding and route to stewardship queue.

Template 13: DSPM Business Case

Purpose

This template helps the organization document the business reason for building a Data Security Posture Management program before selecting or purchasing a platform. It connects data security risk to business outcomes, regulatory obligations, AI readiness, operational efficiency, and measurable risk reduction.

1. Business Case Summary

Field	Response
Business case title	
Prepared by	
Date	
Executive sponsor	
Security owner	
Business owner(s)	
Target approval date	
Requested decision	Approve program funding / approve POC / approve operating model / approve tool selection / other

2. Problem Statement

Describe the business problem the DSPM program is intended to solve.

Example language:

The organization lacks consistent visibility into where sensitive and business-critical data exists, who can access it, how it is exposed, whether it is retained appropriately, and whether AI-enabled systems can access or reuse it. This creates privacy, security, regulatory, operational, and reputational risk.

Question	Response
What data security problem are we trying to solve?	
Why does this matter now?	
What has changed in the business, technology environment, regulatory landscape, or AI strategy?	
What are the consequences of doing nothing?	

3. Current-State Risk

Risk Area	Current Challenge	Business Impact	Evidence Available
Unknown sensitive data			
Overexposed data			
Excessive access			
Stale or duplicate data			
Weak ownership			
Poor classification			
Regulatory exposure			
AI-accessible sensitive data			
Third-party or SaaS exposure			
Lack of reporting evidence			

4. Business Drivers

Select the drivers that apply.

Driver	*Applies?*	Notes
Reduce breach exposure		
Improve privacy and regulatory readiness		
Prepare data for safe AI use		
Improve DLP accuracy and prioritization		
Reduce excessive access		
Improve data ownership and accountability		
Support retention and deletion requirements		
Support audit and compliance evidence		
Reduce manual discovery work		
Improve executive and board reporting		
Support cloud, SaaS, or data warehouse modernization		
Reduce risk from third-party data sharing		

5. Expected Outcomes

Outcome	Success Measure	Target Date	Owner
Identify critical sensitive data repositories			
Assign owners to Tier 1 data stores			
Reduce high-risk exposure findings			
Improve classification coverage			
Identify AI-accessible sensitive data			
Remediate excessive access			
Create risk acceptance workflow			
Establish executive reporting			

6. Scope

Scope Area	*Included?*	Notes
Cloud storage		
SaaS applications		
Collaboration platforms		
Databases		
Data warehouses		
Data lakes		
File shares		
Source code repositories		
Endpoint data		
Backups		
AI tools and copilots		
Vector databases or RAG systems		
Third-party repositories		

7. Cost of Inaction

Risk	Potential Impact	Likelihood	Severity	Notes
Sensitive data exposure				
Regulatory finding				
AI misuse or overexposure				
Delayed breach response				
Failed audit evidence				
Unowned remediation				
Ineffective DLP policy				
Excessive access remains unresolved				

8. Investment Required

Investment Area	Estimated Cost	Notes
DSPM platform		
Professional services		
Internal staffing		
Managed service support		
Integrations		
Training and enablement		
Governance and reporting support		
Ongoing operational maintenance		

9. Required Stakeholders

Function	Required Role	Named Owner
Security	Program owner	
IT/platform operations	Remediation support	
Privacy	Regulatory and data rights guidance	
Legal	Contract, privilege, and legal risk guidance	
Compliance/risk	Control mapping and evidence	
Data governance	Data ownership and classification	

Business unit leadership	Risk ownership and remediation decisions	
Procurement	Vendor and contract support	
Finance	Budget approval	
Executive sponsor	Decision authority and escalation	

10. Recommendation

Example language:

The organization should approve the DSPM program and proceed with a structured evaluation of DSPM capabilities. Approval should include agreement on business objectives, initial scope, ownership model, remediation workflow, risk acceptance process, and executive reporting requirements before final platform selection.

Decision	Recommendation
Proceed with DSPM program?	
Proceed with POC?	
Approve initial scope?	
Approve funding range?	
Approve operating model?	
Approve steering committee?	

11. Approval

Approver	Role	Decision	Date
		Approved / Rejected / Needs Revision	
		Approved / Rejected / Needs Revision	
		Approved / Rejected / Needs Revision	

Template 14: Risk Acceptance Record

Purpose

This template documents a formal decision to temporarily accept a known data security risk. It should be used when a DSPM finding, policy exception, AI access concern, excessive access issue, retention conflict, or remediation delay cannot be resolved immediately.

Risk acceptance should be visible, owned, justified, time-bound, and reviewed.

1. Risk Acceptance Summary

Field	Response
Risk ID	
Risk title	
Date submitted	
Submitted by	
Business owner	
Technical owner	
Security reviewer	
Privacy/legal reviewer	
Approval authority	
Expiration date	
Review cadence	Weekly / Monthly / Quarterly / Other
Status	Pending / Approved / Rejected / Expired / Closed

2. Risk Description

Describe the risk being accepted. Example language:

Restricted customer data remains accessible to a broad internal group because immediate access removal may disrupt active business operations during a system migration.

Question	Response
What is the risk?	
Where does the risk exist?	
What data is affected?	
How sensitive is the data?	
Who or what can access the data?	
Why can the risk not be remediated immediately?	
What business process depends on this access or condition?	

3. Affected Data

Data Element	Description
Data type	Customer / employee / financial / health / intellectual property / credentials / legal / other
Sensitivity level	Public / Internal / Confidential / Restricted
Regulatory category	GDPR / CCPA / HIPAA / GLBA / PCI / NYDFS / SEC / contractual / other
Location	
System or repository	
Data owner	
Approximate volume	
AI-accessible?	Yes / No / Unknown
Externally shared?	Yes / No / Unknown
Subject to retention rule?	Yes / No / Unknown
Subject to deletion rights?	Yes / No / Unknown
Subject to legal hold?	Yes / No / Unknown

4. Risk Rating

Factor	Rating	Notes
Data sensitivity	Low / Medium / High / Critical	
Exposure level	Low / Medium / High / Critical	
Number of users or identities with access	Low / Medium / High / Critical	
External access	Low / Medium / High / Critical	
AI access risk	Low / Medium / High / Critical	
Regulatory impact	Low / Medium / High / Critical	
Business impact	Low / Medium / High / Critical	
Likelihood	Low / Medium / High / Critical	
Overall risk rating	Low / Medium / High / Critical	

5. Reason for Acceptance

Select all that apply.

Reason	*Applies?*	Explanation
Business disruption risk		
Technical limitation		
Legacy system constraint		
Migration in progress		
Regulatory or legal conflict		
Contractual dependency		
Operational dependency		
Resource limitation		
Awaiting vendor support		
Awaiting business decision		
Other		

6. Compensating Controls

Control	*Implemented?*	Owner	Evidence Location
Additional monitoring			
Export restriction			
Access review			
MFA enforcement			
External sharing restriction			
AI indexing blocked			
Encryption enabled			
DLP policy applied			
Alerting enabled			
User notification or training			
Legal or privacy review completed			

7. Conditions of Acceptance

Example language:

This risk is accepted only for the period stated below. Acceptance does not remove accountability for remediation. The risk must be reviewed on the approved cadence and escalated immediately if exposure increases, AI access is introduced, sensitive data volume increases, external sharing occurs, or compensating controls fail.

Condition	Requirement
Acceptance start date	
Acceptance expiration date	
Review cadence	
Required remediation date	
Escalation trigger	
Renewal allowed?	Yes / No
Renewal approval authority	
Evidence repository	

8. Remediation Plan

Remediation Step	Owner	Due Date	Status
			Not Started / In Progress / Complete
			Not Started / In Progress / Complete
			Not Started / In Progress / Complete

9. Approval

Approver	Role	Decision	Date	Notes
	Business owner	Approved / Rejected		
	Security	Approved / Rejected		
	Privacy/legal	Approved / Rejected		
	Risk/compliance	Approved / Rejected		
	Executive sponsor or steering committee	Approved / Rejected		

10. Closure

Field	Response
Closure date	
Final disposition	Remediated / Renewed / Transferred / Accepted Permanently / No Longer Applicable
Evidence location	
Closure approved by	
Notes	

Template 15: Steering Committee Decision Table

Purpose

This template defines the decisions a DSPM steering committee is responsible for making. It helps prevent unclear ownership, delayed remediation, inconsistent exceptions, and unresolved business risk.

The steering committee should not review every DSPM finding. It should make cross-functional decisions that require authority, funding, policy interpretation, exception approval, or escalation.

1. Steering Committee Overview

Field	Response
Committee name	Data Security Steering Committee / DSPM Steering Committee / Other
Executive sponsor	
Committee chair	
Program owner	
Meeting cadence	Weekly / Biweekly / Monthly / Quarterly
First meeting date	
Decision log location	
Reporting audience	CISO / CIO / Risk Committee / Executive Team / Board

2. Committee Members

Function	Representative	Role in Committee
Security		Program ownership, risk prioritization, reporting
IT/platform operations		Remediation execution, integrations, platform changes
Privacy		Privacy obligations, DSAR, deletion, minimization
Legal		Contractual, privilege, regulatory, litigation risk
Compliance/risk		Control mapping, audit evidence, exceptions
Data governance		Data ownership, classification, lifecycle decisions
Business unit leadership		Business context, risk ownership, prioritization
IAM		Access governance, identity controls, access reviews
Procurement/vendor management		Vendor review, contract support
AI governance		AI access, model use, RAG, copilots, agentic workflows
Finance		Budget, funding, investment planning

3. Decision Table

Decision Area	**Decision Needed**	**Decision Owner**	**Required Participants**	**Output**	**Review Cadence**
Program scope	*Which systems, repositories, and data types are in scope first?*	Security leader	IT, data governance, privacy, business owners	Approved scope	Quarterly
Business objectives	*What business outcomes must the DSPM program support?*	Executive sponsor	Security, risk, business leaders	Approved objectives	Quarterly
Critical data definition	*Which data types are restricted, regulated, confidential, or business critical?*	Data governance or privacy leader	Security, legal, compliance, business owners	Critical data standard	Semiannual
Classification model	*What labels and handling rules will be used?*	Data governance	Security, privacy, IT	Classification standard	Semiannual
Data ownership	*Who owns each critical repository or data domain?*	Business sponsor	Security, data governance, IT	Ownership record	Monthly
Risk prioritization	*Which findings require immediate remediation?*	Security leader	Privacy, legal, IT, business owner	Prioritized queue	Monthly
Remediation SLA	*How quickly must findings be addressed by severity?*	Security leader	IT, compliance, business owners	SLA standard	Quarterly
Risk acceptance	*Who may accept unresolved data risk, and for how long?*	Risk/compliance leader	Security, legal, privacy, business owner	Risk acceptance record	Monthly
AI access decisions	*Which data may be indexed, embedded, retrieved, or used by AI systems?*	AI governance lead	Security, privacy, legal, business owner	AI data access decision	Monthly

Exceptions	***Which policy exceptions are allowed, denied, or escalated?***	**Committee chair**	**Security, privacy, legal, affected owner**	**Exception decision**	**Monthly**
Automation	*Which remediation actions may be automated?*	Security and IT leaders	Legal, privacy, business owner	Automation approval matrix	Quarterly
Reporting	*What metrics are reported to executives and the board?*	Security leader	Risk, compliance, privacy, executive sponsor	Executive scorecard	Quarterly
Vendor/tool selection	*Which DSPM capabilities are mandatory before purchase?*	Security leader	IT, procurement, privacy, data governance	Capability requirements	As needed
Funding	*What budget, staffing, or support is required?*	Executive sponsor	Finance, security, IT	Investment decision	Annual or as needed

4. Decision Log

Decision ID	Date	Decision	Owner	Approved By	Due Date	Status
DSPM-DEC-001						Open / Closed
DSPM-DEC-002						Open / Closed
DSPM-DEC-003						Open / Closed

5. Escalation Criteria

The following issues should be escalated to the steering committee or executive sponsor.

Escalation Trigger	Required Action
Critical sensitive data exposure remains unresolved past SLA	Executive review and remediation plan
No business owner assigned to critical data	Ownership decision required
Business unit refuses remediation	Risk acceptance or executive escalation
AI system can access restricted data without approval	Immediate review and access decision
External sharing of restricted data is identified	Security, privacy, and legal review
Regulated data is found in unmanaged repository	Remediation or risk acceptance
Compensating control fails	Reassess risk and escalate
Exception request affects multiple business units	Steering committee decision
Remediation requires new funding	Executive sponsor review
Finding may create material business impact	Executive or board-level review

6. Meeting Cadence

Phase	Recommended Cadence	Purpose
Initial deployment	Weekly	Resolve scope, ownership, and early blockers
Stabilization	Biweekly	Review high-risk findings, exceptions, and remediation progress
Steady state	Monthly	Review trends, overdue risks, metrics, and decisions
Executive reporting	Quarterly	Report risk reduction, AI readiness, and unresolved decisions

7. Committee Success Measures

Measure	Target
Percentage of critical repositories with assigned owners	
Percentage of high-risk findings reviewed within SLA	
Percentage of risk acceptances with expiration dates	
Number of overdue remediation items	
Number of unresolved ownership disputes	
Time to approve or reject exception requests	
Percentage of AI-accessible repositories reviewed	
Executive scorecard delivered on schedule	

Template 16: Minimum Viable Operating Model

Purpose

This template helps smaller organizations build a practical DSPM operating model without creating unnecessary bureaucracy. It defines the minimum roles, processes, decision rights, metrics, and documentation needed to turn DSPM visibility into action.

A smaller organization does not need a large steering committee or complex governance structure to begin. It does need clear ownership, repeatable decisions, and evidence that risk is being reduced.

1. Operating Model Summary

Field	Response
Organization or business unit	
Prepared by	
Date	
Executive sponsor	
Security owner	
Initial scope	
Review cadence	
Reporting audience	

2. Minimum Roles

Role	Named Owner	Responsibility
Executive sponsor		Approves program, resolves blockers, accepts business risk when needed
Security owner		Owns DSPM process, risk prioritization, reporting, and coordination
IT/platform owner		Supports access changes, configuration updates, integrations, and remediation
Data/business owner		Confirms data value, business need, retention needs, and acceptable use
Privacy/legal advisor		Reviews regulated data, deletion, retention, contractual, and AI concerns
Compliance/risk owner		Maps findings to control requirements and tracks evidence
AI governance contact		Reviews AI access, copilots, RAG, prompt use, and AI-enabled workflows

In smaller organizations, one person may fill multiple roles. The responsibility still needs to be documented.

3. Minimum Scope

Environment	*Included in Initial Scope?*	Owner	Notes
Microsoft 365 or Google Workspace			
Cloud storage			
SaaS applications			
File shares			
Databases			
Data warehouse			
Developer repositories			
Backup repositories			
AI tools or copilots			
Third-party shared repositories			

4. Minimum Classification Model

Label	Definition	Example Data	Handling Rule
Public	Approved for public release	Published marketing content	No special restriction
Internal	Business information not intended for public release	Internal procedures, general business documents	Internal access only
Confidential	Sensitive business or operational information	Contracts, financial reports, employee records	Restricted to business need
Restricted	Regulated, high-impact, or highly sensitive data	PHI, payment data, SSNs, secrets, credentials, legal privilege	Strict access, monitoring, approval required

5. Minimum Processes

Process	Minimum Requirement	Owner	Tool or Evidence Location
Discovery intake	Decide which systems are scanned first	Security owner	
Classification review	Confirm data labels and sensitive data types	Data/business owner	
Risk prioritization	Rank findings by sensitivity, exposure, access, and business impact	Security owner	
Remediation workflow	Assign findings, track status, define due dates	IT/platform owner	

Ownership assignment	Assign owner to each critical repository	Executive sponsor	
Exception handling	Document approved exceptions and expiration dates	Risk/compliance owner	
Risk acceptance	Record accepted risks with business justification	Business owner	
AI access review	Review sensitive repositories available to AI systems	AI governance contact	
Reporting	Provide simple progress update to leadership	Security owner	

6. Minimum Decision Rights

Decision	Decision Owner	Required Input
What data matters most?	Executive sponsor	Security, privacy, business owner
What gets scanned first?	Security owner	IT/platform owner
Who owns each repository?	Executive sponsor	Business unit leadership
What must be remediated immediately?	Security owner	Business owner, privacy/legal if regulated
What can be accepted temporarily?	Business owner	Security, risk/compliance, executive sponsor
What data can be exposed to AI tools?	Executive sponsor or AI governance contact	Security, privacy, legal, business owner
What metrics will be reported?	Security owner	Executive sponsor
What requires escalation?	Security owner	Executive sponsor

7. Minimum Risk Prioritization Rules

Priority	Criteria	Required Action
Critical	Restricted data publicly exposed, externally shared, AI-accessible without approval, or accessible by excessive privileged identities	Immediate review and remediation or executive risk acceptance
High	Confidential or restricted data accessible to broad internal groups or stale users	Assign owner and remediate within approved SLA
Medium	Sensitive data found in approved location but with unclear ownership, weak labels, or excessive retention	Review, assign owner, and remediate through normal workflow
Low	Internal data with minor classification or hygiene issue	Track and remediate as capacity allows

8. Minimum Remediation Tracker

Finding ID	Data Location	Risk	Priority	Owner	Due Date	Status	Notes
			Critical / High / Medium / Low			Open / In Progress / Complete / Accepted	
			Critical / High / Medium / Low			Open / In Progress / Complete / Accepted	
			Critical / High / Medium / Low			Open / In Progress / Complete / Accepted	

9. Minimum Risk Acceptance Log

Risk ID	Risk Description	Business Owner	Expiration Date	Compensating Controls	Status
					Pending / Approved / Expired / Closed
					Pending / Approved / Expired / Closed

10. Minimum AI Data Access Log

AI Tool or Workflow	Data Source	*Sensitive Data Present?*	*Approved?*	Owner	Notes
		Yes / No / Unknown	Yes / No / Pending		
		Yes / No / Unknown	Yes / No / Pending		

11. Minimum Metrics

Metric	Current	Target	Notes
Percentage of critical repositories scanned			
Number of restricted data findings			
Number of high-risk exposures			
Percentage of findings with assigned owners			
Number of overdue remediation items			
Number of accepted risks with expiration dates			
Number of AI-accessible sensitive repositories			
Percentage of critical findings closed within SLA			

12. Minimum Operating Cadence

Meeting	Frequency	Participants	Purpose
DSPM working session	Weekly during first 30 to 60 days	Security, IT, data/business owner	Review findings, assign owners, clear blockers
Risk review	Monthly	Security, business owner, privacy/legal, executive sponsor as needed	Review high-risk findings, accepted risks, overdue items, exceptions
Executive update	Quarterly	Security owner, executive sponsor, leadership	Report progress, unresolved risks, funding needs, AI readiness

13. Minimum Documentation Checklist

Document	*Complete?*	Owner	Location
DSPM program charter			
Critical data definition			
Repository scan list			
Data owner list			
Classification standard			
Risk prioritization rules			
Remediation tracker			
Risk acceptance log			
AI data access log			
Executive scorecard			

14. Maturity Path

Phase	Focus	Exit Criteria
Phase 1: Visibility	Scan highest-risk repositories	Sensitive data baseline created
Phase 2: Ownership	Assign owners to critical repositories	Owners assigned to Tier 1 data stores
Phase 3: Remediation	Fix highest-risk exposure first	Critical findings tracked and reduced
Phase 4: Governance	Add exception, risk acceptance, and reporting processes	Decisions are documented and reviewed
Phase 5: Optimization	Add automation, integrations, and advanced reporting	Risk reduction is measurable over time

Key Takeaway

A DSPM program should be designed before a DSPM platform is purchased. The organization must first agree on why the program exists, what business outcomes it needs to support, which data matters most, who owns that data, what risks are unacceptable, who is accountable for remediation, and how success will be measured.

The strongest DSPM programs are not built around scanning everything. They are built around governance, ownership, accountability, risk prioritization, remediation, evidence, and measurable business outcomes. Scanning is important, but it is not the strategy. It is one capability that supports the strategy.

For smaller organizations, the operating model does not need to be complex. It should be simple enough to use and strong enough to create accountability. What matters at the beginning is that sensitive data is discovered, risk is prioritized, owners are assigned, remediation is tracked, exceptions are documented, and leadership can see whether risk is going down.

A DSPM tool should help the business answer its most important data security questions:

- *Where is our critical data?*
- *Who owns it?*
- *Who has access to it?*
- *Is it exposed, duplicated, over-retained, or used outside approved processes?*
- *Which risks should be fixed first?*
- *Who is accountable for fixing them?*
- *How do we prove that risk has been reduced?*

Technology should support the operating model, not define it. A small organization with a basic but consistent operating model is ahead of a large organization with a sophisticated tool and no accountability.

The program comes first. The purchase comes second.

Chapter 5: The DSPM Reference Architecture

5.1 How DSPM Connects Data, Identity, Governance, Detection, Remediation, and Reporting

A DSPM program is not a single tool sitting beside the rest of the security stack. It is an architectural layer that connects data visibility, identity context, governance requirements, detection signals, remediation workflows, and executive reporting.

That distinction matters.

Many organizations begin their DSPM journey by asking a simple question: "Where is our sensitive data?" That is a good place to start, but it is not enough. Knowing where sensitive data lives does not automatically tell the organization whether that data is exposed, whether access is appropriate, whether it violates policy, whether it is tied to a business process, or whether someone is accountable for fixing the risk.

A strong DSPM architecture helps organizations answer more practical questions:

- *Where is sensitive, regulated, or business critical data located?*
- *Who or what can access it?*
- *Why does the data exist?*
- *Is it exposed, over-permissioned, duplicated, stale, or misconfigured?*
- *Which business, security, privacy, or application owner is accountable?*
- *What action needs to happen next?*
- *How can the organization prove that risk is being reduced over time?*

This is where DSPM becomes more than discovery and classification. It becomes a connective layer across security, compliance, privacy, data governance, cloud operations, identity, and business ownership.

The goal of this chapter is to give architects, buyers, and security leaders a practical reference model for understanding where DSPM fits, what it connects to, and how it turns scattered data signals into prioritized risk decisions and measurable remediation.

5.2 Why DSPM Needs Reference Architecture

Most security programs already have many tools that see part of the problem. A cloud security platform may identify exposed storage. A DLP tool may detect sensitive content leaving an approved channel. An identity platform may show who belongs to a group. A SIEM may collect events. A GRC platform may track controls. A CMDB may document applications and assets. A data catalog may describe business data sets. A ticketing system may track remediation work.

Each tool has value, but each tool usually sees the world through its own lens.

DSPM is useful because it connects these lenses around the data itself.

A reference architecture gives the organization a shared way to think about that connection. It helps security teams, privacy teams, infrastructure teams, application owners, and executives understand how DSPM fits into the larger environment. It also helps buyers evaluate whether a DSPM platform can support the way the organization actually works.

Without an architecture view, DSPM can easily be misunderstood as another scanner. That creates a narrow program. The organization discovers sensitive data, produces findings, and maybe builds a dashboard, but the work does not consistently lead to ownership, remediation, evidence, or measurable risk reduction.

A reference architecture prevents that mistake. It shows DSPM as an operating layer that connects data sources, identity context, governance systems, detection tools, workflow engines, remediation systems, and reporting layers.

The key message is simple:

DSPM turns scattered data signals into prioritized risk decisions and measurable remediation.

That is the difference between knowing that sensitive data exists and being able to govern, protect, monitor, and reduce the risk around it.

5.3 The Core DSPM Architecture Model

At its simplest, a DSPM architecture can be represented as a flow from data discovery to business evidence.

Data Sources > DSPM Discovery and Classification > Risk Engine > Ownership and Workflow > Remediation > Evidence and Reporting

This model is intentionally simple. It is not meant to show every integration or technical variation. It is meant to show the operating logic of a mature DSPM program.

The organization first identifies where data lives. The DSPM platform discovers and classifies the data. It enriches those findings with context. It determines risk. It routes work to accountable owners. It supports remediation. Then it produces evidence and reporting for leadership, audit, compliance, privacy, and security operations.

Each stage matters.

Data Sources

Data sources are the places where data lives, moves, accumulates, or is copied. This includes obvious systems such as databases, warehouses, cloud storage, SaaS platforms, and file shares. It also includes less obvious locations such as backups, endpoints, collaboration platforms, AI workspaces, development environments, and shadow data stores created by business teams.

For many organizations, this is where the first surprise appears. Sensitive data is rarely confined to the systems listed in official documentation. It spreads through exports, reports, copies, test data, analytics projects, user uploads, cloud migrations, third party integrations, and AI experimentation.

A DSPM architecture begins by accepting a practical truth: the data estate is usually larger, messier, and more dynamic than the official inventory suggests.

DSPM Discovery and Classification

Discovery identifies where data exists. Classification determines what kind of data it is.

This stage answers questions such as:

- *Does this repository contain personal information?*
- *Does it contain financial data, health data, intellectual property, credentials, secrets, or regulated records?*
- *Is the data business critical?*
- *Is the data stale, redundant, or outside expected locations?*
- *Are there toxic combinations, such as sensitive data mixed with credentials, excessive access, or public exposure?*

Classification must go beyond simple pattern matching. Mature DSPM programs need to understand data sensitivity, data type, business meaning, regulatory relevance, location, volume, ownership, and usage context.

For example, a file containing names may not be highly sensitive by itself. A file containing names, Social Security numbers, account details, and health information is a different risk. A database containing customer records in a tightly controlled production environment may be expected. A copy of the same data in a public storage bucket, unmanaged file share, developer workspace, or AI tool may represent a much higher risk.

Discovery and classification create the foundation. They tell the organization what exists and where it is. The architecture becomes powerful when that visibility is enriched with identity, governance, detection, and business context.

Risk Engine

The risk engine is where DSPM moves from inventory to prioritization.

A list of sensitive data locations is useful, but it can become overwhelming. Large organizations may have thousands or millions of findings. The question is not simply, *"Where is sensitive data?"* The better question is, *"Which sensitive data creates meaningful risk right now?"*

A DSPM risk engine combines multiple factors, including:

- Sensitivity of the data
- Regulatory relevance
- Business criticality
- User and group access
- Service account and nonhuman identity access
- Privileged access
- External exposure
- Public or anonymous access

- Cloud misconfigurations
- Data movement
- Encryption status
- Retention status
- Stale or redundant data
- Detection signals from security tools
- Ownership and business context
- Existing compensating controls

This combination helps the organization distinguish between routine findings and high priority risks.

For example, a data warehouse table containing regulated customer data may not be the highest risk if it is encrypted, monitored, access controlled, owned, and tied to a valid business process. A spreadsheet containing a smaller set of the same data may be much riskier if it is sitting in a broadly shared folder with no clear owner and no retention policy.

DSPM should help teams prioritize based on real exposure and business impact, not just the presence of sensitive data.

Ownership and Workflow

Findings only matter if someone can act on them.

One of the most common failure points in data security is the gap between detection and ownership. Security may find the risk, but the fix may require an application owner, data owner, privacy team, cloud engineer, legal stakeholder, or business process owner. If the architecture does not identify who owns the data and who can approve or perform the change, findings turn into backlog noise.

Ownership and workflow connect DSPM findings to accountable people and teams.

This stage should answer:

- *Who owns the data?*
- *Who owns the application or repository?*
- *Who can approve access changes?*
- *Who can validate business need?*
- *Who can determine whether data should be retained, archived, deleted, masked, encrypted, or moved?*
- *What workflow should be used for remediation?*
- *What service level applies?*

This is where DSPM begins to support an operating model. Instead of sending a generic report to security, the platform should help route the right issue to the right owner with the right context.

Remediation

Remediation is where risk reduction happens. A mature DSPM architecture should support multiple remediation paths. Not every finding should be handled the same way. Some require access changes. Some require encryption. Some require deletion. Some require policy updates. Some require investigation. Some require compensating controls because the risk cannot be immediately removed.

Common remediation actions include:

- Removing public exposure
- Reducing excessive access
- Revoking unnecessary permissions
- Removing stale users or groups
- Reviewing service account access
- Encrypting data
- Masking or tokenizing data
- Moving data to an approved location
- Deleting redundant, obsolete, or trivial data
- Applying retention policies
- Updating DLP, CASB, SSE, or cloud controls
- Creating tickets for infrastructure or application teams
- Launching access reviews or approval workflows
- Documenting risk acceptance where appropriate

The important point is that remediation must be connected to workflow. A dashboard that shows risk is useful. A process that reduces risk is better.

Evidence and Reporting

Evidence and reporting close the loop between security operations, governance, and business accountability. Security teams need operational visibility into data risk. Compliance teams require defensible control evidence. Privacy teams need records of processing, retention, and exposure. Executives need to understand risk trends over time, while boards need concise reporting that connects data exposure to business impact. Auditors, meanwhile, need proof that controls not only exist, but operate consistently and effectively.

Effective DSPM reporting should help organizations answer critical questions, including:

- *What sensitive data was discovered?*
- *What risks were identified?*
- *Which risks were remediated?*
- *Which risks remain open?*
- *Who owns each risk?*
- *How long did remediation take?*
- *Are findings increasing or decreasing over time?*
- *Are policy exceptions documented and approved?*
- *Can the organization demonstrate that controls are functioning as intended?*

Reporting should also capture how risks were discovered. An issue identified proactively through DSPM monitoring carries different operational implications than one uncovered during an audit, reported by a business user, triggered through DLP activity, or discovered after a security incident. Tracking discovery sources helps organizations evaluate control effectiveness, measure operational maturity, and identify areas where visibility or governance may still be weak.

Evidence is not simply a compliance artifact collected for auditors. It is the mechanism by which an organization demonstrates measurable improvement in data security, governance, and risk reduction over time.

5.4 Architecture Inputs

A DSPM reference architecture depends on several categories of inputs. These inputs give the DSPM platform the visibility and context needed to produce useful risk decisions.

The following categories are not meant to be implemented all at once. They provide a practical map of what DSPM may connect to as the program matures.

Data Sources

Data sources are the systems where sensitive, regulated, high value, or risky data may exist.

Typical data sources include:

Architecture Area	Examples	Why It Matters
Cloud storage	Object storage, cloud file storage, cloud drives	Sensitive data is often copied, exported, shared, or exposed through cloud storage.
SaaS platforms	Collaboration, CRM, HR, finance, productivity, ticketing, messaging	Business users often create and share sensitive data outside traditional IT managed repositories.
Databases	Relational, NoSQL, managed databases, self hosted databases	Databases often hold customer, employee, transaction, and operational data.
Data warehouses	Enterprise analytics platforms and reporting stores	Warehouses concentrate large volumes of business critical data.
Data lakes	Raw, semi structured, and unstructured data repositories	Data lakes may contain broad data sets with inconsistent controls and unclear ownership.
File shares	Network shares, shared drives, departmental folders	Legacy file shares often contain stale, overexposed, and poorly classified data.
Endpoints	Laptops, desktops, local storage	Sensitive data may be downloaded, exported, cached, or stored locally.
Backups	Backup platforms, snapshots, archives	Backups can preserve sensitive data long after production systems change.
AI tools and workspaces	AI assistants, model workspaces, prompt repositories, training data locations	AI adoption can create new data flows, copies, and exposure paths.

Data source coverage is one of the first questions architects and buyers should ask. A DSPM platform cannot manage risk in places it cannot see.

However, breadth is not the only concern. Depth matters too. It is not enough to say a platform connects to a data source. Buyers should ask what metadata is collected, how often scans occur, whether permissions are analyzed, whether content is classified, whether lineage or movement is visible, and whether remediation can be initiated.

Identity Sources

Identity context helps DSPM determine who or what can access sensitive data.

Identity sources may include:

Architecture Area	Examples	Why It Matters
Identity providers	Entra ID, Okta, Ping, Google identity services	IdPs help resolve users, groups, roles, and authentication context.
Cloud IAM	AWS IAM, Azure RBAC, Google Cloud IAM	Cloud IAM reveals permissions across cloud resources and data stores.
IGA platforms	Access governance, certification, lifecycle management	IGA context helps connect access risk to reviews, approvals, and ownership.
PAM systems	Privileged access vaults, session controls, elevation workflows	PAM context helps identify privileged paths to sensitive data.
Service accounts	Application accounts, automation accounts, integration accounts	Service accounts often have persistent access and unclear ownership.
Nonhuman identities	Workloads, bots, APIs, tokens, keys, machine identities	Nonhuman identities can access sensitive data at scale and are often overlooked.
API keys and tokens	Secrets, credentials, integration tokens	Exposed secrets can create direct paths to sensitive data.

Identity is essential because data risk is access risk.

A repository containing sensitive data is not automatically a critical exposure. The risk depends on who can access it, how they can access it, whether access is justified, whether accounts are active, whether identities are privileged, whether access is inherited, and whether nonhuman identities have excessive permissions.

A mature DSPM architecture should help teams see the relationship between data and identity. That includes users, groups, roles, service accounts, machine identities, privileged accounts, dormant accounts, external collaborators, and inherited permissions.

Governance Sources

Governance sources provide business, compliance, privacy, legal, and ownership context. These systems may include:

Architecture Area	Examples	Why It Matters
CMDB	Applications, services, owners, business units, environments	CMDB context connects data findings to systems and accountable owners.
Data catalog	Data sets, definitions, lineage, business terms	Data catalogs help map technical data to business meaning.
GRC platform	Controls, risks, policies, compliance obligations	GRC systems connect findings to control requirements and risk management.
Privacy inventory	Processing activities, data subjects, lawful basis, data flows	Privacy inventories help determine regulatory and privacy impact.
Records management	Retention schedules, archive rules, disposition policies	Records context helps determine whether data should be retained or deleted.
Legal holds	Litigation holds, preservation requirements	Legal holds prevent improper deletion of data that must be preserved.
Data retention schedules	Retention periods by data type, region, or business process	Retention context supports defensible deletion and data minimization.

Governance context helps answer one of the most important questions in data security: *should this data be here at all?*

A purely technical finding might say, "Sensitive data exists in this repository." Governance context adds the next layer: "This data belongs to a regulated business process, falls under a seven year retention policy, is owned by Finance, and is subject to an active legal hold."

Or it may reveal the opposite: "This data has no clear owner, no documented business purpose, no retention requirement, and broad access."

That difference matters. Governance context helps the organization make better decisions about remediation, retention, access, and risk acceptance.

Detection Sources

Detection sources connect DSPM findings to active security signals.

Common detection sources include:

Architecture Area	Examples	Why It Matters
SIEM	Security event collection, correlation, investigation	SIEM context can show whether sensitive data exposure is tied to suspicious activity.
SOAR	Automated response playbooks and case management	SOAR workflows can help escalate or automate response actions.

DLP	Data movement, exfiltration attempts, policy violations	DLP signals help identify sensitive data leaving approved paths.
CASB or SSE	SaaS access, cloud application control, web data movement	CASB and SSE tools help monitor data movement through cloud and web channels.
EDR	Endpoint activity, malware, suspicious process behavior	EDR context can connect endpoint compromise to sensitive data exposure.
CNAPP	Cloud posture, workload risk, cloud misconfigurations	CNAPP signals help connect cloud infrastructure risk to sensitive data.
Cloud security tools	CSPM, CWPP, CIEM, cloud native alerts	These tools help identify misconfigurations and access paths in cloud environments.
Threat intelligence	Known malicious indicators, actor behavior, campaign context	Threat intelligence may help prioritize exposed data associated with active threats.

Detection sources make DSPM more actionable.

For example, sensitive data in a storage bucket may be a concern. Sensitive data in a misconfigured bucket with public access is a higher concern. Sensitive data in that same bucket with recent access from an unusual geography, a compromised endpoint alert, or suspicious service account activity is a much higher priority.

The architecture should help security teams connect data risk to threat activity, not treat each signal in isolation.

Threat Modeling Inputs

DSPM architecture should also include threat modeling inputs that help teams understand how sensitive data could be misused, exposed, or moved through business and technical workflows. This is especially important as organizations adopt AI tools, automation, third-party integrations, and more complex data pipelines.

Threat modeling inputs may include:

Architecture Area	Examples	Why It Matters
Data flow threat modeling	Data movement diagrams, lineage maps, ingestion and export paths	Helps identify where sensitive data moves, where controls break down, and where exposure may occur.
AI workflow abuse cases	Unauthorized summarization, data leakage through prompts, unsafe model outputs, unintended training data use	Helps teams evaluate how AI workflows could expose or misuse sensitive data.
Prompt injection considerations	Malicious instructions, indirect prompt injection through documents, poisoned content, tool misuse	Helps assess how AI assistants or agents could be manipulated into revealing, moving, or acting on sensitive data.

Insider misuse scenarios	Privileged user abuse, excessive access, bulk downloads, unauthorized sharing	Helps evaluate risks from trusted users, contractors, administrators, and service accounts.
Third-party data exposure paths	Vendor access, SaaS integrations, shared workspaces, APIs, external collaborators	Helps identify where sensitive data leaves direct organizational control.

Threat modeling helps DSPM move beyond discovery and classification. It allows teams to ask not only, "*Where is the sensitive data?*" but also, "*How could this data be abused, exposed, moved, or accessed outside its intended purpose?*" This context strengthens prioritization, improves remediation planning, and helps security, privacy, architecture, and governance teams align around realistic risk scenarios.

Remediation Systems

Remediation systems turn findings into action.

These systems may include:

Architecture Area	Examples	Why It Matters
Ticketing systems	ServiceNow, Jira, ITSM platforms	Tickets assign work, track progress, and document accountability.
Access review platforms	IGA certifications, access review workflows	Access reviews validate whether permissions are still appropriate.
Workflow automation	Tines, Torq, SOAR, internal automation	Automation can reduce manual effort and speed common remediation actions.
Approval systems	Business owner approval, legal approval, privacy approval	Approval workflows help ensure changes are authorized and documented.
IGA workflows	Joiner, mover, leaver, access request, access certification	IGA workflows help correct excessive or outdated access.
PAM workflows	Privileged access requests, elevation, rotation, session review	PAM workflows help reduce privileged paths to sensitive data.
DevOps and infrastructure workflows	CI/CD, infrastructure as code, cloud engineering queues	Some findings require code, configuration, or infrastructure changes.

Remediation is where architecture becomes operational.

A DSPM platform may identify that sensitive data is overexposed, but the fix may require a cloud engineer to change permissions, a business owner to approve access removal, a legal stakeholder to confirm retention obligations, a privacy leader to validate regulatory impact, or an application owner to change a workflow.

That is why remediation must be designed as part of the architecture, not added later as an afterthought.

Reporting Layers

Reporting layers translate technical findings into useful views for different audiences.

Reporting may include:

Architecture Area	Examples	Why It Matters
Executive dashboards	Risk trends, top exposures, remediation progress	Executives need concise views of business risk and progress.
Security operations dashboards	Active findings, exposure, alerts, remediation status	Security teams need operational detail for investigation and response.
Audit evidence	Control operation, remediation proof, access review records	Auditors need evidence that controls exist and are operating.
Compliance reporting	Regulatory mappings, policy exceptions, control gaps	Compliance teams need traceability to obligations and requirements.
Privacy reporting	Data subject impact, data processing context, retention status	Privacy teams need visibility into personal data handling and exposure.
Board reporting	Material risk themes, trend lines, accountability, investment needs	Boards need business level reporting that supports oversight.
Risk trend reporting	Open risk, remediation age, recurrence, control drift	Trends help measure whether the program is improving.

Reporting should not be an afterthought. It is the mechanism that helps different stakeholders understand the same data risk from their own perspective.

A security analyst may need technical details. A CISO may need risk trends and remediation performance. A privacy officer may need to know whether personal data is exposed or retained too long. An auditor may need evidence. A board may need to understand whether the organization is reducing data risk in a measurable way.

A mature DSPM architecture supports all of these views without forcing each team to recreate the story manually.

5.5 Reference Architecture Diagram

The following words as diagram model shows the DSPM architecture as an end to end flow.

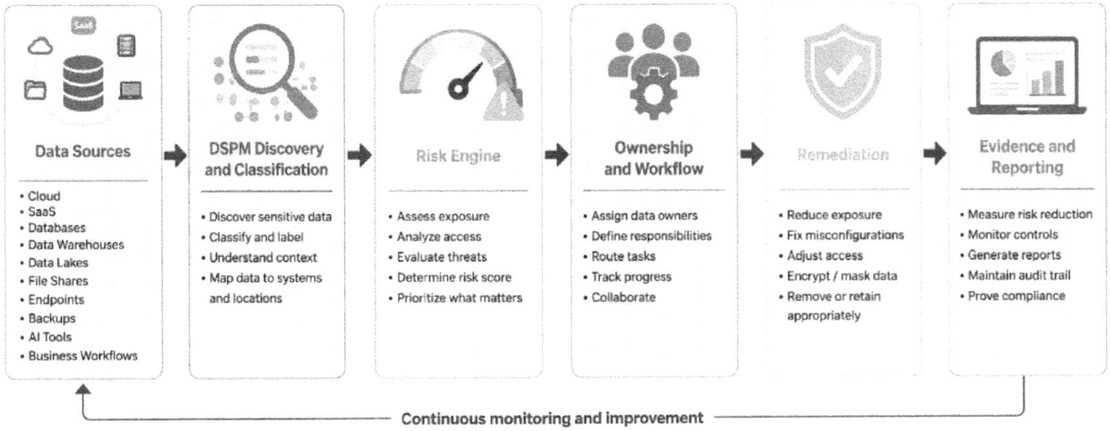

Figure 2: DSPM architecture as an end to end flow.

This diagram shows an important principle: DSPM value increases as context increases.

Discovery alone can identify sensitive data. Classification can describe that data. Identity context shows who can access it. Governance context explains why it exists and what rules apply. Detection context shows whether risk is active or escalating. Workflow connects the findings to accountable owners. Remediation reduces exposure. Reporting proves progress.

Each layer adds value.

5.6 Integration View

Another way to understand DSPM is to place it at the center of the architecture.

This model is useful for architects and buyers because it maps DSPM to systems the organization may already own.

DSPM does not replace every tool in this picture. It connects to them. In some cases, it enriches them. In other cases, it uses their context to make better decisions. In a mature program, DSPM becomes part of the operating fabric of data security.

The practical question for architects is not, *"Does DSPM integrate with everything?"* The better question is, *"Which integrations are necessary to support the outcomes we need first?"*

For example, an organization that is early in its DSPM journey may begin with cloud storage, SaaS platforms, identity provider integration, and ticketing. A more mature organization may add GRC, privacy inventory, SIEM, SOAR, IGA, PAM, CNAPP, and executive reporting.

The architecture should grow with the program.

5.7 How the Architecture Works in Practice

Consider a common scenario.

A DSPM platform discovers a folder in a cloud collaboration platform containing customer contracts, tax forms, bank account details, and employee information. The folder is shared with a large internal group, several external collaborators, and one inactive user account.

Discovery identifies the folder. Classification determines that it contains sensitive and regulated data. Identity context shows broad access and an inactive account. Governance context shows that the data belongs to Finance, should be retained for a defined period, and is not approved for external sharing. Detection context shows recent downloads from an unusual location. The risk engine prioritizes the finding because sensitive data, external access, stale identity, governance violation, and suspicious activity all overlap.

The finding is routed to the Finance data owner, security operations, and the identity team. A ticket is created. External sharing is reviewed. The inactive account is removed. The folder permissions are reduced. The unusual activity is investigated. The remediation is documented. The reporting layer shows the issue was resolved, how long it took, who approved the changes, and whether similar exposure exists elsewhere.

That is DSPM architecture in action.

The value is not just that the platform found sensitive data. The value is that it helped the organization understand the risk, route the work, reduce exposure, and produce evidence.

5.8 Buyer and Architect Questions

A DSPM reference architecture should help buyers and architects ask better questions during evaluation. The following questions can be used in discovery sessions, vendor evaluations, architecture reviews, and implementation planning.

Data Coverage

What repositories, SaaS platforms, databases, file shares, cloud environments, data warehouses, data lakes, endpoints, backups, and AI tools are supported?

Additional questions:

- *Does the platform scan structured, semi structured, and unstructured data?*
- *Does it support cloud, SaaS, on premises, and hybrid environments?*
- *Can it identify data copies, exports, and shadow data stores?*
- *How often does discovery run?*
- *Does the platform support near real time visibility where needed?*
- *What metadata is collected?*
- *What data stays in place and what, if anything, is copied into the DSPM platform?*

Identity Context

Can the platform resolve users, groups, roles, privileged accounts, service accounts, external users, and nonhuman identities?

Additional questions:

- *Can it identify excessive access?*
- *Can it distinguish direct access from inherited access?*
- *Can it identify dormant users or stale permissions?*
- *Can it connect identity risk to sensitive data exposure?*
- *Can it integrate with the organization's IdP, IAM, IGA, and PAM tools?*
- *Can it help launch or inform access reviews?*

Governance Context

Can the platform connect findings to data owners, business processes, regulatory requirements, retention rules, privacy obligations, and legal holds?

Additional questions:

- *Can it map data to applications or business services?*
- *Can it identify whether sensitive data exists in approved or unapproved locations?*
- *Can it support data retention and defensible deletion workflows?*
- *Can it help privacy teams understand personal data exposure?*
- *Can it connect findings to GRC controls or compliance obligations?*

Risk Prioritization

Does the platform only classify data, or does it prioritize risk based on sensitivity, exposure, access, location, business context, and control gaps?

Additional questions:

- *How is risk scored?*
- *Can risk scoring be customized?*
- *Does the platform explain why a finding is high risk?*
- *Can it identify toxic combinations?*
- *Can it correlate data risk with detection signals?*
- *Can it distinguish between accepted business use and unnecessary exposure?*

Remediation

Can findings become tickets, access reviews, approvals, workflow actions, or automated remediation steps?

Additional questions:

- *Which remediation systems are supported?*
- *Can tickets include enough context for owners to act?*
- *Can the platform recommend remediation actions?*
- *Can it automate low risk actions with approval?*
- *Can it track remediation status and aging?*
- *Can it verify whether remediation actually worked?*

Reporting

Can the platform produce executive, security, audit, compliance, privacy, and board level reporting?

Additional questions:

- *Can reporting show risk trends over time?*
- *Can it show remediation performance?*
- *Can it produce evidence for audits?*
- *Can it support regulatory reporting needs?*
- *Can it show program maturity improvement?*
- *Can it translate technical findings into business risk language?*

These questions help keep the evaluation focused on outcomes rather than feature lists. A long integration list may look impressive, but the real test is whether the platform helps the organization reduce data risk in a repeatable way.

5.9 Common Architecture Mistakes

DSPM programs often struggle when the architecture is too narrow, too tool centered, or too disconnected from ownership and workflow. The following mistakes are common and avoidable.

Mistake 1: Treating DSPM as Only a Scanner

Discovery is the starting point, not the operating model.

If DSPM is treated only as a scanner, the organization may learn where sensitive data exists but fail to reduce risk. This usually leads to dashboards, reports, and long lists of findings without meaningful remediation.

A better approach is to define from the beginning how findings will be prioritized, routed, remediated, and measured.

Mistake 2: Ignoring Identity Context

Sensitive data without access context does not give a complete risk picture.

A data store with sensitive information may be acceptable if access is limited, monitored, justified, and aligned to business need. A smaller data set may be much riskier if it is accessible to too many users, external collaborators, privileged accounts, service accounts, or inactive users.

DSPM architecture should connect data risk to identity risk as early as possible.

Mistake 3: Skipping Ownership Mapping

Findings need accountable owners or they become backlog noise.

Security teams can identify data risk, but they do not always own the data, business process, repository, or application. Without ownership mapping, remediation stalls.

A mature DSPM architecture should connect findings to data owners, system owners, application owners, business owners, and control owners.

Mistake 4: Creating Reports Without Remediation Workflows

Dashboards do not reduce risk by themselves.

Reporting is valuable, but only when it reflects action. A dashboard that shows thousands of unresolved findings may create awareness, but it does not create accountability. Reporting should be connected to workflow, ownership, aging, closure, exceptions, and evidence.

The best reports tell a risk reduction story.

Mistake 5: Connecting Too Many Tools Too Quickly

A broad integration strategy can become a distraction if it is not tied to outcomes.

Some organizations try to connect every possible source before they have defined priorities, owners, workflows, or success measures. This creates complexity before value.

A better approach is to start with critical data sources, identity context, and high value remediation workflows. Then expand based on risk, maturity, and business need.

Mistake 6: Forgetting About AI Data Flows

AI tools introduce new data movement and governance challenges.

Employees may upload sensitive data into AI tools. Developers may use production data for model testing. Business teams may create prompt libraries, summaries, embeddings, or training data sets without clear ownership. AI adoption can create new copies of sensitive data that do not fit traditional inventory models.

DSPM architecture should account for AI workspaces, AI enabled SaaS platforms, model development environments, and data flows into approved or unapproved AI tools.

Mistake 7: Treating Compliance as the Finish Line

Compliance is important, but it is not the whole goal.

A DSPM program may support GDPR, HIPAA, PCI DSS, SOX, CCPA, or other requirements, but the architecture should do more than produce compliance reports. It should help the organization reduce exposure, improve governance, support secure innovation, and build trust.

Compliance asks whether required controls exist. Data security also asks whether the organization understands and reduces real risk.

5.10 DSPM Architecture and Maturity

The DSPM architecture should evolve as the organization matures. Not every organization needs to begin at the most advanced level. The right architecture depends on regulatory pressure, budget, resources, data complexity, business risk, and the organization's appetite for automation.

A practical maturity path may look like this:

- Level 1: Manual inventory and limited discovery
- Level 2: Basic DSPM discovery and classification
- Level 3: Identity, ownership, workflow, and ticketing integration

- Level 4: Risk based prioritization, metrics, audit evidence, and automated workflows
- Level 5: Predictive risk, continuous optimization, and business aligned reporting

Level 1: Manual Inventory and Limited Discovery

At Level 1, the organization has limited visibility. Data inventories may be incomplete, outdated, or manually maintained. Sensitive data discovery may happen through interviews, spreadsheets, audits, or one time scans.

The primary architecture goal at this stage is to establish a baseline. The organization should identify major data sources, known sensitive repositories, critical business systems, and obvious exposure points.

Level 2: Basic DSPM Discovery and Classification

At Level 2, the organization begins using DSPM capabilities for discovery and classification. The program can identify sensitive data across selected environments and generate initial findings.

The architecture goal is to expand coverage and improve classification accuracy. The organization should also begin defining ownership, remediation paths, and reporting needs before findings grow too large to manage.

Level 3: Identity, Ownership, Workflow, and Ticketing Integration

At Level 3, DSPM becomes part of the operating model. The platform connects to identity sources, maps findings to owners, and routes work through ticketing or workflow systems.

This is a major maturity step. The organization is no longer just finding risk. It is assigning risk, acting on it, and tracking progress.

Level 4: Risk Based Prioritization, Metrics, Audit Evidence, and Automated Workflows

At Level 4, the organization uses data driven prioritization and measurable performance indicators. DSPM findings are enriched with business, identity, governance, and detection context. Workflows are standardized. Metrics such as remediation aging, policy exceptions, exposure trends, access violations, and control drift are tracked.

The architecture goal is to make data risk measurable and manageable at scale.

Level 5: Predictive Risk, Continuous Optimization, and Business Aligned Reporting

At Level 5, DSPM becomes a continuous improvement capability. The organization uses predictive signals, advanced analytics, automation, and business aligned reporting to reduce risk before it becomes a crisis.

This does not mean every action is fully automated. It means the architecture supports faster decisions, smarter prioritization, better evidence, and continuous refinement of controls.

5.11 Building the Architecture in Phases

A practical DSPM architecture should be built in phases. Trying to do everything at once can slow the program down and frustrate stakeholders.

Phase 1: Establish Visibility

Start with the most important data sources. For many organizations, this means cloud storage, SaaS collaboration platforms, major databases, data warehouses, and file shares.

The goal is to answer:

- *Where is sensitive data?*
- *What types of sensitive data exist?*
- *Where are the obvious exposure points?*
- *Which repositories require immediate attention?*

Phase 2: Add Identity and Access Context

Next, connect identity sources. This allows the program to move from "where is sensitive data" to "who or what can access it."

The goal is to identify excessive access, external sharing, stale permissions, privileged paths, service account exposure, and nonhuman identity risk.

Phase 3: Connect Ownership and Governance

Once the organization can see data and access, it should connect findings to owners and governance context.

The goal is to answer:

- *Who owns the data?*
- *What business process does it support?*
- *What policies or regulations apply?*
- *How long should the data be retained?*
- *Is the data in an approved location?*

Phase 4: Operationalize Remediation

Next, connect ticketing, workflow, approval, access review, and automation systems.

The goal is to make remediation repeatable. Findings should be routed to the right owners with the right context and tracked through closure or documented exception.

Phase 5: Mature Reporting and Evidence

Finally, build reporting layers for different audiences.

The goal is to show risk reduction over time. Reports should help executives, security teams, privacy teams, compliance teams, auditors, and the board understand progress in language that fits their responsibilities.

5.12 Practical Design Principles

The following design principles can help guide DSPM architecture decisions.

Start With Outcomes

Do not begin with the longest possible integration list. Begin with the outcomes the organization needs.

Examples include:

- Reduce public exposure of sensitive data
- Identify over privileged access to regulated data
- Support privacy inventory accuracy
- Improve audit evidence
- Reduce stale sensitive data
- Govern AI data usage
- Improve board reporting on data risk

The architecture should support these outcomes first.

Prioritize High Value Data

Not all data has the same value or risk. Start with repositories that contain regulated, sensitive, business critical, customer, employee, financial, health, legal, or intellectual property data.

The goal is not perfect coverage on day one. The goal is meaningful risk reduction.

Connect Data to Identity Early

Identity context is one of the fastest ways to make DSPM findings actionable. A data finding becomes more useful when the organization can see who has access, whether access is excessive, and whether the access path is direct, inherited, privileged, external, stale, or nonhuman.

Design for Ownership

A finding without an owner is a conversation, not a remediation plan.

Ownership should be part of the architecture from the beginning. That may require integration with a CMDB, data catalog, application inventory, business owner registry, or manual ownership mapping during the early stages.

Make Workflow Part of the Architecture

Workflow determines whether DSPM becomes operational. Decide how findings will become tickets, tasks, access reviews, approvals, investigations, or automated actions.

Do this before the program produces a large backlog.

Measure What Matters

Avoid vanity metrics. The number of findings alone does not tell the full story.

More useful measures include:

- High risk exposures reduced
- Excessive access removed
- Publicly exposed sensitive repositories closed
- Remediation time improved
- Data owner coverage increased
- Stale sensitive data reduced
- Audit evidence produced
- Policy exceptions reviewed
- Repeat findings decreased

Measurement should help the organization understand whether risk is actually going down.

Key Takeaway

DSPM needs a reference architecture because data security is not a single tool problem. Sensitive data lives across cloud, SaaS, databases, data warehouses, lakes, file shares, endpoints, backups, AI tools, and business workflows. Access is shaped by users, groups, roles, privileged accounts, service accounts, and nonhuman identities. Governance depends on ownership, privacy obligations, retention, legal holds, compliance requirements, and business process. Detection tools provide signals. Remediation systems turn findings into action. Reporting proves progress.

A strong DSPM architecture connects these pieces in a practical way. The goal is not to integrate DSPM with every system immediately. The goal is to integrate it with the systems necessary to support the first risk outcomes the organization has committed to reduce.

At its simplest, the DSPM architecture should help the organization move through this flow:

When implemented well, DSPM helps the organization move from discovery to decision, from decision to ownership, from ownership to remediation, and from remediation to evidence. This is what makes DSPM useful to architects, buyers, security teams, privacy teams, and business leaders. It shows where the platform fits, what it must connect to, and how it becomes part of the operating model instead of becoming another disconnected security tool.

The architecture should help the business answer the questions that matter most:

- *What data do we have?*
- *Where is it?*
- *Who or what can access it?*
- *Why does it exist?*
- *Is it exposed, misused, or over-permissioned?*
- *Who owns the risk?*
- *What needs to happen next?*
- *Can we prove that risk is being reduced?*

That is the bridge between DSPM concepts and DSPM execution.

Chapter 6: How to Find the Right DSPM Tool

Finding the right DSPM tool should not start with a vendor demo. It should start with a risk assessment grounded in the organization's real-world data exposure, governance gaps, identity risks, privacy obligations, AI usage patterns, and operational blind spots. The goal is not to buy a platform first. The goal is to understand the problems that actually need to be solved.

Those problems were outlined in Chapter 4: unknown sensitive data, overexposed data, excessive access, weak ownership, poor remediation workflows, privacy exposure, AI and data leakage risk, and the lack of continuous visibility into where sensitive information exists and how it is being used.

The right DSPM platform is not necessarily the most recognizable, the most expensive, or the one with the most polished dashboard. It is the platform that consistently helps the organization answer critical operational questions:

- *Where is sensitive data?*
- *Who has access to it?*
- *Is it exposed or over-permissioned?*
- *Is it being used safely?*
- *Who owns the risk?*
- *What should be remediated first?*
- *Did the remediation actually reduce risk?*

Industry definitions broadly align around these capabilities. Gartner defines DSPM as the ability to discover unknown data across cloud and on-premises environments, classify structured and unstructured data, and assess security, privacy, posture, access, and AI-related risks. Gartner also identifies discovery, classification, and risk/posture management as foundational DSPM capabilities. (Gartner) G2 similarly defines DSPM platforms as solutions that discover and classify sensitive data, identify exposure and policy violations, continuously monitor risk, and support remediation workflows or recommendations. (G2)

One of the biggest mistakes organizations make is spending months or even years comparing tools while sensitive data remains exposed. Analysis paralysis is becoming a security risk of its own. Organizations should identify their non-negotiable requirements, conduct a focused proof of concept, select the platform that best aligns to their current risk profile, and begin reducing exposure as quickly as possible.

The first DSPM decision does not need to be perfect. It needs to be actionable. Adjustments and platform changes may happen over time as the program matures. What matters most is establishing visibility, accountability, and measurable risk reduction before unmanaged data becomes tomorrow's incident.

6.1 Start With the Problems You Are Actually Trying to Solve

Tie the DSPM evaluation directly back to Chapter 4. Do not buy "DSPM" because the market says it is hot. Buy it because it solves specific data security problems that your organization has already identified.

Chapter 4 Problem	What the DSPM Tool Must Prove	Evidence You Should Demand
Unknown sensitive data	*Can it discover sensitive data across cloud, SaaS, databases, file stores, and on-prem systems?*	Inventory of repositories scanned, sensitive data types found, scan success/failure report, unsupported systems list
Shadow data	*Can it find unmanaged, duplicated, abandoned, or copied data stores?*	List of unowned assets, stale datasets, duplicate regulated data, unknown buckets/shares/databases
Excessive access	*Can it show who has effective access, not just who has direct permissions?*	Effective access graph, group nesting, inherited permissions, service accounts, external users, privileged roles
Public or external exposure	*Can it identify internet-facing, anonymous, shared-link, third-party, or cross-tenant exposure?*	Exposure path, sharing source, user/group/app identity, remediation recommendation
Weak data ownership	*Can it map findings to application, data, system, or business owners?*	CMDB/tag ingestion, owner mapping, ticket routing, unresolved-owner report
Poor classification	*Can it distinguish truly sensitive data from noise?*	False-positive and false-negative testing, confidence scores, tuning process, custom classifier support
Too many findings	*Can it prioritize based on sensitivity, exposure, access, business criticality, and activity?*	Risk scoring logic, top 10 actionable findings, deduplication, suppression workflow
Slow remediation	*Can it create tickets, assign owners, track SLAs, and verify closure?*	Jira/ServiceNow integration, workflow demo, before/after validation
AI and GenAI data risk	*Can it identify sensitive data used in AI apps, vector databases, copilots, prompts, or training pipelines?*	AI data exposure report, connector coverage, AI-specific policy findings
Compliance and privacy exposure	*Can it map data to regulatory obligations such as PCI, HIPAA, GDPR, CCPA, GLBA, or internal policies?*	Data-type mapping, policy packs, evidence exports, audit reports
Inability to show progress to leadership	*Can it produce measurable risk reduction over time?*	Baseline score, trend report, remediation metrics, executive dashboard

Key principle: a DSPM tool should not merely find data. It should help the organization reduce data risk.

6.2 DSPM Vendor and Tool Landscape

As of May 2026, the DSPM market is crowded and increasingly blurry. Gartner Peer Insights shows "Products 1–20 of 53" in the DSPM category, while G2 lists 37 DSPM category entries. The market now includes pure-play DSPM vendors, CNAPP platforms, DLP vendors, privacy platforms, SaaS security vendors, backup and cyber resilience providers, identity governance tools, and data governance platforms that have expanded into DSPM-related capabilities.

This is not a ranked recommendation list. It is a broad market map of DSPM and DSPM-adjacent technologies identified through public vendor documentation, analyst references, product listings, and market guides.

The important point is that "DSPM" is now simultaneously:

- A standalone platform category
- A feature set
- A security capability integrated into broader ecosystems

Some vendors were born as DSPM platforms. Others added DSPM capabilities into cloud security, privacy, governance, identity, backup, or AI security offerings. Organizations should evaluate solutions based on operational outcomes, visibility, risk reduction, and remediation capabilities rather than relying solely on category labels.

Pure-Play DSPM Platforms

These vendors primarily focus on discovering, classifying, monitoring, and reducing sensitive data exposure risks across cloud, SaaS, hybrid, and enterprise environments.

Vendor / Product	Market Position to Evaluate
Arexdata DSPM	DSPM, data audit, classification, permissions, traceability
Cyera Platform	AI-native DSPM and enterprise data security
Eureka Security DSPM	Cloud-focused DSPM platform
Fasoo DSPM	Enterprise DSPM and data-centric security
Polymer DSPM	DSPM and adaptive data controls
Sentra	Cloud-native DSPM and exposure management
Satori Data Security Platform	DSPM, DDR, access governance, real-time enforcement
Symmetry Systems DataGuard	Hybrid-cloud DSPM and data flow visibility
Teleskope	DSPM/DLP for SaaS, cloud, AI, and databases
TrustLogix / TrustDSPM	DSPM with policy-based access management

CNAPP + DSPM Platforms

These vendors originated in cloud security posture management, workload protection, or CNAPP markets and later expanded into DSPM capabilities.

Vendor / Product	Market Position to Evaluate
Check Point CloudGuard	CNAPP with DSPM integrations
Cortex Cloud / Prisma Cloud	Cloud security with DSPM capabilities
CrowdStrike Falcon Cloud Security	Cloud security posture and data exposure visibility
Netskope DSPM	SASE/cloud security with DSPM functionality
Wiz	CNAPP with DSPM capabilities
Zscaler DSPM	Cloud exposure monitoring and data protection

Data Governance + DSPM Platforms

These vendors focus heavily on governance, metadata management, classification, ownership, and compliance workflows alongside DSPM functionality.

Vendor / Product	Market Position to Evaluate
AvePoint Confidence Platform	M365, SaaS governance, collaboration security
BigID Next	Discovery, governance, privacy, DSPM
IBM Guardium DSPM	Database security and governance
Lepide Data Security Platform	Auditing, permissions, governance
LightBeam	Data mapping and privacy automation
Spirion	Sensitive data discovery and governance
Varonis Unified Data Security Platform	Permissions, behavior analytics, data governance

Privacy + DSPM Platforms

These platforms emphasize privacy operations, regulatory compliance, consent management, and exposure reduction.

Vendor / Product	Market Position to Evaluate
DataForesight by Whitehats Technologies	Privacy and compliance visibility
OneTrust Privacy Automation	Privacy governance and data mapping
Relyance AI	AI-native privacy and continuous compliance
Securiti / Veeam Data Command Center	Privacy, governance, AI trust, DSPM

Backup / Cyber Recovery + DSPM Platforms

These vendors originated in resilience, backup, or cyber recovery and expanded into data posture visibility and risk management.

Vendor / Product	Market Position to Evaluate
Commvault Cloud	Cyber resilience with DSPM capabilities
Rubrik DSPM	Cyber recovery integrated with DSPM and posture management
SpinOne by SpinAI	SaaS backup, collaboration security, DSPM-adjacent

Identity and Data Access Governance Platforms

These vendors focus on identity-aware access visibility, permissions, insider risk, and governance.

Vendor / Product	Market Position to Evaluate
Netwrix 1Secure / Access Analyzer / Auditor	Access governance and auditing
SailPoint	Identity security with data access governance
Qostodian by Qohash	Unstructured data monitoring and insider risk

SaaS and Collaboration Data Security Platforms

These vendors focus heavily on SaaS ecosystems, collaboration security, insider risk, and user-driven exposure.

Vendor / Product	Market Position to Evaluate
Cyberhaven	Insider risk and data detection/response
Forcepoint DSPM	DSPM integrated with DLP
Proofpoint DSPM	Data security and insider threat protection
Strac	SaaS, cloud, and GenAI data discovery and protection

AI-Native Data Security Platforms

These vendors heavily emphasize AI governance, AI-assisted classification, GenAI protection, and AI-related data risks.

Vendor / Product	Market Position to Evaluate
Bedrock Data	AI-native data governance and security
Concentric AI Semantic Intelligence	AI-driven classification and governance
Matters.AI	AI-native DSPM, DDR, DAM, DLP
Ray Security Predictive Data Security Platform	Predictive data security analytics

Open-Source and Budget-Conscious DSPM Foundations

Not every organization can immediately invest in a commercial DSPM platform. Smaller organizations, public-sector entities, startups, educational institutions, healthcare providers, and budget-constrained security teams may begin with open-source or lower-cost tooling to improve visibility and establish foundational governance practices.

It is important to recognize that there are currently very few mature open-source platforms that provide full enterprise-grade DSPM capabilities across:

- Discovery
- Classification
- Exposure analysis
- Identity-aware access mapping
- Continuous monitoring
- Automated remediation workflows
- AI risk analysis
- Data posture scoring

However, organizations can still establish meaningful visibility and reduce risk using combinations of:

- Open-source discovery and classification tooling
- Open-source data cataloging platforms
- Open-source governance frameworks
- OSS-assisted DSPM foundations paired with existing security controls

Open-Source Tool	Common Usage
Apache Atlas	Metadata governance and data lineage
OpenMetadata	Data cataloging and metadata management
DataHub	Data discovery, ownership, lineage, governance
OpenDLP	Historical open-source sensitive data discovery tool

These platforms may help organizations:

- Discover sensitive data repositories
- Build initial data inventories
- Establish ownership models
- Improve metadata visibility
- Support classification efforts
- Demonstrate business value before larger investments

Organizations should avoid assuming that open-source tooling alone provides the same operational maturity, automation, scalability, remediation capabilities, identity integration, or continuous risk analysis as modern commercial DSPM platforms.

In many environments, open-source tooling becomes an early visibility and governance layer that later supports adoption of a broader enterprise DSPM strategy.

6.3 Budget: Important, But Do Not Let It Narrow the Market Too Early

Budget is a real constraint, but it should not be the first filter. Many organizations eliminate the "high-price leader" before understanding whether that vendor can solve the problem faster, reduce labor, reduce breach exposure, or consolidate other tools. Vendors also adjust pricing based on strategic goals, timing, expansion potential, competitive pressure, reference value, and partner involvement.

Budget Area	What to Ask	Why It Matters
Pricing metric	*Is pricing based on data volume, number of repositories, cloud accounts, users, identities, connectors, assets, or modules?*	A tool that looks affordable in a small POC may become expensive at enterprise scale.
Scan costs	*Will scanning create cloud API, compute, storage, egress, or SaaS API costs?*	"Agentless" does not always mean "costless."
Connector licensing	*Are SaaS, on-prem, databases, file shares, backups, and AI systems included?*	Some vendors price coverage separately.
Classification depth	*Are advanced classifiers, custom labels, OCR, source-code scanning, or GenAI classifiers extra?*	Basic discovery may not solve the real problem.
Support	*What level of support is included? Is implementation support included?*	DSPM value depends heavily on deployment quality.
Professional services	*How many services hours are required? Who pays for connector setup and tuning?*	Budget must include time-to-value, not just license price.
Remediation workflow	*Are ticketing, API access, SOAR integration, or auto-remediation included?*	Visibility without workflow can create shelfware.
Data retention	*How long are findings, samples, metadata, logs, and historical trends retained?*	Retention may affect cost, privacy, and auditability.
Expansion pricing	*What happens when the data estate grows 30%, 50%, or 100%?*	Data grows faster than security budgets.
Exit rights	*Can you export findings, history, labels, policies, and evidence at contract end?*	Avoid being trapped in a system you cannot leave cleanly.

Selection rule: budget should shape negotiation, not blind the evaluation. First identify the tools that can solve the problem. Then negotiate.

6.4 The Value Added Reseller Matters More Than Most Teams Expect

A good VAR can be as important as the tool itself. DSPM implementations fail not only because a tool lacks features, but because the customer never gets the right connectors deployed, never tunes classification, never maps owners, never operationalizes ticketing, and never gets past dashboard admiration.

What a Strong VAR Does	What a Weak VAR Does
Helps translate your data risk problems into vendor requirements	Repeats the vendor's sales deck
Knows which vendors work well in your environment type	Pushes the vendor with the best margin
Helps structure a realistic POC	Lets the vendor define success
Provides implementation support	Disappears after the purchase order
Escalates support problems	Tells you to open a ticket and wait
Helps negotiate pricing and terms	Only forwards quotes
Understands security, privacy, risk, and board reporting needs	Treats DSPM like another IT tool
Helps with adoption after deployment	Focuses only on closing the sale

Questions to ask the VAR:

Question	What You Are Testing
How many DSPM deployments have you supported in the last 12 months?	Real implementation experience
Which DSPM vendors have you replaced and why?	Honesty and field knowledge
Which vendor is best for our environment and which is worst?	Willingness to advise, not just sell
Who supports us when the connector fails?	Post-sale accountability
Can you help run the POC scorecard?	Ability to keep the process objective
Can you provide references from customers with similar data architecture?	Relevance
How do you handle vendor escalations?	Support leverage
Are your incentives different across vendors?	Conflict of interest

Common Vendor Claims vs. Reality

Vendor Claim	Reality	How to Validate It
"We deploy in minutes."	Initial cloud connection may take minutes. Meaningful coverage, access review, tuning, and remediation take longer.	Ask for time-to-first-scan, time-to-first-actionable-finding, and time-to-first-remediation.
"We are agentless."	Agentless reduces friction, but still requires permissions, APIs, scanning architecture, cost controls, and change approval.	Review required roles, read permissions, data access model, logs accessed, and cloud cost impact.
"We cover everything."	No one covers everything deeply. Coverage may be broad but shallow.	Ask for exact connector list, supported versions, limitations, unsupported data stores, and roadmap dependencies.
"Our classification is 95% accurate."	Accuracy depends on data type, language, context, file format, custom patterns, and tuning.	Test precision and recall using known datasets and seeded false positives/false negatives.
"AI solves classification."	AI can improve context, but it can also hallucinate, mislabel, or produce inconsistent results without governance.	Ask how models are trained, whether data leaves your environment, how confidence is calculated, and how tuning works.
"We prioritize risk automatically."	Risk scoring may reflect vendor assumptions, not your business priorities.	Demand transparent scoring factors and the ability to adjust weights.
"We integrate with your SIEM and ticketing."	Integration may mean basic alert forwarding, not operational workflow.	Create and close a real ticket during the POC. Send real findings to SIEM. Validate fields, severity, ownership, and closure state.
"We remediate automatically."	Auto-remediation is often limited to specific systems and can create outages if misused.	Test one low-risk remediation end to end. Require approval workflow and rollback.
"No sensitive data leaves your environment."	Vendors may store snippets, metadata, hashes, embeddings, labels, or samples.	Review architecture, data processing agreement, retention settings, encryption, and tenant isolation.
"Single pane of glass."	A dashboard is not a program. Teams still need ownership, workflow, prioritization, and accountability.	Ask how findings become assigned work and how leadership sees risk reduction over time.

6.5 Agentless vs. Agent-Based Tradeoffs

Agentless is attractive, but it is not automatically better. Agent-based is heavier, but it may provide deeper visibility or enforcement. Many mature programs use a hybrid model.

Approach	Strengths	Weaknesses	Best Fit
Agentless cloud/API scanning	Fast onboarding, lower operational friction, good for cloud storage, SaaS, databases, metadata, permissions	Limited by APIs, rate limits, permissions, snapshot timing, and vendor connector depth	Cloud-first organizations that need rapid discovery and posture visibility
Lightweight connector or scanner	More control over scan location, useful for on-prem, private networks, file shares, large databases	Requires deployment, network access, patching, and operational ownership	Hybrid environments with regulated data and private systems
Agent-based endpoint/server scanning	Deep local visibility, endpoint context, offline/local file discovery, potential enforcement	Heavier deployment, endpoint performance concerns, agent conflicts, change management	Endpoint-heavy environments, regulated workstations, local file exposure
Inline/proxy/access broker	Real-time control, policy enforcement, masking, access governance	More architecture change, potential latency, app compatibility concerns	Data access control, analytics platforms, Snowflake/Databricks/database enforcement
Hybrid DSPM model	Balances fast discovery with deeper enforcement where needed	More design and integration work	Enterprises with cloud, SaaS, on-prem, endpoint, and AI workloads

Rule of thumb: agentless is excellent for starting fast. It is not always sufficient for finishing the job.

6.6 Depth vs. Breadth: Cloud, SaaS, On-Prem, and AI Coverage

A vendor may say it covers "AWS, Azure, GCP, SaaS, and on-prem." That statement means almost nothing until you inspect depth.

Coverage Area	Breadth Question	Depth Question
Cloud object storage	*Do you support S3, Azure Blob, ADLS, GCS?*	*Can you identify public exposure, cross-account access, encryption state, stale data, owner, and data sensitivity?*
Cloud databases	*Do you support RDS, Aurora, DynamoDB, Cosmos DB, Cloud SQL, BigQuery, Redshift, Synapse?*	*Can you classify structured data, analyze permissions, detect excessive access, and avoid production performance impact?*
Data warehouses/lakes	*Do you support Snowflake, Databricks, BigQuery, Redshift, Synapse, Athena, lakehouses?*	*Can you map roles, inherited privileges, external shares, data lineage, and active usage?*
SaaS	*Do you support Microsoft 365, Google Workspace, Salesforce, Slack, ServiceNow, Box, Dropbox, GitHub, Jira?*	*Can you inspect sharing links, external collaborators, sensitive documents, app integrations, and stale permissions?*
On-prem file shares	*Do you support Windows file servers, SMB, NFS, NAS, NetApp, SharePoint on-prem?*	*Can you handle ACL inheritance, nested groups, stale shares, owners, and remediation?*
On-prem databases	*Do you support SQL Server, Oracle, PostgreSQL, MySQL, MongoDB, DB2?*	*Can you scan without performance harm and map real user/application access?*
Backups	*Do you inspect backup repositories and snapshots?*	*Can you identify sensitive data in recoverable copies and prioritize clean recovery?*
Endpoints	*Do you find sensitive data on laptops/desktops?*	*Can you distinguish local copies, synced cloud files, browser downloads, and removable media risk?*
AI systems	*Do you support vector databases, RAG pipelines, copilots, prompts, model stores, and agent workflows?*	*Can you show what sensitive data is accessible to AI tools and prevent unsafe use?*

Breadth gets you inventory. Depth gets you risk reduction.

6.7 Classification Accuracy vs. Volume of Findings

A DSPM tool that finds millions of "sensitive" files can look impressive in a demo and become useless in production. Security teams do not need more noise. They need prioritized, trusted findings.

Metric	What It Means	Why It Matters
Precision	*Of the items labeled sensitive, how many are truly sensitive?*	Low precision creates alert fatigue.
Recall	*Of all truly sensitive items, how many did the tool find?*	Low recall creates dangerous blind spots.
Confidence score	How certain the tool is about a classification	Helps route findings based on confidence.
Business context	Whether the tool understands customer data, employee data, source code, contracts, IP, credentials, secrets, health data, payment data	Generic labels are not enough.
Toxic combinations	Sensitive data plus public exposure, external access, stale owner, no encryption, privileged access, or active exfiltration path	This is where risk becomes actionable.
Deduplication	Whether repeated copies are grouped logically	Prevents inflated finding counts.
Suppression/tuning	Whether known acceptable patterns can be tuned out	Prevents recurring noise.
False-negative testing	Whether seeded sensitive data is missed	Most vendors prefer showing what they found, not what they missed.

POC test: give each vendor a known test set with examples of true sensitive data, fake data, edge cases, internal identifiers, secrets, contracts, source code, HR files, customer data, and benign lookalikes. Make them report what they found, what they missed, and what they mislabeled.

6.8 Identity and Access Context Maturity

DSPM without identity context is incomplete. The real risk is not just that sensitive data exists. The real risk is that the wrong people, apps, service accounts, third parties, or AI systems can access it.

Maturity Level	Capability	What It Looks Like
Level 0: No identity context	Finds sensitive data only	"This bucket contains PII."
Level 1: Basic permissions	Shows direct permissions	"These users/groups have access."
Level 2: Effective access	Resolves inherited, nested, and group-based access	"These 4,200 users effectively have access through nested groups."
Level 3: Privilege and exposure context	Adds admin roles, public access, external sharing, cross-account access	"This sensitive data is accessible by external collaborators and cloud admins."
Level 4: Activity context	Adds access frequency, last accessed, unusual access, dormant access	"Only 12 users accessed this in 180 days; 3,000 can access it."
Level 5: Risk path and enforcement	Maps attack paths and supports remediation or policy enforcement	"Remove this group, revoke this token, disable this public link, enforce masking, create ticket."

Ask vendors to prove they can answer:

Who can access this data right now, how did they get access, when did they last use it, and what exact change would reduce risk without breaking the business?

6.9 Integration Requirements

DSPM should become part of the security operating model, not another dashboard that people forget to check.

Integration Area	Examples	Why It Matters	POC Test
IAM / IdP	Entra ID, Okta, Google Workspace, AWS IAM, Azure RBAC, GCP IAM	Effective access, identity risk, owner mapping	Show direct and inherited access for a sensitive repository.
IGA	SailPoint, Saviynt, Omada	Access reviews, certification, joiner/mover/leaver process	Send excessive-access findings into an access review.
SIEM	Microsoft Sentinel, Splunk, Chronicle, QRadar	Alerting, correlation, incident response	Send a high-risk data exposure event with useful fields.
SOAR	Cortex XSOAR, Splunk SOAR, Tines, Torq	Automated triage and response	Trigger a workflow for public sensitive data.

CNAPP / CSPM / CIEM	Wiz, Prisma Cloud, Orca, Lacework, CrowdStrike, Zscaler	Cloud asset risk, misconfigurations, attack paths	Correlate sensitive data with public exposure or toxic IAM.
DLP	Microsoft Purview DLP, Proofpoint, Netskope, Forcepoint, Zscaler, Symantec	Enforcement and data movement controls	Use DSPM classification to inform DLP policy.
Data catalogs	Collibra, Alation, Atlan, Microsoft Purview	Data ownership, lineage, business glossary	Map findings to business owner and data domain.
Privacy tools	OneTrust, BigID, Securiti, TrustArc	Privacy records, RoPA, DSAR, regulatory mapping	Connect sensitive data discovery to privacy inventory.
Ticketing	ServiceNow, Jira, Azure DevOps	Operational remediation	Create, assign, update, and close a real ticket.
CMDB / asset inventory	ServiceNow CMDB, cloud tags, asset inventory	Ownership and prioritization	Route findings by app owner or system owner.
Messaging	Slack, Teams, email	Notifications	Notify the right owner without exposing sensitive content.
Data platforms	Snowflake, Databricks, BigQuery, Redshift, SQL Server, Oracle	Structured data visibility and access analysis	Prove role mapping and query/access context.

A DSPM tool that cannot integrate into remediation workflows will become a reporting tool, not a risk reduction platform.

6.10 Time to Value vs. Time to Deploy

Do not let vendors define success as "connected." A connected tool is not the same as an operational tool.

Milestone	What It Means	Good Target
Time to connect	First connector is authorized	Hours to days
Time to first scan	First data store is scanned	Hours to days
Time to first finding	Tool produces discovery/classification results	Same week
Time to first actionable risk	Team agrees a finding is real, important, and fixable	Week 1–2
Time to first remediation	Owner takes corrective action	Week 2–3
Time to verified closure	Tool confirms risk is reduced	Week 3–4

Time to repeatable workflow	Findings route to owners with SLA and reporting	30–60 days
Time to enterprise rollout	Core repositories onboarded with operating model	60–120+ days depending on scope
Deployment Type	Time-to-Value Pattern	Watch Out For
Cloud-only agentless	Fastest initial findings	Cloud permission design, API limits, scan cost
SaaS API connectors	Fast for M365/Google/Salesforce if permissions are ready	API throttling, incomplete sharing context
Data warehouse connectors	Medium	Role complexity, performance controls, admin approvals
On-prem file shares	Slower	Network routes, scanners, service accounts, ACL complexity
Endpoint agents	Slower	Endpoint deployment, performance, change approvals
Inline enforcement	Slowest but potentially highest control	Architecture change, app impact, rollback planning

6.11 Questions to Ask in a POC That Vendors Do Not Want Asked

POC Question	Why It Matters
Show us what you missed.	Vendors prefer to show true positives, not false negatives.
What data types are you bad at classifying?	Every classifier has weak spots.
Which connectors are generally available, beta, roadmap, or partner-delivered?	Roadmap coverage is not coverage.
What permissions do you require and why?	Overprivileged DSPM tools can become a new risk.
Do you read data content, metadata only, samples, snippets, hashes, or embeddings?	Data handling affects privacy, legal, and security review.
Where is customer data processed and stored?	Data residency and vendor risk.
Can we disable sample retention?	Sensitive snippets in a vendor platform may create new exposure.
Can we bring our own classifiers?	Internal data types often matter more than generic PII.
Can we tune risk scoring?	Vendor severity may not match business risk.
Can you prove effective access through nested groups?	Direct permissions are not enough.

Can you identify service accounts and non-human identities?	Machine identities often have broad access.
Can you show stale access?	"Can access" plus "never uses" is a remediation opportunity.
Can you create and close a ServiceNow/Jira ticket?	This proves operational workflow.
Can you verify remediation after the owner acts?	Closure must be evidence-based.
What happens if a connector fails silently?	Failed scans create false confidence.
How do you handle very large repositories?	Scale breaks many tools.
What is the expected cloud/SaaS API cost?	Scanning can have hidden cost.
Can we export all findings and history?	Avoid lock-in.
Can you support least-privilege deployment of the DSPM tool itself?	The tool should not become a super-admin blind spot.
What customer similar to us can we speak with?	Reference relevance matters.

6.12 Red Flags During Evaluation

Red Flag	What It Usually Means
Vendor will only demo against their own sample environment	They may not perform well on messy real-world data.
They avoid false-negative testing	Classification quality may be overstated.
They cannot explain required permissions clearly	Security architecture may be immature.
They claim "no data leaves your environment" but cannot prove it	Data handling may be more complex than sales says.
They show thousands of findings but cannot prioritize the top 10	The tool may create noise instead of action.
They cannot map findings to owners	Remediation will stall.
They cannot integrate with ticketing	Findings will remain dashboard items.
They cannot show effective access	Access risk will be incomplete.
They cannot support your highest-risk repository type	The tool may be impressive but irrelevant.
They depend heavily on roadmap features	You may be buying promises.
They resist security review	The vendor may not be enterprise-ready.
The POC requires broad admin privileges without justification	The tool itself may increase risk.
Pricing is vague until the end	Commercial risk is being hidden.

The VAR disappears during technical issues	Post-sale support will likely be weak.
Every answer is "yes"	No vendor is strong at everything.

6.13 Why Most DSPM POCs Fail

Most POCs fail because the organization treats the POC like a product trial instead of a decision process.

Why POCs Fail	How to Prevent It
No clear success criteria	Define must-haves, nice-to-haves, scoring, and disqualifiers before demos.
Vendor chooses the scope	Customer chooses representative systems, including messy data.
POC is too broad	Test a small number of high-value repositories deeply.
POC is too narrow	Include at least one cloud, one SaaS, one structured data source, and one ownership/remediation workflow if relevant.
Classification is not tested scientifically	Seed known data and measure false positives and false negatives.
No remediation test	Require one real ticket, one real owner, one real fix, and one verified closure.
Identity context is skipped	Require effective access, nested groups, external users, and service accounts.
Security review happens too late	Review architecture, permissions, data handling, and legal terms early.
Procurement starts after technical selection	Start commercial review early enough to avoid surprise pricing.
No executive decision date	Set a decision date and enforce it.
No post-POC owner	Assign a platform owner, remediation owner, and executive sponsor before purchase.

6.14 How to Run a DSPM POC Correctly

POC Charter

Item	Recommendation
Duration	30–45 days for most organizations
Vendors	2–3 vendors maximum
Scope	Representative, not exhaustive
Systems	Include your highest-risk data locations
Success criteria	Defined before kickoff
Evaluation team	Security, privacy, risk, data platform, cloud, IAM, IT ops, legal/procurement

Output	Buy / do not buy / revisit later decision
Required proof	Discovery, classification, access context, prioritization, workflow, remediation verification

Suggested POC Scope

Environment	Example Target
Cloud object storage	One high-risk S3/Azure Blob/GCS location
SaaS	Microsoft 365, Google Workspace, Salesforce, or Box
Structured data	Snowflake, Databricks, BigQuery, SQL Server, Oracle, or PostgreSQL
On-prem or file share	One sensitive file share or NAS location
Identity	Entra ID, Okta, cloud IAM, privileged groups
Workflow	ServiceNow or Jira
Security telemetry	SIEM or SOAR integration
Business ownership	CMDB, tags, data catalog, or manual owner mapping

POC Scorecard

Category	Weigh t	What Good Looks Like
Problem fit	20%	Solves the Chapter 4 risks that matter most
Coverage depth	15%	Covers priority repositories deeply, not just broadly
Classification quality	15%	Strong precision/recall, tunable, explainable
Identity/access context	15%	Effective access, external users, service accounts, stale access
Risk prioritization	10%	Top findings are actionable and business-relevant
Remediation workflow	10%	Tickets, owners, SLAs, verification
Deployment effort	5%	Realistic permissions, low friction, scalable architecture
Integrations	5%	Works with IAM, SIEM, CNAPP, catalog, ticketing
Vendor/VAR support	3%	Responsive, knowledgeable, accountable
Commercial fit	2%	Pricing model aligns with expected growth

A vendor that scores poorly on a must-have should not win because it scores well on nice-to-haves.

6.15 Minimum Viable DSPM Requirements

To avoid analysis paralysis, define the minimum bar. A company can always mature later.

Requirement	Minimum Acceptable Standard
Discovery	Finds sensitive data in the highest-risk environments
Classification	Produces trusted results with manageable false positives
Access context	Shows who can access sensitive data and how
Exposure detection	Identifies public, external, excessive, stale, or toxic access
Prioritization	Ranks findings by business risk, not just count
Ownership	Maps findings to responsible teams or owners
Workflow	Creates tickets and tracks remediation
Verification	Confirms whether risk was actually reduced
Reporting	Shows risk trends for leadership
Deployment model	Can be operated by your team without constant vendor dependency
Governance and Risk Review	Confirms the platform aligns with legal, privacy, security, architecture, vendor risk, data governance, and operational ownership requirements
Commercial model	Predictable enough to scale

6.16 Practical Decision Guidance

Use this decision model:

If Your Main Problem Is...	Prioritize Vendors Strong In...
Cloud data exposure	Cloud DSPM, CNAPP integration, cloud IAM, object storage/data warehouse coverage
SaaS oversharing	M365/Google/Salesforce/Box/Slack depth, external sharing analysis, SaaS DLP integration
On-prem file share risk	ACL analysis, Windows/NAS support, owner mapping, remediation workflows
Data warehouse access risk	Snowflake/Databricks/BigQuery/Redshift/SQL role mapping and activity context
Privacy compliance	Data mapping, subject data discovery, RoPA/DSAR support, privacy tool integration
AI data risk	AI app visibility, vector database support, prompt/RAG/data pipeline governance
Excessive access	Effective permissions, identity graph, IGA integration, stale access analysis
Incident response	SIEM/SOAR integration, activity telemetry, data blast-radius analysis
Ransomware resilience	Backup visibility, sensitive data in recoverable copies, clean recovery prioritization
Board reporting	Executive dashboards, measurable risk reduction, trend reporting

6.17 Minimum Viable Buyer Requirements

Before an organization evaluates DSPM platforms, it should define the minimum capabilities required for the platform to be useful in its environment. These requirements should be based on the organization's risk profile, data footprint, regulatory obligations, staffing model, and AI adoption plans.

The goal is not to create a perfect feature checklist. The goal is to prevent the organization from buying a platform that looks impressive in a demo but cannot support the outcomes the program actually needs.

At a minimum, buyers should evaluate whether the platform can support the following requirements:

Requirement	What to Validate
Business Fit	The platform aligns with the organization's industry, data risk profile, regulatory obligations, and operating model.
Data Source Coverage	The platform can discover and classify data across the organization's most important environments, including cloud, SaaS, databases, warehouses, lakes, file shares, collaboration platforms, and AI-connected repositories.
Classification Maturity	The platform supports structured and unstructured classification, context-aware classification, confidence scoring, regulatory mapping, and drift monitoring.

Identity Integration Depth	The platform can connect data exposure to users, groups, nested groups, service accounts, OAuth grants, machine identities, SaaS permissions, and privileged roles.
AI Readiness	The platform can identify AI-accessible data, risky AI-connected repositories, prompt or upload exposure paths, and data that may be inappropriate for AI use.
Privacy Alignment	The platform supports privacy use cases such as data minimization, retention, deletion, DSAR support, RoPA alignment, and approved-use validation.
Governance Features	The platform supports ownership assignment, exception tracking, policy alignment, approval workflows, audit evidence, and executive reporting.
Workflow and Remediation	The platform can route findings to accountable owners, integrate with ticketing systems, support remediation tracking, and provide evidence of closure.
Deployment Model	The platform's deployment model aligns with the organization's architecture, security requirements, data residency expectations, and operational constraints.
Data Residency	The organization can validate where platform data, metadata, logs, samples, prompts, and support data are stored and processed.
Vendor Access to Customer Data	The organization understands what the vendor can access during normal operations, troubleshooting, support, model improvement, or managed service delivery.
Open API Support	The platform provides APIs, webhooks, export options, and integration capabilities that allow the organization to connect DSPM findings into existing security, governance, privacy, and reporting workflows.
Managed Service Support	Smaller or resource-constrained teams can access implementation support, tuning assistance, operational guidance, or managed service options if internal staffing is limited.
Reporting and Evidence	The platform can produce operational, compliance, executive, and board-level reporting that shows risk reduction over time.
Cost and Scalability	The pricing model is understandable, scalable, and aligned to the organization's expected growth, data volume, and coverage needs.

A platform that cannot meet the organization's minimum viable requirements may still be impressive, but it may not be useful.

Open-Source and Budget-Constrained Environments

Not every organization has the budget or maturity to begin with a commercial DSPM platform. Smaller organizations, nonprofits, public-sector entities, startups, and budget-constrained security teams may need to build foundational data visibility before they can justify a larger investment.

Open-source tools can help with parts of the DSPM journey, especially around data cataloging, metadata management, governance foundations, discovery, and classification. Examples may include tools such as Apache Atlas, OpenMetadata, DataHub, and other open-source or community-supported data governance technologies.

However, buyers should be careful with positioning.

Most open-source tools are not full enterprise DSPM platforms. They may help an organization understand where data exists, improve metadata visibility, support cataloging, or demonstrate the value of data governance. They may not provide mature coverage for identity-aware exposure analysis, SaaS permissions, AI data access, remediation workflows, privacy mapping, behavioral risk, or enterprise-grade reporting.

A practical way to frame open-source options is this:

Open-source tooling may help an organization build DSPM foundations, prove value, and prepare for a future commercial platform. It should not be assumed to provide the same depth, automation, support, or risk prioritization capability as a mature enterprise DSPM solution.

For some organizations, this is still a very good starting point. Visibility is better than guessing, and an open-source-assisted approach may help security leaders demonstrate need, build internal support, and justify future investment.

The key is honesty. Open source can support a DSPM journey, but it should not be oversold as a complete substitute for a governed, enterprise-ready DSPM capability.

Managed Service Support for Smaller Teams

A DSPM platform can create visibility, but visibility still requires people to interpret findings, tune policies, assign ownership, manage workflows, and drive remediation.

Smaller security teams should evaluate whether the vendor, reseller, or partner ecosystem can provide managed service support. This may include implementation assistance, connector setup, classification tuning, false-positive review, reporting support, remediation planning, executive readout support, or ongoing operational guidance.

This matters because many organizations do not fail at DSPM because the tool cannot find risk. They fail because no one has time to operationalize the findings.

For smaller teams, managed service support may be the difference between a platform that becomes useful and a platform that becomes another dashboard no one has time to manage.

Buyers should ask:

- *Does the vendor or partner provide implementation support?*
- *Can they help tune classification and severity models?*
- *Can they assist with data owner mapping and workflow design?*
- *Can they help prepare executive reporting?*
- *Can they support remediation planning?*
- *Can they help the organization mature over time instead of simply deploying the tool and leaving?*

Managed service support should not replace internal ownership, but it can help organizations build momentum while internal processes mature.

Data Residency, Deployment Model, and Vendor Access

CISOs should pay close attention to where the DSPM platform runs, where data is processed, and what the vendor can access.

DSPM platforms may collect or process highly sensitive information, including metadata, classification results, file samples, database schemas, access paths, identity information, prompt-related data, logs, secrets, regulated data indicators, and evidence of misconfiguration or exposure. Even when the platform claims not to store full content, the metadata alone may reveal sensitive business information.

Organizations should validate:

- *Where is the DSPM platform hosted?*
- *Is the platform SaaS, self-hosted, private cloud, hybrid, or agent-based?*
- *Where is customer metadata stored?*
- *Are sensitive samples collected or retained?*
- *Are prompts, logs, embeddings, or AI-related artifacts analyzed?*
- *Can the vendor access customer data during support?*
- *Can support engineers view metadata, file paths, labels, findings, or samples?*
- *Is customer data used for model training, product improvement, or analytics?*
- *Can customer data leave the approved region?*
- *Are government, regulated, or sovereign cloud requirements supported?*
- *Can access by vendor personnel be logged, restricted, approved, and reviewed?*

This review should include legal, privacy, procurement, architecture, and security stakeholders. It is not only a technical deployment question. It is a data governance and vendor risk question.

A CISO should assume that DSPM data is sensitive until proven otherwise.

The platform may not contain the original regulated record, but it may expose where sensitive data lives, who can access it, where controls are weak, and which repositories are most valuable to an attacker. That intelligence must be protected accordingly.

6.18 Decision Matrix: Selecting the Right DSPM Platform

Organizations evaluating DSPM platforms often struggle because many vendors appear similar during demonstrations. Most platforms can discover sensitive data, generate dashboards, classify content, and produce risk findings. The differences usually emerge later during implementation, integration, governance, operationalization, and long-term program maturity.

A successful DSPM evaluation should not rely solely on feature lists or vendor demonstrations. Organizations should build a decision matrix that scores platforms against operational, technical, governance, privacy, AI, and business requirements.

The goal is not to identify the "best" DSPM platform in the market. The goal is to identify the platform that best aligns with the organization's risk profile, operational maturity, business priorities, regulatory obligations, AI strategy, and long-term governance model.

A structured decision matrix helps:

- Reduce emotional or marketing-driven purchasing decisions
- Align stakeholders around evaluation criteria
- Compare vendors consistently

- Document selection rationale
- Identify operational tradeoffs
- Prevent feature-focused tunnel vision
- Connect technical capabilities to business outcomes

Recommended Evaluation Categories

The following categories are commonly useful when evaluating DSPM platforms.

Evaluation Area	Questions to Consider
Business Fit	*Does the platform align with the organization's industry, regulatory environment, operating model, risk profile, and business priorities?*
AI Readiness	*Can the platform identify AI-related data exposure, monitor AI-connected repositories, evaluate prompt or upload risks, and support AI governance initiatives?*
Privacy Alignment	*Does the platform support privacy operations such as retention, deletion workflows, DSAR support, data minimization, regulatory mapping, and approved-use validation?*
Identity Integration Depth	*How well does the platform integrate with IAM, Entra ID, Okta, Active Directory, SaaS permissions, group structures, privileged access, machine identities, and identity context analysis?*
Classification Maturity	*Does the platform support context-aware classification, ML-assisted classification, entity extraction, structured and unstructured discovery, confidence scoring, and classification drift monitoring?*
Workflow Maturity	*Can findings be routed effectively through ticketing, remediation, ownership assignment, escalation, approval, exception handling, and automation workflows?*
Governance Features	*Does the platform support ownership tracking, exception management, policy alignment, evidence collection, audit support, decision rights, and reporting maturity?*
Managed Service Support	*Does the vendor or partner provide implementation, tuning, reporting, remediation, or operational support for teams without deep internal capacity?*
Deployment Model	*Is the platform SaaS, self-hosted, private cloud, hybrid, agentless, agent-based, or connector-based? Does that model align with the organization's architecture and risk tolerance?*
Deployment Complexity	*How difficult is implementation? How much tuning, professional services, infrastructure preparation, connector setup, or operational overhead is required?*
Data Residency	*Where are metadata, findings, logs, samples, prompts, and support artifacts stored and processed? Can the platform meet regional, sovereign cloud, or regulatory residency requirements?*
Vendor Access to Customer Data	*What can vendor personnel access during support, troubleshooting, managed service delivery, product analytics, or model improvement? Is that access logged, approved, limited, and contractually governed?*
Sensitive Metadata Protection	*Does the platform protect metadata, file paths, schemas, access maps, classification results, and exposure findings as sensitive security intelligence?*

Open API Support	*Does the platform provide mature APIs, webhook support, export options, automation integration, and extensibility into existing security and governance workflows?*
Integration Coverage	*Does the platform support the organization's cloud providers, SaaS platforms, databases, collaboration tools, AI systems, identity providers, DLP, SIEM, SOAR, GRC, and hybrid environments?*
Open-Source Fit	*Could open-source discovery, cataloging, or governance tooling support early maturity, prove value, or reduce cost before a commercial DSPM purchase?*
Support for Regulated Environments	*Can the platform support healthcare, financial services, government, defense, education, or other regulated environments with appropriate controls, reporting, deployment options, and audit evidence?*
Reporting and Metrics	*Can the platform provide meaningful operational, executive, compliance, and board-level reporting that shows risk reduction over time?*
Scalability	*Can the platform handle enterprise-scale environments, large data volumes, global operations, multi-cloud architectures, and future AI-connected data growth?*
Cost	*What are the licensing, implementation, storage, support, managed service, operational, and professional services costs over time?*
Vendor Stability	*Does the vendor demonstrate financial stability, product maturity, roadmap clarity, support quality, customer references, and long-term viability?*

Sample DSPM Decision Matrix

Organizations may score categories using weighted scoring models based on business priorities.

Category	Weight	Vendor A	Vendor B	Vendor C
Business Fit	High	8	6	9
AI Readiness	High	9	5	8
Privacy Alignment	Medium	7	8	6
Identity Integration Depth	High	9	6	7
Classification Maturity	High	8	7	8
Workflow Maturity	Medium	6	9	7
Governance Features	High	8	5	7
Deployment Complexity	Medium	5	8	7
Open API Support	Medium	9	6	8
Cost	Medium	4	8	6

The exact scoring model matters less than the discipline of evaluating platforms consistently.

Not Every Organization Needs the Same DSPM Platform

A heavily regulated healthcare organization may prioritize:

- Privacy workflows
- PHI classification
- Retention governance
- Audit support
- Identity controls

A cloud-native technology company may prioritize:

- API integration
- Developer workflow visibility
- AI readiness
- Data lake coverage
- Automation capabilities

A global enterprise may prioritize:

- Scalability
- Cross-border governance
- Multi-cloud support
- Operational reporting
- Role-based access delegation

A smaller organization may prioritize:

- Ease of deployment
- Operational simplicity
- Managed services support
- Lower administrative overhead
- Faster time to value

The right platform depends heavily on organizational maturity and operational reality.

Avoid Overweighting Demonstration Features

Many DSPM demonstrations emphasize:

- Beautiful dashboards
- Massive discovery counts
- AI-generated risk summaries
- Automated remediation claims
- Executive reporting visuals

These capabilities can be valuable, but organizations should focus equally on operational realities such as:

- Classification accuracy

- Identity context quality
- Workflow usability
- False-positive rates
- Governance flexibility
- Reporting quality
- API maturity
- Long-term maintainability

A platform that produces millions of findings without operational clarity may create more work than value.

Evaluate the Operating Model, Not Just the Tool

Organizations should also evaluate:

- Internal staffing requirements
- Ownership expectations
- Workflow maturity
- Governance readiness
- Executive sponsorship
- Privacy involvement
- Legal involvement
- Data ownership accountability

A mature DSPM program requires more than technology deployment.

The platform must fit the organization's ability to operationalize findings, govern data consistently, and sustain remediation workflows over time.

Practical Recommendation

Build the decision matrix before the vendor demonstrations begin.

Without predefined evaluation criteria, organizations often make decisions based on:

- Brand familiarity
- Marketing language
- Executive influence
- Fear of missing features
- Visual dashboards
- Analyst rankings
- Short-term proof-of-concept impressions

The strongest DSPM evaluations are grounded in risk reduction, operational fit, governance maturity, and long-term usability.

The best DSPM platform is not necessarily the most expensive, the most famous, or the most feature-rich.

It is the platform the organization can realistically govern, operationalize, sustain, and use to measurably reduce data risk over time.

Key Takeaways

The right DSPM tool is the one that helps the organization move from unknown risk to measurable risk reduction.

Do not spend years chasing the perfect tool. Prioritize the must-haves, run a disciplined POC, choose the tool that best fits your data environment and operating model, and begin reducing exposure. You may need to course-correct later, but that is acceptable. What is not acceptable is letting sensitive data remain exposed while the organization debates endlessly.

The goal is not to buy DSPM. The goal is to secure the data.

Chapter 7: How to Discover and Classify Data Without Drowning in Findings

One of the fastest ways to overwhelm a data security program is to scan everything at once without a clear plan for what happens next. DSPM tools can surface thousands or even millions of findings across cloud storage, SaaS platforms, databases, data warehouses, collaboration platforms, and AI-connected environments. While that visibility is valuable, it can quickly become noise if the organization has not defined priorities, ownership, validation steps, and remediation workflows.

The goal of discovery and classification is not simply to find as much data as possible. The goal is to identify where sensitive and critical data exists, understand the risk around that data, validate the accuracy of the findings, and take action in a controlled, repeatable way.

A practical way to approach this is through a crawl, walk, run model. This allows the team to start small, build confidence, tune the DSPM tool, and gradually expand coverage without drowning in findings.

7.1 Crawl: Start Small and Prove Value

The crawl phase should begin with a focused proof of concept or a limited deployment. If the vendor offers a formal POC, use that opportunity to test the tool against a meaningful but manageable scope. The objective is not to scan the entire enterprise immediately. The objective is to prove that the tool can discover important data, classify it accurately enough to be useful, and produce findings your team can act on.

If a vendor-led POC is not part of the process, start with one target area. Ideally, choose a target that meets one of the following criteria:

- It contains a large portion of the organization's critical or sensitive data.
- It is quick to scan and easy to access.
- It has similar configuration patterns to other environments.
- It has clear business ownership.
- It represents a common data store type that will be scanned again later.

For example, the team may choose a high-value cloud storage bucket, a business-critical SaaS platform, a data warehouse, or a shared drive used by a department that routinely handles sensitive information. The best starting point is usually not the largest environment. It is the environment where the team can learn quickly and show value without creating unnecessary operational burden.

Starting small allows the security, privacy, data governance, and IT teams to become familiar with the chosen DSPM tool. They can learn how the tool connects, how it scans, how it classifies data, how findings are presented, and how results should be interpreted.

During the crawl phase, focus on answering a few foundational questions.

Can the DSPM tool successfully connect to the target environment?
Before worrying about classification accuracy or remediation, confirm that the tool can

authenticate, scan, and collect the expected metadata without disrupting business operations.

Is the tool discovering the data stores, objects, files, tables, or records expected?
Discovery results should be compared against known inventories, platform views, or input from data owners. This helps identify permission gaps, blind spots, or misconfigurations in the tool deployment.

Are sensitive data types being identified correctly?
The team should review a sample of findings for common sensitive data categories such as personal information, financial data, health data, authentication secrets, intellectual property, customer data, or regulated data.

Are the findings actionable?
A finding is only useful if someone can understand what it means, who owns it, why it matters, and what should happen next.

The crawl phase should result in a small number of validated insights, not a giant backlog of unresolved findings.

7.2 Walk: Validate and Tune the Findings

The walk phase begins after initial discovery. This is where the team validates findings, tunes classification logic, and decides which results should drive action.

Discovery tells you where data exists. Classification tells you what kind of data it likely is. Validation determines whether the tool's conclusions are accurate and useful enough to support business decisions.

This phase is critical because automated classification will never be perfect out of the box. A DSPM tool may correctly detect patterns that resemble sensitive data, but business context still matters. A number may look like a national identifier but actually be a test value. A file may contain customer information but be located in an approved system with the correct controls. A stale data set may look risky, but the business may have a legitimate retention requirement.

Validation helps separate true risk from noise.

During the walk phase, the team should review findings with the right stakeholders. This often includes security, privacy, compliance, legal, data governance, application owners, infrastructure owners, and business data owners. The purpose is not to pull every stakeholder into every finding. The purpose is to confirm that findings are being interpreted correctly and routed to the right owners.

Key activities in the walk phase include the following.

1. Validate Classification Accuracy

Review samples of classified data to determine whether the tool is correctly identifying sensitive data types. Look for both false positives and false negatives.

False positives create noise and reduce trust in the tool. False negatives create blind spots and can leave critical data unprotected. The team should tune detection rules, confidence thresholds, custom classifiers, and exclusions where appropriate.

2. Confirm Data Ownership

Findings need owners. Without ownership, DSPM results become another dashboard that no one acts on.

Use the walk phase to map findings to business units, application owners, data owners, or platform teams. Where ownership is unclear, treat that as a governance issue. Unknown ownership is often a risk signal by itself.

3. Prioritize by Risk, Not Volume

A common mistake is trying to resolve findings in the order they appear. Instead, prioritize based on risk.

A useful prioritization model may include:

- Sensitivity of the data
- Exposure level
- Access permissions
- Business criticality
- Regulatory impact
- Data age
- Whether the data is production or test data
- Whether the data is actively used
- Whether the location is approved for that data type
- Whether the data is accessible to AI systems or copilots

For example, a small number of sensitive records exposed through a public or broadly shared link may be more urgent than a large volume of sensitive data stored in a properly controlled production system.

4. Tune Policies and Rules

Use what the team learns during validation to tune the tool. This may include creating custom data classifiers, adjusting severity levels, suppressing expected findings, excluding known test data, defining approved storage locations for certain data types, or adjusting confidence thresholds.

The walk phase is where the organization moves from "the tool found data" to "the tool is producing results we trust."

5. Define Response Paths

Before scaling scans across the enterprise, define what happens when certain findings appear.

For example:

- Public exposure of sensitive data may trigger immediate security review.
- Sensitive data in an unapproved location may trigger a data owner review.

- Stale data may trigger retention or deletion review.
- Excessive access may trigger permission cleanup.
- Secrets or credentials may trigger incident response or key rotation.
- AI-accessible restricted data may trigger AI governance review.

The output of the walk phase should be a validated and tuned process for reviewing, prioritizing, and routing DSPM findings.

7.3 Run: Scale Coverage and Automate Carefully

The run phase begins when the team has enough confidence in the tool, the findings, and the workflow to expand coverage and automate selected actions.

If the organization started with a small target area, this is where additional environments are onboarded. Expansion should still be controlled. The team can onboard similar systems first, using the lessons learned from the initial scan. For example, if the first target was a cloud storage environment, the team may next scan other buckets, accounts, or projects with similar configuration patterns.

The run phase is also where automation becomes valuable. However, automation should be introduced only after the team has validated the findings and understands the potential business impact.

Automation can include actions such as:

- Removing "share with everyone" or public access links
- Revoking stale or excessive permissions
- Opening tickets for data owners
- Notifying business owners of sensitive data in unapproved locations
- Quarantining files in specific high-risk scenarios
- Tagging or labeling sensitive data
- Moving data to approved locations
- Triggering retention review for stale data
- Escalating critical findings to incident response
- Creating recurring reports for governance and compliance teams

Start with low-risk, high-confidence automations. Automatically creating a ticket for a validated finding is usually safer than automatically deleting data. Removing broad sharing links may be appropriate when the organization has confirmed that such links violate policy and the DSPM tool can identify them with high confidence.

Automation should be governed by clear rules. The team should know what action is being taken, when it is being taken, who approved it, how it is logged, and how it can be reversed if needed.

The goal of the run phase is not to automate everything. The goal is to reduce repeatable risk at scale while keeping humans involved where judgment is required.

7.4 Automated Data Classification

As organizations expand DSPM programs across cloud platforms, SaaS applications, AI systems, collaboration environments, APIs, data lakes, data warehouses, and hybrid infrastructure, manual classification approaches quickly become operationally unsustainable. Sensitive data no longer remains in a single database or controlled repository. It moves continuously between systems, users, workflows, integrations, third parties, and AI-enabled services, often faster than security teams can manually review or govern it.

In the AI era, organizations generate, copy, transform, and share data at massive scale. Sensitive information may be embedded in datasets, pasted into prompts, duplicated across collaboration tools, transformed through pipelines, synchronized between platforms, or exposed through shadow IT and unsanctioned AI workflows. Traditional classification methods based only on static labels, keywords, or regex pattern matching cannot keep pace with this level of scale, complexity, and contextual change.

Automated data classification has therefore become a foundational capability within modern DSPM programs. Modern platforms increasingly combine pattern matching, metadata analysis, contextual awareness, identity correlation, behavioral signals, entity extraction, and machine learning models to improve classification accuracy, reduce operational overhead, and maintain visibility as data changes across the environment.

But automated classification should not be treated as infallible.

A classification decision can trigger downstream actions across DLP, access control, retention, privacy workflows, legal hold, incident response, AI access, and executive reporting. If data is under-classified, sensitive information may be exposed, shared, retained improperly, or made available to AI systems without proper controls. If data is over-classified, business workflows may be blocked, users may lose access unnecessarily, retention policies may be misapplied, and security teams may create friction that drives people toward shadow processes.

The goal is not only to classify more data. The goal is to classify data accurately enough, consistently enough, and with enough governance that downstream security, privacy, and business decisions can rely on it.

Key Components of Automated Data Classification

ML-Assisted Classification

Machine learning-assisted classification helps identify sensitive data patterns that may not match traditional deterministic rules. Rather than relying exclusively on exact strings or predefined regular expressions, ML models can identify probable sensitive content based on structure, language patterns, relationships, and usage context.

Examples include:

- Identifying legal contracts without explicit labels
- Detecting healthcare records with inconsistent formatting
- Recognizing intellectual property documents

- Discovering sensitive financial discussions in collaboration platforms
- Identifying AI training datasets containing regulated information
- Finding sensitive data in unstructured notes, transcripts, tickets, and documents

ML-assisted classification is particularly valuable for unstructured data, where traditional pattern matching often produces high false-positive or false-negative rates.

That does not mean the machine gets the final word.

ML-assisted classification must operate under human governance. The organization should define when automated classification is trusted, when human review is required, when a classification can trigger enforcement, and when the result should be treated only as a signal.

Human governance is especially important when classification decisions affect:

- DLP blocking or quarantine
- Access removal
- Legal hold
- Retention or deletion
- Privacy rights fulfillment
- Regulatory reporting
- Incident response
- AI indexing or retrieval
- Executive risk metrics
- Business process interruption

A practical rule is simple: the more disruptive, legally significant, or business-impacting the downstream action, the more governance should be required before automation acts.

Automated classification should support judgment, not replace it.

Context-Aware Classification

Context-aware classification evaluates the surrounding environment of the data rather than analyzing content alone.

This may include:

- File ownership
- Data source location
- Access patterns
- Business unit association
- Cloud repository type
- Sharing exposure
- Identity and permission relationships
- Associated applications or workflows
- Regulatory context
- AI accessibility

For example, a spreadsheet containing employee IDs stored in an HR repository may carry significantly different risk than a similar file located in a public collaboration workspace.

Context transforms raw discovery into meaningful risk prioritization.

Entity Extraction

Entity extraction capabilities identify and classify specific types of sensitive information within structured and unstructured content.

Examples include:

- Personally identifiable information
- Protected health information
- Payment card data
- API keys and secrets
- Source code references
- Customer identifiers
- Legal terms
- Geographic locations
- Intellectual property references
- Authentication tokens or credentials

Advanced DSPM solutions may also perform relationship mapping between extracted entities to better understand business impact and exposure pathways.

Behavioral Classification

Behavioral classification analyzes how data is accessed, shared, modified, copied, or transmitted over time.

This allows organizations to identify:

- Unusual access behavior
- Data staging before exfiltration
- Excessive sharing activity
- Abnormal AI prompt interactions
- Risky collaboration behavior
- Insider misuse patterns
- Third-party exposure risks
- Bulk download or export behavior

Behavioral analysis helps shift DSPM from static inventory management toward dynamic risk intelligence.

Continuous Classification Drift Monitoring

Data classification is not a one-time event.

Data changes constantly:

- Files are modified.
- Ownership changes.
- Permissions expand.
- Repositories move.
- AI workflows evolve.
- Sensitive content accumulates over time.
- Business context changes.
- Regulatory obligations change.

Classification drift occurs when previously classified data no longer accurately reflects its current sensitivity, exposure level, ownership, or business context.

Continuous classification drift monitoring helps organizations:

- Detect newly sensitive data
- Identify stale or outdated labels
- Reassess exposure risk
- Monitor permission creep
- Track data lifecycle changes
- Validate policy effectiveness
- Maintain regulatory alignment
- Confirm whether AI access remains appropriate

Without continuous monitoring, classification programs rapidly become inaccurate and operationally unreliable.

Classification Maturity Model

Classification maturity matters because classification decisions influence enforcement, reporting, risk prioritization, and business operations. A weak classification program can create downstream failures. A mature classification program creates a more reliable foundation for DLP, privacy, retention, access governance, incident response, and AI security.

Maturity Level	Description	Common Approach	Strengths	Risks
Level 1: Manual	Classification depends on users or data owners applying labels manually.	User-applied labels, folder naming, business owner input.	Simple to start and useful for known high-value data.	Inconsistent, subjective, incomplete, and difficult to scale.
Level 2: Rule-Based	Classification uses predefined rules, patterns, dictionaries, and regular expressions.	Regex, keywords, file properties, structured data patterns.	Good for known data types such as SSNs, credit cards, account numbers, or health identifiers.	Can miss context, create false positives, and struggle with unstructured or transformed data.
Level 3: Context-Aware	Classification considers surrounding context, location, ownership, metadata, access, and business process.	Content plus metadata, repository type, owner, system purpose, access patterns.	Better accuracy and more useful risk prioritization.	Requires good metadata, ownership, and tuning.
Level 4: ML-Assisted	Machine learning models help identify sensitive data, entities, patterns, and relationships that rules may miss.	Entity extraction, semantic similarity, document understanding, clustering, confidence scoring.	Scales better across large and diverse data environments and helps find unknown sensitive data.	Requires human governance, confidence thresholds, validation, and error handling.
Level 5: Governed and Adaptive	Classification is continuously monitored, tuned, reviewed, and connected to policy decisions.	ML-assisted classification with human review, confidence thresholds, appeal process, drift monitoring, and audit evidence.	Supports defensible decisions across DLP, privacy, retention, access, and AI governance.	Requires ownership, process discipline, and regular review.

The organization does not need to reach Level 5 immediately. Early maturity may begin with manual labels and rule-based discovery. What matters is that classification decisions become more accurate, more contextual, and more governed over time.

Classification Confidence Thresholds

DSPM programs should define classification confidence thresholds before automated findings are connected to enforcement workflows.

A confidence threshold is the level of certainty required before a classification result can be used for a specific action. Not all actions require the same level of confidence.

Confidence Level	Example Range	Recommended Use	Governance Expectation
Low confidence	0–59%	Discovery signal, backlog review, tuning input.	Do not trigger enforcement. Use for investigation or model improvement.
Medium confidence	60–79%	Review queue, owner validation, sampling, enrichment of risk scoring.	Human review recommended before action.
High confidence	80–94%	Finding creation, workflow routing, reporting, DLP policy suggestion, access review trigger.	Human review required before disruptive action.
Very high confidence	95–100%	Automated labeling, low-risk workflow routing, approved control action where policy allows.	Periodic sampling and audit required. Human review still needed for high-impact actions.

These ranges are examples. Each organization should define its own thresholds based on risk tolerance, data type, business impact, regulatory obligations, and the maturity of the classification engine.

Some data types may require stricter thresholds than others. A Social Security number pattern may be easier to classify with high confidence than a document containing trade secrets, privileged legal advice, source code, merger activity, or sensitive strategy. Highly regulated or high-impact data should have stronger review requirements, especially when classification affects retention, deletion, legal hold, privacy requests, access removal, or AI exposure.

Classification Error Handling

Classification errors are not a minor inconvenience. They can break other parts of the data security program.

An under-classified file may bypass DLP, remain broadly accessible, avoid retention controls, or become available to AI tools. An over-classified file may trigger unnecessary restrictions, overwhelm security teams, block legitimate work, or cause business users to distrust the program.

The DSPM operating model should define how classification errors are identified, reviewed, corrected, and used to improve the system.

Error Type	Example	Potential Impact	Required Response
False positive	A harmless document is classified as regulated data.	Unnecessary DLP alerts, blocked workflows, user frustration, inflated risk reporting.	Review, correct label, tune rule or model, document decision.

False negative	Regulated data is not classified as sensitive.	Exposure, privacy risk, DLP bypass, AI access, audit failure.	Escalate, correct label, assess exposure, review similar data, tune controls.
Over-classification	Internal business content is labeled Restricted.	Excessive controls, business disruption, retention errors, alert fatigue.	Review classification criteria and downstream policies.
Under-classification	Confidential or regulated data is labeled Internal.	Insufficient controls, excessive access, improper sharing, AI exposure.	Reclassify, assess access, apply controls, review related repositories.
Context error	Data is classified correctly by content but incorrectly by purpose or ownership.	Wrong owner assigned, wrong retention rule, wrong policy decision.	Validate with business owner and update metadata.
Drift error	A previously accurate classification becomes inaccurate as data changes.	Stale controls, inaccurate reporting, policy mismatch.	Perform periodic review and drift monitoring.

Classification error handling should be built into the workflow from the beginning. Users, data owners, privacy teams, legal teams, and security analysts should have a clear way to challenge, correct, or escalate classification decisions.

Appeal and Review Process

A mature classification program needs an appeal and review process. This gives users and data owners a safe, documented way to challenge classifications they believe are wrong.

The appeal process should not be viewed as resistance to security. It is an important quality-control mechanism. Business users often understand context that automated systems cannot see. Security teams understand risk patterns that business users may miss. Privacy and legal teams understand obligations that neither group should decide alone.

A practical classification appeal process should include:

Step	Description	Owner
1. Submit appeal	User, owner, or reviewer challenges a classification decision.	Requester
2. Capture rationale	Requester explains why the label appears incorrect or harmful.	Requester
3. Review evidence	Security reviews content signals, metadata, access, location, and policy impact.	Security or DSPM owner
4. Validate business context	Data owner confirms business purpose, sensitivity, and handling expectations.	Data owner
5. Consult privacy/legal if needed	Required when regulated data, legal hold, deletion, privilege, or contractual obligations are involved.	Privacy/legal

6. Decide outcome	Classification is upheld, changed, downgraded, upgraded, or sent for further review.	Classification owner or steering committee
7. Update controls	Labels, DLP rules, retention policies, access controls, or AI permissions are adjusted if needed.	Security, IT, data owner
8. Document evidence	Decision, rationale, approver, and date are recorded.	DSPM program owner
9. Tune classification logic	Rule, model, or policy is updated when the appeal reveals a recurring issue.	DSPM/tool owner

The appeal process should be time-bound. For example, high-impact appeals may require review within five business days, while lower-risk appeals may be reviewed during the normal monthly classification review cycle.

When Human Review Should Be Required

Human review should be required before classification triggers actions that could create legal, regulatory, operational, or business impact.

Human review is strongly recommended when:

- The classification affects regulated data.
- The classification affects legal hold, deletion, or retention.
- The classification could restrict access for a business-critical process.
- The classification would trigger DLP blocking or quarantine.
- The classification would allow or deny AI indexing.
- The classification affects privileged, legal, HR, security, or executive content.
- The finding has medium or low confidence but high potential impact.
- The system has recently changed classification rules or ML models.
- The classification result conflicts with business-owner input.
- The classification may affect customer, employee, patient, student, or financial data.

Human review does not mean every decision must become a committee meeting. It means the organization must define where automation is safe and where human judgment is required.

Practical Considerations

Automated classification should augment human governance, not replace it.

Organizations should establish:

- Classification governance standards
- Confidence thresholds
- Human review workflows
- Appeal and review processes
- False-positive and false-negative handling procedures
- Regulatory mapping validation
- Data ownership accountability
- AI governance oversight

- Sampling and quality assurance procedures
- Classification drift monitoring

Security teams should also recognize that classification accuracy directly impacts downstream controls such as:

- DLP enforcement
- Access governance
- Encryption policies
- Retention decisions
- Privacy workflows
- Legal hold
- AI usage restrictions
- Incident response prioritization
- Executive reporting

Poor classification quality creates cascading security failures.

The goal is not perfect classification. The goal is continuously improving visibility, prioritization, governance, and operational decision-making at enterprise scale.

Recommended Governance Language

The following language can be adapted for the organization's DSPM charter, classification policy, or operating model.

Automated and ML-assisted classification may be used to identify, label, prioritize, and route sensitive data findings. Classification results must be governed based on confidence level, data sensitivity, business impact, and downstream action. Automated classification may support discovery, prioritization, and workflow routing, but high-impact decisions involving DLP enforcement, access removal, retention, deletion, legal hold, privacy rights, regulatory reporting, or AI access require defined review and approval.

The organization will maintain classification confidence thresholds, sampling procedures, appeal workflows, and periodic review processes to identify and correct classification errors. Classification errors must be documented, reviewed, and used to improve rules, models, policies, and training data. Automated classification supports human judgment; it does not eliminate accountability.

Practical Recommendation

Start with automation where the risk of being wrong is low and the value of visibility is high.

Use automated classification to discover, group, prioritize, and route findings. Add human review where the decision affects rights, obligations, access, deletion, retention, AI exposure, or business continuity. As the program matures, expand automation only where classification accuracy, confidence thresholds, exception handling, and audit evidence are strong enough to support it.

The goal is not blind automation. The goal is governed classification that the organization can trust.

7.5 Avoiding Finding Fatigue

Finding fatigue happens when the DSPM program produces more results than the organization can realistically review or remediate. This can cause teams to ignore alerts, lose confidence in the tool, or treat DSPM as a compliance checkbox rather than an operational capability.

To avoid drowning in findings, the program should focus on meaningful prioritization.

Not every finding is equal. A file containing sensitive data is not automatically a critical risk. The risk depends on where the data is stored, who has access to it, whether the location is approved, how old the data is, whether the data is still needed, whether AI systems can access it, and whether compensating controls are in place.

The team should avoid measuring success only by the number of findings discovered. Better measures include:

- Number of critical data stores discovered
- Percentage of high-risk findings validated
- Reduction in public or broadly shared sensitive data
- Reduction in stale sensitive data
- Number of unknown data owners resolved
- Time to remediate critical findings
- Improvement in classification accuracy
- Reduction in false positives and false negatives
- Expansion of scan coverage across priority systems
- Number of repeatable workflows automated
- Number of AI-accessible sensitive repositories reviewed

These metrics show whether the DSPM program is improving security outcomes, not just generating activity.

7.6 Recommended Crawl, Walk, Run Model

A simple operating model can look like this:

Phase	Primary Goal	Key Activities	Expected Outcome
Crawl	Prove value in a limited scope.	Connect one target, run discovery, review initial classifications, identify obvious risks.	Team understands the tool and validates that it can produce useful findings.
Walk	Validate and tune.	Review findings with owners, tune classifiers, reduce false positives, define confidence thresholds, create prioritization and response workflows.	Findings become trusted, actionable, and tied to ownership.
Run	Scale and automate.	Expand to more environments, automate low-risk actions, integrate ticketing and reporting, monitor drift, track metrics.	DSPM becomes an operational program rather than a one-time scan.

7.7 Practical Example

An organization may begin by scanning a single cloud storage environment used by the finance team. The DSPM tool discovers files containing financial records, personal information, and old exports from business applications.

In the crawl phase, the security team confirms the tool can connect successfully, scan the storage location, and identify sensitive data. They review a sample of findings and confirm that some files are accurately classified.

In the walk phase, the team meets with the finance data owner to validate whether the files are expected, whether they are stored in an approved location, and whether the access permissions are appropriate. The team discovers that several folders are shared too broadly and that some old exports are no longer needed. They tune the classification rules to reduce false positives, define confidence thresholds for finance data, and create a workflow for reviewing similar findings.

They also establish a simple appeal process. If finance users believe a classification is wrong, they can submit the finding for review. Security reviews the evidence, the finance data owner confirms business context, and privacy or legal is consulted if regulated data, retention, deletion, or legal hold obligations are involved.

In the run phase, the organization expands scanning to other finance storage locations and then to similar department-managed repositories. Once confidence is high, the team automates ticket creation for sensitive data in unapproved locations and automatically removes certain "share with everyone" links that violate policy. Higher-impact actions, such as deletion, retention changes, access removal from critical workflows, or AI indexing decisions, still require human review.

This approach produces measurable risk reduction without overwhelming the team or blindly trusting automation.

Key Takeaways

Discovery and classification should be rolled out deliberately. Start small, validate what the tool finds, tune the results, and then scale.

The crawl phase builds familiarity and proves value. The walk phase validates findings, establishes ownership, creates confidence thresholds, and builds trust. The run phase expands coverage and introduces automation carefully.

Automated classification is essential at enterprise scale, but it must be governed. ML-assisted classification, context-aware classification, entity extraction, behavioral signals, and drift monitoring can improve visibility and prioritization, but they should not replace human judgment.

Classification errors matter because they can affect DLP, privacy workflows, retention, legal hold, access governance, AI usage, incident response, and executive reporting. Mature programs define confidence thresholds, human review requirements, appeal processes, and error-handling procedures before classification results are used for high-impact enforcement.

A successful DSPM program does not try to fix everything at once. It focuses on the most important data, the highest-risk exposure, and the workflows that can be repeated safely.

The goal is not blind automation. The goal is governed classification that helps the organization move from visibility to action without drowning in findings.

Chapter 8: How to Prioritize Data Risk Using Exposure, Identity, Sensitivity, & Business Context

Data risk is not the same for every company.

One of the first mistakes people make in DSPM is assuming that every organization values the same data in the same way. That is simply not true. I have worked with companies that, after completing discovery, cared more about financial data than client data. I have a strong opinion about that course of action, but I will leave that alone for now.

The important point is this: business context matters.

A file containing customer data may be the highest-risk asset in one company, while financial forecasts, board materials, source code, or acquisition plans may represent the greatest risk in another. DSPM programs need to account for that reality. Sensitivity alone does not determine priority. Exposure, identity, access, and business impact all need to be evaluated together.

One thing I always caution teams about is getting too wrapped up in being perfectly accurate everywhere. The saying is, "Perfect is the enemy of good." That applies directly to data risk programs.

You do not need a perfect risk model to start reducing risk. You need a practical model that helps you identify where the organization is most exposed and where action will reduce the most risk.

That means prioritization should focus on questions like:

- *Is the data sensitive?*
- *Who has access to it?*
- *Is it exposed broadly?*
- *Is access tied to risky identities?*
- *Is the data important to the business?*
- *Could the exposure create regulatory, financial, reputational, or operational harm?*

The goal is not to debate every finding forever. The goal is to reduce meaningful risk.

8.1 Be Careful How You Define a False Positive

I also caution teams to be very careful when labeling DSPM findings as false positives.

In one client environment, the team was extremely concerned about what they believed were false positives. I was brought in to level set the situation and determine what was actually happening.

When we looked at the links and files they had labeled as false positives, the DSPM tool was not wrong.

From a hacker's standpoint, those findings were valid.

The files existed. The access had been open. In many cases, the files were still shared broadly. However, somewhere behind the scenes, another security control was preventing the file from being read. In other words, the file was still exposed from a permissions standpoint, but another layer of security was blocking access at runtime.

That additional layer of protection is good. Defense in depth is a positive thing.

But that does not mean the DSPM finding was wrong.

The DSPM identified that the file was shared too broadly. That was true. The fact that another tool blocked the read action does not erase the exposure. It only means there was a compensating control in place.

From an attacker's perspective, I would still pay attention to that finding. I would look at the access message, investigate the control blocking access, and try to understand what was happening underneath. Broad sharing is still a signal. It may not mean the data is immediately readable, but it does mean there is something worth investigating.

This is why organizations need to distinguish between:

- **A true false positive**
  The finding is incorrect. The file does not exist, the data classification is wrong, or the access condition being reported is not real.
- **A mitigated exposure**
  The finding is technically accurate, but another control reduces or blocks exploitation.
- **An accepted risk**
  The finding is accurate, but the business has decided not to remediate it for a documented reason.
- **A priority issue**
  The finding is accurate and meaningful, but it may not be the most urgent risk compared to other exposures.

Lumping all of these into "false positive" creates confusion. It also weakens the DSPM program because teams start dismissing real risk simply because another control exists somewhere else in the environment.

8.2 Prioritization Requires Multiple Signals

A mature DSPM program does not prioritize risk based on one factor alone.

A sensitive file sitting in a locked-down location may be lower priority than a moderately sensitive file shared with the entire company. A file owned by a privileged user may be more important than the same file owned by a low-risk identity. A business-critical dataset exposed to external collaborators may require faster action than a stale internal document with limited impact.

Good prioritization combines several signals:

- Sensitivity tells you what the data is.
- Exposure tells you where the data can go and who can reach it.

- Identity context tells you whether the users, groups, service accounts, or external identities involved increase the risk.
- Business context tells you how much the data matters to the organization.

When these signals come together, the DSPM team can move from a long list of findings to a meaningful risk-based action plan.

The objective is not to chase every alert. The objective is to identify the exposures that matter most and take action before they become incidents.

Key Takeaways

Do not confuse imperfect data with useless data, and do not confuse mitigated exposure with a false positive.

DSPM findings should be evaluated through the lens of real-world attack paths, business impact, and compensating controls. The tool may not always tell the full story, but broad access to sensitive or business-critical data is still a risk signal worth understanding.

The best DSPM programs do not wait for perfect accuracy. They use available context to make better decisions, reduce unnecessary exposure, and focus remediation where it matters most.

Chapter 9: How to Remediate Common Patterns of Risk

Effective DSPM remediation requires three things working together:

People, process, and technology.

A DSPM platform can identify risks, prioritize findings, and recommend remediation steps, but the organization still needs trained people, repeatable processes, and supporting technologies to reduce risk in a consistent way.

Remediation should not be treated as a one-time cleanup activity. It should be treated as an ongoing operating model for protecting data.

9.1 People: Train the Users, Administrators, and Managers

Remediation starts with people.

The tool is only as good as the people using it. Security, system, data, cloud, and network administrators all need to be trained on how to use the DSPM platform and how to respond to its findings.

This includes teams such as:

Role	Responsibility
Security administrators	Review DSPM findings, validate risk, and coordinate remediation
System administrators	Fix access, configuration, and ownership issues
Data administrators	Understand data location, data quality, and data ownership
Cloud administrators	Remediate storage, sharing, and cloud access risks
Network administrators	Support secure connectivity and access control
Compliance and governance teams	Validate regulatory, privacy, and policy requirements
Business data owners	Approve access, confirm business need, and accept or reject risk

These users need to understand how the DSPM tool discovers sensitive data, how risk is scored and prioritized, how to investigate findings, how to remediate excessive access, how to validate that remediation was successful, when to escalate an issue, and when a risk exception may be appropriate.

The broader employee population also plays an important role. Employees must understand how to handle sensitive data before it becomes a security issue.

Employees should complete training on the following areas:

1. Security awareness

Users need to understand the basic principles of protecting company data, including phishing risks, oversharing, improper permissions, and unsafe file movement.

2. Data security

Users should know what types of data are considered sensitive, regulated, confidential, or restricted.

3. AI security

Employees must understand the risks of entering company data, customer data, intellectual property, credentials, source code, regulated information, or confidential documents into AI tools.

4. File labeling and classification

Users should be trained to label files correctly so security tools, policies, and downstream users can apply the correct protections.

5. Secure data handling

Employees need clear guidance on where data should be stored, how it should be shared, and what actions are prohibited.

Manager Accountability

Managers play a critical role in data security because they shape priorities, approve access, reinforce expectations, and influence how employees behave under pressure.

A user's manager is often the person best positioned to confirm whether access is still needed, whether a workflow is legitimate, whether a risky behavior reflects a business need, and whether a user needs coaching, process support, or formal escalation.

Manager accountability should be part of DSPM remediation because many data risks are created or sustained by business decisions, not technical failures alone. A manager may ask a team to move faster, share broadly, use a new tool, export data, or collaborate with a third party without fully understanding the security implications. If the security team is the only group held accountable, the organization misses the business pressure that caused the behavior in the first place.

Managers should understand what sensitive data their teams handle, which repositories, tools, and workflows are approved, how to validate whether access is still needed, when to escalate unusual data access or sharing behavior, how to reinforce secure use of AI tools, how to support remediation without blaming users, and how productivity pressure can lead to control bypass.

Manager-level reporting can also help reinforce accountability. If one department repeatedly creates high-risk findings, stores sensitive data in unmanaged locations, or bypasses approved AI workflows, the issue may not be an individual awareness problem. It may be a leadership, workflow, or resourcing problem.

Remediation is not only about training users to behave better. It is also about ensuring managers create conditions where secure behavior is realistic.

Remediation is not only a technical function. It is also a behavior change program. If users and managers do not understand the sensitivity of the data they work with, the organization will continue to recreate the same risks even after the DSPM platform identifies and remediates them.

9.2 Process: Create a Repeatable Remediation Workflow

People need a clear process to follow.

A DSPM program should define how findings move from discovery to remediation, validation, and continuous improvement. Without a process, findings may be reviewed inconsistently, ownership may be unclear, and high-risk issues may remain unresolved.

A strong remediation process should include the following steps.

Step 1: Discover and Classify the Data

The first step is to understand what data exists and how sensitive it is.

The organization should identify where sensitive data is located, what type of data was found, whether the data is regulated, confidential, proprietary, or public, whether the data has the correct classification label, whether the data is stored in an approved location, and whether the data is being used by approved applications and users.

This step is critical because remediation depends on classification. You cannot apply the right control if you do not understand the data.

Step 2: Assign Ownership

Every high-risk data finding needs an owner.

The owner may be a business unit, application owner, data steward, system administrator, or security team member. Without ownership, remediation work can stall.

The process should define who owns the data, who owns the system where the data resides, who can approve or deny access, who is responsible for remediation, and who accepts the risk if remediation is delayed.

For example, if sensitive customer data is found in a shared cloud folder, the security team may identify the risk, but the business owner may need to confirm whether the users with access still have a legitimate business need.

Step 3: Prioritize the Risk

Not all findings have the same urgency.

DSPM findings should be prioritized based on business impact, data sensitivity, exposure, and likelihood of misuse.

Common prioritization factors include:

Factor	Why It Matters
Data sensitivity	Regulated or confidential data creates higher risk
Exposure level	Public or external access increases urgency
Number of users with access	Larger access groups increase risk
User type	Third-party, guest, or inactive users may increase risk
Data location	Sensitive data in unapproved locations may violate policy
Business criticality	Critical systems may require faster response
Regulatory impact	Privacy, financial, or healthcare data may require strict handling
AI exposure	Data sent to unauthorized AI tools may create confidentiality risk

A file containing public marketing content may not need urgent action. A file containing customer records that is shared publicly should be treated as a high-priority remediation item.

Step 4: Select the Remediation Action

Once the data is understood, the correct remediation action should be selected.

Common remediation actions include:

Risk Pattern	Remediation Action
Sensitive data exposed to too many users	Remove excessive permissions and apply least privilege
Publicly shared files containing sensitive data	Disable public links and restrict sharing
Regulated data stored in the wrong location	Move data to an approved repository
Unlabeled sensitive files	Apply the correct classification label
Data copied into unauthorized AI tools	Remove the data, investigate exposure, and reinforce AI usage policy
Old or abandoned sensitive data	Archive, delete, or transfer ownership
Sensitive data owned by inactive users	Reassign ownership and remove stale access
Excessive administrator access	Reduce privileges and require approval workflows
Data shared with external parties	Validate business need, apply contracts, or revoke access
Secrets or credentials found in files	Rotate credentials and remove exposed secrets
Duplicate sensitive data	Remove unnecessary copies and retain the authoritative source
Sensitive data in development or test environments	Mask, tokenize, or remove production data

Misclassified files	Correct the label and apply the right policy
Sensitive data in personal storage	Move to approved corporate storage

The remediation action should match the risk. The goal is not to remove access blindly. The goal is to reduce unnecessary exposure while preserving legitimate business use.

Step 5: Validate the Fix

Remediation is not complete until the fix is verified.

The organization should confirm that excessive access was removed, public links were disabled, data was moved to the correct location, labels were applied correctly, credentials were rotated, external sharing was reviewed, unauthorized AI exposure was investigated, and the DSPM finding is no longer active.

Validation may be performed through the DSPM platform, ticketing system, access review process, SIEM, cloud logs, DLP alerts, or manual review.

Step 6: Document the Outcome

Every remediation activity should leave an audit trail.

Documentation should include the original finding, the data owner, the risk rating, the remediation decision, the action taken, the date completed, the person or team responsible, any exception or accepted risk, and evidence that the fix was validated.

This is important for compliance, governance, audits, and future investigations.

Step 7: Improve the Control

The final step is to prevent the same issue from recurring.

For example, if the organization repeatedly finds sensitive files shared publicly, the answer may not be to keep closing public links one by one. The better long-term remediation may be to change the sharing policy, require approval for public links, apply automated DLP controls, or train users on proper sharing practices.

Process improvement questions include:

- *Why did this risk occur?*
- *Was the user trained?*
- *Was the policy clear?*
- *Did the technology allow unsafe behavior?*
- *Was there an approval gap?*
- *Did leadership pressure contribute to the behavior?*
- *Should this control be automated?*
- *Should the classification policy be updated?*
- *Should users, managers, or executives receive additional training?*

Strong DSPM programs use findings to improve the security program over time.

9.3 Technology: Use the Right Tools to Enforce and Automate Controls

Technology enables remediation at scale.

A DSPM platform is the central tool for discovering sensitive data, identifying exposure, prioritizing risk, and recommending remediation. However, DSPM works best when it is integrated with the broader security and IT ecosystem.

Important supporting technologies include:

Technology	Role in Remediation
DSPM	Discovers sensitive data, identifies exposure, prioritizes risk, and recommends remediation
IAM	Controls user access, roles, groups, and privileged permissions
PAM	Manages and restricts administrator access
DLP	Prevents sensitive data from leaving approved locations
CASB / SSE	Controls cloud application access and data movement
SIEM	Collects logs and supports investigation
SOAR	Automates response workflows
Ticketing system	Tracks remediation ownership and completion
Data classification tools	Applies labels and policies to sensitive files
Encryption and KMS	Protects sensitive data at rest and in transit
Data catalog	Helps identify data owners, data lineage, and business context
CNAPP / CSPM	Identifies cloud misconfigurations and risky storage exposure
MDM / endpoint security	Controls data movement on user devices
AI security controls	Monitor and restrict sensitive data use in AI tools

The DSPM platform should not operate in isolation. It should connect to the tools that can enforce remediation.

For example, if DSPM identifies sensitive data with public access, IAM or cloud storage controls may remove the public permission. If DSPM finds regulated data in the wrong repository, workflow automation may create a ticket for the data owner. If DSPM detects sensitive data being sent to an unauthorized AI tool, DLP or SSE controls may block the transfer. If DSPM finds credentials in a file, the incident response process may trigger secret rotation. If DSPM discovers excessive access by inactive users, IAM automation may remove access.

Technology should support both detection and enforcement.

9.4 The Human Layer of Data Security

Most data security programs spend a great deal of time on technology, policy, and process, but the human layer is where many data risks become real. People create, copy, move, share, download, upload, retain, and delete data every day. They make decisions in email, collaboration platforms, SaaS applications, code repositories, cloud storage, databases, ticketing systems, analytics tools, and AI platforms.

That does not mean employees are the problem. More often, they are operating inside environments that have become too complex to understand without help. Data is scattered across too many systems. Permissions are inherited from groups no one remembers creating. Sensitive files are duplicated into personal drives, shared workspaces, exports, test environments, and unmanaged repositories. Business teams are expected to move quickly, while security teams are expected to make sure every movement is safe.

The human layer of data security is about understanding how people interact with data in the real world, then using that context to guide better decisions. It moves security awareness away from generic reminders and toward practical, risk-based intervention.

9.5 Security Friction, Shadow AI, and Control Avoidance

Most users are not trying to violate policy. They are trying to complete their work efficiently.

When security controls create excessive friction, users often route around them through personal devices, unsanctioned SaaS platforms, unmanaged collaboration tools, browser extensions, personal email, or public AI services. In many organizations, shadow AI adoption is driven less by malicious intent and more by productivity pressure, workflow friction, unrealistic approval processes, and the perception that official tools are too slow or restrictive.

This creates one of the most important operational realities in modern data security:

Users will often choose productivity over policy when the business pressure is high enough.

That does not mean organizations should weaken security controls. It means security programs must be designed with operational usability in mind.

Traditional cybersecurity programs sometimes assume that stronger controls automatically produce better security outcomes. In practice, overly restrictive controls can unintentionally increase risk by pushing users toward unmanaged workflows that security teams cannot monitor, govern, or protect.

Examples include:

- Employees pasting confidential information into public AI chat tools because approved internal tools are unavailable
- Teams sharing files through personal cloud storage because corporate collaboration systems are too restrictive
- Developers using unauthorized AI coding assistants to accelerate delivery deadlines

- Business users exporting sensitive reports locally to avoid slow access approval processes
- Employees forwarding files to personal email accounts to work around DLP restrictions
- Teams creating duplicate datasets outside governed platforms because official analytics environments are difficult to access

In each case, the user often believes they are solving a business problem, not creating a security incident.

Shadow AI Is Often a Governance Problem Before It Is a Technology Problem

Shadow IT has existed for decades, but AI has dramatically accelerated the problem.

Public generative AI platforms, AI-enabled SaaS features, browser plugins, AI meeting assistants, automated summarization tools, transcription services, and AI copilots allow users to process large volumes of data with little technical effort. Many of these tools provide immediate business value, which makes them highly attractive to users operating under time pressure.

The problem is that sensitive data frequently follows the user.

Organizations may prohibit certain AI tools while failing to provide secure alternatives. They may block approved workflows without understanding how employees actually work. In these situations, users often create unofficial processes outside governance boundaries.

This is especially common when organizations ban AI usage without defining acceptable alternatives, require excessive approval cycles for collaboration, make secure sharing significantly harder than insecure sharing, deploy overly aggressive DLP controls without tuning, create complicated access request processes, lack modern collaboration tooling, fail to explain why controls exist, or focus on punishment instead of enablement.

Security programs that rely entirely on restriction often struggle because users continue seeking ways to complete their work.

Secure Enough to Not Bypass

One of the most important design principles in modern data security is this:

Controls that are technically secure but operationally unusable often fail in practice because users route around them.

An effective DSPM program must balance governance with usability.

That does not mean lowering standards. It means building controls that align with how people actually work. Organizations should strive to create workflows where the secure path is also the easiest or fastest reasonable option.

Examples include:

- Providing approved enterprise AI tools instead of relying only on bans
- Using context-aware DLP rather than blocking every upload attempt
- Implementing just-in-time education during risky behavior

- Creating faster access review and approval workflows
- Reducing unnecessary permission complexity
- Automating low-risk remediation actions
- Providing secure collaboration environments that meet business needs
- Building clear data handling guidance into daily workflows

Security that ignores user experience often creates more shadow IT, more shadow AI, and less visibility.

Productivity Pressure Changes User Behavior

Modern employees operate under constant pressure to move faster, collaborate broadly, and produce immediate results. AI tools amplify this pressure because users quickly see how much time automation can save.

When leadership prioritizes speed without defining acceptable guardrails, employees often make their own decisions about acceptable risk.

This is not solely a training problem. It is also a governance, culture, and leadership problem.

Organizations should clearly define which AI tools are approved, which data types may be used with AI systems, which workflows require additional review, which activities are prohibited, how sensitive data should be handled, what monitoring occurs, what responsibilities users carry, and what escalation paths exist when uncertainty arises.

Clear guidance reduces uncertainty and helps users make safer decisions under pressure.

Executive Behavior Shapes User Behavior

User behavior is shaped by leadership expectations.

If executives demand speed while ignoring governance, employees will often interpret that pressure as permission to work around controls. This is especially true when teams are rewarded for fast delivery, broad collaboration, AI adoption, revenue acceleration, or customer responsiveness, but are not equally held accountable for data handling, privacy obligations, retention requirements, or approved-use boundaries.

Employees pay attention to what leaders reward.

If the organization celebrates speed at any cost, users may begin to treat security requirements as obstacles. If leaders use unsanctioned AI tools, bypass approved workflows, share sensitive files informally, or pressure teams to "just get it done," those behaviors become informal permission structures. The policy may say one thing, but leadership behavior teaches another.

This creates a serious governance problem.

Security teams can train users, deploy DLP, implement DSPM, publish AI policies, and create secure workflows, but those controls will struggle if executive behavior sends a different message. Leadership must model the behavior they expect from the rest of the organization.

Executives and senior leaders should be accountable for supporting approved AI and data handling workflows, avoiding pressure that encourages unsafe shortcuts, reinforcing that governance is part of delivery, funding secure alternatives when business teams need speed, holding managers accountable for repeated control bypass, and treating data security as a business responsibility rather than only a security function.

This does not mean leaders should slow the business unnecessarily. It means they should make it clear that speed and governance must operate together.

A mature DSPM program helps leadership see where business pressure is creating data risk. If risky behavior clusters around a department, project, executive priority, or business process, the right response may not be another awareness module. The better response may be to fix the workflow, provide a secure alternative, clarify ownership, adjust incentives, or address the leadership expectation driving the behavior.

Security culture is not created by posters, policies, or annual training alone. It is created by what leaders tolerate, reward, fund, and model.

Training Must Reflect Reality

Traditional annual awareness training often fails because it focuses on generic policy language rather than real operational behavior. It also often focuses only on individual users, while ignoring the manager and leadership expectations that shape user behavior in the first place.

Modern training should address:

- Shadow AI usage
- Prompt handling risks
- Sensitive data uploads
- SaaS oversharing
- Collaboration risks
- Data ownership responsibilities
- Manager accountability for team data handling
- Executive expectations around secure AI and data use
- AI-generated output validation
- Third-party data exposure
- Business-context decision making

Training should also explain why controls exist, not simply list prohibited activities.

Users are far more likely to support governance when they understand the regulatory risk, the privacy implications, the business consequences, the customer impact, the intellectual property concerns, and the operational recovery challenges.

Security awareness becomes more effective when it reflects the reality of modern workflows instead of treating users as adversaries.

DSPM Helps Reduce Friction Through Context

One advantage of mature DSPM programs is that they can reduce unnecessary friction by improving contextual understanding.

Rather than applying identical restrictions to all data, DSPM allows organizations to make more informed decisions based on sensitivity, exposure, identity context, data ownership, business criticality, regulatory obligations, sharing patterns, AI usage, and behavioral risk indicators.

This enables organizations to focus stronger controls where the risk is highest while reducing unnecessary disruption elsewhere.

Better context creates better governance decisions.

The Goal Is Not Perfect User Behavior

No organization completely eliminates shadow IT, shadow AI, or risky user behavior.

The goal is to reduce unnecessary friction, improve visibility, create safer workflows, enable secure productivity, detect risky behavior earlier, educate users continuously, and build governance into daily operations.

Effective DSPM programs recognize an important truth:

People are not separate from the security architecture.

They are part of it.

9.6 Why Traditional Awareness Fails

Traditional security awareness training often fails because it treats all users, all risks, and all behaviors as if they are the same.

Most employees have sat through annual training that tells them not to click suspicious links, not to share passwords, and not to mishandle sensitive data. The content may be technically correct, but it is usually disconnected from the employee's actual job, actual systems, and actual data exposure. A finance analyst exporting payroll data, a developer cloning production data into a test environment, and a sales manager sharing customer files with a partner do not need the same lesson at the same time.

Generic awareness training also suffers from poor timing. People are trained once or twice a year, but risky data decisions happen every day. By the time an employee encounters a real situation, the training may be long forgotten or too abstract to apply.

The result is predictable. Employees may technically "complete" training without changing behavior. Security teams may be able to prove compliance with a training requirement, but not prove a reduction in actual data exposure.

Traditional awareness often answers the wrong question. It asks, "*Did the user complete the training?*" A stronger data security program asks, "*Did the user understand the risk in the moment where their behavior mattered?*"

Behavior vs. Intent

A mature human-layer strategy separates behavior from intent.

Not every risky action is malicious. An employee who downloads sensitive customer records may be preparing a business report. A developer who copies production data into a lower environment may be trying to troubleshoot a performance issue. A manager who shares a folder externally may be trying to speed up collaboration with a partner. These actions can create serious exposure, but the intent may be entirely legitimate.

This distinction matters because security responses should be proportional. Treating every risky behavior as hostile can create friction, resentment, and alert fatigue. Ignoring risky behavior because the user is trusted can create silent exposure.

DSPM helps bridge that gap by providing context. It can show what data was involved, where it was located, who had access, whether the access was appropriate, how the data moved, and whether the exposure violated policy or regulatory expectations. That context allows security teams to respond based on risk rather than assumption.

For example, a user accessing sensitive data they normally work with may require no action. A user downloading a large volume of sensitive data before leaving the company may require investigation. A user sharing regulated data externally with a known business partner may require policy validation and access review. A user placing confidential data into an unmanaged AI tool may require immediate intervention and education.

The behavior may look similar at a surface level, but the intent, context, and risk can be very different.

The goal is not to assume the worst. The goal is to understand enough to respond intelligently.

Training Based on Real Data Exposure

DSPM changes security education because it gives organizations visibility into actual data exposure, not just theoretical risk.

Instead of delivering the same generic message to everyone, security teams can tailor education based on real patterns. If DSPM identifies that a department routinely stores sensitive files in overexposed collaboration folders, training can focus on safe sharing, access review, and data minimization. If developers are using production data in test environments, education can focus on masking, tokenization, synthetic data, and approved development workflows. If business users are uploading confidential files to unsanctioned SaaS or AI tools, training can address approved tools, acceptable use, and safer alternatives.

This makes training more relevant and more credible. Users are more likely to listen when the guidance reflects their actual work.

DSPM-driven training can answer questions such as:

- *Which teams are handling the most sensitive data?*
- *Where are users creating the most exposure?*
- *Which applications or repositories are most frequently involved?*
- *Are users over-sharing data because permissions are too complex?*
- *Are risky behaviors concentrated in one team, workflow, tool, or business process?*

This shifts awareness from a broad compliance activity to a targeted risk reduction mechanism.

For example, a healthcare organization may discover that care coordination teams are storing patient information in shared folders with excessive permissions. Rather than sending everyone a generic HIPAA reminder, the organization can provide focused guidance to those teams on patient data handling, minimum necessary access, and secure collaboration. The training becomes specific, timely, and grounded in what is actually happening.

That is a very different experience from annual awareness training. It feels less like a checkbox and more like useful guidance.

9.7 Just-in-Time Education vs. Annual Training

Annual training is not useless. It can establish baseline expectations, communicate policy, and satisfy compliance obligations. But annual training alone is too slow and too broad to manage modern data risk.

Just-in-time education brings guidance closer to the moment of risk.

If a user attempts to share sensitive data externally, they can receive a prompt explaining why the action may be risky. If an employee uploads regulated data into an unapproved tool, they can be redirected to an approved workflow. If a developer tries to move production data into a non-production environment, they can be reminded of masking requirements before the exposure occurs.

This type of education works because it is immediate, contextual, and actionable. It does not rely on the user remembering a policy from months ago. It helps them make a better decision while they are making the decision.

A strong program often uses multiple layers of education and accountability:

- Annual or periodic training establishes the foundation.
- Role-based training addresses job-specific data responsibilities.
- Manager training reinforces accountability for team behavior and access decisions.
- Executive guidance sets expectations for secure AI use, approved workflows, and governance-aware delivery.
- Just-in-time prompts guide users during risky actions.
- Targeted coaching helps teams correct repeated exposure patterns.
- Manager-level reporting reinforces accountability without creating a culture of blame.

The best education does not simply tell users what they did wrong. It explains the risk, offers a safer path, and makes the secure behavior easier than the risky one.

For example, instead of saying, "You are not allowed to share this file," a better message might say, "This file contains regulated customer information and is currently shared outside the company. Use the approved secure sharing workspace or request a partner access review."

That message teaches, redirects, and preserves business momentum.

9.8 Insider Risk Overlap

The human layer of data security naturally overlaps with insider risk, but the two should not be treated as identical.

Insider risk includes malicious insiders, negligent users, compromised accounts, departing employees, contractors, third parties, and business processes that unintentionally expose sensitive data. DSPM contributes to insider risk programs by providing data context that many traditional tools lack.

User behavior analytics may show that an employee downloaded an unusual number of files. Identity tools may show that the user authenticated successfully. Endpoint tools may show that files were copied to a device. DSPM adds another critical question: *What data was involved?*

That question changes everything.

Downloading thousands of public marketing images is not the same as downloading customer financial records, source code, merger documents, patient data, employee records, or credentials. Accessing a folder is not the same as accessing a folder containing regulated or business-critical data. Sharing a file externally is not the same as sharing a file containing trade secrets.

DSPM helps insider risk teams prioritize based on sensitivity, exposure, access, and business impact.

It can also help identify non-malicious insider risk patterns, such as users retaining access after changing roles, former project teams keeping access to sensitive workspaces, contractors with broad access after an engagement ends, shared accounts or service accounts touching sensitive data, employees using personal storage or unsanctioned tools for convenience, and business units creating shadow repositories outside governed environments.

The overlap between DSPM and insider risk should be handled carefully. Organizations should avoid building a surveillance culture where every user feels watched or distrusted. The message should be centered on protecting people, customers, and the business. Transparency, clear policy, proportional response, and privacy-aware monitoring are essential.

The goal is not to accuse employees. The goal is to reduce unnecessary exposure, detect meaningful risk, and intervene before harm occurs.

9.9 Bringing the Human Layer Into the DSPM Program

A mature DSPM program does not stop at discovery and classification. It uses those insights to improve how people work with data.

That means security teams should partner with business leaders, legal, privacy, HR, compliance, and IT to define acceptable data behaviors. They should identify where users need better workflows, where policies are unclear, where managers need better visibility, and where technology is creating friction.

Sometimes the right answer is not more training. Sometimes the right answer is fixing permissions, simplifying approved sharing methods, automating access reviews, improving labeling, reducing unnecessary data copies, changing leadership expectations, or funding a secure alternative that makes the approved path easier.

Human-layer data security is most effective when it is practical and empathetic. People usually want to do the right thing, but they need clear guidance, usable tools, timely feedback, and leadership that reinforces secure behavior.

DSPM gives organizations the visibility to make that possible. It turns abstract awareness into behavior-focused security. It helps teams move from "users are the weakest link" to a better and more accurate message:

People are part of the control environment. Give them context, guide them at the right moment, and design systems that make secure behavior the natural path.

9.10 How AI Improves DSPM Remediation

AI has significantly improved the DSPM space because it helps security teams understand context.

Traditional data discovery tools often rely on pattern matching. For example, they may detect credit card numbers, Social Security numbers, API keys, or specific keywords. While this is useful, it does not always explain what the data means or how risky it is in context.

AI can help determine whether data is sensitive based on surrounding content, usage, ownership, location, and business meaning.

A common example is the word "Jordan."

When someone says "Jordan," *what do they mean?*

They could mean Jordan the country, the Jordan River, a person named Jordan, Michael Jordan, or the Jordan brand or shoe. Each meaning has a different security concern and may require a different classification.

Term	Possible Meaning	Potential Risk
Jordan	A person	Personal data, employee data, or customer data
Jordan	A country	Geographic, operational, legal, or regulatory concern
Jordan River	Location or historical reference	Usually low sensitivity unless tied to business operations
Michael Jordan	Public figure or marketing reference	Public information, marketing content, copyright, or branding concern
Jordan shoes	Product or brand reference	Intellectual property, vendor data, pricing, product strategy, or commercial concern

The word alone is not enough. The context determines the risk.

This is where AI becomes valuable in DSPM. AI can look beyond the keyword and evaluate the surrounding information to determine what the data likely represents, how it should be classified, and what remediation action may be appropriate.

For example, AI can help determine whether "Jordan" appears in an employee record, a customer support case, a product roadmap, a marketing document, a travel request, a legal contract, a vendor invoice, or a brand strategy document.

Each case may require a different label, policy, owner, and remediation workflow.

AI helps reduce false positives, improve classification accuracy, and guide security teams toward the right response.

9.11 People, Process, and Technology Working Together

The strongest remediation programs combine all three pillars.

Pillar	Purpose	Example
People	Ensure users, managers, administrators, and leaders understand the risk and their responsibilities	Employees are trained not to paste sensitive data into unauthorized AI tools, and managers reinforce approved workflows
Process	Create a repeatable workflow for remediation and validation	High-risk DSPM findings are assigned, tracked, remediated, and verified
Technology	Detect, enforce, automate, and monitor controls	DSPM integrates with IAM, DLP, SIEM, SOAR, and ticketing systems

A failure in any one area weakens the entire program.

If the technology detects risk but no owner is assigned, remediation stalls. If the process exists but users are not trained, the same risk keeps recurring. If people understand the policy but technology does not enforce it, sensitive data may still be exposed. If automation removes access without business review, legitimate work may be disrupted. If leaders demand speed without governance, users may bypass controls even when the right tools and processes exist.

DSPM remediation must balance security, business need, compliance, leadership expectations, and usability.

Key Takeaways

Effective DSPM remediation requires people, process, and technology working together.

People must be trained to understand data risk and use the tools correctly. Processes must define how findings are reviewed, prioritized, assigned, remediated, validated, and documented. Technology must detect risk, enforce policy, automate response, and provide visibility across the data environment.

The human layer matters because data risk is often created through ordinary business behavior. Users create, copy, share, upload, download, and retain data every day, often under pressure to move quickly. Most risky behavior is not malicious. It is usually shaped by unclear guidance, workflow friction, productivity pressure, poor tooling, or business expectations that reward speed without reinforcing governance.

Managers and executives are part of the control environment. Managers help validate business need, reinforce team behavior, approve access, and identify when repeated data exposure reflects a workflow problem rather than an individual training failure. Executives shape culture through the priorities they set, the behavior they model, and the pressure they create. If leaders demand speed while ignoring governance, users may interpret that pressure as permission to bypass controls.

AI strengthens DSPM by adding context. It helps teams understand not just what data was found, but what the data means and how it should be protected.

The goal is not simply to find sensitive data. The goal is to understand the data, reduce unnecessary exposure, enforce the right controls, create usable secure workflows, and prevent the same risks from recurring.

People are not separate from the security architecture.

They are part of it.

Chapter 10: How DSPM Fits into the Modern Security Ecosystem

Data Security Posture Management, or DSPM, is not meant to replace the security, privacy, governance, and cloud tools organizations already use. Its value is different. DSPM gives those tools the data context they often lack.

Most enterprise security programs already have systems for managing identity, protecting cloud infrastructure, detecting events, automating response, enforcing policy, managing audits, supporting privacy obligations, and cataloging business data. Yet many of those tools still struggle to answer a deceptively simple set of questions:

- *Where is our sensitive data?*
- *What kind of sensitive data is it?*
- *Who or what can access it?*
- *Is that access appropriate?*
- *Is the data exposed, duplicated, stale, misconfigured, or outside policy?*
- *Which data risks should we fix first?*

DSPM sits at the center of those questions. It creates a data-centric view of risk across cloud, SaaS, databases, data lakes, warehouses, file stores, collaboration platforms, and, in some cases, on-premises environments. It helps security and governance teams move from protecting systems in the abstract to protecting the data that actually matters.

A useful way to frame DSPM is this:

DSPM makes the rest of the security stack data-aware.

That does not mean DSPM becomes the system of record for everything. Identity tools still manage identities. CNAPP platforms still manage cloud-native risk. DLP tools still help prevent leakage. SIEMs still collect and correlate events. SOAR platforms still automate workflows. GRC platforms still manage controls and audit evidence. Privacy platforms still manage privacy obligations. Data catalogs still manage business metadata and lineage.

DSPM adds the missing connective tissue: sensitive data discovery, classification, exposure analysis, access context, and risk prioritization.

10.1 DSPM as the Data Intelligence Layer

DSPM platforms typically perform five core functions.

First, they discover where data lives. This may include object storage, databases, data warehouses, file shares, SaaS applications, developer platforms, collaboration tools, and data lakes.

Second, they classify sensitive data. A DSPM platform may identify personal data, protected health information, payment card data, financial records, intellectual property, credentials, source code, legal documents, employee records, customer data, and other regulated or business-critical information.

Third, they map access. DSPM tools look at which users, groups, roles, service accounts, applications, third parties, and machine identities can access sensitive data.

Fourth, they identify risky conditions. These may include public exposure, excessive permissions, stale data, unauthorized replication, unencrypted data stores, misconfigured repositories, dormant accounts with access, sensitive data in non-production environments, or data located outside approved regions or systems.

Finally, DSPM supports remediation. Depending on the platform and integration model, it may create tickets, trigger workflows, notify owners, recommend access reductions, feed findings into GRC systems, enrich SIEM alerts, support DLP policies, or initiate SOAR playbooks.

The key distinction is that DSPM starts with the data. Instead of asking only whether an asset is vulnerable, a bucket is public, or a user has access, DSPM asks whether sensitive data is involved and how much that changes the risk.

For example, a cloud security tool may identify three public storage buckets. DSPM can determine that one contains public marketing assets, one contains customer personally identifiable information, and one contains credentials in log files. The technical misconfiguration may look similar across all three, but the business risk is very different.

That is where DSPM changes prioritization.

10.2 DSPM and IAM

Identity and Access Management, commonly called IAM, governs digital identities and access. IAM tools manage users, groups, roles, authentication, authorization, single sign-on, multi-factor authentication, provisioning, deprovisioning, privileged access, access reviews, and identity governance.

IAM answers questions such as:

- *Who is this user?*
- *What applications or systems can they access?*
- *What groups or roles do they belong to?*
- *Are they required to use multi-factor authentication?*
- *Should their access be removed or changed?*
- *Are they overprivileged?*

Common IAM-related platforms include Okta, Microsoft Entra ID, SailPoint, Saviynt, CyberArk, Ping Identity, BeyondTrust, and the native IAM services in AWS, Azure, and Google Cloud.

IAM is excellent at managing identity and access decisions. However, IAM does not always understand the sensitivity of the data behind those permissions. It may know that a contractor has access to a Snowflake database, an S3 bucket, or a SharePoint site. It may not know that the database contains customer financial records, the bucket contains payment data, or the SharePoint site contains employee medical information.

DSPM gives IAM programs better data context.

With DSPM, access reviews become more meaningful. Instead of asking, *"Should this user still have access to this system?"* the reviewer can ask, *"Should this user still have access to this system containing regulated customer data?"*

DSPM also helps identify excessive access to sensitive data. This includes broad group permissions, dormant accounts, unnecessary privileged access, third-party access, service account overreach, and nested group exposure that may otherwise be difficult to see.

The relationship is straightforward:

IAM governs identities. DSPM shows what those identities can do to sensitive data.

Together, IAM and DSPM help organizations move closer to least privilege, not as an abstract access-control goal, but as a data-risk reduction strategy.

10.3 DSPM and CNAPP

Cloud-Native Application Protection Platform, or CNAPP, is a broad cloud security category. CNAPP platforms commonly combine cloud security posture management, workload protection, cloud infrastructure entitlement management, container security, Kubernetes security, infrastructure-as-code scanning, cloud vulnerability management, runtime detection, and cloud compliance monitoring.

Examples include Wiz, Prisma Cloud, Orca Security, Lacework, Microsoft Defender for Cloud, CrowdStrike Falcon Cloud Security, Check Point CloudGuard, and Tenable Cloud Security.

CNAPP tools usually start with cloud assets, configurations, identities, workloads, containers, and infrastructure. They identify issues such as public storage, exposed virtual machines, vulnerable workloads, overprivileged cloud roles, unencrypted databases, insecure Kubernetes clusters, missing logging, and risky security group rules.

DSPM starts from a different place: the data.

This distinction matters because not every cloud finding carries the same level of business risk. A public bucket containing generic website images is not the same as a public bucket containing patient records or customer payment data. A vulnerable workload with no access to sensitive data is not the same as a vulnerable workload that can assume a role with access to regulated data.

DSPM improves CNAPP by adding data sensitivity to cloud risk prioritization. It helps cloud security teams identify which misconfigurations, vulnerabilities, or attack paths could expose critical data.

A practical combined workflow may look like this:

1. CNAPP identifies a public cloud storage bucket.
2. DSPM determines that the bucket contains regulated customer data.
3. IAM or CIEM analysis shows that several service accounts also have excessive permissions.
4. SOAR or ticketing opens a high-priority remediation workflow.
5. GRC records the issue as a control violation with evidence.

CNAPP secures the cloud environment. DSPM tells the organization which cloud risks matter most because sensitive data is involved.

10.4 DSPM and DLP

Data Loss Prevention, or DLP, focuses on detecting, monitoring, and preventing sensitive data from being leaked, shared, copied, uploaded, emailed, printed, or otherwise exfiltrated. DLP tools may operate across email, endpoints, web traffic, SaaS applications, cloud storage, file shares, collaboration tools, and network channels.

DLP tools commonly detect patterns such as Social Security numbers, credit card numbers, health records, source code, confidential documents, financial records, or custom sensitive-data patterns. They can alert, block, quarantine, encrypt, redact, warn users, apply labels, prevent external sharing, or create incidents.

DLP is powerful, but it has historically been difficult to tune. Many organizations struggle with false positives, false negatives, alert fatigue, inconsistent classification, incomplete data visibility, and limited business ownership.

10.5 DSPM and DLP are closely related, but they are not the same.

DLP is often strongest when data is in motion or in use. It watches for sensitive data leaving, being shared, or being handled in risky ways. DSPM is strongest at discovering where sensitive data lives, how it is exposed, who can access it, and where the riskiest data conditions exist before exfiltration occurs.

DSPM can make DLP more effective by improving classification, identifying high-priority repositories, clarifying ownership, and helping teams decide where DLP controls should be applied first.

For example, DSPM may discover that sensitive HR files are broadly accessible in a collaboration platform. DLP can then help prevent those files from being emailed externally or shared outside the organization. IAM can reduce unnecessary access. SOAR can open tickets. GRC can track the control issue.

DSPM finds and prioritizes sensitive data risk. DLP helps enforce controls that prevent sensitive data from leaving or being misused.

Because DLP is such an important and often misunderstood category, the next chapter will provide a deeper reference on DLP tools, including how they work, where they fit, common deployment models, strengths, limitations, and how to evaluate them in a modern data security program.

10.6 DSPM and SIEM

Security Information and Event Management, or SIEM, collects, normalizes, correlates, searches, and analyzes logs and events from across the enterprise. SIEM platforms are central to many security operations programs.

Examples include Splunk, Microsoft Sentinel, Google SecOps, IBM QRadar, Elastic Security, Sumo Logic, LogRhythm, and Devo.

SIEM tools ingest logs from identity providers, firewalls, EDR platforms, cloud services, SaaS applications, databases, applications, servers, DLP tools, CNAPP platforms, VPNs, proxies, and network devices. They help detect suspicious activity such as failed logins, impossible travel, privilege escalation, lateral movement, cloud control-plane changes, unusual downloads, account compromise, and potential exfiltration.

The challenge is that SIEM alerts often lack data sensitivity context. A SIEM may detect that a user downloaded 10,000 files from SharePoint. Without DSPM, the analyst may not know whether those files were public documents, internal project notes, patient records, executive compensation files, or legal documents.

DSPM enriches SIEM alerts with data context. It can add sensitivity labels, data owner information, exposure status, risk scores, regulatory tags, and identity-to-data access context.

That enrichment improves triage. Suspicious activity involving sensitive data deserves faster attention than suspicious activity involving low-risk data.

Together, SIEM and DSPM answer a better investigation question:

Did suspicious activity involve sensitive data, and what is the potential impact?

DSPM can also support more precise detection rules. For example, a SOC may create alerts for large downloads from repositories containing PHI, access to regulated data by dormant accounts, privileged access to sensitive data outside business hours, or service account activity outside normal behavior.

SIEM tells the organization what happened. DSPM helps explain whether what happened matters to sensitive data.

10.7 DSPM and SOAR

Security Orchestration, Automation, and Response, or SOAR, automates security workflows across tools. SOAR platforms use playbooks, triggers, integrations, and decision logic to help teams respond consistently and quickly.

Examples include Palo Alto Cortex XSOAR, Splunk SOAR, Tines, Swimlane, Torq, D3 Security, and Microsoft Sentinel playbooks using Logic Apps.

A SOAR workflow may enrich an alert, query identity systems, open a ticket, disable a user, revoke access, notify an owner, quarantine a file, update a SIEM case, collect evidence, or route an approval.

DSPM gives SOAR better triggers and better context.

For example, if DSPM detects that a publicly exposed storage bucket contains customer PII, SOAR can launch a response workflow. That workflow may validate the exposure, identify the owner, restrict public access if policy allows, open a ticket, notify the data owner, escalate to compliance, send evidence to GRC, and confirm remediation after the finding is resolved.

Without DSPM, the automation may know that a bucket is public. With DSPM, the automation knows the bucket contains sensitive data and should be treated as a higher-risk event.

DSPM finds risky data conditions. SOAR helps automate what happens next.

10.8 DSPM and GRC

Governance, Risk, and Compliance, or GRC, provides the structure for managing policies, controls, risks, audits, exceptions, evidence, regulatory obligations, and compliance reporting.

Examples include ServiceNow GRC, Archer, OneTrust GRC, AuditBoard, Drata, Vanta, Hyperproof, LogicGate, ZenGRC, and MetricStream.

GRC platforms manage frameworks and obligations such as NIST CSF, NIST 800-53, ISO 27001, SOC 2, HIPAA, PCI DSS, GDPR, CCPA/CPRA, SOX, CIS Controls, HITRUST, and COBIT.

GRC defines what should be true. DSPM helps show what is actually true about sensitive data.

For example, a control may state that sensitive customer data must be encrypted, access-restricted, and stored only in approved locations. DSPM can provide evidence showing where that data exists, whether encryption is enabled, who has access, whether access is excessive, whether public exposure exists, and whether data has drifted into unapproved locations.

This turns governance from a periodic documentation exercise into a more continuous evidence-based process.

DSPM can support GRC through risk-register updates, control testing, audit evidence, issue tracking, exception management, remediation reporting, data-risk metrics, and compliance dashboards.

Instead of recording a generic risk such as "cloud data exposure," DSPM can help define a measurable risk such as:

Twelve repositories containing regulated customer data are accessible by broad internal groups. Three are externally shared. Two contain stale data beyond the approved retention period.

That level of detail gives governance teams something they can assign, track, measure, and report.

10.9 DSPM and Privacy Platforms

Privacy platforms help organizations manage obligations related to personal data. These obligations may include data subject rights, consent, records of processing activities, privacy assessments, data retention, cookie governance, vendor privacy reviews, cross-border transfers, and breach notification support.

Examples include OneTrust, BigID, Securiti, TrustArc, Transcend, DataGrail, and MineOS.

Privacy teams care about where personal data lives, why it is collected, how it is used, who it is shared with, how long it is retained, whether consent or another lawful basis applies, and whether individuals can exercise their rights.

Privacy inventories are often based on business process documentation, application owner input, questionnaires, or declared data flows. Those are useful, but they may not reflect technical reality.

DSPM helps validate where personal data actually exists.

It may discover customer data in analytics environments, production data in test systems, employee files in shared drives, personal data in unmanaged SaaS applications, stale records beyond retention policy, or sensitive data shared with external users.

This is especially valuable for privacy operations such as data subject access requests, data minimization, retention enforcement, privacy impact assessments, and breach impact analysis.

During an incident, privacy teams need to know whether personal data was involved, what categories of data were affected, whether the data was encrypted, who had access, whether regulated jurisdictions are implicated, and whether notification thresholds may apply. DSPM can help answer those questions faster and with better evidence.

Privacy platforms manage personal-data obligations. DSPM discovers and validates where personal data lives and how exposed it is.

10.10 DSPM and Data Catalogs

Data catalogs inventory data assets and make data easier to understand, govern, and use. They are commonly used by data governance, analytics, business intelligence, data engineering, and AI teams.

Examples include Collibra, Alation, Microsoft Purview Data Catalog, Informatica, Atlan, DataHub, Apache Atlas, Google Dataplex, AWS Glue Data Catalog, and Unity Catalog.

Data catalogs manage metadata such as table names, column names, data lineage, business glossary terms, ownership, stewardship, data domains, usage patterns, certified datasets, data quality scores, schema details, and approved business definitions.

Their purpose is often to make data understandable, trustworthy, and usable.

DSPM adds security and risk context to that metadata.

A catalog may know that a dataset is owned by Finance, used for revenue reporting, and certified for analytics. DSPM may add that the dataset contains customer PII, is accessible by too many users, is replicated into a development environment, and includes stale data outside retention policy.

The integration also works in the other direction. Data catalogs can help DSPM by providing business ownership, stewardship, lineage, criticality, approved usage, data domains, and system-of-record context.

Together, DSPM and data catalogs help organizations answer:

What does this data mean, who owns it, how is it used, and how risky is it?

This relationship becomes even more important as organizations adopt generative AI and machine learning. AI governance depends on knowing which datasets are being used, whether sensitive or regulated data is included, whether usage is approved, whether lineage is understood, and whether controls are appropriate.

Data catalogs make data understandable and usable. DSPM makes data safer and risk-aware.

10.11 A Practical Ecosystem Example

Consider an organization that stores customer data in Snowflake, AWS S3, Microsoft 365, Salesforce, and Databricks. It uses Okta and SailPoint for identity, Wiz for cloud security, Microsoft Purview DLP, Splunk for SIEM, Tines for SOAR, ServiceNow GRC, OneTrust for privacy, Collibra for data cataloging, and a DSPM platform for data security posture.

DSPM scans the environment and discovers customer PII in Snowflake, payment-like data in S3, employee records in SharePoint, secrets in developer storage, and production data copied into a test environment.

CNAPP identifies a public S3 bucket and an overprivileged AWS role. DSPM determines that the bucket contains customer PII and payment-like data. That finding is no longer just a cloud misconfiguration; it is a data exposure risk.

IAM shows that hundreds of users have access to sensitive Snowflake tables through nested groups. DSPM identifies which of those tables contain regulated data and which accounts are dormant or overprivileged.

DLP policies are tuned to monitor and restrict external sharing of the highest-risk data. SIEM alerts are enriched with sensitivity and ownership context. SOAR workflows notify owners, open tickets, revoke risky access, and validate remediation. GRC records the control violation and tracks closure. Privacy teams assess whether personal data obligations are triggered. The data catalog updates ownership, lineage, and sensitivity metadata.

The tools work better together because DSPM gives them shared data context.

10.12 Understanding Overlap Between Tool Categories

Modern security platforms increasingly overlap. Some CNAPP platforms include DSPM-like discovery. Some DSPM platforms include cloud posture and access analysis. Some DLP tools include discovery and labeling. Some privacy platforms include data mapping and classification. Some data catalogs include governance and sensitivity tagging.

This overlap is not necessarily a problem, but it does require clear operating decisions.

The practical question is not always, "Which category owns this capability?"

A better question is:

Which platform is the system of record for this decision, and which platforms provide supporting evidence?

For identity lifecycle decisions, IAM or IGA is usually the system of record. DSPM provides sensitive-data context.

For cloud misconfiguration remediation, CNAPP or the cloud security team may own the workflow. DSPM helps prioritize based on data exposure.

For leakage prevention, DLP enforces policy. DSPM improves discovery, classification, and targeting.

For investigation, SIEM manages the event timeline. DSPM enriches the case with data sensitivity and exposure details.

For automated response, SOAR runs the playbook. DSPM supplies the trigger and data-risk context.

For compliance and audit, GRC manages controls and evidence. DSPM validates whether data controls are operating as expected.

For privacy operations, the privacy platform manages obligations. DSPM supports discovery and exposure analysis.

For data stewardship and business metadata, the data catalog is often the system of record. DSPM adds security posture and risk.

Clear ownership prevents tool sprawl from becoming operational confusion.

10.13 What DSPM Should Not Replace

DSPM is a powerful category, but it should not be positioned as a replacement for the entire security stack.

DSPM should not replace IAM because it does not usually manage authentication, single sign-on, provisioning, or the full identity lifecycle.

It should not replace CNAPP because it does not usually cover all workload, container, Kubernetes, infrastructure-as-code, and runtime cloud risk.

It should not replace DLP because it does not usually provide the same real-time endpoint, email, web, SaaS, and network enforcement controls.

It should not replace SIEM because it does not serve as the central log collection, correlation, and detection platform.

It should not replace SOAR because it does not orchestrate every security response workflow across the enterprise.

It should not replace GRC because it does not manage the full policy, audit, risk, exception, and compliance lifecycle.

It should not replace privacy platforms because it does not usually manage the complete privacy operations process, including consent, DSAR fulfillment, and records of processing.

It should not replace data catalogs because it does not usually own business glossary, stewardship, certified datasets, analytics enablement, and enterprise lineage.

DSPM is strongest when it is used as the data security posture layer that connects these tools and improves their decisions.

10.14 Integration Priorities for a DSPM Program

Organizations do not need to integrate everything at once. A practical DSPM program can mature in phases.

Phase 1: Visibility and Ownership

Start by connecting the most important data environments, cloud platforms, SaaS repositories, file stores, data warehouses, and identity provider. The goal is to understand where sensitive data lives, who owns it, and who can access it.

Phase 2: Risk Prioritization

Integrate DSPM with IAM, CNAPP, ticketing, and GRC. The goal is to prioritize the riskiest findings, assign ownership, and begin structured remediation.

Phase 3: Detection and Response

Integrate DSPM with SIEM, SOAR, and DLP. The goal is to enrich alerts, automate response, and prevent sensitive data from being misused or exfiltrated.

Phase 4: Governance and Optimization

Integrate DSPM with privacy platforms, data catalogs, retention processes, AI governance workflows, and executive reporting. The goal is to turn DSPM into a sustainable data governance and risk capability.

Key Takeaways

DSPM helps organizations protect data by giving the broader security and governance ecosystem better context.

IAM controls who has access. DSPM shows whether that access reaches sensitive data.

CNAPP secures cloud environments. DSPM identifies which cloud risks could expose sensitive data.

DLP helps prevent sensitive data from leaving or being misused. DSPM improves DLP targeting through discovery, classification, and posture context.

SIEM detects and investigates events. DSPM enriches those events with sensitivity, ownership, and exposure information.

SOAR automates response. DSPM supplies data-risk triggers and remediation context.

GRC manages governance, risk, controls, and audit evidence. DSPM validates whether data controls are actually working.

Privacy platforms manage personal-data obligations. DSPM helps locate personal data and assess exposure.

Data catalogs manage business metadata, ownership, lineage, and stewardship. DSPM adds sensitivity and risk context.

The simplest way to remember the relationship is this:

DSPM tells every other tool what data matters, where it lives, who can reach it, and how exposed it is.

In the next chapter, we will take a deeper look at Data Loss Prevention tools. DLP deserves its own focused discussion because it is one of the most established, most valuable, and most challenging data security controls to implement well. The next chapter will explain how DLP tools work, where they fit, how they differ from DSPM, and how to evaluate them as part of a modern data security architecture.

Chapter 11: DLP in the Real World: What Still Matters and What Doesn't

Data Loss Prevention has been declared dead more times than most security technologies.

And yet, it keeps showing up.

It shows up in Microsoft Purview. It shows up in Google Workspace. It shows up in Box. It shows up in CASB, SSE, endpoint security, email security, insider risk, cloud platforms, and compliance conversations. Even organizations that say they "moved past DLP" usually still have some version of it running somewhere.

That tells us something important.

DLP is not dead.

But the old idea of DLP is.

For a long time, organizations treated DLP like a magic net that could be stretched across the enterprise to catch sensitive data before it escaped. The promise was simple: identify sensitive data, write policies, block risky movement, and prevent data loss.

In practice, it was rarely that clean.

Security teams ended up with noisy alerts, frustrated users, excessive exceptions, duplicate policies, and controls that were either too weak to matter or too strict to survive contact with real business workflows. DLP became one of those tools everyone wanted for compliance, but few people loved operationally.

The problem was not always the technology. The problem was often the expectation.

DLP is not a complete data security program. It does not automatically know which data matters most. It does not understand every business process. It cannot fix poor data ownership, excessive access, unmanaged repositories, bad retention habits, or years of shadow data growth.

What DLP can still do is enforce specific controls at specific points of risk.

That distinction matters.

Modern DLP works best when it is not asked to be the brain of the data security program. It should be an enforcement layer, informed by better intelligence from data discovery, classification, identity, access governance, user behavior, business context, and DSPM.

DLP should not decide the entire strategy.

DLP should help enforce the strategy.

11.1 What DLP Actually Does Well

DLP is strongest when the use case is clear, the data type is identifiable, the user action is observable, and the control point is close to where the risk occurs.

In plain terms, DLP works best when the organization can answer these questions:

- *What data are we trying to protect?*
- *Where is it moving?*
- *Who is moving it?*
- *Where is it going?*
- *What should happen when the movement is risky?*

When those answers are clear, DLP can still provide meaningful control.

DLP does well at identifying common regulated data types such as Social Security numbers, credit card numbers, health information, bank account numbers, tax identifiers, and other structured data patterns. It can detect when this information appears in email, documents, file shares, cloud storage, endpoint activity, or collaboration platforms.

DLP also does well at controlling obvious egress points. These include emailing sensitive attachments externally, uploading files to unmanaged cloud storage, copying files to USB drives, printing sensitive documents, pasting regulated content into web forms, publicly sharing files, or downloading sensitive records from SaaS applications.

Another area where DLP still has value is user coaching. A well-designed DLP warning can stop accidental exposure before it happens.

For example, a user attempting to email a spreadsheet containing patient information to an external address might receive a message that says:

This file appears to contain protected health information. Confirm that the recipient is authorized before sending.

That kind of warning can be more effective than another annual security awareness course because it appears at the exact moment of risk.

DLP also helps with regulatory enforcement. It can support policies tied to PCI DSS, HIPAA, GLBA, GDPR, CCPA, SOX, contractual data handling obligations, and internal confidentiality requirements. It does not make an organization compliant by itself, but it can provide control evidence, enforcement history, alert records, user justifications, and audit trails.

That evidence matters when the organization needs to answer uncomfortable questions:

- *Who attempted to share the data?*
- *What data was involved?*
- *Where was it going?*
- *Was the action blocked?*
- *Did the user override the warning?*
- *Was a business justification provided?*
- *Was this a one-time mistake or part of a repeated behavior pattern?*

At its best, DLP gives security, privacy, legal, compliance, and business leaders a clearer view into risky data movement.

At its worst, it creates thousands of alerts that nobody trusts.

The difference usually comes down to design.

Move Beyond Pattern Matching

Traditional DLP platforms often rely heavily on pattern matching, regular expressions, fingerprints, dictionaries, and predefined policy rules. These approaches remain useful, particularly for detecting well-structured sensitive information such as payment card data, Social Security numbers, healthcare identifiers, or regulated document types.

However, modern DLP programs increasingly require contextual awareness rather than simple pattern detection alone.

A mature DLP program should integrate with DSPM, data classification systems, identity platforms, and authoritative data repositories to confirm whether data is actually sensitive rather than simply matching a pattern. This allows organizations to move beyond basic content inspection toward higher-confidence data protection decisions.

For example, a sequence of numbers matching a credit card pattern may not actually represent regulated payment data. A spreadsheet containing customer IDs sourced from a classified financial database likely represents confirmed sensitive information. A file copied from a regulated healthcare repository may carry significantly different risk than a similar file located in a public collaboration space. AI-generated summaries may contain sensitive business context even when traditional regex patterns are absent.

Modern DLP maturity increasingly depends on integrating data classification systems, DSPM findings, identity context, repository sensitivity, business ownership, access patterns, governance metadata, and regulatory mapping.

The goal is not simply identifying patterns. The goal is understanding whether the data is actually confidential, regulated, business-critical, or improperly exposed.

11.2 Where DLP Fails

DLP fails when it is expected to understand business context it does not actually have.

A traditional DLP engine might be able to detect that a spreadsheet contains credit card numbers. It may not know whether that spreadsheet is a legitimate finance reconciliation report, a customer support export, a test file, a fraud investigation artifact, or an unauthorized copy of production data.

Those distinctions matter.

DLP often mistakes pattern matching for understanding.

A policy that says "block files containing credit card numbers" sounds reasonable until finance, fraud, billing, customer service, audit, and compliance teams all explain that they have legitimate business workflows involving payment-related data.

If the policy is too strict, business stops.

If the policy is too loose, risk remains.

If exceptions are added without governance, the policy slowly becomes meaningless.

DLP also struggles because sensitivity is not the same as business criticality.

A file with one test Social Security number is not the same as a database export containing 250,000 customer records. A board presentation may not contain regulated data, but it may be highly confidential. A source code repository may not contain obvious PII, but it may contain credentials, proprietary logic, architecture details, or intellectual property.

Traditional DLP has trouble with these distinctions unless it is enriched by classification, ownership, access, exposure, identity, and business process context.

DLP also breaks when classification is wrong.

If a file is labeled "Public" but contains regulated information, DLP may allow risky activity. If a file is labeled "Confidential" but contains harmless information, DLP may create unnecessary friction. If labels are missing, stale, manually applied, inconsistently used, or poorly governed, the DLP program inherits those weaknesses.

Bad classification creates bad DLP.

DLP also fails when it becomes an exception engine.

This is one of the most common real-world failure patterns. A policy starts with good intent. Then users complain. Then business units request exceptions. Then more exceptions are added. Eventually, no one knows which exception is valid, who approved it, whether it still has a business purpose, or whether the original risk still exists.

At that point, DLP becomes less of a control and more of a policy landfill.

Most importantly, DLP cannot fix poor data governance.

It cannot fix unknown data owners, excessive access, unmanaged SaaS usage, stale data, poor retention, shadow IT, weak identity governance, or a lack of data lifecycle management.

DLP may expose symptoms of those problems, but it does not solve the root cause.

DLP Visibility Failures in the Real World

The 2017 Equifax breach demonstrated how security monitoring failures can undermine even large enterprise security environments.

According to the U.S. House Oversight Committee investigation, attackers issued approximately 9,000 database queries across 48 databases and successfully located unencrypted personally identifiable information hundreds of times. The attackers exfiltrated sensitive data from the environment without detection because a device responsible for monitoring network traffic had been inactive for approximately 19 months due to an expired security certificate.

Once the certificate was renewed, Equifax immediately detected suspicious traffic activity.

The lesson is not simply that Equifax lacked security tools. The lesson is that security controls require continuous operational validation, monitoring integrity, asset awareness, classification visibility, governance oversight, and lifecycle management.

DLP, monitoring, and detection technologies are only effective when organizations continuously validate that the controls are operational, properly integrated, monitored, maintained, and aligned to the actual locations of sensitive data.

This is one reason DSPM and contextual data visibility have become increasingly important. Organizations cannot effectively protect sensitive data if they do not continuously understand where sensitive data exists, whether it is encrypted, who can access it, which repositories contain regulated information, whether monitoring controls remain operational, whether data movement is visible, and whether AI systems can access or process the data.

11.3 The Implementation Reality: Powerful Tools Still Require Heavy Setup

One of the biggest misconceptions about modern DLP is that embedded platforms make the problem easy.

They do not.

Tools like Microsoft Purview, Google Workspace DLP, Box Shield, CASB DLP, and endpoint DLP can be powerful, but they require significant planning, configuration, testing, tuning, rollout management, and ongoing governance.

This is especially true for platforms like Microsoft Purview.

Purview can cover a broad Microsoft ecosystem, including Microsoft 365 services, Exchange, SharePoint, OneDrive, Teams, endpoints, and other integrated Microsoft security and compliance capabilities. That breadth is valuable. It is also one of the reasons implementations can become complicated.

The challenge is not simply turning on DLP.

The challenge is deciding what should happen, where, to whom, under which conditions, with which exceptions, with which labels, with which alerting workflow, with which business owners, and with which measurable outcome.

That is a much harder problem.

A Purview-style DLP program may require decisions around sensitivity label taxonomy, sensitive information types, trainable classifiers, data locations, endpoint onboarding, device groups, user groups, policy scoping, alert thresholds, policy tips, override permissions, business justifications, exception handling, audit logging, incident routing, integration with Microsoft Defender, integration with Sentinel or a SIEM, integration with ServiceNow, Jira, or another ticketing system, role-based administration, testing and simulation, user communications, and policy lifecycle management.

That is a lot of setup before the organization gets to durable value.

The tool may technically support the control, but technical support does not equal operational success.

This is why many organizations should define a realistic DLP success model before implementation. The goal should not be "100 percent prevention of data loss." That is not realistic. A better goal is measurable risk reduction in specific, high-value areas.

For example, a DLP program may aim to reduce external sharing of regulated data by a defined percentage, reduce repeat DLP violations from high-risk departments, reduce sensitive data uploads to unmanaged cloud applications, increase the percentage of high-severity alerts tied to known data owners, reduce false positives over time, ensure all DLP exceptions have an owner, reason, and expiration date, improve response time for high-risk data movement events, or decrease sensitive data stored in unauthorized locations.

There is no universal percentage of success that applies to every DLP program. A tool cannot honestly promise that 80 percent, 90 percent, or 95 percent of data loss will be prevented across every environment. Success depends on the quality of discovery, classification, policy design, business participation, identity context, endpoint coverage, user behavior, and operational follow-through.

A better way to think about DLP effectiveness is this:

DLP success is not measured by how many policies exist.

It is measured by whether risky data movement decreases without breaking the business.

A poorly configured DLP tool with broad policies may generate thousands of alerts and still miss the most important risks. A well-designed DLP program with fewer policies may create better outcomes because it focuses on the data, users, repositories, and workflows that matter most.

That is the uncomfortable truth about tools like Purview: the platform may be capable, but capability does not remove the need for architecture.

In fact, the more capable the platform, the more important the architecture becomes.

11.4 Endpoint, Network, and Cloud DLP Realities

DLP is not one thing. It is a collection of controls deployed at different inspection and enforcement points.

Each type has value. Each type has limits.

Endpoint DLP

Endpoint DLP monitors and controls user activity on managed devices. It is closest to the human behavior that often creates exposure.

Endpoint DLP can help control actions such as copying files to USB drives, printing, moving files to local folders, uploading files to cloud storage, copying content into web forms, using restricted applications, or downloading sensitive files.

This makes endpoint DLP useful for insider risk, accidental exposure, contractor environments, regulated workflows, and unmanaged egress paths.

Its strength is proximity to the user.

Its weakness is operational complexity.

Endpoint DLP depends on agent deployment, operating system support, browser coverage, device health, application compatibility, policy tuning, and user experience. It may struggle with unmanaged devices, mobile workflows, virtual desktops, developer tools, encrypted applications, or users working outside standard corporate patterns.

Endpoint DLP is best used for specific, high-risk user actions involving sensitive data. It is not a universal answer to every data protection problem.

Network DLP

Network DLP inspects traffic moving across network boundaries. Historically, this included email gateways, web proxies, firewalls, secure web gateways, and dedicated inspection appliances.

Network DLP can still provide value at centralized egress points, especially for outbound email, web uploads, FTP, SFTP, and traffic leaving known corporate networks.

But the world changed.

Users are remote. Applications are SaaS-based. Traffic is encrypted. Devices may connect directly to cloud services. Data often moves between platforms without crossing traditional network choke points.

That does not make network DLP useless, but it does make it less central than it used to be.

Network DLP is best for specific outbound channels, legacy environments, regulated traffic inspection, and organizations that still route traffic through controlled inspection points.

Cloud DLP

Cloud DLP applies controls inside SaaS platforms, cloud storage, email systems, collaboration platforms, and cloud security ecosystems.

This includes tools like Microsoft Purview DLP, Google Workspace DLP, Box Shield, CASB DLP, and other platform-native controls.

Cloud DLP is powerful because it lives where users increasingly work. It can understand native sharing models, user identities, file permissions, collaboration activity, and platform-specific actions.

Its limitation is scope.

Microsoft is strongest in Microsoft environments. Google is strongest in Google Workspace. Box is strongest inside Box. Salesforce controls are strongest inside Salesforce. GitHub secret scanning is strongest inside GitHub.

Each native control understands its own world. None of them automatically understands the entire enterprise data estate.

That is why cloud DLP is valuable, but fragmented.

11.5 Embedded DLP: Microsoft Purview, Google Workspace, Box, and Native Platform Controls

Embedded DLP has become more important because sensitive data now lives inside platforms. Users do not just move files across a network. They collaborate in SaaS applications, share links, sync folders, co-author documents, export reports, upload datasets, and connect platforms together.

The control needs to live where the data lives.

But embedded DLP also creates a new problem: every platform has its own version of DLP, and they do not all mean the same thing. Even more importantly, the license required to "have DLP" is not always the same as the license required to use the DLP capabilities the business actually expects.

This distinction matters.

A company may say, "We already own Microsoft Purview," or "Google has DLP built in," or "Box has Shield," but that does not automatically mean they have the right licensing, configuration, staffing, policy model, reporting, endpoint coverage, or incident response workflow to operate DLP effectively.

DLP licensing should always be validated against the specific use case.

A basic external sharing policy is not the same as endpoint DLP. A sensitive data detector is not the same as insider risk management. A platform-native control is not the same as enterprise-wide data protection. A purchased license is not the same as an operational program.

Microsoft Purview DLP

Microsoft Purview DLP is one of the most comprehensive embedded DLP ecosystems, particularly for organizations heavily invested in Microsoft 365.

Its biggest advantage is breadth. Purview can support DLP across major Microsoft workloads such as Exchange Online, SharePoint Online, OneDrive for Business, Teams, endpoints, and other Microsoft security and compliance services. For Microsoft-centric organizations, that is a major benefit. It allows DLP to connect with identity, sensitivity labels, endpoint controls, audit logs, investigation workflows, Microsoft Defender, and other compliance capabilities.

Purview is especially useful when an organization wants to control activities such as external email containing sensitive data, sensitive file sharing in SharePoint or OneDrive, endpoint copying, printing, or uploading, Teams-related data exposure, regulated data handling, policy tips and user coaching, business justification prompts, and audit and investigation workflows.

However, Purview is not simple.

The same breadth that makes it powerful also makes it complex to implement. Organizations often underestimate the planning required to configure labels, policies, locations, sensitive information types, endpoint settings, user groups, exceptions, alerts, and response workflows.

Purview can become very effective, but usually only after careful setup and tuning.

A common mistake is to enable broad DLP policies too quickly. That often produces high alert volume, user frustration, and emergency exceptions. Another mistake is assuming Microsoft's built-in templates will map cleanly to the organization's actual business workflows. Templates can provide a starting point, but they are not a substitute for understanding how sensitive data actually moves through the business.

The real concern with Purview is not whether it can enforce DLP. It can.

The concern is how much configuration is required to get meaningful success and how the organization defines that success.

A Purview DLP implementation may technically be complete because policies are enabled, but operationally immature because alerts are noisy, exceptions are unmanaged, labels are inconsistent, and business owners are not involved.

What Must Be Purchased or Licensed

Microsoft Purview licensing can be confusing because capabilities vary significantly across Microsoft commercial, government, and regulated cloud environments. Many discussions focus primarily on Microsoft 365 E3 and E5 licensing, but government and highly regulated organizations may instead operate within GCC, GCC High, or DoD environments using G3 and G5 licensing models. Feature availability, retention options, Insider Risk Management capabilities, eDiscovery functionality, AI governance controls, and integration support may differ across these environments and should be validated carefully during planning and deployment.

In practical terms, Microsoft 365 E3-level licensing can provide useful baseline DLP functionality for core Microsoft 365 workloads such as Exchange Online, SharePoint Online, and OneDrive for Business. Many organizations already own some meaningful DLP capability without realizing it.

However, more advanced DLP, governance, and insider risk use cases typically require Microsoft 365 E5, Microsoft Purview Suite licensing, or targeted Purview add-ons.

The practical distinction is usually this: Microsoft 365 E3, G3, or equivalent baseline licensing generally supports core DLP capabilities for Exchange Online, SharePoint Online, and OneDrive for Business. Microsoft 365 E5, G5, Purview Suite licensing, or additional Purview add-ons are often required for more advanced capabilities such as Teams chat DLP, Endpoint DLP, advanced Information Protection, Insider Risk Management, advanced eDiscovery, Advanced Audit, data lifecycle governance, adaptive protection, AI governance, and compliance workflows.

For smaller and midsize organizations, Microsoft 365 Business Premium may provide useful foundational security and compliance controls, but many advanced Purview capabilities still require additional licensing or business-focused Purview packages.

The important lesson is that "we own Microsoft 365" is not enough information.

Organizations should validate which Microsoft 365 licensing tier is deployed, which Purview capabilities are actually enabled, which users are licensed for those controls, which workloads are covered, whether government cloud limitations apply, and whether AI governance features are supported in the organization's environment.

Licensing assumptions frequently create gaps between expected security capabilities and the controls actually operating in production.

Practical Buying Guidance

Before assuming Purview DLP is "already owned," the organization should validate whether users are licensed for Microsoft 365 E3, E5, Business Premium, Frontline, Government, or Education equivalents; whether the required DLP use case is core Microsoft 365 DLP or advanced DLP; whether endpoint DLP is required; whether Teams chat DLP is required; whether Insider Risk Management is required; whether Defender for Cloud Apps integration is required; whether advanced audit, eDiscovery, or communication compliance features are part of the desired workflow; and whether all users benefiting from the service are properly licensed.

This last point is easy to overlook. Some Microsoft services technically expose features in a portal even when the licensing model is more nuanced. A visible button should never be treated as proof that the organization is properly licensed.

Implementation Warning

Purview is often marketed as part of the Microsoft ecosystem, which can create the impression that deployment is straightforward. In reality, successful Purview DLP requires architecture.

The organization needs to decide which data types matter most, which labels are authoritative, which repositories are in scope, which users and groups are in scope, which policies run in audit mode first, which policies warn users, which policies allow override, which policies block without override, who reviews alerts, who approves exceptions, how exceptions expire, and what success looks like.

Without those decisions, Purview can easily become a technically enabled but operationally noisy control.

The goal should not be to turn on every policy available. The goal should be to reduce risky data movement in measurable ways.

Google Workspace DLP

Google Workspace DLP is designed for organizations that live heavily in Gmail, Drive, Docs, Sheets, Slides, and Chat.

Its strength is that it is native to Google collaboration workflows. It can help prevent users from sharing sensitive information externally, exposing regulated data, or mishandling sensitive content inside Google's ecosystem.

Google Workspace DLP is especially useful for cloud-native organizations, education, startups, and companies that use Google Workspace as their primary productivity environment.

Its strengths include native fit for Google Drive and Gmail workflows, external sharing controls, sensitive data detection, admin visibility, investigation through Google security tools, and better user experience inside Google-native workflows.

But it is not enterprise-wide DLP by itself.

It does not control everything happening in Microsoft 365, Box, Slack, Salesforce, GitHub, endpoints, databases, data lakes, or unmanaged SaaS applications. It also depends on the organization's Google Workspace edition and configuration maturity.

Google Workspace DLP is best for protecting sensitive data inside Google's collaboration environment. It should be paired with broader discovery, SaaS visibility, endpoint controls, and DSPM for a more complete program.

What Must Be Purchased or Licensed

Google Workspace DLP availability depends on the Workspace edition.

For many commercial enterprise customers, Google Workspace DLP is available in Enterprise Standard and Enterprise Plus. Depending on the edition and configuration, DLP may apply across Gmail, Drive, and Chat.

This means Google Workspace DLP is not always limited only to the highest enterprise tier. Enterprise Standard may be enough for many DLP use cases, especially where the core requirement is to protect Gmail, Drive, and Chat from accidental or unauthorized sharing of sensitive information.

However, Enterprise Plus may still matter if the organization needs adjacent advanced security, investigation, encryption, compliance, or data governance capabilities.

The distinction is important. An organization may have enough licensing for basic DLP but not enough licensing for the broader security and compliance ecosystem it expects to build around DLP.

Practical Buying Guidance

Before assuming Google Workspace DLP is available, the organization should validate which Google Workspace edition is deployed, whether Gmail DLP, Drive DLP, and Chat DLP are all required, whether Enterprise Standard is sufficient or Enterprise Plus is needed for adjacent controls, whether DLP is needed for education, frontline, enterprise, or essentials users, whether investigation, alerting, audit, and export requirements are covered, and whether Google-only DLP is enough or whether CASB, SSE, endpoint DLP, or DSPM is also needed.

Google Workspace DLP can define sensitive content, scan files or messages, generate alerts, warn users, or block risky activity depending on the use case and configuration.

As with any DLP tool, policies should be tested before broad enforcement. Audit-only or monitor-first rollouts are usually safer than immediate blocking.

Implementation Warning

Google Workspace DLP can be easier to consume than some legacy DLP tools because it is embedded in the admin experience and native to Google collaboration. But it still requires careful design.

The organization needs to decide which organizational units and groups are in scope, which sharing patterns are allowed, which external domains are trusted, which sensitive data detectors should be used, which custom detectors are needed, when to warn versus block, how incidents are reviewed, how false positives are handled, and how DLP integrates with broader investigation processes.

Google Workspace DLP can reduce accidental exposure inside Google, but it should not be mistaken for full enterprise DLP. It is strongest where Google Workspace is the primary collaboration environment.

Box Shield

Box Shield is Box's native security and DLP-oriented control layer for content stored and shared in Box.

Its strength is content-centric protection. Box is often used for legal documents, customer files, regulated documents, contracts, partner collaboration, healthcare files, financial records, and other sensitive content. Shield gives organizations a way to classify content, restrict risky sharing, detect suspicious activity, and apply controls directly inside Box.

Box Shield is useful when organizations need to control external collaboration, public link sharing, downloads of sensitive files, classification-based access, suspicious sessions, anomalous downloads, possible insider activity, and content-based policy violations.

It can also integrate with broader security ecosystems, including SIEM and CASB tools, which helps organizations include Box activity in larger investigation workflows.

The limitation is obvious: Box Shield protects Box.

It does not replace Microsoft Purview, Google Workspace DLP, endpoint DLP, network DLP, CASB DLP, or DSPM. It is a strong embedded control for a specific platform.

Box Shield is best for organizations where Box is a major content repository or external collaboration platform.

What Must Be Purchased or Licensed

Box Shield is not the same as simply having a standard Box content collaboration license. It is an additional Box security capability that must be included in the customer's Box package or purchased according to Box's commercial model.

Box Shield provides security controls focused on content classification, access policies, threat detection, anomalous behavior, and data leak prevention within Box.

Box Shield Pro is an additional advanced offering layered on top of Box Shield. It is generally positioned around enhanced AI-powered classification and advanced content threat protection capabilities.

The practical distinction is that a standard Box license should not be assumed to include Box Shield. Box Shield is needed for Box-native security and DLP-style controls. Box Shield Pro may be needed for more advanced AI-powered classification and enhanced protection capabilities.

This means organizations need to validate whether they have Box only as a collaboration platform, Box Shield as a content security control, or Box Shield Pro for more advanced classification and protection capabilities.

Practical Buying Guidance

Before assuming Box has DLP coverage, the organization should validate whether Box Shield is included in the current Box agreement, whether Box Shield Pro is required for AI-powered classification and advanced threat capabilities, whether the organization is on Enterprise Plus, Enterprise Advanced, or another Box plan, whether the required control is classification, access policy, threat detection, ransomware detection, or alerting, whether SIEM, CASB, or SOAR integrations are needed, whether Microsoft sensitivity label interoperability is part of the desired design, and whether Box is a primary sensitive content store or only one repository among many.

Implementation Warning

Box Shield can be very useful when Box is a major system of record for documents and collaboration. It is less useful if the organization treats it as a general DLP replacement.

The organization still needs to decide which Box folders contain regulated or confidential data, which classification labels should exist, which content should be auto-classified, which users can share externally, which domains are trusted, which downloads should be restricted, which anomalous behaviors should trigger investigation, who owns Box security incidents, and how Box findings connect to broader DSPM and DLP workflows.

Box Shield is strongest when the organization has clear ownership of Box content and knows which collaboration patterns are acceptable.

Other Native Controls

Many other platforms now include DLP-like or data protection capabilities.

Examples include Salesforce Shield, GitHub secret scanning, AWS Macie, Snowflake governance capabilities, Slack enterprise controls, ServiceNow data controls, CASB DLP, SSE DLP, and cloud-native security features.

These controls are valuable because they understand the platform they live in.

They are limited because they usually do not understand the entire data estate.

That is the pattern with embedded DLP:

Native context is good.

Enterprise-wide context is still missing.

What Must Be Purchased or Licensed

For other native controls, licensing varies significantly by platform. In many cases, the data protection feature is tied to an enterprise tier, advanced security tier, governance add-on, cloud security module, or consumption-based service.

Organizations should ask five buying questions before relying on native DLP:

- *Is the capability included in the current license, or is it an add-on?*
- *Is it licensed per user, per workload, per repository, per event, or by consumption?*
- *Does it protect only that platform, or does it extend into other platforms?*
- *Does it detect sensitive data, enforce policy, or only generate alerts?*
- *Does it integrate with the organization's SIEM, SOAR, DSPM, ticketing, and identity systems?*

Implementation Warning

Native DLP controls are easy to overestimate.

A platform may provide excellent protection inside its own walls while leaving major gaps elsewhere. Salesforce controls do not protect Box. Box controls do not protect Google Drive. Google DLP does not protect SharePoint. Microsoft Purview does not automatically govern every SaaS application, database, or data lake with equal depth.

This is why tool ownership and control boundaries must be explicit.

Licensing Reality Check

A useful way to summarize embedded DLP licensing is this:

Platform	Baseline DLP Availability	Advanced Capabilities Usually Require	Key Buying Warning
Microsoft Purview	Core DLP for Exchange Online, SharePoint Online, and OneDrive may be available in Microsoft 365 E3/E5, G3/G5, and some other plans	Microsoft 365 *5, Microsoft Purview Suite, or add-ons such as Information Protection and Governance for Endpoint DLP, Teams chat DLP, and advanced Purview capabilities	E3 or G3 may provide useful DLP, but E5, G5, or add-ons are often needed for the controls buyers assume they are getting
Google Workspace DLP	Available in supported editions, commonly including Enterprise Standard and Enterprise Plus	Enterprise Plus may be needed for adjacent advanced security, compliance, encryption, or investigation capabilities	Validate the exact Workspace edition and whether Gmail, Drive, and Chat DLP are all in scope
Box Shield	Requires Box Shield entitlement or appropriate Box package	Box Shield Pro may be required for AI-powered classification and advanced threat capabilities	Standard Box collaboration licensing should not be assumed to include Shield or Shield Pro
Other Native Controls	Varies by platform	Usually enterprise, security, governance, or consumption-based add-ons	Native controls are usually platform-specific and should not be treated as enterprise-wide DLP

The Licensing Trap

One of the easiest mistakes in DLP modernization is assuming that because a feature exists in a platform, the organization owns it, is licensed to use it, and is prepared to operate it.

Those are three different things.

A feature can be visible but not properly licensed. A feature can be licensed but not configured. A feature can be configured but not tuned. A feature can be tuned but not governed. A feature can be governed but still not reduce meaningful risk.

This is especially important with platforms like Microsoft Purview, where E3 or G3 licensing may provide core DLP capabilities, while E5, G5, or Purview add-ons may be needed for more advanced use cases like endpoint DLP, Teams DLP, insider risk, advanced audit, or broader compliance workflows.

The better buying question is not:

"Do we have DLP?"

The better question is:

"Do we have the specific DLP capability, license, configuration, ownership model, and operational process required for the risk we are trying to reduce?"

That question saves money, avoids disappointment, and keeps DLP tied to business outcomes instead of feature checklists.

11.6 Policy Sprawl and Alert Fatigue

DLP programs often begin with a sincere goal: protect sensitive data.

Then reality happens.

The security team enables broad detection rules. Alerts start flowing. Business users complain. False positives appear. Exceptions are added. More policies are created. Different teams configure different tools. Over time, no one has a clean view of which policies exist, which ones matter, which ones overlap, or which ones are still valid.

This is policy sprawl.

Policy sprawl is one of the most damaging conditions in a DLP program because it quietly destroys trust. Analysts stop trusting alerts. Users stop reading warnings. Business units assume security does not understand their workflows. Leaders see dashboards filled with activity but not meaningful risk reduction.

Common signs of DLP policy sprawl include too many policies with unclear ownership, duplicate policies across tools, policies created in response to one incident and never reviewed again, exceptions without expiration dates, inconsistent enforcement across platforms, overlapping alerts from multiple tools, no mapping between policies and business objectives, no retirement process for stale policies, and no defined owner for policy tuning.

Alert fatigue follows close behind.

A DLP program suffering from alert fatigue often has analysts ignoring low-severity alerts, users overriding warnings without reading them, repeated violations from the same departments, and no meaningful remediation workflow.

The organization may be generating thousands of DLP alerts while reducing very little actual risk.

The answer is not always more tuning. Sometimes the answer is fewer, better policies.

Every DLP policy should be able to answer:

- *What data are we protecting?*
- *Why does this data matter?*
- *Which business process uses it?*
- *Who owns it?*
- *Which movement is allowed?*
- *Which movement is risky?*
- *What action should occur?*
- *Who reviews the alert?*
- *What happens after review?*
- *When should this policy be revised or retired?*

If those questions cannot be answered, the policy probably needs to be redesigned.

11.7 Why Classification Without Context Breaks DLP

The future of DLP depends less on isolated pattern matching and more on contextual understanding driven by DSPM, identity awareness, repository sensitivity, behavioral analysis, and governance intelligence.

Classification is necessary, but classification alone is not enough.

A label can tell a system what something is supposed to be. Context tells the system whether the current action is risky.

A document labeled "Confidential" may be safely shared with outside counsel, but not with a personal email account. A spreadsheet containing employee compensation data may be appropriate in an HR-restricted workspace, but not in a public Teams channel. A customer export may be acceptable in a sanctioned analytics platform, but not in a user's downloads folder.

The same data can be acceptable in one situation and dangerous in another.

Classification-only DLP asks whether the file contains sensitive data, what label is applied, and whether the policy allows or blocks the action.

Context-aware DLP asks who is taking the action, what their role is, whether they normally access this data, whether the device is managed, whether the destination is approved, whether the recipient is trusted, whether the file is business-critical, whether the data is regulated, whether the volume is normal, whether the activity is part of an approved workflow, whether the repository is already overexposed, and whether the user has shown risky behavior recently.

This is where DSPM changes the model.

DSPM helps reveal where sensitive data lives, who has access, how exposed it is, whether it is properly classified, whether it is duplicated, whether it is stale, whether it is externally shared, and whether the current location aligns with business expectations.

DLP without DSPM sees sensitive data.

DLP with DSPM sees sensitive data in context.

That context is what turns DLP from a noisy detection tool into a targeted enforcement mechanism.

11.8 Where DLP Still Provides Real Control

Despite its limitations, DLP still provides meaningful value when deployed thoughtfully and connected to broader governance, identity, and data-security programs.

DLP is most effective when used to control sensitive data movement, shape user behavior, enforce regulatory handling requirements, generate operational and compliance evidence, and reduce inappropriate data exposure.

The goal is not to stop every possible data movement event. The goal is to reduce meaningful business risk while maintaining operational usability.

Egress Control

One of the clearest and most effective DLP use cases remains controlling sensitive data leaving a managed environment.

Examples include blocking customer records from being uploaded to personal cloud storage, preventing regulated data from being emailed to unauthorized recipients, restricting public sharing of confidential documents, stopping sensitive files from being copied to USB devices, preventing bulk downloads from sensitive repositories, blocking uploads to unsanctioned SaaS applications, and warning users before data is pasted into public AI tools.

Egress control works well because the risk is relatively understandable: sensitive data is moving somewhere it should not go.

Modern DLP platforms increasingly extend this capability into SaaS platforms, endpoints, browsers, AI workflows, collaboration tools, and cloud environments.

User Behavior Control

DLP can also help shape user behavior.

Not every event requires immediate blocking. In many cases, the better response may be a warning, a policy reminder, a business justification requirement, a notification to a data owner, enhanced monitoring, or manager escalation.

For example, a first-time policy violation may generate a warning. A repeat offender may trigger manager notification. A privileged user may receive additional monitoring. A departing employee downloading large volumes of data may trigger escalation. A user sending regulated data externally may be required to provide a business justification.

This is where DLP increasingly overlaps with Insider Risk Management, User and Entity Behavior Analytics, and broader governance programs.

Behavioral context matters because accidental activity, negligent behavior, and intentional misuse often look very different over time.

Regulatory Enforcement

DLP can also support regulatory and contractual enforcement requirements.

Examples include preventing PCI data from being emailed externally, restricting PHI sharing outside approved healthcare workflows, preventing employee tax documents from being stored in public locations, blocking customer personal data uploads into unmanaged SaaS platforms, restricting export-controlled documents from unauthorized geographic sharing, and applying retention or handling rules to regulated information.

DLP should not be confused with the compliance program itself, but it can serve as an important technical enforcement and evidence layer within broader governance initiatives.

DLP Works Both Directions

Many organizations think of DLP primarily as an outbound control designed to prevent employees from emailing, uploading, copying, or exfiltrating sensitive data.

Modern DLP programs increasingly need to address inbound data exposure as well.

Customers, partners, vendors, and external users frequently upload sensitive information into systems that were never designed to store confidential or regulated data.

Examples include customers uploading medical records into support portals, users attaching tax documents to helpdesk tickets, clients submitting payment card data through unsecured forms, sensitive legal documents uploaded into collaboration platforms, regulated information pasted into chatbot interfaces, and source code or credentials submitted through public intake workflows.

In many cases, the user is not acting maliciously. They may simply believe they are providing the information necessary to complete a task quickly.

This creates both security and governance challenges.

Organizations may unintentionally store regulated data in unmanaged systems, expand compliance scope unexpectedly, retain sensitive data without appropriate governance controls, expose confidential information to unnecessary users, increase regulatory and breach risk, or feed sensitive data into AI workflows unintentionally.

Modern DLP and tracing technologies can help reduce this risk by blocking inappropriate uploads, quarantining risky attachments, warning users before submission, redirecting users to approved secure workflows, masking sensitive content, and applying classification and governance controls at ingestion time.

Examples include blocking payment card uploads into non-PCI systems, preventing PHI uploads into general support environments, warning users before sensitive information is pasted into AI tools, redirecting users toward approved secure upload portals, and automatically quarantining risky submissions.

This is another reason context matters.

Effective inbound DLP requires organizations to understand not only what the data is, but whether the destination system is appropriate for storing, processing, governing, or exposing that type of information.

Control Evidence

DLP also creates operational evidence.

Those records can support audits, investigations, legal review, incident response, privacy inquiries, compliance reporting, executive reporting, and board-level governance metrics.

Useful DLP evidence may include policy matches, blocked actions, allowed actions, user overrides, business justifications, alert history, repeat activity, destination details, file details, user details, and remediation actions.

In a mature program, DLP evidence should not simply prove that alerts occurred.

It should demonstrate whether risk is actually decreasing, whether behavior is improving, whether governance controls are effective, and whether sensitive data exposure is being reduced over time.

11.9 DLP Policy Exception Governance

DLP exceptions are sometimes necessary.

A business may need to share regulated data with an approved partner. A legal team may need to transfer confidential documents to outside counsel. A finance team may need to send tax files through a controlled workflow. A support team may need to receive sensitive customer documentation. A developer may need temporary access to troubleshoot a production issue.

The problem is not that exceptions exist.

The problem is when exceptions become invisible, permanent, poorly documented, or disconnected from risk ownership.

CISOs do not just need DLP controls. They need a way to manage business exceptions without losing accountability.

A mature DLP exception process should answer several questions:

- *Who is requesting the exception?*
- *What data is involved?*
- *Why is the exception needed?*
- *Which business process does it support?*
- *Who owns the data?*
- *Who owns the risk?*
- *What compensating controls are required?*
- *How long should the exception last?*
- *Who approved it?*

- *When will it be reviewed?*
- *What evidence proves the exception is still appropriate?*

Every DLP exception should have a named owner, business justification, expiration date, compensating control, approval record, and review cadence.

Exceptions should not be open-ended unless there is a formally approved business requirement and recurring governance review.

Examples of compensating controls may include limiting the exception to specific users, approved domains, managed devices, encrypted channels, named repositories, specific file types, defined business workflows, or monitored transfer methods. In some cases, the right answer is not a DLP exception at all. The better answer may be to create an approved secure transfer process, provision a partner workspace, improve labeling, implement encryption, use a managed file exchange platform, or redesign the workflow.

Exception governance should also distinguish between temporary exceptions and durable business requirements.

A temporary exception may be appropriate for a time-limited project, investigation, migration, audit, legal matter, or incident response need. A durable requirement may indicate that the business process itself needs an approved secure design rather than repeated exceptions.

A simple exception lifecycle should include:

Step	Purpose
Request	Capture who needs the exception, what data is involved, and why it is needed
Review	Evaluate sensitivity, destination, user role, business purpose, regulatory obligations, and available alternatives
Approval	Require approval from the appropriate data owner, business owner, security, privacy, legal, or compliance stakeholder
Compensating Controls	Define controls such as encryption, approved recipient domains, monitoring, limited scope, or managed transfer methods
Expiration	Set a clear end date or review date
Monitoring	Track usage, overrides, repeat activity, and unusual behavior
Recertification	Confirm the exception is still needed and still aligned with business purpose
Retirement	Remove exceptions that are no longer justified

DLP exception governance should be reviewed regularly by security, privacy, legal, compliance, IT, and affected business owners. This does not need to become a heavy committee process, but it does need ownership.

Unmanaged exceptions are one of the fastest ways for a DLP program to lose credibility.

A policy full of permanent exceptions is not a policy. It is a memory of what the organization once intended to protect.

11.10 How DSPM Should Inform DLP Policies

DLP should not drive the data security strategy.

DSPM should inform where DLP is needed.

Traditional DLP starts with policies and looks for violations. DSPM starts with the data estate and identifies where risk actually exists.

That is a major shift.

The older model looks like this:

- Create DLP policy.
- Detect sensitive data movement.
- Generate alert.
- Investigate event.
- Tune policy.

A better model looks like this:

- Discover sensitive data.
- Classify and enrich it with context.
- Identify exposure and access risk.
- Prioritize business-critical data.
- Map legitimate workflows.
- Create focused DLP policies.
- Monitor outcomes.
- Tune based on risk reduction.

DSPM should help answer the questions DLP cannot answer by itself:

- *Where does sensitive data actually live?*
- *Which repositories are overexposed?*
- *Who has excessive access?*
- *Where is regulated data outside approved locations?*
- *Which data stores are externally shared?*
- *Which files are unlabeled or mislabeled?*
- *Which data is stale and should be deleted?*
- *Which users have unusual access or behavior?*
- *Which business processes require legitimate sharing?*
- *Which data movement creates the most real risk?*

Once those answers are known, DLP can be applied with more precision.

For example, instead of creating a global policy that alerts on every file containing PII, an organization might use DSPM findings to create a focused policy around customer records stored in overexposed SharePoint sites, downloaded by users outside the customer operations team, or shared with external domains.

That is a better policy.

It is more specific. It is more defensible. It is easier to tune. It is more likely to reduce real risk.

DSPM can also help reduce false positives by giving DLP better context.

A file with one employee ID in a restricted HR folder may not need the same treatment as a spreadsheet with 50,000 employee records in a public collaboration site. A customer export in a sanctioned analytics workspace may be normal. The same export in a personal OneDrive folder may be risky.

DLP sees the pattern.

DSPM helps explain the risk.

11.11 Common DLP Failure Patterns

Most DLP failures are predictable.

Starting Too Broad

The organization enables too many sensitive information types across too many locations and too many users.

The result is an alert flood.

A better approach is to start with a small number of high-risk data types, high-risk repositories, high-risk user groups, and high-risk egress channels.

Blocking Before Monitoring

The organization moves directly to enforcement without understanding business impact.

The result is disruption, complaints, emergency exceptions, and loss of trust.

A better approach is to start in monitor or simulation mode, study the impact, tune the policy, communicate with users, and then gradually increase enforcement.

Treating All Sensitive Data the Same

The organization applies the same policy to every sensitive data match.

The result is poor prioritization.

A better approach is to combine sensitivity with location, volume, owner, access, exposure, user role, destination, and business context.

No Business Ownership

Security owns every DLP decision, even though business units own the processes.

The result is conflict.

A better approach is to assign data owners and business process owners who can help define appropriate use, approved sharing paths, exception rules, and escalation requirements.

Permanent Exceptions

Exceptions are approved once and never reviewed.

The result is policy erosion.

A better approach is to require every exception to have an owner, business justification, expiration date, compensating control, and review cycle.

No Feedback Loop

The DLP team reviews alerts but does not improve classification, access, retention, training, or data architecture.

The result is the same alerts forever.

A better approach is to treat DLP events as signals. Repeated alerts may indicate that data is in the wrong place, access is too broad, a workflow is broken, a policy is poorly designed, or users need a safer approved process.

Tool Overlap Without Rationalization

Microsoft, Google, Box, CASB, endpoint DLP, email security, and SSE tools may all inspect similar data using different policies.

The result is duplicate alerts, inconsistent enforcement, and user confusion.

A better approach is to define which platform owns which control point.

11.12 How to Rationalize or Modernize an Existing DLP Program

Modernizing DLP does not always mean replacing the tool. Sometimes the best move is to simplify the program, improve context, and clarify control ownership.

Step 1: Inventory the Current DLP Estate

Start by documenting every DLP-like capability currently in use.

This may include endpoint DLP, email DLP, network DLP, CASB or SSE DLP, Microsoft Purview DLP, Google Workspace DLP, Box Shield, cloud provider controls, SaaS-native controls, data discovery tools, classification tools, DSPM platforms, and SIEM or SOAR integrations.

For each capability, document who owns it, what it covers, what policies exist, what data types are monitored, what actions are enforced, how many alerts are generated, how exceptions are handled, which business units are affected, what integrations exist, what gaps remain, and what the licensing costs.

Many organizations discover they have more DLP than they realized.

Step 2: Map Policies to Control Objectives

Every DLP policy should map to a clear business, regulatory, or security objective.

Examples include preventing PCI data from leaving approved payment workflows, preventing PHI from being shared externally without authorization, preventing source code from being uploaded to unmanaged SaaS, preventing confidential board documents from being publicly shared, detecting bulk download of customer records, and requiring justification for external sharing of sensitive files.

If a policy cannot be mapped to a clear objective, it should be reviewed, merged, or retired.

Step 3: Identify Duplicate and Conflicting Policies

Look for overlap.

For example, Microsoft Purview and an email gateway may both inspect outbound email. A CASB and Box Shield may both alert on Box external sharing. Endpoint DLP and SSE may both block uploads to personal cloud storage. Google Workspace DLP and a CASB may both alert on Drive sharing.

Overlap is not always bad, but unmanaged overlap creates noise.

The organization should decide which tool is authoritative for each control point.

Step 4: Reduce Policy Count

A mature DLP program usually has fewer policies than people expect.

Instead of creating a unique policy for every business exception, organize policies around data category, risk tier, user population, destination type, regulatory requirement, business process, and control action.

Fewer policies are easier to test, explain, tune, govern, and defend.

Step 5: Use Risk-Based Enforcement

Not every event should be blocked.

A practical enforcement ladder might look like this:

- Monitor
- Notify
- Coach with policy tip
- Require business justification
- Notify data owner
- Block with override
- Block without override
- Quarantine
- Escalate to insider risk or incident response

The enforcement action should become stronger as risk increases.

For example, one employee ID in an internal HR process may only require monitoring. A spreadsheet containing thousands of employee records sent externally may require blocking. A customer database export uploaded to personal cloud storage may require blocking and escalation. A departing employee downloading large volumes of sensitive data may require insider risk review.

Step 6: Use DSPM to Target the Highest-Risk Areas

Use DSPM findings to decide where DLP should focus first.

Priority areas may include overexposed sensitive repositories, externally shared regulated data, sensitive data in unmanaged locations, high-risk departments, privileged users, dormant but accessible data, public cloud storage exposure, shadow data stores, AI and analytics workflows, and sensitive data without clear ownership.

This helps the DLP program focus on actual risk instead of theoretical sensitivity.

Step 7: Fix the Data Problem, Not Just the Alert

When the same DLP alert appears repeatedly, the right question is not only, *"How do we tune the alert?"*

The better question is, *"What condition is causing this?"*

Maybe too many users have access. Maybe the data is in the wrong repository. Maybe the file should be deleted. Maybe the workflow needs an approved transfer method. Maybe the label is wrong. Maybe the destination should be sanctioned. Maybe the user needs training. Maybe the policy is too broad.

DLP should trigger improvement, not just tickets.

Step 8: Create DLP Governance

DLP needs governance, but that does not mean it needs bureaucracy.

A lightweight monthly review with security, privacy, legal, compliance, IT, and business data owners can be enough to keep the program healthy.

The group should review top DLP alerts, repeat violations, policy changes, exception requests, false positive trends, high-risk data movement, DSPM findings that require DLP updates, policies that should be retired, user experience issues, and regulatory changes.

The goal is to keep DLP aligned with the business, not frozen in time.

Step 9: Measure Outcomes, Not Alert Volume

Alert volume is a poor measure of success.

A DLP team that generates 20,000 alerts is not automatically doing a good job. It may simply be generating 20,000 interruptions.

Better metrics include reduction in externally shared regulated data, reduction in public sensitive files, reduction in repeat policy violations, reduction in false positives, percentage of exceptions with expiration dates, percentage of high-severity alerts tied to known owners, mean time to review high-risk DLP events, number of risky workflows redesigned, reduction in sensitive data stored in unmanaged locations, and reduction in unauthorized uploads to personal cloud applications.

The goal is not more alerts. The goal is less risk.

11.13 Simple DLP Modernization Roadmap

A DLP modernization effort does not need to begin with a full platform replacement. In many organizations, the better starting point is to stabilize what already exists, reduce noise, improve context, and reconnect DLP to business outcomes.

A simple modernization roadmap can help security leaders move from reactive control management to measurable data risk reduction.

Phase	Focus	Practical Actions
Phase 1: Stabilize	Reduce noise and understand the current state	Inventory DLP tools, policies, alerts, exceptions, owners, control points, and licensing. Identify duplicate policies and high-noise rules.
Phase 2: Prioritize	Focus on the highest-risk data and workflows	Use DSPM, classification, identity, and business context to identify regulated data, externally shared data, high-risk repositories, sensitive exports, and AI-related exposure.
Phase 3: Rationalize	Simplify policies and clarify ownership	Retire stale policies, merge duplicates, define authoritative control points, assign policy owners, and map policies to business or regulatory objectives.
Phase 4: Govern Exceptions	Preserve business flexibility without losing accountability	Require exception owners, business justification, compensating controls, expiration dates, approval records, and review cadence.
Phase 5: Tune Enforcement	Apply the right control at the right moment	Move from broad blocking to risk-based enforcement such as monitor, warn, require justification, notify owner, block with override, block without override, quarantine, or escalate.
Phase 6: Integrate	Connect DLP to the broader data security ecosystem	Integrate DLP with DSPM, IAM, SIEM, SOAR, ITSM, insider risk, data catalog, GRC, and privacy workflows.
Phase 7: Measure	Prove risk reduction	Track reduction in risky data movement, repeat violations, false positives, unmanaged exceptions, public sensitive files, unauthorized uploads, and time to review high-risk events.
Phase 8: Optimize	Improve the business process, not just the policy	Use repeated DLP findings to improve data architecture, approved workflows, user guidance, labeling, access governance, and secure collaboration paths.

The most important modernization principle is simple:

Do not modernize DLP by adding more rules to an already noisy program.

Modernize DLP by adding context, ownership, governance, and measurable outcomes.

The future of DLP is not bigger policy libraries. It is better decision-making.

11.14 A Practical DLP Maturity Model

Level 1: Reactive DLP

At this level, DLP is noisy and mostly reactive. Policies are broad, alerts are manual, exceptions are ad hoc, and business context is limited.

The goal at Level 1 is stabilization.

Reduce noise. Identify owners. Document existing policies. Stop unmanaged exceptions. Focus on the highest-risk data movement first.

Level 2: Defined DLP

At this level, policies are mapped to known data types, regulations, and business requirements. There is some tuning, some ownership, and a basic exception process.

The goal at Level 2 is structure.

Use simulation before blocking. Define policy intent. Assign owners. Establish review cycles. Start tracking useful metrics.

Level 3: Risk-Based DLP

At this level, DLP is informed by DSPM, classification, access, exposure, and business context. High-risk locations receive stronger controls. Exceptions expire. Alerts route to owners.

The goal at Level 3 is targeted control.

Move from "alert on sensitive data" to "control risky movement of important data."

Level 4: Context-Aware DLP

At this level, DLP policies consider user role, device trust, destination trust, data sensitivity, exposure, volume, behavior, and business process.

DLP integrates with DSPM, IAM, SIEM, SOAR, ITSM, CASB, SSE, and insider risk workflows.

The goal at Level 4 is precision.

Apply the right control at the right moment.

Level 5: Adaptive Data Protection

At this level, DLP becomes part of an adaptive data security operating model. Discovery is continuous, policies are dynamically adjusted, risk scoring is automated, and remediation workflows become more intelligent.

The goal at Level 5 is continuous optimization.

DLP is no longer a standalone program. It is one enforcement layer in a larger data security strategy.

11.15 What Still Matters

DLP still matters for regulated data egress, external sharing control, endpoint data movement, cloud collaboration guardrails, user coaching, business justification capture, audit evidence, high-risk user behavior, regulatory enforcement, reducing accidental exposure, and inbound protection against inappropriate sensitive data submissions.

These are real use cases. They are not going away.

Organizations still need ways to prevent sensitive data from being emailed externally, uploaded to personal cloud drives, shared publicly, copied to USB, moved into unauthorized tools, or submitted into systems not designed to store confidential information.

DLP can help with that.

But only when the policies are focused and context-aware.

11.16 What Matters Less Than People Think

DLP is less useful as a standalone data security strategy, a complete insider threat program, a replacement for DSPM, a replacement for access governance, a replacement for encryption, a replacement for retention and deletion, a universal SaaS control, a reliable classification engine by itself, a way to compensate for poor data architecture, or a "set it and forget it" compliance tool.

This is where many programs go wrong. They expect DLP to solve problems that belong to governance, architecture, identity, data management, legal, privacy, or business process owners.

DLP cannot carry all of that weight.

11.17 The Real Future of DLP

The future of DLP is not more rules.

The future of DLP is better context.

The old model was built around broad detection and broad enforcement. Find sensitive data. Block movement. Generate alerts. Tune later.

That model created too much noise.

The modern model needs to be more intelligent:

Discover the data. Understand the sensitivity. Understand the owner. Understand the access. Understand the exposure. Understand the business workflow. Understand the destination. Understand the user behavior. Then enforce.

This is why DSPM matters.

DSPM helps answer the questions that DLP was never designed to answer by itself. It shows where sensitive data lives, who has access, whether the access is appropriate, whether the data is exposed, whether it is mislabeled, whether it is duplicated, whether it is stale, and whether it is sitting in a risky location.

With that context, DLP policies become sharper.

Instead of blocking everything, the organization can block what matters. Instead of alerting on every match, it can prioritize real risk. Instead of creating endless exceptions, it can redesign broken workflows. Instead of treating DLP as the strategy, it can treat DLP as enforcement.

That is the shift.

DLP should enforce the decision.

DSPM should help determine what the decision should be.

Key Takeaways

DLP is not dead.

Bad DLP is dead.

The old model of broad policies, brittle detection, noisy alerts, unmanaged exceptions, and security-owned enforcement is no longer good enough. Modern DLP must be targeted, governed, measurable, and informed by data context.

Tools like Microsoft Purview, Google Workspace DLP, and Box Shield can provide meaningful embedded controls, but they are not magic. They require significant setup, thoughtful configuration, policy tuning, business participation, proper licensing, and ongoing governance.

A powerful platform can still fail if the organization has weak classification, unclear ownership, excessive access, unmanaged exceptions, and no definition of success.

Licensing also matters. Microsoft 365 E3 and G3 may provide some useful baseline DLP capabilities, but E5, G5, or Purview add-ons may be needed for endpoint DLP, Teams DLP, insider risk, advanced audit, and deeper compliance workflows. Google Workspace DLP depends on the Workspace edition and the services in scope. Box Shield and Box Shield Pro require the right Box security entitlements and should not be assumed to come with standard content collaboration licensing.

DLP also works in both directions. It can help prevent sensitive data from leaving approved environments, and it can help prevent customers, partners, vendors, and users from uploading sensitive data into systems that were never designed to store or govern it.

CISOs do not just need DLP controls. They need DLP governance. That means policies must have owners, exceptions must have business justification and expiration dates, and DLP evidence must show whether risk is actually decreasing.

The goal is not to build the biggest DLP program.

The goal is to reduce risky data movement without breaking the business.

That requires fewer, better policies. It requires context from DSPM. It requires clear ownership. It requires exception governance. It requires a practical understanding of where DLP works, where it does not, what must be licensed, and what must be operationalized.

DLP still matters. But it matters most when it knows its place.

Chapter 12: Identity, Access, and the Real Data Attack Surface

Identity is easy to treat as someone else's problem.

The identity team owns the directory. The cloud team owns IAM roles. The SaaS owners manage their own permissions. The security team watches alerts. The data team knows where important information lives. Legal and compliance care about who should have access. Procurement knows which vendors were approved. Human resources knows who joined, moved, or left.

That division of responsibility makes sense on an org chart.

It does not make sense to sensitive data.

Data does not care which team created the permission. It does not care whether access came from a direct assignment, a nested group, an OAuth grant, a service account, a SaaS integration, a shared link, a contractor account, a cloud workload role, or an AI system inheriting permissions from a user or service account.

If the path exists, the exposure exists.

This is why identity deserves its own chapter in any serious conversation about Data Security Posture Management. DSPM can discover sensitive data, classify it, identify exposures, and help prioritize remediation. But without identity depth, DSPM stops too early. It tells you where risk may exist, but not enough about who or what can act on that risk.

The real question is not just:

Where is our sensitive data?

The better question is:

Who and what can reach this data, under what conditions, with what level of privilege, and does that access still make business sense?

That is the identity layer of DSPM.

This framing is also important for adoption. Many organizations already fund identity governance, access reviews, privileged access management, conditional access, and zero trust initiatives. DSPM becomes easier to justify when it is positioned as an extension of those programs. Identity teams already know access matters. DSPM helps show which access matters most because it connects identity decisions to sensitive data risk.

12.1 Identity Is the Control Plane for Data Risk

Most organizations have spent years improving authentication. They implemented single sign-on, multifactor authentication, conditional access, privileged access management, and identity governance workflows. Those controls matter. Strong authentication reduces the likelihood that an attacker can impersonate a legitimate user or gain unauthorized access through stolen credentials.

But authentication only answers part of the problem.

It answers the question:

Is this identity allowed to sign in?

Modern data security requires a second question:

After sign-in, what can this identity actually do?

An employee with strong MFA may still have excessive access. A contractor may retain access long after a project ends. A service account may have broader permissions than the team that created it realizes. A SaaS application may hold delegated access to files no human has reviewed in years. A machine identity may move data between systems continuously without ever appearing in a traditional user access review. An AI assistant may inherit a user's access and summarize sensitive content from repositories that were never intended for that use.

Identity has become the control plane for data exposure.

In modern environments, identity is no longer limited to employees. It includes employees, contractors, vendors, partners, customers, service accounts, APIs, applications, workloads, cloud services, devices, robotic process automation systems, AI assistants and copilots, autonomous agents and agentic AI workflows, and machine identities operating across distributed environments.

Every one of these identities can become a path to sensitive data.

As organizations adopt AI-enabled workflows, the definition of identity continues to expand beyond human users. AI systems may retrieve data, summarize information, trigger actions, access APIs, orchestrate workflows, interact with other systems, and make operational decisions using permissions delegated by the organization.

In many environments, AI systems effectively operate as highly privileged machine identities.

This creates important governance and security questions:

- *What data can the AI access?*
- *What actions can it perform?*
- *What repositories can it search?*
- *What systems can it interact with?*
- *What prompts or workflows are logged?*
- *What outputs are retained?*
- *Can the AI expose regulated or confidential information?*
- *Can the AI operate beyond its intended purpose?*
- *Who owns accountability for AI-driven actions?*

These are no longer hypothetical concerns. As AI adoption accelerates, organizations increasingly grant AI systems broad access to collaboration platforms, document repositories, messaging systems, ticketing environments, analytics platforms, code repositories, and business workflows. In many cases, the AI inherits the access rights of the user, service account, connector, or application identity connected to it. That inherited permission model can unintentionally amplify existing overpermissioning problems.

This is why identity governance can no longer focus solely on human users.

Modern identity governance must address human identities, non-human identities, delegated access, service-to-service trust, SaaS integrations, API permissions, automation workflows, AI-connected systems, and machine-driven decision paths.

Identity is no longer just an authentication problem.

It is a data-governance problem.

That is why DSPM should not treat identity as a simple enrichment field attached to a finding. Identity is part of the data attack surface itself.

12.2 The Data Attack Surface Is Also an Identity Attack Surface

The phrase "data attack surface" often brings to mind exposed storage buckets, public shares, unencrypted databases, unmanaged repositories, and sensitive data copied into the wrong place. Those are important. But many data exposures are not caused by a missing firewall rule or a public internet setting.

They are caused by legitimate access that no longer makes sense.

A folder may not be public, but it may be accessible to a group that contains nearly the whole company. A database may not be internet facing, but a service principal may have read and export rights. A file may not be directly shared externally, but an approved SaaS app may have permission to read it through an API. A cloud bucket may not allow anonymous access, but a workload role may allow broad access across accounts or subscriptions. A copilot may not create new permissions, but it may make existing overexposure searchable, summarizable, and usable at scale.

From the data's perspective, these are exposure paths.

This is a shift in thinking. Traditional security teams often separate identity, cloud posture, SaaS posture, endpoint security, and data security into different programs. Attackers do not. AI systems do not. Business workflows do not. They chain these systems together.

An attacker may compromise an identity, enumerate accessible data, find overpermissive groups, abuse an app grant, use a stale token, pivot through a service account, or pull data through an approved integration. A user may connect an AI tool to a repository and unintentionally expose everything that identity can read. A business unit may deploy a workflow automation tool that inherits broad access from a service account. The exposure may look like normal access until someone asks whether that access should have existed in the first place.

DSPM becomes stronger when it can connect sensitive data to identity reality.

12.3 Effective Access: The Question Beneath the Question

Access reviews often ask, *"Who has access?"*

That sounds simple.

It is not.

In most organizations, access is layered. A person may have direct access to a repository, inherited access through a group, additional access through a nested group, temporary access through a privileged role, standing access through an admin assignment, indirect access through a SaaS application, data movement access through a service account, and AI-enabled access through a copilot or agent that inherits that user's permissions.

Effective access means the access that actually exists after all those layers are resolved.

It answers questions such as:

- *Can this identity read the data?*
- *Can it modify, delete, export, share, or administer the data?*
- *Is access direct or inherited?*
- *Did access come from a role, group, link, app, token, policy, or exception?*
- *Is the identity internal, external, privileged, dormant, temporary, or non-human?*
- *Does access require MFA or device compliance?*
- *Is access standing or just in time?*
- *Is access limited by time, network, geography, workload, or approval?*
- *Can the identity grant access to others?*
- *Can the identity move the data somewhere else?*
- *Can an AI tool inherit or use this access to summarize, retrieve, or expose the data?*

Effective access is where DSPM starts to become operationally useful. A classification engine can tell you that a file contains regulated data. An identity-aware DSPM capability can tell you that the file is accessible by a stale contractor group, a vendor-owned guest account, three privileged administrators, a third-party OAuth app with broad read permissions, and an AI assistant that inherits access from overprivileged users.

That changes the conversation from awareness to action.

12.4 Identity Risk Patterns: Data Risk and Control

Identity risk becomes easier to prioritize when it is mapped directly to data risk. The same identity weakness may be tolerable in a low-risk environment and unacceptable when it touches regulated, confidential, business-critical, or AI-accessible data.

Identity Risk Pattern	Data Risk	Practical Control
Broad group access to sensitive repositories	Too many users can read, copy, export, or expose regulated or confidential data	Resolve effective access, reduce group membership, apply least privilege, and assign a data owner
Nested groups hiding	Reviewers approve a parent group without	Expand nested groups during review

external or stale users	seeing risky members deeper in the chain	and require owner approval for sensitive data access
Contractors retaining access after project end	Temporary access becomes persistent exposure	Tie access to contract end dates, sponsor reviews, and automated expiration
Service accounts with excessive access	Non-human identities can read, copy, or move large volumes of sensitive data	Assign owners, reduce scope, rotate credentials, monitor activity, and review access regularly
OAuth apps with broad scopes	Third-party or internal apps may read, export, or synchronize sensitive content	Review app grants, limit scopes, require admin approval, and remove unused apps
SaaS local roles outside central IAM	Users may have sensitive access not visible in the identity provider	Integrate SaaS permission reviews with DSPM and IGA workflows
Standing privileged access	Administrators can access or export sensitive data without approval or time limits	Use PAM, just-in-time access, session monitoring, and privileged access reviews
Dormant identities with sensitive access	Abandoned accounts increase compromise and insider risk	Disable stale identities and remove access to sensitive repositories
Machine identities with long-lived secrets	Tokens, keys, or certificates may allow durable access to sensitive data	Use vaulting, managed identities, rotation, short-lived credentials, and monitoring
AI inherited permissions	AI assistants, copilots, or agents can expose data through permissions granted to users, connectors, or service accounts	Review AI-accessible repositories, reduce excessive permissions, restrict connectors, and monitor AI usage
Shared links or unmanaged collaboration	Sensitive data may be reachable outside intended business boundaries	Restrict external sharing, expire links, require approvals, and monitor downloads
Temporary access without expiration	Short-term business need becomes long-term privilege creep	Require expiration dates, recertification, and automated removal

This table is not a replacement for a full identity governance program. It is a prioritization tool. It helps leaders focus on the identity patterns that create the most meaningful data risk.

12.5 Nested Groups: Where Simple Permissions Go to Hide

Nested groups are one of the most common ways access gets out of hand.

A nested group is a group inside another group. It sounds harmless. It is often convenient. It allows teams to reuse access structures instead of assigning every user individually. But over time, nested groups can create permission chains that no one fully understands.

For example, a finance folder may grant access to "Finance Reporting." That group may include "Finance Contractors." Finance Contractors may include "Quarter End Support." Quarter End Support may include several external identities added for a project two years ago.

On the surface, the folder appears restricted to finance. In reality, the effective access path may include external users, temporary workers, dormant accounts, and people who no longer need the data.

Nested groups create four common problems.

First, they create hidden inheritance. Access looks appropriate at the top level, but risky identities appear deeper in the chain.

Second, they create ownership confusion. No one knows who owns the parent group, child group, or business approval.

Third, they create review fatigue. Access reviewers approve familiar group names without seeing the actual members.

Fourth, they create privilege accumulation. Users collect access as they move roles, join projects, or inherit group-based permissions that are never removed.

A mature DSPM program should not stop at the visible permission. It should resolve the chain. It should show the business owner, technical owner, group nesting path, member identities, account status, privilege level, and relationship to sensitive data.

The phrase "Finance only" is not enough.

Which finance identities? Which inherited groups? Which external accounts? Which service accounts? Which apps? Which exceptions? Which AI tools inherit access to that content?

That is the difference between apparent access and effective access.

12.6 Service Accounts: Useful, Powerful, and Often Forgotten

Service accounts are created to let systems do work. They run jobs, connect applications, pull reports, sync directories, move files, back up databases, process payments, publish logs, and support automation.

They are necessary.

They are also risky.

A service account often has more access than a normal user because it needs to operate across systems. It may be exempt from MFA. It may use a password, secret, certificate, or token that is rarely rotated. Its owner may be unclear. It may not be tied to a living employee. It may continue working long after the application, project, or vendor relationship has changed.

This creates a quiet form of privilege drift.

The account was created for a legitimate reason. The reason changed. The access remained.

For DSPM, service accounts matter because they frequently sit close to data. They read from databases, write to storage, copy files, generate reports, feed analytics platforms, and move sensitive information between environments. If the service account is overprivileged, stale, shared, or poorly governed, the data it can access inherits that risk.

Service accounts also matter for AI because many AI connectors, indexing jobs, retrieval systems, RAG pipelines, and automation workflows depend on service or application identities. If those identities have excessive access, the AI system may inherit that access and expose sensitive data through search, summarization, or generated output.

A good DSPM identity model should flag service accounts that have access to sensitive or regulated data, broad read/write/export/admin privileges, no clear business or technical owner, no recent activity but retained access, long-lived secrets or credentials, exclusions from normal access policies, shared use across multiple applications or teams, access across production and non-production environments, ability to create/share/replicate/delete data, or no documented purpose.

Service accounts should not be treated as background noise. In many environments, they are among the most powerful identities in the business.

12.7 OAuth App Grants: The Consent Layer No One Reviews Enough

OAuth app grants are a major blind spot in data security.

OAuth is commonly used to let applications access resources without sharing a user's password. That is a good thing. It enables modern SaaS integrations, delegated access, automation, mobile applications, reporting, workflow tools, and identity federation.

The risk is not OAuth itself.

The risk is poorly governed consent.

A user may approve an application that requests permission to read email, access files, manage calendars, read directory information, or act on the user's behalf. In some environments, administrators can grant organization-wide consent. Some applications receive delegated permissions tied to a user. Others receive application permissions that allow the app to operate independently of a user session.

For data security, this matters a great deal.

A user may lose access to a file when they change roles, but an application grant may continue to provide access through an API. A file may not be directly shared externally, but an integration may read it, index it, summarize it, export it, or copy it into another platform. A SaaS application may be approved for one business purpose, then quietly accumulate access to more data over time.

OAuth app grants also create AI inherited permission risk. Many AI tools and productivity assistants rely on connectors, app grants, plugins, or integrations. If those grants are broad, the AI-enabled tool may access much more data than the business intended.

DSPM should understand OAuth and app permissions because they answer an uncomfortable question:

What can access sensitive data besides people?

High-risk OAuth and SaaS app patterns include broad scopes such as read all files, read all mail, or directory-wide access; applications with organization-wide consent but unclear business ownership; apps approved by users without security review; apps with access to sensitive repositories but no current usage; apps created by unknown or unverified publishers; apps with long-lived refresh tokens; apps that can export, sync, or replicate data; apps connected to departed users or stale admin accounts; apps that bridge corporate data into unmanaged environments; and apps with permissions that exceed their stated purpose.

A mature DSPM program should help security teams see not just user access, but application access. It should correlate app grants with sensitive data, data movement, user behavior, AI usage, and business purpose.

The question is simple:

Would we still approve this app if we knew exactly which sensitive data it could touch?

12.8 SaaS Permissions: The New Enterprise File System

For many organizations, the most sensitive data no longer lives only in traditional databases or file shares. It lives in SaaS platforms.

Customer records live in CRM systems. Contracts live in document platforms. Support tickets contain personal information, screenshots, logs, credentials, and customer history. Engineering workspaces contain source code, secrets, architecture diagrams, and incident notes. Collaboration platforms contain discussions, attachments, decisions, and files. Data warehouses contain extracts from everything.

SaaS permissions are now part of the data security perimeter.

The challenge is that each SaaS platform has its own permission model. Some use workspaces. Some use projects. Some use channels. Some use folders. Some use object-level permissions. Some have admin roles that bypass normal access controls. Some allow external sharing. Some allow app marketplace integrations. Some allow data export through APIs. Some use group sync from the identity provider, while others maintain local groups inside the application.

This creates a fragmented access picture.

The identity provider may show that a user has access to the SaaS platform. It may not show which sensitive records, projects, channels, repositories, dashboards, tickets, or exports the user can reach inside the platform.

That distinction matters.

A user's ability to log in to a SaaS application is not the same as their ability to access sensitive data inside that application.

This becomes even more important when SaaS platforms add AI features. An AI assistant embedded inside a SaaS application may inherit the platform's permission model. If the underlying permissions are too broad, the AI feature may make overexposed data easier to discover, summarize, and reuse.

DSPM should help bridge this gap by mapping SaaS permissions to data sensitivity. It should help identify where sensitive information is exposed through local roles, shared workspaces, public links, external collaborators, app integrations, AI connectors, and administrative permissions.

In practice, this means asking:

- *Which SaaS platforms contain sensitive data?*
- *Which identities can access that data inside each platform?*
- *Which permissions are local to the SaaS app and not visible in the identity provider?*
- *Which SaaS apps can export or sync data elsewhere?*
- *Which marketplace apps or integrations have access?*
- *Which AI features or copilots can search, summarize, or process the data?*
- *Which admins can bypass normal controls?*
- *Which data owners can approve or revoke access?*

SaaS security without data context becomes a list of configuration issues.

DSPM without SaaS identity context becomes an incomplete map.

12.9 Contractors and External Collaborators: The Edges of Trust

Contractors and external collaborators are part of modern work. They help build systems, support customers, conduct audits, manage campaigns, implement tools, provide legal advice, and deliver specialized expertise.

They also create identity complexity.

Contractors may need access quickly. They may work across multiple clients. They may use unmanaged devices. Their accounts may be sponsored by business owners who later move roles. They may be added to groups for convenience. They may retain access after a project ends because no one wants to interrupt business operations.

External collaborators create a similar challenge. A shared folder for a project can become a permanent access path. A guest account can remain active long after the contract expires. A partner workspace can accumulate documents from multiple teams. A vendor may receive access to production data for troubleshooting, then keep that access because the next issue might happen soon.

The issue is not that external access is always wrong. It is that external access should be visible, intentional, time-bound, and proportional to the data involved.

A strong DSPM program should treat external access as a risk dimension. Sensitive data shared with an external party should receive more scrutiny than non-sensitive collaboration content. Access should be tied to purpose, owner, expiration, and review cadence.

Useful controls include sponsored guest ownership, time-limited access, external sharing approvals based on data sensitivity, separate contractor groups with clear naming and ownership, automated expiration for project-based access, reviews focused on sensitive repositories first, strong authentication and device requirements, restrictions on download/copy/sync/forwarding where appropriate, removal tied to contract end date rather than employment status, and alerting when external users access unusual data volumes.

For DSPM, the priority is context. An external collaborator in a low-risk marketing folder is different from an external collaborator in a repository containing regulated personal data, source code, contracts, merger documents, credentials, or customer exports.

That distinction becomes even more important when AI systems can search across collaboration platforms. External access that once looked isolated may become part of a larger exposure pattern if an AI tool can retrieve or summarize content across shared workspaces.

Identity risk is not only about who someone is.

It is about what they can reach.

12.10 Machine Identities and Non-Human Identities

One of the biggest changes in modern security is that non-human identities now outnumber human users in many environments.

Applications talk to applications. Cloud workloads assume roles. Containers pull secrets. Pipelines deploy infrastructure. APIs call other APIs. SaaS platforms sync with data warehouses. Automation scripts collect logs. Bots open tickets. Certificates authenticate services. Tokens authorize access.

These are machine identities and non-human identities. They are essential to digital business. They are also difficult to govern because they do not behave like employees.

They do not complete security training. They do not respond to access review emails. They do not leave the company in a way that triggers HR offboarding. They may not have a manager. They may not have a clear owner. They may authenticate thousands of times a day or only once a quarter. They may be embedded in code, stored in a vault, copied into a pipeline, or forgotten in a configuration file.

From a DSPM perspective, non-human identities deserve special attention because they often enable data movement at scale.

A user may download a few files. A workload identity may replicate an entire database. A user may access one project. A service principal may enumerate every storage account. A developer may view a report. An API token may export customer records every night. An AI indexing service may ingest entire repositories based on the permissions granted to a connector identity.

Non-human identity risk usually appears in one of five forms.

First, excessive privilege. The identity can access more data than its function requires.

Second, weak ownership. No accountable business or technical owner exists.

Third, credential risk. Secrets, keys, certificates, or tokens are long-lived, exposed, unrotated, or stored insecurely.

Fourth, lack of lifecycle management. The identity persists after the workload, vendor, or integration is no longer needed.

Fifth, limited monitoring. Behavior is treated as system noise, even when it touches sensitive data.

DSPM should help make non-human identities visible. It should show which data they can access, what they have accessed, whether access matches purpose, whether an AI workflow inherits their permissions, and whether the identity is governed with the same seriousness as a privileged human account.

12.11 Privileged Access Governance: The Blast Radius Problem

Privileged access deserves special treatment because it changes the blast radius of every data exposure.

Privileged users can often bypass normal controls, change permissions, export large volumes of data, approve access for others, disable protections, view sensitive repositories, create tokens, configure integrations, or alter logs and monitoring settings. In SaaS, cloud, data platforms, and AI-connected environments, privileged access may also allow a user or service to connect new data sources, enable broad indexing, or grant AI systems access to sensitive repositories.

This is why privileged access governance cannot be treated as a routine access review.

Business owners may validate the operational need for access, but privileged access decisions should remain under centralized security and IT governance authority. Administrative access, elevated permissions, cross-environment privileges, bulk export rights, data platform administration, AI connector administration, and sensitive platform configuration rights require stricter oversight because they significantly increase organizational risk.

A clear privileged access governance model should require:

- Defined privileged role categories
- Named business and technical owners
- Security approval for high-risk administrative access
- Just-in-time access where practical
- Time-bound elevation
- Strong authentication and device requirements
- Session logging or monitoring for high-risk activity
- Separation of duties for sensitive workflows
- Review of privileged access to AI-connected repositories
- Approval before privileged roles can grant data access to AI tools or connectors
- Emergency access with after-action review
- Regular recertification and removal of unused privileged access

Privileged access should be treated as a data risk control, not only an infrastructure control.

A privileged identity that can access sensitive data, export repositories, approve broad sharing, or configure AI indexing can create more risk than a normal user account with the same authentication strength.

DSPM can help prioritize privileged access reviews by showing where privileged rights intersect with sensitive data, external sharing, regulated repositories, AI-accessible content, or high-risk data movement.

The key question is not simply:

Who is an administrator?

The better question is:

Which administrators, privileged roles, service accounts, and AI-connected identities can reach sensitive data, change its exposure, or expand who else can use it?

12.12 Just-in-Time Access: Less Standing Privilege, More Intentional Access

Standing privilege is comfortable.

It is also dangerous.

A user who might need access someday often receives access today. Administrators keep persistent rights because outages happen. Developers keep production access because troubleshooting is easier. Contractors keep access because removing and restoring it later feels inefficient.

Just-in-time access offers a better pattern.

Instead of granting permanent access, organizations can require users to request elevated or sensitive access when needed. The request can include business justification, approval, duration, scope, ticket number, and stronger authentication. Access expires automatically after the approved window.

For DSPM, just-in-time access becomes especially powerful when it is tied to data sensitivity.

Access to low-risk operational data may follow normal business workflows. Access to regulated data, intellectual property, sensitive financial records, legal documents, large customer exports, or AI-connected repositories may require stronger approval, shorter duration, session monitoring, or additional controls.

The goal is not to slow the business down.

The goal is to make access intentional.

Good just-in-time programs usually include clear criteria for when JIT is required, sensitive data classification as an input to access policy, approval by a data owner or business owner, time-limited access with automatic removal, strong authentication and device checks, logging of session activity where appropriate, emergency access paths with after-action review, integration with ticketing and change management, and metrics showing reduction in standing privilege.

JIT should not be limited to administrator roles. It should also apply to sensitive data access, bulk export rights, production data access, privileged SaaS roles, cloud data administration, AI connector administration, and high-impact non-human operations.

Least privilege becomes more practical when access can be granted quickly, safely, and temporarily.

12.13 The Identity Graph and the Data Graph

DSPM becomes more useful when it connects two graphs: the identity graph and the data graph.

The data graph shows where sensitive data lives, how it is classified, who owns it, where it moves, how it is protected, and which repositories contain risk.

The identity graph shows users, groups, roles, accounts, apps, machines, service principals, tokens, keys, permissions, ownership, activity, trust relationships, and AI-connected identities.

The real power comes from joining them.

When the graphs are connected, security teams can answer questions that neither graph can answer alone:

- *Which identities can access our most sensitive data?*
- *Which sensitive repositories have excessive group-based access?*
- *Which contractors can access regulated data?*
- *Which external collaborators have access to confidential documents?*
- *Which service accounts can export customer records?*
- *Which OAuth apps can read sensitive files?*
- *Which dormant identities still have access to crown jewel data?*
- *Which privileged users have access they do not use?*
- *Which SaaS admins can bypass normal data controls?*
- *Which machine identities can move sensitive data across environments?*
- *Which AI tools, copilots, agents, or connectors inherit access to sensitive data?*

This is the point where DSPM moves from inventory to intelligence.

A flat list of sensitive files is useful.

A prioritized list of sensitive files with risky effective access is much more useful.

12.14 Toxic Combinations: Where Identity and Data Create Real Risk

Not every access issue deserves the same urgency. Security teams do not have enough time to fix every imperfect permission at once. DSPM should help prioritize the combinations that create real exposure.

A toxic combination is a set of conditions that becomes risky when combined.

Examples include:

- Sensitive data plus external access
- Sensitive data plus public link sharing
- Sensitive data plus broad group access
- Sensitive data plus dormant user access
- Sensitive data plus privileged admin access without JIT
- Sensitive data plus unmanaged device access

- Sensitive data plus unreviewed OAuth app grants
- Sensitive data plus service accounts with no owner
- Sensitive data plus non-human identities with long-lived secrets
- Sensitive data plus ability to export, sync, or share externally
- Sensitive data plus access from users outside the data owner's business function
- Sensitive data plus local SaaS permissions not governed by central IAM
- Sensitive data plus AI inherited permissions
- Sensitive data plus AI connectors with broad repository access
- Sensitive data plus copilots that index stale, overexposed, or ownerless repositories

This is how identity depth improves prioritization.

A folder containing public marketing material and a broad group may not be urgent. A folder containing customer personal data and the same broad group is a different matter. A dormant account with no access is low priority. A dormant account with access to sensitive exports is not. An OAuth app with calendar read access may be acceptable. An OAuth app with access to all files and no owner deserves attention. A copilot connected to well-governed repositories may support productivity. A copilot connected to stale, overexposed, sensitive content may create immediate data risk.

Risk is contextual.

DSPM should make that context visible.

12.15 Identity Lifecycle: Joiner, Mover, Leaver Is Not Enough

Identity governance programs traditionally focus on joiner, mover, and leaver workflows. That is the right starting point.

A new employee joins and receives access. An employee changes roles and their permissions should change. An employee leaves and access should be removed.

The problem is that modern identity risk rarely fits neatly into those three events.

Access changes continuously.

People join projects without formally changing jobs. Contractors extend engagements. Employees support temporary initiatives. Executives gain indirect access through assistants and shared mailboxes. Developers receive emergency access during incidents and retain it afterward. Users approve SaaS integrations. Machine identities are created automatically through orchestration workflows. Vendors receive access outside standard HR processes. Data is copied into new platforms, shared with new groups, or exposed through new AI-enabled workflows.

Modern environments are dynamic, and identity exposure evolves constantly alongside them.

One of the most common sources of excessive access is temporary privilege expansion that never gets reversed.

Organizations frequently grant additional access when an employee covers for someone on leave, a contractor temporarily supports another team, a user assists during an incident or audit, a project requires short-term elevated access, a manager changes roles but retains prior permissions, or an employee is promoted and performs two jobs simultaneously during a transition period.

In many organizations, temporary access quietly becomes permanent because there is no defined expiration date, ownership review, or cleanup process.

Operational convenience often overrides governance discipline.

A common example occurs during promotions or organizational transitions. An employee may retain access associated with their former role while also receiving permissions needed for their new responsibilities. Over time, that user accumulates layered access across departments, repositories, applications, business units, and sensitive data environments.

The organization may view the arrangement as temporary, but temporary access without clear review timelines often becomes long-term privilege accumulation.

There is an old operational reality in identity governance:

Nothing is more permanent than temporary access with no firm end date.

This creates significant risk: excessive data exposure, violations of least privilege, expanded insider risk, segregation-of-duties conflicts, regulatory noncompliance, increased AI overexposure risk, and larger blast radius during account compromise.

AI systems amplify this problem further.

An overprivileged user no longer needs to manually search dozens of repositories to locate sensitive information. AI assistants, copilots, enterprise search tools, and agentic workflows can summarize, correlate, extract, and combine information across all accessible systems within seconds. Access that once seemed operationally tolerable may become dangerous when AI can rapidly aggregate data at scale.

This is why modern identity governance cannot rely solely on periodic access reviews or calendar-based recertification.

A DSPM-aligned identity program should support event-driven access governance.

Useful review triggers include sensitive data discovered in a broadly accessible repository, a data set changing classification level, a user changing departments or managers, a contractor engagement expiring, a temporary project ending, a group receiving access to regulated data, an external collaborator accessing unusual information, a dormant service account remaining active, a new OAuth application receiving high-risk permissions, a machine identity gaining cross-environment access, a user receiving privileged access to a data platform, an AI tool gaining access to a sensitive repository, or a repository becoming externally shared.

Annual access reviews are rarely sufficient for sensitive data environments. By the time a scheduled review occurs, excessive exposure may have existed for months or years.

DSPM helps make identity governance more precise by identifying where review efforts should focus first. By correlating identity roles, repository access, data sensitivity, permission inheritance, group membership, historical access patterns, organizational changes, AI access paths, and behavioral activity, DSPM and identity governance platforms can help organizations identify where privilege accumulation quietly increases long-term data exposure risk.

Identity governance is no longer only about provisioning and deprovisioning accounts.

It is about continuously understanding who, what, and which systems can access sensitive data, and whether that access still makes sense.

12.16 Access Reviews as a Security Control

Access reviews should not be treated as a compliance exercise performed once per year to satisfy an audit requirement.

In mature environments, access reviews function as an active security and governance control designed to continuously validate whether access remains appropriate, justified, and aligned with business need.

The central question is not simply:

Does this user still have access?

The more important question is:

Should this user still have access to this data, for this purpose, under current business conditions?

That distinction matters because access often persists long after the original justification has changed.

Effective access reviews require participation from multiple stakeholders because no single group fully understands both the technical and business implications of access decisions.

At minimum, sensitive data access reviews should involve the data owner, the user's supervisor or manager, the data custodian or IT owner, and security and governance teams where appropriate.

Each party provides different context. The data owner understands business sensitivity and appropriate usage. The manager validates operational necessity. IT understands technical permissions and inherited access paths. Security and governance teams evaluate risk, regulatory obligations, segregation-of-duties concerns, and policy alignment.

Access decisions should not rely solely on technical ownership or historical permissions.

This becomes especially important for privileged access.

While business stakeholders may validate operational need, privileged access decisions should remain under centralized security and IT governance authority. Administrative access, elevated permissions, cross-environment privileges, sensitive platform administration rights, bulk export rights, data platform administration, and AI connector administration require stricter oversight because they significantly increase organizational risk.

Access reviews should also evaluate whether the original business justification still exists, whether temporary access should expire, whether permissions accumulated through prior roles remain necessary, whether AI systems inherit excessive access, whether group membership still aligns to business function, whether dormant or unused access should be removed, and whether AI-connected workflows still align with approved use.

Modern DSPM platforms can improve access reviews by providing visibility into actual data exposure, effective permissions, external sharing, sensitive repositories, behavioral activity, stale or orphaned access, AI-accessible data, and overpermissioned environments.

This allows organizations to prioritize reviews around the highest-risk data rather than reviewing all access equally.

Data Ownership Transfer Matters

Organizations also need formal processes for transferring data ownership when employees leave, change roles, or organizational responsibilities shift.

One of the most common governance failures occurs when sensitive repositories, SaaS platforms, shared drives, analytics environments, AI workflows, or collaboration spaces lose a clearly accountable owner.

Orphaned ownership creates significant risk. No one validates access requests. Sensitive data becomes stale or unmanaged. Retention decisions are ignored. AI-connected repositories remain exposed. Oversharing persists unnoticed. Governance exceptions accumulate without accountability.

Ownership transfer should be treated as part of the identity lifecycle process, not as an afterthought.

When ownership changes, organizations should review repository permissions, external sharing settings, AI integrations, retention requirements, classification accuracy, data minimization requirements, regulatory obligations, and existing governance exceptions.

Data without accountable ownership frequently becomes data without effective governance.

12.17 Ownership: The Missing Link in Remediation

Finding risky access is easier than fixing it.

Remediation requires ownership. Someone needs to know whether access is needed. Someone needs authority to approve removal. Someone needs to understand the business process. Someone needs to accept the risk if access remains.

Many data security findings stall because ownership is unclear.

The identity team can remove access, but they may not know whether the access is legitimate. The security team can flag the risk, but they may not own the business process. The data team may own the platform, but not the users. The application owner may own the tool, but not the content inside it. The business owner may own the data, but not understand the access model.

DSPM should help connect findings to accountable owners.

For identity-related data risk, ownership may include the data owner, business process owner, application owner, system owner, group owner, service account owner, OAuth app owner, contractor sponsor, external collaborator sponsor, cloud account owner, SaaS workspace owner, AI system owner, AI connector owner, and security risk owner.

The best owner is not always the person with administrative access.

It is the person who can decide whether access is appropriate.

Ownership turns a finding into a workflow.

12.18 Practical Identity Controls for DSPM Programs

A mature DSPM program does not replace IAM, IGA, PAM, SaaS security, cloud security, or secrets management. It makes those programs smarter by adding data context.

The following controls are especially important.

First, build a unified identity inventory. Include employees, contractors, vendors, guests, service accounts, machine identities, OAuth apps, SaaS integrations, cloud roles, API keys, certificates, AI assistants, AI agents, AI connectors, and break-glass accounts. Tag each identity by type, owner, status, privilege level, source system, and business purpose.

Second, resolve effective access. Do not rely only on direct permissions. Resolve nested groups, inherited permissions, local SaaS roles, cloud roles, shared links, application permissions, delegated access, AI inherited permissions, and policy exceptions.

Third, correlate access to data sensitivity. Access risk should be evaluated differently when the data is public, internal, confidential, regulated, business-critical, or AI-accessible. Sensitive data should drive stronger access controls and faster remediation.

Fourth, govern external access tightly. External access should be sponsored, approved, time-bound, monitored, and reviewed. Sensitive data shared externally should receive additional scrutiny.

Fifth, reduce standing privilege. Use just-in-time access for privileged roles, production data access, bulk export rights, sensitive SaaS administration, cloud data administration, AI connector administration, and high-risk troubleshooting.

Sixth, manage OAuth and SaaS app consent. Review app grants, scopes, publishers, owners, usage, and data access. Remove unused apps. Limit broad permissions. Require admin approval for high-risk scopes. Tie app access to data sensitivity and AI usage.

Seventh, treat non-human identities as privileged assets. Assign owners. Rotate secrets. Use vaulting. Prefer managed identities where possible. Limit scope. Monitor usage. Remove stale identities. Avoid shared credentials.

Eighth, govern AI inherited permissions. Identify which AI tools, copilots, agents, connectors, and retrieval systems can access sensitive data. Confirm whether they inherit user permissions, service account permissions, application permissions, or connector permissions. Reduce excessive access before enabling broad AI search or summarization.

Ninth, align access reviews to risk. Do not review everything the same way. Prioritize reviews where sensitive data, excessive access, external users, dormant identities, privileged rights, non-human identities, or AI access overlap.

Tenth, monitor data access behavior. Look for unusual downloads, bulk exports, new sharing behavior, access outside normal patterns, dormant account activity, service account anomalies, OAuth app activity against sensitive data, and AI retrieval or summarization against sensitive repositories.

Eleventh, automate remediation where safe. Automation can remove stale access, expire guest accounts, disable unused app grants, revoke dormant service accounts, open tickets, notify owners, enforce policy, and restrict AI access where governance conditions are not met. Use approvals where business impact is possible.

12.19 Identity Metrics That Matter

Metrics should help leaders see whether identity-related data risk is improving. Avoid vanity metrics that count activity without showing risk reduction.

Useful metrics include:

- Number of sensitive repositories with broad access
- Number of sensitive repositories with external access
- Number of sensitive repositories with unresolved nested group exposure
- Percentage of sensitive data with an assigned data owner
- Percentage of high-risk access findings remediated within SLA
- Number of dormant identities with access to sensitive data
- Number of contractors with access beyond contract end date
- Number of external collaborators with access to sensitive data
- Number of service accounts with no owner
- Number of service accounts with access to regulated data
- Number of non-human identities using long-lived credentials
- Number of OAuth apps with high-risk scopes
- Number of SaaS apps with organization-wide consent and no owner
- Percentage of privileged data access using just-in-time workflows
- Number of AI systems with access to sensitive repositories
- Number of AI connectors using broad service account permissions
- Number of repositories exposed to AI systems without assigned data owners
- Mean time to revoke inappropriate access
- Reduction in standing privileged access over time
- Number of sensitive data access exceptions accepted by the business

The best metrics connect access decisions to data risk. They help answer whether the organization is reducing real exposure, not just closing tickets.

12.20 Maturity Model for Identity-Aware DSPM

Identity depth can be assessed using the same maturity thinking as the broader DSPM program.

Level 1: Initial

Identity and data security are mostly separate. Access reviews are manual or inconsistent. Sensitive data is discovered without reliable effective access context. Contractors, external collaborators, service accounts, OAuth apps, machine identities, AI systems, and AI connectors are poorly inventoried. Remediation depends on individual knowledge.

At this level, the priority is visibility. Build the inventory. Identify sensitive data with broad access. Find external sharing. Locate stale accounts and ownerless service accounts. Identify AI-connected repositories. Start with the highest-risk data.

Level 2: Defined

Basic identity governance processes exist. Joiner, mover, and leaver workflows are documented. Some group ownership exists. Sensitive data repositories are reviewed periodically. External access is tracked in certain platforms. Service account standards exist but may not be consistently enforced. AI access may be governed through policy, but not consistently validated through effective access analysis.

At this level, the priority is consistency. Standardize ownership, naming, review cadence, and risk criteria. Begin correlating sensitive data with access paths across major platforms.

Level 3: Managed

Identity and data context are integrated across key systems. Effective access is resolved for important repositories. Nested groups, external collaborators, SaaS permissions, service accounts, machine identities, OAuth apps, and AI connectors are part of regular review. Findings are routed to owners through workflow tools. Remediation is risk-based.

At this level, the priority is scale. Expand coverage across SaaS, cloud, data platforms, non-human identities, and AI-connected systems. Use automation to route and track remediation.

Level 4: Quantitatively Managed

The organization measures identity-related data exposure with clear KPIs. Sensitive data access risk is scored based on effective access, identity type, privilege, exposure, activity, business context, and AI accessibility. Just-in-time access is used for high-risk scenarios. OAuth grants, SaaS permissions, service accounts, machine identities, and AI inherited permissions are continuously monitored.

At this level, the priority is optimization. Use metrics to reduce standing access, improve remediation times, limit broad AI access, and align access policy to risk appetite.

Level 5: Optimizing

Identity-aware DSPM is adaptive and predictive. Access policies adjust based on sensitivity, behavior, business context, AI usage, and risk signals. Non-human identities are governed continuously. High-risk access can be remediated automatically or routed for approval. AI systems are governed as machine identities with clear ownership, approved access boundaries, and monitored usage. Leadership uses identity and data metrics to guide investment, compliance, and operational resilience.

At this level, the priority is continuous improvement. The program learns from incidents, exceptions, usage patterns, business changes, and AI adoption.

The goal is not to force every organization to Level 5. The goal is to reach the level that fits the organization's regulatory burden, risk appetite, operational complexity, and resources.

12.21 A Field Example: The Folder That Was Never Public

Consider a company that discovers a folder containing customer contracts, pricing terms, tax forms, and personal contact information. The folder is not public. It is not indexed on the internet. It requires authentication. On paper, it looks protected.

A basic DSPM scan classifies the folder as sensitive.

An identity-aware review tells a different story.

The folder is accessible to a group called "Sales Operations." That group includes another group called "Revenue Support." Revenue Support includes a contractor group created during a system migration. Several contractors still have active guest accounts. One external collaborator account belongs to a vendor whose contract ended last year. A service account used for reporting has read and export permissions. An OAuth app approved for productivity analytics can read files in the workspace. Two administrators have standing access and do not use just-in-time elevation. A copilot can summarize the folder contents because it inherits access from users and connectors tied to that workspace.

No single issue looks dramatic by itself.

Together, they create meaningful risk.

The remediation plan is practical:

Confirm the business owner for the folder
Remove stale contractor and vendor access
Break apart nested groups that obscure membership
Convert broad access to role-based access by job function
Review and reduce the reporting service account permissions
Revoke or constrain the OAuth app grant
Move administrators to just-in-time access
Review whether AI tools should be able to index or summarize the folder
Add quarterly review because the folder contains sensitive customer data
Monitor for bulk download, external sharing, unusual access, and AI retrieval activity

The folder was never public.

It was still overexposed.

That is the kind of risk identity-aware DSPM is meant to reveal.

12.22 Common Mistakes

Mistake 1: Confusing authentication strength with access appropriateness

MFA is important, but MFA does not make excessive access acceptable. A strongly authenticated identity can still access data it should not have.

Mistake 2: Reviewing groups without expanding them

Approving a group name is not the same as approving the members, nested groups, external users, service accounts, and AI-connected access paths inside it.

Mistake 3: Ignoring local SaaS permissions

Central identity provider access does not always show what a user can do inside a SaaS application. Local roles, workspaces, channels, projects, object permissions, and AI-enabled SaaS features matter.

Mistake 4: Treating non-human identities as exceptions

Service accounts, machine identities, OAuth apps, API tokens, AI agents, and connector identities should not live outside governance. They often have broad and durable access.

Mistake 5: Relying on annual access reviews

Annual reviews are too slow for sensitive data exposure. Reviews should be triggered by data sensitivity, access changes, external sharing, role changes, AI enablement, and risky activity.

Mistake 6: Removing access without business context

Blind revocation can break business processes. The better pattern is owner-driven, risk-based remediation with automation where safe.

Mistake 7: Treating DSPM and IAM as separate programs

DSPM identifies data risk. IAM controls identity and access. IGA governs entitlement lifecycle. PAM reduces privileged access. SaaS and cloud security tools expose platform-specific posture. These programs become stronger when connected.

Mistake 8: Ignoring AI inherited permissions

AI tools often do not create new access paths from nothing. They inherit existing access from users, service accounts, app grants, connectors, or platform permissions. If those permissions are excessive, the AI system can amplify the exposure.

12.23 Practical Questions for Leaders

Leaders do not need every technical detail. They need questions that reveal risk and drive accountability.

Ask:

- *Which identities can access our most sensitive data?*
- *How much of that access is direct, inherited, privileged, external, or non-human?*
- *Which sensitive repositories have broad or unclear access?*
- *Which contractors and external collaborators can access regulated data?*

- *Which service accounts and machine identities can read, export, or move sensitive data?*
- *Which OAuth apps and SaaS integrations can access sensitive content?*
- *Which sensitive data access is standing, and which is just in time?*
- *Which privileged users can change access to sensitive repositories?*
- *Which AI systems, copilots, agents, or connectors can access sensitive data?*
- *Which AI tools inherit permissions from overprivileged users or service accounts?*
- *Who owns each high-risk access path?*
- *How quickly can we remove inappropriate access?*
- *How do we prove access is appropriate to auditors, customers, and leadership?*

These questions turn identity from an IT function into a data risk conversation.

12.24 Action Plan: Building Identity Depth into DSPM

Organizations do not need to solve every identity problem at once. Start where identity risk and data sensitivity overlap.

Step 1: Pick the crown jewel data sets

Start with the data that would matter most if exposed. This may include customer data, employee data, payment data, health data, legal data, financial records, source code, credentials, intellectual property, strategic business documents, or sensitive data that may be exposed through AI tools.

Step 2: Map effective access

For each data set, identify direct access, inherited access, nested groups, privileged roles, external collaborators, service accounts, OAuth apps, SaaS integrations, machine identities, shared links, AI systems, AI connectors, and AI inherited permissions.

Step 3: Identify toxic combinations

Prioritize sensitive data with broad access, external access, dormant users, stale contractors, ownerless service accounts, high-risk app grants, standing privilege, unmanaged sharing, AI indexing, or AI inherited permissions.

Step 4: Assign owners

Every high-risk access path needs a business owner and, where appropriate, a technical owner. Ownership should be visible and auditable. AI-connected access paths should also have accountable system, data, and business owners.

Step 5: Remediate in risk order

Remove stale access first. Reduce broad groups. Break risky nested group chains. Revoke unused app grants. Constrain service accounts. Apply JIT for privileged access. Add expiration to contractor and external access. Limit AI access to sensitive repositories until permissions are cleaned up.

Step 6: Automate repeatable controls

Automate expiration, access review triggers, owner notifications, ticket creation, stale access detection, OAuth review, service account attestation, AI connector review, and policy enforcement where safe.

Step 7: Measure improvement

Track reduction in broad access, external exposure, dormant access, standing privilege, ownerless non-human identities, high-risk app grants, and AI-accessible sensitive repositories. Report progress in business language.

12.25 The Human Side of Identity

Identity can sound technical, but the hard part is often human.

People ask for access because they are trying to get work done. Managers approve access because they trust their teams. Administrators grant access because tickets need to close. Developers create service accounts because applications need to run. Vendors retain access because no one wants to delay support. Business teams share files because collaboration is how work happens. AI tools are connected because users and leaders want speed, productivity, and easier access to information.

Most excessive access is not malicious.

It is the residue of speed, convenience, unclear ownership, and weak cleanup.

A successful DSPM program should respect that reality. It should not shame teams for messy access. It should make the risk visible, explain it clearly, and give people a practical way to fix it.

The tone matters.

"You did this wrong" creates resistance.

"Here is sensitive customer data that is accessible through a stale contractor group, and here is the safest way to clean it up" creates action.

The same is true for AI inherited permissions. Saying "AI is dangerous" is too vague to help. Saying "This copilot can summarize customer contracts because it inherits access from an overbroad group, and here is how we reduce that exposure before expanding AI use" creates a path forward.

Identity-aware DSPM works best when it helps people make better decisions without forcing them to become access model experts.

Key Takeaways

Identity is a core part of DSPM. Sensitive data is not only at risk because of where it lives or how it is classified. It is at risk because of who, and what, can access it.

Access may come from users, groups, contractors, external partners, service accounts, SaaS tools, OAuth apps, machine identities, privileged roles, AI systems, inherited permissions, or temporary access that was never removed.

AI makes this risk bigger. Assistants, copilots, agents, and connectors may inherit access from users, apps, service accounts, or platforms. If access is too broad, AI can make sensitive data easier to find, summarize, combine, and expose.

A strong DSPM program connects the data graph to the identity graph. Organizations need to know who can access sensitive data, how they got access, whether they still need it, who owns the decision, and what should be fixed first.

Privileged access needs extra care. Admin rights, bulk export rights, platform owner roles, cross-environment access, data administration, and AI connector administration can greatly increase exposure. These rights should be approved, limited, monitored, reviewed, and removed when no longer needed.

Access governance should be an active security control, not just a compliance task. Reviews should include the data owner, the user's manager, IT or the data custodian, and security or governance teams when needed.

Organizations should have clear processes for temporary access, privileged access, job changes, contractor offboarding, OAuth and SaaS permissions, machine identities, AI inherited access, and data ownership changes. Without ongoing review, temporary access often becomes permanent.

DSPM should support identity governance, not compete with it. Identity programs already have tools, funding, processes, and executive attention. DSPM makes those efforts stronger by connecting access decisions to sensitive data risk.

The goal is not perfect access. That is not realistic.

The goal is intentional access: access that is visible, justified, limited, owned, monitored, and removed when it is no longer needed.

When DSPM includes identity context, it becomes more than a discovery tool. It becomes a decision tool for data risk.

Chapter 13: Privacy Operations in Practice

The early regulatory chapter explains what GDPR, CCPA/CPRA, HIPAA, GLBA, NYDFS, SEC, and the EU AI Act require. This chapter focuses on how an organization operationalizes privacy under pressure, especially when data is scattered across SaaS, cloud, endpoints, collaboration tools, security telemetry, AI systems, backups, archives, and third-party platforms.

Privacy operations is where legal, security, data governance, records management, compliance, and business teams meet. The goal is not just to "know the regulation." The goal is to prove, quickly and defensibly, what personal data exists, where it flows, who can access it, why it is retained, how it is protected, whether its use is approved, and what evidence supports the organization's decisions.

Privacy operations also forces the organization to ask two deceptively simple questions:

Does this constitute a sale, sharing, or monetization of data?

Is this an approved use of the data?

Those questions matter because modern privacy risk is not always caused by unauthorized access. Sometimes the access is technically allowed, but the use is inappropriate, undisclosed, excessive, or outside the purpose the individual, customer, regulator, or contract expected.

In the AI era, that distinction becomes even more important. Data may be collected for support, billing, security, HR, or customer service, then later reused for analytics, model improvement, training, personalization, enrichment, automation, or AI-assisted decision-making. The organization may still "have access" to the data, but that does not automatically mean the new use is approved.

Approved access does not always equal approved use.

13.1 Why Privacy Operations Needs Its Own Chapter

Most privacy failures are not caused by a lack of policy. They happen because the organization cannot answer practical questions fast enough:

- *Where is this person's data?*
- *Can we delete it, or is it under legal hold?*
- *Was regulated data involved in the incident?*
- *Which systems must be searched for a DSAR?*
- *Do we have evidence that this vendor was assessed?*
- *Can we prove our retention and deletion decisions?*
- *Did data leave the approved geography?*
- *Was AI trained on personal, regulated, or confidential data?*
- *Was this data used for an approved purpose?*
- *Does this activity constitute a sale, sharing, or monetization of data?*

That is the work of privacy operations.

Regulators increasingly expect organizations to show operational evidence, not just policy language. GDPR requires accountability and records of processing. CCPA gives California residents privacy rights, including rights related to sale and sharing. HIPAA requires breach notification for unsecured protected health information. GLBA requires safeguards for customer information. NYDFS requires timely cybersecurity incident reporting. SEC rules require public companies to disclose material cybersecurity incidents and cyber risk governance.

The practical takeaway is simple: privacy operations must be built as a repeatable, evidence-producing function.

Privacy operations is also where the organization validates whether data use still matches business purpose, customer expectations, privacy notices, contracts, consent, regulatory obligations, and internal governance approvals.

The central privacy question is no longer only:

Can we access the data?

It is increasingly:

Should this data be used this way at all?

13.2 Core Privacy Operations Capabilities

A mature privacy operations program should include the following capabilities:

Capability	Practical Outcome
DSAR operations	Locate, review, export, correct, delete, or restrict personal data within required timelines
RoPA management	Maintain defensible records of processing activities
DPIA and risk assessment	Identify privacy risks before deploying new systems, analytics, AI, or data-sharing programs
Breach notification readiness	Determine whether notification is required, to whom, and by when
Privilege handling	Protect attorney-client and work-product materials during investigations
Legal hold	Preserve data when litigation, investigation, audit, or regulatory inquiry is reasonably anticipated
eDiscovery support	Search, preserve, collect, review, and produce data defensibly
Cross-border transfer governance	Track data movement and access across jurisdictions and validate transfer mechanisms
Retention conflict management	Resolve conflicts between deletion rights, legal holds, regulatory retention, and business need
Approved-use governance	Validate that data is being used for an approved purpose, not merely accessed by an approved system
Sale, sharing, and	Determine whether data use, disclosure, enrichment, analytics, or third-party

monetization review	processing creates privacy obligations
AI privacy governance	Track training data, prompts, outputs, embeddings, logs, vendor use, and human oversight
Regulator-ready evidence	Produce artifacts that demonstrate compliance decisions and controls

Privacy operations should not be treated as a purely legal function. It is an operating discipline. It requires systems, workflows, owners, evidence, and repeatable decisions.

13.3 DSAR: Data Subject Access Request Operations

A DSAR process is not just a legal intake workflow. It is a data discovery, identity verification, review, redaction, fulfillment, and evidence process.

Under GDPR, individuals have rights involving access, rectification, erasure, restriction, portability, objection, and certain protections related to automated decision-making. Under CCPA/CPRA, California residents have rights that include knowing what personal information is collected, deleting certain information, correcting inaccurate information, opting out of sale or sharing, limiting use of sensitive personal information, and non-discrimination for exercising rights.

DSAR Operating Model

A practical DSAR workflow should include the following steps.

1. Intake

Capture the requester, request type, jurisdiction, identity evidence, date received, deadline, and communication channel.

2. Verification

Confirm identity using a risk-based approach. Higher-risk requests, such as access to sensitive data, deletion of an account, or requests involving minors, should require stronger verification.

3. Scope Determination

Determine whether the request applies to customer, employee, applicant, patient, prospect, vendor, or business contact data.

4. System Search

Search structured and unstructured repositories, including CRM, HRIS, ticketing, email, collaboration platforms, cloud storage, security logs, data warehouses, backups where feasible, AI systems, prompt logs, embeddings where applicable, and vendor-managed systems.

5. Approved-Use and Sale/Sharing Review

Determine whether the data has been used beyond its original purpose, shared with third parties, used for analytics or AI, sold, monetized, enriched, or disclosed in ways that create additional privacy obligations.

6. Review and Redaction

Remove or withhold data that belongs to other individuals, privileged material, security-sensitive information, trade secrets, or information exempted by law.

7. Fulfillment

Deliver the response securely and in a usable format. Track whether the request was fulfilled, partially fulfilled, denied, or extended.

8. Evidence Capture

Preserve evidence of request handling, searches performed, systems checked, exemptions applied, approvals, response dates, communications, sale/sharing analysis, and approved-use decisions.

DSAR Evidence Checklist

The organization should be able to show:

Evidence	Why It Matters
Request intake record	Proves when the clock started
Identity verification method	Shows the organization avoided improper disclosure
System search log	Demonstrates reasonable search scope
Data map reference	Shows how systems were identified
AI system search scope	Shows whether prompts, outputs, embeddings, logs, or AI-connected repositories were considered
Approved-use review	Shows whether data was used for the purpose originally allowed
Sale/sharing analysis	Supports opt-out, disclosure, and regulatory obligations
Redaction notes	Explains withheld information
Legal review notes	Supports exemptions and privilege decisions
Fulfillment record	Shows timely completion
Exception or extension rationale	Supports defensibility

Common DSAR Failure Points

The most common DSAR issues are incomplete data maps, unmanaged SaaS repositories, weak identity verification, no audit trail, poor redaction discipline, uncertainty around backups or archived data, and lack of visibility into AI-connected repositories.

A growing failure point is not knowing whether personal data was used in AI workflows. A DSAR process that searches the CRM but ignores AI meeting assistants, prompt logs, support chat summaries, data science workspaces, or AI-enabled SaaS platforms may miss meaningful data use.

For cybersecurity and data governance teams, the DSAR lesson is this:

You cannot fulfill privacy rights against data you cannot find.

13.4 RoPA: Records of Processing Activities

A RoPA is the organization's operating inventory of personal data processing. It should not be treated as a static spreadsheet created once for compliance. It should be tied to business processes, systems, vendors, data categories, purposes, legal bases, retention rules, transfer mechanisms, AI use, and approved-use decisions.

GDPR Article 30 requires certain controllers and processors to maintain records of processing activities. EDPB guidance continues to treat records of processing and international transfer documentation as key accountability artifacts.

Practical RoPA Fields

A useful RoPA should include:

Field	Example
Business process	Customer support ticket handling
System or repository	Zendesk, Salesforce, Snowflake
Data owner	VP Customer Operations
Privacy owner	Privacy Counsel
Security owner	Application Security
Data subjects	Customers, prospects, support contacts
Data categories	Contact info, account identifiers, support history
Sensitive data	Payment fragments, health details, government IDs, credentials, biometric data
Purpose	Support, fraud prevention, account administration
Approved use	Support case handling and account administration only
Prohibited use	Model training, unrelated analytics, resale, enrichment without approval
Sale/sharing/monetization review	Not sold; shared only with approved subprocessors
Legal basis or lawful purpose	Contract, consent, legitimate interest, legal obligation
Retention period	7 years after account closure
Vendors or subprocessors	Support platform, analytics provider
Countries accessed from	United States, Ireland, India
Transfer mechanism	Adequacy, SCCs, BCRs, derogation
Security controls	Encryption, RBAC, logging, DLP
AI use	Summarization only; no training; logs retained 30 days
DSAR searchable	Yes, partially, no
Deletion supported	Native delete, soft delete, manual workflow, vendor ticket
Legal hold capable	Yes/no
Evidence location	GRC record, ticket, contract repository

RoPA Improvement Recommendation

RoPA should be maintained through change management. Any new system, vendor, AI use case, data lake ingestion, major integration, new geography, analytics initiative, or data-sharing arrangement should trigger a RoPA review.

A strong operational control is to block production launch until the data owner answers:

What personal data is processed, why, where does it go, how long is it retained, who can access it, is this an approved use, and could this constitute a sale, sharing, or monetization of data?

This may feel like a lot of questions, but they are much easier to answer before launch than during an incident, audit, DSAR, regulatory inquiry, or lawsuit.

13.5 DPIA: Data Protection Impact Assessment

A DPIA is a structured assessment used to identify and reduce privacy risk before processing begins. Under GDPR, DPIAs are required where processing is likely to result in high risk to individuals. The UK ICO describes DPIAs as a way to identify and minimize data protection risks, especially for high-risk processing.

A DPIA should not be paperwork after the decision is already made. It should influence design.

DPIA Triggers

A DPIA should be required for:

Trigger	Example
Sensitive data processing	Health, biometric, financial, children's data
Large-scale monitoring	Employee monitoring, behavioral analytics
Automated decisioning	Fraud scoring, hiring filters, credit decisions
AI or machine learning	Model training, inference, profiling, retrieval, summarization
New data sharing	New vendor, affiliate sharing, data clean room
Sale, sharing, or monetization	Data enrichment, ad tech sharing, model improvement, resale, brokered data
Cross-border transfer	New processing or access from another jurisdiction
New surveillance capability	Logging, endpoint monitoring, user behavior analytics
High-impact security tooling	Decryption, packet capture, insider risk systems
Secondary use of data	Using data for a purpose beyond the original collection reason

DPIA Practical Questions

A DPIA should answer:

1. *What data is being collected?*
2. *Is it necessary and proportionate?*

3. *What is the lawful basis or business justification?*
4. *Who are the data subjects?*
5. *What harm could occur?*
6. *What security controls protect the data?*
7. *Can the data be minimized, masked, tokenized, aggregated, or deleted sooner?*
8. *Does the processing involve automated decisions or AI?*
9. *Are vendors or subprocessors involved?*
10. *Are cross-border transfers involved?*
11. *Does this constitute a sale, sharing, or monetization of data?*
12. *Is this an approved use of the data?*
13. *Does the intended use match the privacy notice, consent, contract, and customer expectation?*
14. *What residual risk remains?*
15. *Who accepted the risk?*

DPIA Evidence

Good DPIA evidence includes the completed assessment, architecture diagram, data flow map, threat model, vendor review, legal review, security control validation, approved-use determination, sale/sharing analysis, residual risk decision, and approval record.

The key point is simple: a DPIA should help the organization design safer processing before the data is already in motion.

13.6 Authorized Access vs. Approved Use

One of the most important privacy distinctions is the difference between authorized access and approved use.

A user, system, vendor, AI tool, or business process may have technical access to data. That does not automatically mean the data may be used for any purpose.

For example, a customer support system may contain customer emails, contact details, support history, product issues, and attached files. The support team may be authorized to access that data to resolve customer cases. That does not necessarily mean the same data can be reused for unrelated marketing analytics, AI model improvement, employee performance scoring, product telemetry enrichment, or resale to a partner.

The access may be authorized.

The use may still be inappropriate.

This issue appears frequently in AI, analytics, and SaaS environments because data can be repurposed quickly. A dataset collected for one business reason may later become attractive for training, personalization, automation, fraud detection, product optimization, or customer segmentation.

Privacy operations must help the organization ask:

- *Was the data collected for this purpose?*
- *Was this use disclosed?*
- *Is consent required?*

- *Is opt-out required?*
- *Is this use covered by contract?*
- *Does this use create a sale, sharing, or monetization issue?*
- *Does this use involve sensitive personal information?*
- *Does this use affect individuals' rights or expectations?*
- *Is the data minimized for this purpose?*
- *Is there a safer way to achieve the same business goal?*

This is where privacy operations becomes more than compliance administration. It becomes business governance.

The organization should not wait for a DSAR, audit, or incident to discover that data was technically accessible but used in a way no one had approved.

13.7 Breach Notification Operations

Breach notification is where privacy operations and incident response collide.

Different regimes have different thresholds, timelines, and notification recipients. HIPAA's Breach Notification Rule requires covered entities and business associates to provide notification following a breach of unsecured protected health information. NYDFS Part 500 requires covered entities to notify the Superintendent as promptly as possible and no later than 72 hours after determining a cybersecurity incident has occurred. The FTC GLBA Safeguards Rule requires notification to the FTC as soon as possible and no later than 30 days after discovery for certain events involving unencrypted customer information of at least 500 consumers. Public companies subject to SEC rules must disclose material cybersecurity incidents on Form 8-K.

Breach Decision Workflow

A breach notification workflow should include the following steps.

1. Incident Intake

Capture event source, detection time, affected systems, suspected data types, and initial severity.

2. Data Impact Analysis

Identify whether the incident involved personal data, PHI, financial data, customer information, credentials, minors' data, regulated records, confidential business information, AI training data, prompts, outputs, embeddings, or AI vendor logs.

3. Jurisdiction Mapping

Determine impacted individuals' locations, applicable contracts, sector rules, state laws, and international requirements.

4. Legal Threshold Analysis

Decide whether the event meets the definition of a reportable breach, cybersecurity incident, security event, material cyber incident, contractual notification event, or AI-related privacy incident.

5. Approved-Use and Disclosure Analysis

Determine whether the data was accessed, disclosed, processed, or used outside approved purpose. This includes evaluating whether a vendor, AI system, analytics tool, or third party used the data beyond permitted terms.

6. Notification Clock Tracking

Track when the organization discovered the event, when it determined reportability, and when each notification deadline starts.

7. Regulator and Individual Notification

Prepare regulator notices, individual notices, customer notices, contractual notices, law enforcement coordination, and public disclosures as needed.

8. Evidence Preservation

Preserve logs, forensic images, communications, decision records, legal analysis, containment actions, notification artifacts, vendor communications, and AI system evidence where relevant.

Breach Evidence Checklist

Evidence	Purpose
Incident timeline	Proves discovery, containment, and decision timing
Data classification results	Shows what regulated data was involved
Impacted population analysis	Supports notification scope
Legal threshold memo	Explains reportability decision
Approved-use analysis	Shows whether data was used or disclosed beyond permitted purpose
AI system evidence	Shows whether prompts, outputs, embeddings, logs, or training data were involved
Forensic report	Supports facts and root cause
Communications log	Tracks regulator, customer, and individual notices
Board or executive briefings	Supports governance evidence
Remediation plan	Shows corrective action
Lessons learned	Supports continuous improvement

Important Operational Point

The privacy team cannot wait until after forensics are complete. Notification decisions often need to be made while facts are still developing. The best organizations maintain a live "known facts, assumptions, unknowns" record so decisions are clear and defensible.

Privacy operations should also document whether the issue was an unauthorized access event, an unauthorized disclosure, an inappropriate use of data, or a vendor/AI processing issue. Those distinctions matter for legal analysis, regulatory notification, customer communications, and remediation.

13.8 Privilege in Privacy and Cyber Investigations

Privilege must be designed into sensitive investigations from the beginning. Poor handling can expose investigation materials, legal analysis, draft reports, and internal communications during litigation or regulatory inquiry.

Practical Privilege Controls

Control	Practical Use
Counsel-directed investigation	Helps establish legal purpose
Clear engagement letters	Defines whether consultants are retained to assist counsel
Privilege labels	Marks legal advice and attorney work product
Need-to-know distribution	Reduces waiver risk
Separate business and legal workstreams	Avoids mixing routine operations with legal analysis
Draft control	Limits uncontrolled copies of sensitive reports
Communication discipline	Prevents speculative or inflammatory statements

What Teams Often Miss

Security teams often document too casually during incidents. Messages such as "we failed to patch this for months" or "this was definitely negligence" can become problematic if they are inaccurate, incomplete, or discoverable.

Better practice:

Current evidence indicates the affected system had not yet received the April patch. Root cause remains under investigation.

This preserves accuracy without overstating conclusions.

13.9 Legal Hold

Legal hold is the process of preserving relevant information when litigation, investigation, audit, subpoena, regulatory inquiry, or enforcement action is reasonably anticipated.

Legal hold directly conflicts with deletion, retention, DSAR erasure, and data minimization obligations. That conflict must be managed, not ignored.

Legal Hold Workflow

1. Identify the matter.
2. Define why the data is under legal hold.
3. Define custodians, systems, time periods, and data types.
4. Issue hold notices.
5. Suspend deletion for in-scope data.
6. Confirm custodian acknowledgment.

7. Preserve relevant repositories.
8. Monitor compliance.
9. Release the hold when authorized.
10. Resume retention and deletion rules where appropriate.
11. Revisit whether retained data is still needed after the hold is released.

The question *"why is this data under legal hold?"* should be documented clearly. A legal hold should not become a permanent reason to keep data forever.

Once the hold is released, the organization should revisit the entire retention process to determine whether the data is still required, should return to normal retention rules, should be archived, should be minimized, or should be defensibly deleted.

Legal Hold Evidence

Evidence	Why It Matters
Triggering event	Shows why the hold was issued
Custodian list	Defines scope
Hold notice	Shows instructions were communicated
Acknowledgments	Shows custodians received and accepted obligations
Preservation actions	Shows systems were protected
Exception log	Tracks inaccessible or unavailable data
Release notice	Shows hold was ended properly
Post-release disposition	Shows deletion resumed when appropriate

Privacy Operations Lesson

When a person asks for deletion, the organization must check legal hold before deleting. The DSAR response should explain, where legally appropriate, that some data cannot be deleted because it must be retained for legal, regulatory, security, or contractual reasons.

Legal hold should preserve what is required. It should not become a blanket excuse for uncontrolled retention.

13.10 eDiscovery

eDiscovery is the defensible process of identifying, preserving, collecting, processing, reviewing, and producing electronically stored information.

Privacy operations matters because eDiscovery often includes personal data, sensitive personal data, PHI, financial records, employee communications, customer records, and confidential business data.

eDiscovery and Privacy Control Points

Stage	Privacy Risk	Control
Identification	Overbroad search scope	Use targeted custodians, dates, systems, and keywords
Preservation	Excessive data retention	Scope holds carefully
Collection	Pulling unnecessary personal data	Use filtering and minimization
Processing	Data transferred to review vendors	Validate contracts, security, and transfer mechanisms
Review	Exposure to reviewers	Apply access controls and confidentiality terms
Production	Producing third-party personal data	Redact, withhold, or seek protective orders
Disposition	Data kept too long after matter closes	Enforce post-matter destruction

eDiscovery Evidence

A defensible eDiscovery process should preserve chain of custody, collection logs, search terms, review decisions, redaction logs, production history, privilege logs, and destruction certificates.

The privacy function should be involved before data leaves the organization, not after production is complete.

13.11 Cross-Border Transfers

Cross-border transfer governance ensures that personal data does not move to another country without an approved legal mechanism, risk assessment, contract, and security control.

Under GDPR, transfers outside the EEA may rely on an adequacy decision or, absent adequacy, appropriate safeguards such as enforceable rights and legal remedies. The EDPB also recognizes derogations for specific situations where neither adequacy nor appropriate safeguards apply.

Transfer Inventory

Every cross-border transfer should document:

Field	Example
Exporting entity	EU subsidiary
Importing entity	U.S. parent company
Data subjects	Customers, employees
Data categories	Contact, usage, billing, support
Sensitive data	Health, financial, biometric, children's data
Purpose	Support and analytics
Approved use	Customer support and analytics under documented controls

Countries	Ireland to United States
Transfer mechanism	SCCs, adequacy, BCRs, derogation
Transfer impact assessment	Completed, not required, pending
Supplementary controls	Encryption, access controls, pseudonymization
Vendor contract	DPA, SCCs, subprocessors
AI processing location	Region where prompts, outputs, embeddings, telemetry, or logs are processed
Review cadence	Annual or upon material change

Common Cross-Border Gaps

Organizations often miss remote administrative access from another country, support access by offshore vendors, logs copied into global SIEM platforms, SaaS subprocessors, AI model training or inference outside the approved region, data warehouse replication, backup and disaster recovery locations, and collaboration tools where files are shared globally.

The practical rule is this:

Data access can be a transfer, even if the primary database never moves.

AI makes this harder because data may cross borders without looking like a traditional transfer. A user prompt, retrieved document chunk, embedding, model evaluation record, support log, or AI vendor telemetry event may create sovereignty concerns even when the original system of record remains in an approved region.

Privacy operations must therefore track not only where data is stored, but where AI systems process, cache, index, infer from, and retain that data.

13.12 Retention Conflicts

Retention is one of the most difficult areas of privacy operations because multiple obligations can point in different directions.

A person may request deletion. A regulation may require retention. A contract may require records. Litigation may require preservation. Security may need logs. Finance may need transaction records. AI governance may require model evidence. Privacy law may require minimization.

The answer is not always "delete" or "keep."

The answer is controlled disposition with documented rationale.

Retention Conflict Matrix

Scenario	Privacy Operation Response
DSAR deletion request, no legal need to retain	Delete or de-identify within workflow
DSAR deletion request, legal hold applies	Preserve in-scope data and document exception
DSAR deletion request, financial record retention applies	Retain required records, delete unnecessary data
Security logs contain personal data	Retain for defined security period, restrict access
Backups contain deleted user data	Suppress restoration or delete on backup expiration cycle
AI model trained on personal data	Assess whether deletion, retraining, suppression, or opt-out controls apply
AI prompt or output contains personal data	Apply retention, access, deletion, and review rules based on approved use
Regulator inquiry pending	Suspend deletion for relevant data
Contract requires longer retention than privacy policy	Escalate to legal and records governance
Data no longer has an approved purpose	Delete, de-identify, archive under approved controls, or document exception

Retention Evidence

The organization should maintain a retention schedule, legal basis for retention, system-level deletion capability, exception register, legal hold register, deletion certificates, backup retention policy, data owner approvals, and records of defensible deletion.

Practical Recommendation

Retention rules should be embedded into systems where possible. A policy that says “delete after three years” is weak if no system owner knows how deletion actually happens.

Retention should also be tied to approved use. If the business no longer has a valid purpose for retaining personal data, and no legal, regulatory, contractual, security, or litigation obligation applies, the data should not remain simply because storage is cheap.

Cheap storage is not a privacy strategy.

13.13 EU AI Act and Privacy Operations

The EU AI Act adds another reason privacy operations must become more practical. It is not only about personal data rights. It is also about evidence, risk assessment, transparency, governance, monitoring, and accountability for AI systems.

The European Commission describes the AI Act as Regulation (EU) 2024/1689 and the first comprehensive legal framework on AI worldwide. High-risk AI systems have obligations tied to risk management, data governance, technical documentation, recordkeeping, transparency, human oversight, accuracy, robustness, and cybersecurity. Certain deployers of high-risk AI systems must also perform a fundamental rights impact assessment.

AI Privacy Operations Questions

Privacy operations should ask:

1. *Does the AI system process personal data?*
2. *Was personal data used for training, fine-tuning, prompting, retrieval, evaluation, or monitoring?*
3. *Does the system make or support decisions about people?*
4. *Does it use sensitive data or infer sensitive attributes?*
5. *Can individuals exercise access, correction, deletion, objection, or opt-out rights?*
6. *Are prompts, outputs, embeddings, and logs retained?*
7. *Can the organization explain data lineage?*
8. *Are cross-border transfers involved?*
9. *Are vendors using submitted data for model improvement?*
10. *Does the use constitute sale, sharing, or monetization?*
11. *Is the AI use approved for this data category and business purpose?*
12. *Is there regulator-ready documentation?*

AI Evidence Artifacts

Evidence	Why It Matters
AI system inventory	Shows what AI exists
Use case assessment	Shows purpose and risk level
Approved-use record	Shows that the data may be used for this AI purpose
Data lineage	Shows what data feeds the system
Model card or system card	Summarizes intended use and limitations
DPIA or AI impact assessment	Documents privacy and rights risks
Human oversight procedure	Shows accountable review
Testing and validation evidence	Supports accuracy and robustness claims
Vendor terms	Confirms data use restrictions
Prompt and output logging policy	Shows monitoring and retention decisions
Sale/sharing analysis	Supports privacy rights and disclosure obligations
Incident response plan	Supports handling of harmful or unlawful outputs

13.14 AI Privacy Incident Example: Authorized Access, Inappropriate Use

Consider a company that deploys an AI summarization tool for customer support. The tool is approved to summarize open support cases so agents can respond faster. It connects to the support platform using an integration account with broad read access.

At first, the deployment appears successful. Support response times improve. Agents like the tool. Leadership sees productivity gains.

Then privacy and security teams discover that the integration account can access not only open support tickets, but also archived tickets, identity verification attachments, payment screenshots, health-related customer notes, and escalated legal complaints. The AI tool is not training on the data, but it is summarizing more information than the approved use case requires. Some summaries are stored in logs for quality review. A vendor support team can access those logs.

This may not be a classic breach. No attacker broke in. No employee intentionally stole data. The access may even be technically authorized.

But the use is still a privacy problem.

The organization now needs to answer difficult questions:

- *Was the AI tool approved to process these categories of data?*
- *Were customers told their data could be used this way?*
- *Did the vendor terms prohibit model training and secondary use?*
- *Are support logs retained longer than necessary?*
- *Is sensitive information being summarized into new records?*
- *Does the vendor access create a cross-border transfer?*
- *Does this use trigger DPIA, RoPA, DSAR, or deletion obligations?*
- *Does the workflow constitute sale, sharing, or monetization under applicable law?*
- *Can the company prove what data was processed and why?*

The remediation is not simply "turn off AI."

A better response may include narrowing the integration account permissions, excluding sensitive ticket categories, reducing retention of summaries, updating the RoPA, completing a DPIA, revising vendor terms, masking sensitive fields, improving logging, notifying governance stakeholders, and documenting the approved use.

This example illustrates one of the most important lessons in AI-era privacy operations:

The absence of malicious access does not mean the use was appropriate.

13.15 Regulator-Ready Evidence

Regulator-ready evidence means the organization can produce clear, consistent, dated, approved, and traceable records that show what happened and why.

It does not mean creating perfect paperwork after the fact. It means privacy operations generates evidence as work happens.

Evidence Principles

Good evidence should be:

Principle	Meaning
Dated	Shows when action occurred
Owned	Identifies accountable person or team
Approved	Shows decision authority
Traceable	Links to system, process, ticket, or record
Complete enough	Explains decision and supporting facts
Consistent	Aligns with policy, contracts, and technical reality
Preserved	Available during audit, inquiry, litigation, or incident response

Regulator-Ready Evidence Library

A privacy operations evidence library should include:

1. Data inventory.
2. RoPA.
3. DPIAs and AI impact assessments.
4. DSAR logs.
5. Breach analysis records.
6. Incident response timelines.
7. Vendor assessments.
8. DPAs and SCCs.
9. Transfer impact assessments.
10. Retention schedule.
11. Legal hold records.
12. Deletion certificates.
13. Access reviews.
14. Training records.
15. Policy exceptions.
16. Approved-use determinations.
17. Sale, sharing, and monetization analyses.
18. Board or executive reporting.
19. Risk acceptance records.
20. Audit findings and remediation evidence.
21. AI system inventory.
22. AI vendor terms and data-use restrictions.
23. Security control validation.Regulator-ready evidence should show not only that a control existed, but that the organization made a thoughtful, documented, and defensible decision.

13.16 Operating Model: *Who Owns What?*

Privacy operations is cross-functional. Clear ownership prevents missed deadlines and finger-pointing.

Function	Primary Responsibilities
Privacy Legal	Rights interpretation, regulatory thresholds, exemptions, notices
Security	Incident response, data discovery, access controls, logs, containment
Data Governance	Data inventory, classification, lineage, ownership
Records Management	Retention schedule, legal hold coordination, defensible deletion
IT	System search, deletion execution, access management
Compliance/GRC	Evidence tracking, control testing, audit readiness
Procurement	Vendor intake, contracts, subprocessors
Business Owners	Purpose, necessity, data accuracy, approved use, process ownership
Legal/Litigation	Privilege, legal hold, eDiscovery, regulatory inquiries
AI Governance	AI inventory, model risk, human oversight, AI documentation
Marketing/Product/Revenue Teams	Data monetization, analytics, personalization, customer communications, sale/sharing review inputs

RACI Snapshot

Activity	Legal	Privacy	Security	IT	Records	Business	GRC
DSAR intake	C	A/R	C	R	C	I	C
DSAR system search	C	A	C	R	C	R	I
DPIA	A/C	R	C	C	C	R	I
Approved-use review	A/C	R	C	C	C	R	I
Sale/sharing analysis	A/C	R	C	C	C	R	I
Breach analysis	A	R	R	C	I	I	C
Legal hold	A/R	C	C	R	R	I	C
eDiscovery	A/R	C	C	R	C	I	C
Retention schedule	C	C	C	C	A/R	R	I
Regulator evidence	A	R	R	C	C	I	R
AI privacy assessment	A/C	R	C	C	C	R	I

A = accountable, R = responsible, C = consulted, I = informed

13.17 Practical Maturity Model

Level 1: Reactive

Privacy requests are handled manually. Data maps are incomplete. DSAR searches depend on tribal knowledge. Breach decisions are slow. Retention exceptions are undocumented. AI and analytics use may be reviewed informally or not at all.

Level 2: Defined

Core workflows exist for DSAR, DPIA, breach review, vendor assessment, legal hold, and retention. Evidence is captured, but much of it remains manual. Approved-use and sale/sharing reviews may exist, but they are inconsistent.

Level 3: Operationalized

Systems are mapped. Data owners are assigned. DSAR search scope is repeatable. DPIAs are tied to intake and change management. Legal holds suspend deletion. Breach notification decisions are tracked. AI and analytics use cases trigger privacy review before launch.

Level 4: Measurable

Metrics show request volume, deadline performance, search coverage, deletion completion, DPIA cycle time, incident notification timelines, overdue vendor reviews, retention exceptions, approved-use reviews, sale/sharing analyses, and AI privacy assessments.

Level 5: Automated and Defensible

Data discovery, classification, workflow routing, evidence capture, deletion orchestration, access review, approved-use review, AI assessment, and regulator reporting are integrated. Privacy operations can respond quickly and prove its decisions.

13.18 Metrics That Matter

Privacy operations should be measured with practical metrics, not vanity metrics.

Metric	Why It Matters
DSAR completion within deadline	Measures operational readiness
Average DSAR search completion time	Shows data discovery efficiency
Percentage of systems mapped to data owners	Shows accountability
Percentage of processing activities with current RoPA entries	Measures inventory health
DPIA completion before launch	Shows privacy by design
Number of overdue DPIA remediations	Shows unresolved risk
Breach assessment time	Measures incident decision readiness
Notification deadline adherence	Measures regulatory exposure
Legal hold acknowledgment rate	Shows preservation discipline

Retention exceptions by reason	Reveals conflict areas
Deletion completion rate	Shows actual data minimization
Vendor privacy review coverage	Shows third-party risk control
Cross-border transfers with approved mechanism	Shows transfer governance
AI systems with completed impact assessment	Shows AI governance maturity
Approved-use reviews completed before launch	Shows purpose governance maturity
Sale/sharing analyses completed for data-sharing initiatives	Shows readiness for privacy rights and disclosure obligations
Number of AI systems using personal data without approved-use documentation	Reveals AI privacy governance gaps
Number of systems with unclear data purpose	Reveals retention and minimization risk

Metrics should help leaders understand whether privacy operations is becoming faster, more defensible, and better aligned to actual data use.

13.19 Tabletop Exercise: Privacy Operations Under Pressure

Scenario

A ransomware investigation finds evidence that an attacker accessed a cloud file-sharing platform. The platform contains HR files, customer contracts, support exports, security logs, and a folder used by the data science team for AI experimentation.

A California employee submits a deletion request the same day. Legal receives notice of a pending lawsuit. The company also has EU customers, a healthcare business unit, a financial services product line, and NYDFS-regulated operations.

During the investigation, the team discovers that some customer support exports were uploaded into an AI analytics tool to summarize complaint trends. The tool was approved for internal analytics, but no one is sure whether it was approved for customer personal data, whether the vendor can use submitted data for product improvement, or whether the workflow creates sale, sharing, or cross-border transfer concerns.

Exercise Questions

1. *Which systems must be preserved?*
2. *Does legal hold override deletion?*
3. *Which data types are involved?*
4. *Are PHI, customer financial information, or California resident data present?*
5. *Are EU residents impacted?*
6. *Did data cross borders?*
7. *Is notification required under HIPAA, GLBA, NYDFS, GDPR, CCPA, contracts, or SEC rules?*
8. *Was AI training, prompting, retrieval, summarization, or analytics involved?*
9. *Was the AI use approved for that data category?*

10. *Does the AI workflow constitute sale, sharing, or monetization?*
11. *What evidence must be preserved?*
12. *Who approves the final notification decision?*
13. *What remediation is required after the immediate incident response?*

Expected Learning

The exercise should show that privacy operations is not a back-office function. It is part of incident response, litigation readiness, regulatory response, AI governance, and data protection architecture.

It should also reinforce that privacy incidents are not limited to unauthorized access. Inappropriate, excessive, undisclosed, or unapproved use of data can create serious privacy risk even when systems are functioning as designed.

13.20 Actionable Recommendations

1. Build a unified data inventory

Tie systems, data owners, data categories, retention periods, vendors, transfer locations, AI systems, and approved uses together.

2. Make DSAR search scope repeatable

Create pre-approved system search playbooks by data subject type. Include AI-connected repositories, prompt logs, outputs, embeddings, and vendor-managed systems where applicable.

3. Connect DPIA to procurement and change management

Do not rely on teams to remember privacy review after launch. New systems, vendors, data sharing, analytics, and AI use cases should trigger review before production.

4. Create a breach notification decision matrix

Include GDPR, HIPAA, GLBA, NYDFS, SEC, CCPA, state breach laws, contractual triggers, and AI-related data exposure scenarios.

5. Coordinate legal hold and deletion

DSAR deletion workflows must check legal hold and retention obligations before action. When a legal hold is released, revisit retention and deletion obligations instead of allowing data to remain indefinitely.

6. Map cross-border access, not just storage

Remote support, offshore administration, SIEM ingestion, AI processing, prompts, outputs, embeddings, and model telemetry processed outside approved jurisdictions can create transfer issues.

7. Document retention conflicts

Maintain an exception register showing why data was retained, restricted, deleted, suppressed, de-identified, or preserved under legal hold.

8. Treat AI systems as privacy systems

Track training data, prompts, outputs, embeddings, logs, vendor use, human oversight, and approved-use boundaries.

9. Ask the two privacy governance questions early

Before launching a new data use case, ask: *Does this constitute a sale, sharing, or monetization of data? Is this an approved use of the data?*

10. Preserve privilege intentionally

Use counsel-directed workflows for sensitive incidents and investigations.

11. Design for regulator-ready evidence

Every workflow should produce dated, approved, traceable records.

12. Validate authorized access against approved use

Do not assume that technical access means the use is appropriate. Review whether the current use matches purpose, notice, consent, contract, retention, and data minimization expectations.

Key Takeaways

Privacy operations turns regulatory obligations into daily practice.

A strong program can answer:

- *What data do we have?*
- *Why do we have it?*
- *Where is it?*
- *Who has access?*
- *How long do we keep it?*
- *Can we delete it?*
- *Is this an approved use of the data?*
- *Does this constitute a sale, sharing, or monetization of data?*
- *Can we prove what we did?*

The organizations that handle privacy well are not the ones with the longest policies. They are the ones that can produce reliable evidence quickly, especially during incidents, DSARs, audits, litigation, regulatory inquiries, and AI governance reviews.

Modern privacy risk is not only about unauthorized access. It is also about authorized but inappropriate use.

In the AI era, that distinction matters more than ever.

Chapter 14: Destroy and Retire: Closing the Data Lifecycle Safely

Opening Thought: The Data You Keep Still Has a Vote

A security team can do almost everything right and still carry unnecessary risk.

They can discover sensitive data, classify it, govern it, protect it, monitor it, and report on it. They can invest in AI-driven alerts, modern identity controls, cloud monitoring, and incident response playbooks. But if old, duplicated, abandoned, orphaned, or legally expired data remains scattered across the environment, the organization is still defending information it may no longer need.

That is the uncomfortable truth of data security:

Data does not become harmless just because the business forgot about it.

Destroy and retire is the final stage of the DSPM lifecycle, but it is not a housekeeping task. It is a security control. It is a compliance function. It is an operational discipline. Most importantly, it is one of the few controls that permanently reduces the amount of sensitive data an attacker, insider, misconfiguration, or third-party failure can expose.

NIST SP 800-88 Rev. 2 defines media sanitization as a process that renders access to target data infeasible for a given level of effort. The same guidance emphasizes that organizations should establish a media sanitization program using appropriate techniques and controls based on the sensitivity of the information.

That point matters. Destruction is not simply pressing delete. It is a controlled decision about whether data should continue to exist, where it exists, what obligations apply, how it should be removed, and what evidence proves the action was completed correctly.

14.1 Why Destroy and Retire Deserves Its Own Lifecycle Stage

Many data security programs treat destruction as a footnote under retention.

That is a mistake.

Retention answers the question:

How long must we keep this?

Destroy and retire answers a different question:

When this data no longer has a valid purpose, how do we safely remove it from risk?

Those are related, but they are not the same.

A retention schedule may say a record can be deleted after seven years. A safe destruction process must still confirm that no legal hold applies, why the data was retained, whether the data owner has approved disposition, whether the system of record is known, whether downstream copies are accounted for, whether backups and snapshots are understood, and whether the destruction method is appropriate for the sensitivity and storage type.

A mature DSPM program must therefore treat destruction as a first-class lifecycle stage, equal in importance to discover, classify, govern, protect, monitor, and report.

Destroy and retire is where gaps in the broader program become obvious. You cannot safely destroy what you have not discovered. You cannot prioritize destruction without classification. You cannot delete data under legal hold. You cannot prove destruction without governance. You cannot confirm success without monitoring and evidence. You cannot safely dispose of AI-era data unless you understand prompts, embeddings, vector stores, logs, model artifacts, and downstream copies.

Core Vocabulary

Before building a destruction process, the organization needs shared language.

Term	Meaning in a DSPM Program
Retention	The period data must be preserved for business, legal, regulatory, contractual, or operational reasons.
Legal hold	A restriction that prevents data from being deleted or altered because it may be needed for litigation, investigation, audit, or regulatory inquiry.
Disposition	The approved decision about what happens to data at the end of its useful or required life. Disposition may include retention, archival, minimization, de-identification, deletion, sanitization, or destruction.
ROT data	Redundant, obsolete, or trivial data that no longer provides meaningful business value.
Stale data	Data that has not been accessed, modified, used, or validated within a defined period. Stale data is not always safe to delete, but it should be reviewed.
Orphaned data	Data without a clear business owner, system owner, active user, or accountable steward.
Legal hold release	The formal approval to end preservation obligations for a matter and return eligible data to normal retention and disposition rules.
Deletion	A logical action that removes a file, object, record, or reference from ordinary use. Deletion alone may not prevent recovery.
Sanitization	A controlled process that makes access to target data infeasible for a defined level of effort.
Destruction	A sanitization method that makes target data recovery infeasible and renders the storage media unusable for future data storage.
Derived data	Data created from, transformed from, inferred from, summarized from, or enriched by another data source.
Embeddings	Mathematical representations of data used by AI and search systems. They may not look like the original record but can still carry sensitivity or enable reconstruction, inference, or retrieval.

The most important distinction is this:

Deletion is an action, but destruction is an assurance outcome.

A deleted file may sit in a recycle bin, version history, archive, backup, replica, log, object version, endpoint cache, email attachment, AI prompt log, vector database, embedding store, exported notebook, or unmanaged report. A destroyed or properly sanitized data set has gone through a process designed to prevent practical recovery.

14.2 NIST Foundation: Clear, Purge, and Destroy

NIST SP 800-88 Rev. 2 defines three sanitization methods: clear, purge, and destroy. It also distinguishes logical techniques, which generally leave information storage media usable, from physical techniques, which often leave media unusable.

Method	What It Means	When It Fits
Clear	Uses logical techniques to sanitize data in user-addressable storage locations, protecting against simple, non-invasive recovery using the normal user interface.	Lower-risk reuse scenarios where the storage type supports reliable clearing and the residual risk is acceptable.
Purge	Uses physical or logical techniques to make target data recovery infeasible using state-of-the-art laboratory techniques, while potentially preserving the media for reuse.	Higher-assurance reuse scenarios, especially when the organization wants stronger protection but does not need to physically destroy the media.
Destroy	Makes target data recovery infeasible using state-of-the-art laboratory techniques and makes the media unusable for future data storage.	End-of-life media, hard copy, failed or obsolete devices, highly sensitive data, or cases where clear or purge cannot be trusted or applied.

NIST notes that purge should be used instead of clear when possible, and that cryptographic erase can be especially important for logical or virtual storage, including cloud storage, where the data owner may not have direct access to the underlying physical media.

NIST also warns against false confidence. For example, degaussing should not be used for non-magnetic media such as SSDs, and some destructive techniques may damage a device without making recovery infeasible.

That is why destroy and retire must be policy-driven, not tool-driven.

14.3 The Safe Destroy and Retire Workflow

A practical DSPM destruction process should follow a repeatable workflow.

1. Identify Candidate Data

Start with discovery.

Candidate data for destruction may include ROT data, stale repositories, orphaned shares, abandoned SaaS workspaces, expired project data, outdated exports, duplicated sensitive data, old database extracts, unmanaged spreadsheets, legacy application data, retired system storage, obsolete AI training sets, expired prompt logs, unused vector stores, stale embeddings, and abandoned analytics workspaces.

DSPM tooling can help identify this data by combining sensitivity, age, access, ownership, location, exposure, activity, retention status, and business context.

A useful first question is not:

Can we delete this?

It is:

Why does this still exist?

2. Classify the Data and Its Risk

Classification determines how carefully the data must be handled. Public marketing content and regulated health records should not follow the same disposition path.

The classification review should consider sensitivity, confidentiality impact, privacy obligations, business value, contractual restrictions, jurisdiction, system criticality, and whether the data appears in multiple environments.

For AI and analytics environments, classification should also consider whether the data was used to train, fine-tune, prompt, retrieve, summarize, embed, label, evaluate, or enrich another system. The original data may no longer be the only risk. The derived data may now carry sensitivity of its own.

NIST's sanitization decision process is based on the confidentiality of the information first. The media type then influences the technique used to achieve the sanitization goal.

3. Check Retention, Legal Hold, Ownership, and Business Need

No destruction should occur until the organization confirms that the data is eligible for disposition.

This is where legal, privacy, records management, compliance, security, IT, and business owners must be part of the process. A security team should not unilaterally destroy data just because it appears old or risky.

The pre-destruction review should answer:

Question	**Why It Matters**
Is the retention period complete?	Data may be required for legal, financial, regulatory, contractual, or operational reasons.
Is there a legal hold?	Data under hold must not be destroyed, even if it is old or risky.
Why is the data under legal hold?	The organization needs to understand the matter, scope, custodians, systems, time period, and preservation basis.
Has the legal hold been released?	Once released, the data should return to normal retention and disposition review.
Who owns the data?	Ownership is needed for approval, context, accountability, and disposition decisions.
Is ownership orphaned or unclear?	Orphaned ownership is a blocker. Data should not be destroyed without assigning an accountable owner or disposition authority.

Is the data used by another system?	Deleting a source, export, index, or reference file can break downstream processes.
Are copies stored elsewhere?	Destroying one copy does not reduce risk if replicas, backups, exports, SaaS sync copies, AI artifacts, or analytics outputs remain.
Is the data part of an investigation?	Security, HR, legal, audit, regulatory, or ethics investigations may require preservation.
Has the data been used in AI or analytics workflows?	Prompts, outputs, embeddings, vector stores, training sets, feature stores, and model evaluation data may need separate disposition review.

If the answer is unclear, the data should be placed in a review queue, not destroyed.

Orphaned Ownership Is a Disposition Blocker

Orphaned data creates two risks at once.

First, no one is accountable for deciding whether the data is still needed. Second, no one is accountable for approving its safe disposition.

Sensitive data without an owner should not be ignored, but it also should not be casually destroyed. The correct response is to assign disposition authority. That may mean identifying a new business owner, assigning ownership to a successor team, escalating to records management, or routing the decision through a governance body.

Orphaned ownership should trigger review of:

- Business purpose
- Retention status
- Legal hold status
- Access permissions
- External sharing
- AI or analytics use
- Downstream copies
- System dependencies
- Required evidence

Data without accountable ownership frequently becomes data without effective governance.

4. Map Dependencies, Copies, and Derived Data

One of the most common destruction failures is assuming the visible copy is the only copy.

Modern data moves across cloud storage, SaaS platforms, collaboration tools, data lakes, warehouses, backups, snapshots, endpoints, logs, developer environments, AI training sets, embeddings, prompt logs, analytics models, and reporting exports. DSPM must help trace where sensitive data lives and where it has moved.

For high-risk data, the destruction workflow should include:

Area	What to Check
Primary system	Database, application, file share, object store, SaaS repository, endpoint, or system of record.
Replicas	Read replicas, disaster recovery copies, regional replication, sync clients, and mirrored storage.
Backups and snapshots	Retention periods, immutability settings, restore points, backup indexes, and expiration timelines.
Logs and telemetry	Application logs, access logs, debug logs, SIEM ingestion, DLP events, API traces, and AI system logs.
Exports	CSV files, spreadsheets, reports, BI extracts, email attachments, temporary files, and user downloads.
AI and analytics	Training sets, fine-tuning sets, embeddings, vector databases, feature stores, prompt logs, outputs, model evaluation data, notebooks, labels, and derived summaries.
Third parties	Processors, managed service providers, legal vendors, auditors, SaaS providers, AI vendors, and analytics vendors.

This does not mean every backup must be surgically altered. In many environments, backups are protected, immutable, and expire according to policy. But the organization still needs to know whether destroyed data can reappear through restoration, replication, unmanaged exports, AI retrieval, or analytics reuse.

5. Choose the Disposition Path

Not all end-of-life data should be destroyed immediately. The right action depends on business purpose, risk, and obligations.

Disposition Path	Use When
Retain	The data still has a valid business, legal, regulatory, contractual, or operational purpose.
Archive	The data must be kept but does not need to remain broadly accessible.
Minimize	The organization only needs part of the data, not the full record or full data set.
De-identify or anonymize	The organization needs analytical value but not direct identifiers, and the method is appropriate for the use case.
Suppress	The data cannot be fully removed from a backup, model, or archive immediately, but it should not be restored, queried, reused, or surfaced.
Clear	Lower-assurance sanitization is acceptable and supported by the media or platform.
Purge	Stronger assurance is needed, but reuse is still desired.
Destroy	The data or media should not be recoverable or reused.

The goal is not to destroy everything as quickly as possible. The goal is to reduce the greatest risk first without creating legal, operational, compliance, or evidentiary harm.

6. Execute With the Right Method

Execution should follow the approved method, the storage type, and the organization's policy.

For cloud and SaaS data, execution may involve retention labels, lifecycle rules, administrative deletion, object version removal, tenant-level purge workflows, customer-managed key destruction, vendor-supported deletion workflows, contractual deletion requests, or platform-specific hard-delete mechanisms.

For databases, execution may involve approved record deletion, partition drops, table purges, transaction log handling, replica synchronization, index cleanup, and backup expiration management.

For AI and analytics systems, execution may involve deletion of training data, removal from feature stores, deletion or regeneration of embeddings, vector store purge, prompt and output log deletion, notebook cleanup, model evaluation data deletion, suppression from retrieval, or vendor deletion requests. In some cases, the organization may need to assess whether retraining, re-indexing, re-embedding, model rollback, or output suppression is required.

For endpoints and physical media, execution may involve clear, purge, cryptographic erase, shredding, pulverizing, incineration, or other approved destruction methods.

For hard copy, execution may involve shredding, pulping, incineration, or a certified destruction vendor.

The method should match the risk. A factory reset may be acceptable in one context and completely inadequate in another.

7. Verify and Validate

NIST separates verification and validation, and that distinction is useful.

Verification asks:

Did the selected technique complete successfully?

Validation asks:

Do we accept the result as effective for this data, this media, and this risk?

NIST describes sanitization assurance as the process of verifying the adequacy or effectiveness of sanitization outcomes. If results are acceptable, the sanitization is accepted. If not, the process should be repeated or escalated to a more secure method.

That means a destruction workflow should include evidence of completion, review of errors or anomalies, confirmation that the method matched the target data, and approval that residual risk is acceptable.

Validation should fail when:

Failure Condition	Example
Wrong method	Degaussing an SSD or using simple deletion for highly sensitive regulated data.
Wrong scope	Deleting only a folder while copies remain in object versions, exports, replicas, vector stores, or prompt logs.
Unqualified execution	A vendor or employee used unapproved tools or undocumented procedures.
Missing evidence	No record of who approved, performed, verified, or validated the action.
Unresolved exception	Data was under legal hold, tied to an active business process, or part of an investigation.
Orphaned ownership	No accountable owner or disposition authority approved the action.
AI derivative gap	Original data was deleted, but embeddings, summaries, training sets, outputs, or model artifacts were not reviewed.

8. Capture Evidence

Destruction without evidence is hard to defend.

NIST recommends completing a certificate of sanitization according to organizational policy. It identifies details such as manufacturer, model, serial number, media type, source, confidentiality categorization, sanitization method, technique, tool version, verification method, and information about the individuals performing verification and validation.

For DSPM, evidence should extend beyond physical media. A strong evidence record should include:

Evidence Field	Example
Data asset	Repository, table, object bucket, SaaS workspace, file share, endpoint, device, AI workspace, vector store, or hard copy batch.
Data classification	Public, internal, confidential, restricted, regulated, or custom classification.
Business owner	Person or team accountable for the data.
Disposition authority	Person, role, or governance body authorized to approve action when ownership is unclear.
Legal and retention result	Retention complete, no legal hold, legal hold released, approved exception, or blocked disposition.
Legal hold rationale	Matter name, scope, custodians, data types, and reason preservation was required.
Post-hold disposition result	Returned to normal retention, archived, minimized, destroyed, or retained under new obligation.
Approved action	Archive, minimize, suppress, clear, purge, destroy, or vendor deletion request.

AI/analytics review	Training data, embeddings, vector stores, prompt logs, outputs, feature stores, notebooks, and derived data reviewed.
Method used	Lifecycle policy, cryptographic erase, secure deletion, vector store purge, re-indexing, physical destruction, purge workflow, or other approved method.
Executor	Internal team, automation, vendor, platform admin, records manager, system owner, or AI platform owner.
Verifier	Person or system that confirmed completion.
Validator	Person or role that accepted the result.
Timestamp	Date and time of approval, execution, verification, and validation.
Residual risk	Known copies, backup expiration date, blocked systems, AI artifacts, or accepted limitation.

The evidence record is what turns destruction from an informal cleanup activity into an auditable control.

14.4 Prioritizing Destroy and Retire Work

Most organizations cannot remediate all stale and risky data at once. The action plan must be prioritized.

A practical prioritization model should weigh the following:

Factor	Higher Priority When
Sensitivity	The data contains PII, PHI, PCI, financial records, credentials, source code, trade secrets, legal data, or regulated content.
Exposure	The data is public, externally shared, broadly accessible, or stored in a misconfigured repository.
Access	The data is available to too many users, dormant accounts, third parties, service accounts, unmanaged identities, or AI tools.
Age and activity	The data is old, inactive, stale, or no longer tied to an active business process.
Ownership	The data is orphaned, has unclear accountability, or is owned by a departed employee or defunct team.
Duplication	The data exists in many unmanaged copies, exports, reports, or AI-derived stores.
Environment	The data spans cloud, SaaS, on-prem, endpoint, backup, third-party, AI, or analytics systems.
Compliance impact	The data is past retention or creates unnecessary privacy, eDiscovery, or regulatory exposure.
AI reuse	The data appears in training sets, prompts, outputs, embeddings, vector databases, notebooks, summaries, or model evaluation data.

Legal hold, active investigation, required retention, unresolved dependency, and unclear ownership are not priority boosters. They are gates. If one applies, destruction stops until the restriction is resolved or an authorized disposition decision is made.

A simple priority model is:

Priority	Description	Action
Critical	Sensitive data, expired retention, no legal hold, excessive access, external exposure, or no owner.	Immediate review, owner assignment, and disposition plan.
High	Sensitive stale data with clear owner and no known hold.	Business approval and scheduled destruction, minimization, or archival.
Medium	Internal data with low exposure but no clear ongoing use.	Owner review and cleanup campaign.
Low	Non-sensitive stale data with limited access.	Automate based on policy where appropriate.
Blocked	Legal hold, active retention, unresolved dependency, unclear ownership, or AI derivative uncertainty.	Preserve, assign owner, document exception, and resolve blocker.

The organization should not buy advanced monitoring for data it cannot classify, and it should not automate destruction for data it cannot legally approve.

14.5 Destroy and Retire Across the DSPM Lifecycle

Destroy and retire depends on every earlier stage of the lifecycle.

DSPM Stage	Contribution to Safe Destruction
Discover	Finds data stores, copies, exports, orphaned repositories, AI artifacts, and unknown sensitive data.
Classify	Determines sensitivity and required handling.
Govern	Defines retention, legal hold, ownership, approved use, disposition authority, and evidence requirements.
Protect and Control	Limits access while data is awaiting review or destruction.
Monitor and Respond	Detects failed deletion, reappearing data, policy drift, unauthorized destruction, and AI reuse.
Destroy and Retire	Removes data safely when it no longer has valid purpose.
Report	Provides evidence, metrics, exceptions, residual risk, and audit readiness.

This is why destroy and retire should not be bolted on at the end of a project. NIST states that the need and methods for media sanitization should be identified before the disposal phase, and that sanitization controls should be developed, documented, and deployed early in the system lifecycle.

For DSPM, that means destruction planning begins when data is created, collected, stored, approved for use, or connected to AI and analytics systems.

14.6 Maturity Model for Destroy and Retire

Level	Characteristics	Next Step
Level 1: Initial	Deletion is manual, inconsistent, and reactive. Retention rules are unclear. Legal hold checks are informal. Evidence is weak or missing. AI-derived data is usually not considered.	Identify high-risk ROT, stale, orphaned, and AI-derived data. Assign owners and document basic disposition decisions.
Level 2: Defined	Basic retention schedules and deletion procedures exist. Reviews are scheduled but mostly manual. Evidence is collected inconsistently.	Create a formal destruction workflow with approval, legal hold checks, ownership validation, classification mapping, AI artifact review, and required evidence.
Level 3: Managed	DSPM findings, retention rules, ownership, and ticketing workflows are connected. Destruction is risk-based and repeatable.	Integrate cloud, SaaS, database, endpoint, backup, AI, and analytics workflows. Standardize verification and validation.
Level 4: Quantitatively Managed	Metrics track eligible data, destroyed data, exceptions, verification failures, backup expiration, policy drift, legal hold releases, AI artifact cleanup, and time to disposition.	Use dashboards and automated playbooks for approved low-risk destruction paths.
Level 5: Optimizing	Destruction is continuously improved using predictive risk scoring, automated policy recommendations, continuous evidence, and business-aligned metrics.	Tune policies based on incidents, audits, business change, regulatory change, AI adoption, and measured risk reduction.

The target is not always Level 5. A startup, healthcare provider, bank, law firm, SaaS company, and manufacturer may all need different maturity targets. The right target depends on risk appetite, regulatory burden, data sensitivity, budget, staffing, and business operating model.

14.7 Special Considerations

Cloud Storage

Cloud platforms make data easy to duplicate, version, replicate, and retain. Destruction workflows must account for object versioning, lifecycle policies, replication rules, retention locks, snapshots, customer-managed keys, and provider deletion behavior.

Cryptographic erase may be especially important where the underlying physical storage is abstracted from the customer. NIST specifically notes that for logical or virtual storage, such as cloud storage, cryptographic erase may be the only viable purge technique, and organizations should understand their options before storing sensitive data there.

SaaS Applications

SaaS destruction depends on platform capabilities. Some platforms support retention labels, legal holds, eDiscovery preservation, recycle bins, permanent purge, and administrative deletion. Others provide limited tenant visibility.

A DSPM program should document what each SaaS platform can and cannot do. The absence of a reliable purge mechanism should affect vendor risk decisions.

Backups and Snapshots

Backups are difficult. They are designed to preserve data, not remove it selectively.

The goal is usually to prevent destroyed data from being restored into production without control. This can be handled through backup retention expiration, restore procedures, post-restore deletion rules, encryption key management, and documented exceptions.

Immutable backups should not be weakened casually to satisfy a deletion request. Instead, the organization should document the backup retention period, protect the backup from unauthorized access, and ensure the data is not reintroduced after restoration.

Legal Hold Release and Post-Hold Disposition

Legal hold should preserve data only for as long as the legal, regulatory, investigative, or audit obligation requires.

When a hold is released, the organization should not simply leave the preserved data in place forever. The release should trigger a post-hold disposition review.

That review should determine:

- Whether the data still has a valid business purpose
- Whether normal retention has already expired
- Whether the data should be archived, minimized, deleted, sanitized, or destroyed
- Whether copies exist in legal platforms, review tools, exports, email collections, or vendor systems
- Whether privileged or confidential investigation materials require special handling
- Whether AI, analytics, or search indexes were created from the preserved data
- What evidence is needed to show that retention and disposition were handled properly

A legal hold is a preservation control. It should not become permanent storage by accident.

AI, Analytics, and Derived Data

Destroy and retire must now include analytics and AI pipelines. Sensitive data may appear in training sets, fine-tuning sets, feature stores, vector databases, embeddings, prompt logs, generated outputs, model evaluation data, exported notebooks, shared reports, dashboards, labels, and derived summaries.

The hard question is not only:

Where is the original record?

It is also:

Where did this record teach, enrich, label, index, summarize, or influence another system?

That matters because deleting the original record may not remove the risk. A customer record may have been transformed into an embedding. A support transcript may have been summarized into a case note. A health record may have been included in a test dataset. A confidential document may have been indexed for retrieval. A prompt may have been stored in logs. A generated output may reproduce sensitive facts.

Disposition decisions for AI and analytics should consider:

AI or Analytics Artifact	Disposition Question
Training set	*Does the data need to be removed, minimized, retrained, or suppressed?*
Fine-tuning data	*Was the data approved for model improvement or adaptation?*
Embeddings	*Can embeddings be deleted, regenerated, or isolated from retrieval?*
Vector database	*Does the vector store contain sensitive or regulated data chunks?*
Prompt logs	*Are prompts retained, searchable, or accessible to vendors or administrators?*
Outputs	*Did the system generate new records containing sensitive information?*
Feature store	*Are derived attributes still tied to individuals or sensitive business entities?*
Model evaluation data	*Does test or benchmark data contain regulated or confidential content?*
Notebooks and exports	*Did analysts create unmanaged copies outside governed systems?*
Search indexes	*Can deleted or restricted content still be surfaced through retrieval?*

DSPM programs should add AI and analytics data flows to disposition planning, especially for regulated, confidential, customer-sensitive, or employee-sensitive data.

The organization may not always be able to surgically remove every influence from a model. In those cases, it should document the limitation, assess residual risk, apply compensating controls, and determine whether retraining, suppression, access restriction, or vendor escalation is required.

Third-Party and Vendor Systems

Destroy and retire does not stop at the organization's boundary.

Vendors, managed service providers, legal vendors, auditors, SaaS providers, AI vendors, and analytics partners may retain copies, logs, exports, support bundles, backups, derived data, or customer-specific processing artifacts.

A mature program should define contractual deletion obligations, evidence requirements, response timelines, support data handling, subcontractor obligations, and certification of destruction expectations.

Vendor deletion evidence should be treated as part of the organization's own evidence library.

14.8 Metrics That Matter

Executives do not need a report that says, "We deleted files."

They need to know whether data risk is going down.

Useful destroy and retire metrics include:

Metric	Why It Matters
Sensitive data past retention	Shows where expired sensitive data still exists.
ROT data volume	Tracks unnecessary data footprint.
Orphaned sensitive repositories	Highlights ownership gaps.
Time to disposition	Measures how long eligible data remains unresolved.
Legal hold exceptions	Shows where destruction is blocked for valid reasons.
Post-hold review completion	Shows whether released holds return to normal retention and disposition.
Verified destruction rate	Measures evidence-backed completion.
Failed validation rate	Identifies tooling, process, or vendor issues.
Reappearing data incidents	Detects restored, replicated, re-created, or re-indexed data.
Backup expiration coverage	Shows whether destroyed production data still exists in backups and for how long.
AI artifact cleanup coverage	Shows whether embeddings, prompt logs, vector stores, and derived data are included in disposition workflows.
Risk reduction by repository	Connects destruction activity to reduced exposure.

A mature report should tell a story: what risk was found, what was prioritized, what was safely destroyed, what remains blocked, what legal holds were released, what AI artifacts were reviewed, and what decision leadership needs to make next.

14.9 Sample Destroy and Retire Policy Statement

Organizations can adapt the following language:

Data that no longer has an approved business, legal, regulatory, contractual, or operational purpose must be reviewed for disposition. Before destruction, the organization must confirm ownership, classification, retention status, legal hold status, business dependency, known copies, downstream dependencies, and AI or analytics-derived artifacts. If data ownership is unclear, disposition must be escalated to an authorized owner or governance body before action is taken. Approved destruction must use a method appropriate to the sensitivity of the data and the storage medium. Destruction must be verified, validated, and supported by evidence sufficient for audit, compliance, privacy, legal, and risk management purposes. When a legal hold is released, the data must be returned to normal retention and disposition review.

That short policy sets the tone. It makes destruction a governed decision, not an informal cleanup habit.

Key Takeaways

Destroy and retire is the lifecycle stage where data security becomes risk removal.

Discovery shows what exists. Classification explains what it is. Governance defines what should happen. Protection limits who can reach it. Monitoring watches for misuse. Reporting proves progress.

But destroy and retire asks the final question:

Should this data still exist at all?

When the answer is no, the organization needs more than deletion. It needs a safe, prioritized, evidence-backed destruction process aligned to business value, legal obligations, data sensitivity, ownership, and technical reality.

Legal hold must be respected, but it should not become permanent storage by accident. Organizations should document why data is under hold, preserve what is required, release holds when authorized, and revisit retention and disposition once the hold ends.

Orphaned data is not just messy. It is a governance failure. Sensitive data without an accountable owner should trigger ownership assignment, review, and disposition planning.

AI and analytics make destruction more complicated. The organization must consider not only the original record, but also training sets, embeddings, vector stores, prompt logs, outputs, summaries, feature stores, indexes, and derived data.

The strongest DSPM programs do not simply protect data forever.

They know when to let data go, and they can prove they did it safely.

Chapter 15: Governing Enterprise Search, Brand Content, and Copilot Readiness

Copilot Search Branding is the practice of making an organization's approved brand knowledge, terminology, assets, and messaging easy for Microsoft 365 Copilot Search to find, rank, and return accurately.

This is not simply putting a logo in Copilot. It is a governance discipline that connects brand management, enterprise search, Microsoft 365 administration, data security, and content lifecycle management.

In simple terms, Copilot Search Branding helps ensure that when employees ask questions like, *"What is our current company boilerplate?"* or *"Which logo should I use for this presentation?"* the answer comes from approved, current, and properly governed sources.

15.1 Why Copilot Search Branding Matters

In traditional enterprise search, a user types a keyword and reviews a list of links. In Copilot Search, users increasingly ask business questions in natural language and expect useful answers.

That changes the risk.

If the organization has old brand decks, abandoned messaging documents, duplicate logos, outdated product names, or overshared strategy files, Copilot Search may surface material that is technically accessible but not appropriate, current, or approved.

Copilot Search Branding matters because it helps organizations protect their reputation, reduce confusion, and keep employees aligned to the current voice of the business.

1. Protect brand consistency

Employees should be able to find approved voice, tone, templates, logos, taglines, and product descriptions instead of copying from an old deck or recycling language from a previous campaign.

2. Reduce misinformation and outdated messaging

Curated search results can guide users toward official answers, approved documents, and current brand guidance. This is especially important when product names, positioning, legal language, or company messaging changes over time.

3. Improve employee productivity

Sales, marketing, HR, legal, communications, and executive teams often lose time hunting for the "right" version of brand content. A governed search experience helps employees find what they need faster.

4. Support security and compliance

Sensitive strategy documents, unreleased campaign material, pricing details, merger-related content, customer statements, or regulated claims should not become casually discoverable because of poor permissions or oversharing.

5. Prepare the organization for AI-driven work

Copilot is only as useful as the knowledge foundation underneath it. A messy brand repository creates messy AI-assisted output. A governed brand knowledge foundation helps Copilot return answers that are current, approved, and safe to use.

15.2 What Copilot Search Branding Includes

Copilot Search Branding should cover more than visual assets. A mature program includes brand identity, brand language, product terminology, search curation, and data governance.

Area	Examples
Brand identity	Logos, colors, fonts, templates, imagery, design rules
Brand language	Boilerplate, tone of voice, messaging pillars, tagline usage
Product naming	Current product names, retired names, approved abbreviations
Corporate terminology	Internal acronyms, department names, initiative names
Sales messaging	Approved value propositions, industry messaging, competitive positioning
Legal and compliance language	Disclaimers, trademark rules, privacy language, regulated claims
Search curation	Bookmarks, acronyms, Q&A-style answers, authoritative result ranking
Data governance	Permissions, sensitivity labels, retention, ownership, review cycles

The point is not to make every brand-related file searchable. The point is to make the right content searchable for the right people, while outdated, sensitive, or unapproved content is archived, restricted, or clearly marked.

15.3 How Copilot Search Branding Works

1. Establish the Brand Source of Truth

The first step is deciding where official brand knowledge lives.

This may include:

- A SharePoint brand center
- A digital asset management platform
- Approved PowerPoint templates
- Legal-approved boilerplate language
- Product naming guidance
- Campaign messaging libraries
- Partner or channel marketing content
- Customer-facing security and compliance statements

The goal is to make approved content easy to identify and outdated content easy to suppress, archive, or remove.

A practical rule: if a user would be embarrassed to use it in front of a customer, executive, regulator, or partner, it should not be treated as an authoritative brand source.

2. Curate Search Answers

Search curation is where branding becomes operational.

User searches	Curated result should point to
"company boilerplate"	Current approved company description
"logo"	Official logo library
"sales deck"	Approved sales presentation template
"DSPM messaging"	Current approved product or solution messaging
"privacy statement"	Legal-approved external statement
"brand colors"	Current brand guideline document

This prevents employees from relying on whatever document happens to rank first because it was edited recently, shared broadly, or accidentally indexed.

3. Manage Acronyms and Internal Language

Acronyms are a common source of confusion in large organizations. The same acronym may mean different things in sales, engineering, finance, legal, security, and operations.

For branding, this matters because acronyms often shape how people describe the company externally.

Examples:

- "MDR" could mean managed detection and response.
- "DDR" could mean data detection and response.
- "SAM" could mean software asset management or SharePoint Advanced Management.
- A product codename may not be approved for external use.

A Copilot Search Branding program should define which acronyms are approved, which are internal only, and which should redirect users to formal terminology.

4. Connect External Brand Repositories Carefully

Not all brand content lives inside Microsoft 365. Many organizations store brand assets and product knowledge in platforms such as digital asset management tools, CRM systems, ServiceNow, Confluence, Jira, or custom knowledge bases.

Connectors can help Copilot Search find approved content outside Microsoft 365, but they also introduce governance questions:

- *Who owns the connected data?*
- *Are permissions mapped correctly?*
- *Are external repositories clean and current?*
- *Should draft content be searchable?*
- *Are old campaigns archived?*
- *Are sensitive files labeled or restricted?*

A connector is not a cleanup strategy. It is an amplifier. If the source is messy, the search experience becomes messy too.

5. Use Brand Kits and Approved Templates

Brand kits and approved templates help users create content aligned to organizational brand rules.

This is especially useful for:

- PowerPoint decks
- Event posters
- Internal announcements
- Sales collateral
- Executive presentations
- Partner marketing material
- HR and recruiting content

The key is ownership. Marketing, brand, legal, and communications teams should control what is official, while IT and security help make the assets available safely.

15.4 Security and Governance Considerations

Copilot Search Branding sits directly on top of data governance.

Copilot experiences are influenced by the data users can access, which means bad permissions can become both a branding problem and a data exposure problem.

Risk	Why it matters	Recommended control
Overshared brand folders	Users may find draft, old, or confidential messaging	Review permissions and remove broad access
Outdated templates	Employees reuse old logos, taglines, or legal language	Apply expiration dates and owner reviews
Duplicate content	Copilot Search may surface inconsistent answers	Consolidate authoritative sources
Sensitive strategy files	Future campaigns or M&A messaging may become discoverable	Use sensitivity labels and restricted access
Poor connector governance	External systems may expose stale or sensitive data	Validate permissions and connector scope
Trademark misuse	Improper use of Microsoft, partner, or company marks can create legal risk	Follow trademark and brand guidelines

For sensitive content, organizations should consider controls such as sensitivity labels, data loss prevention, restricted search scopes, access reviews, retention policies, and clear ownership of authoritative brand repositories.

15.5 Example Scenarios

Scenario 1: The Old Logo Problem

A sales team searches Copilot for "company logo" and finds a folder from three years ago. The deck goes to a customer with outdated colors and a retired tagline.

With Copilot Search Branding, the search result points to the official brand kit, current logo library, and approved sales template.

Scenario 2: The Product Rename Problem

A product was renamed after an acquisition, but old documentation still uses the legacy name. Employees keep using the old name in proposals.

With curated acronyms, bookmarks, and official naming guidance, searches for the old name can redirect users to the current approved product language.

Scenario 3: The Sensitive Strategy Problem

A user searches for "new market launch messaging" and finds a confidential draft stored in a broadly shared SharePoint site.

With proper permissions, sensitivity labels, and search governance, draft strategy content is restricted while approved launch messaging is available to the right audience.

Scenario 4: The New Employee Problem

A new employee asks Copilot Search, *"What does DDR mean here?"* The organization has several meanings for DDR across security, data, and operations teams.

With curated acronym answers, the employee sees the approved definition, context, owner, and related policy or training material.

Scenario 5: The Customer Response Problem

A customer asks for the company's official AI security statement. An account executive searches Copilot and finds three similar documents.

With Copilot Search Branding, the account executive is directed to the legal-approved version, the latest customer-facing FAQ, and the correct internal owner.

15.6 Recommended Operating Model

Copilot Search Branding should be jointly owned. It is not just an IT project.

Role	Responsibility
Brand or marketing owner	Defines official brand rules, assets, messaging, and templates
Legal or compliance	Approves regulated language, disclaimers, and trademark usage
Microsoft 365 admin	Configures Copilot Search, Microsoft Search, connectors, and access
Security team	Reviews permissions, labels, DLP, oversharing, and sensitive data exposure

Data governance team	Defines ownership, lifecycle, metadata, and retention
Business content owners	Keep department-specific brand content current

A simple governance model should answer:

- *Who owns each official brand asset?*
- *Where does the approved version live?*
- *How often is it reviewed?*
- *What content should be searchable?*
- *What content should be restricted?*
- *How are outdated assets retired?*
- *Who approves connector access?*
- *How are search analytics reviewed*

15.7 Maturity Model for Copilot Search Branding

Level	Description
Level 1: Ad Hoc	Brand assets are scattered across Teams, SharePoint, email, and local folders. Users rely on memory or old decks.
Level 2: Defined	A central brand location exists, but search curation, permissions, and lifecycle reviews are inconsistent.
Level 3: Managed	Official brand content is curated through bookmarks, acronyms, approved templates, brand kits, and assigned ownership.
Level 4: Measured	Search analytics, content reviews, access reviews, and usage metrics are used to improve accuracy and reduce outdated results.
Level 5: Optimizing	Brand knowledge, permissions, lifecycle management, and Copilot readiness are continuously governed with automation and strong cross-functional ownership.

15.8 Actionable Recommendations

1. Create a single authoritative brand hub.
2. Archive or restrict outdated brand content.
3. Configure bookmarks for high-value brand searches.
4. Define approved acronyms, product names, and internal terminology.
5. Publish official templates and brand kits.
6. Review permissions on brand, strategy, and campaign repositories.
7. Use sensitivity labels for confidential or pre-release content.
8. Validate connector scope before exposing third-party repositories.
9. Assign content owners and review dates.
10. Track search analytics, failed searches, outdated results, and user feedback.

Key Takeaway

Copilot Search Branding is not about making search prettier. It is about making the right answer discoverable, current, approved, and safe.

As organizations adopt Microsoft 365 Copilot, brand governance becomes part of data governance. The same issues that create security risk, such as oversharing, stale content, unclear ownership, and poor classification, also create brand risk.

A strong Copilot Search Branding program helps employees move faster without turning outdated files, draft language, or sensitive strategy into the organization's accidental voice.

Chapter 16: Securing Data Before AI Uses It

AI Does Not Change the Importance of Data Security. It Raises the Stakes.

Artificial intelligence is forcing organizations to revisit an uncomfortable truth: most companies do not understand their data as well as they think they do.

For years, security teams have been working through familiar problems: too much data, too many repositories, inconsistent classification, excessive permissions, unclear ownership, stale files, unmanaged SaaS applications, shadow IT, weak retention, and gaps between security, privacy, legal, compliance, data governance, and the business.

Those issues were already risky before AI became part of the enterprise technology stack.

AI makes them harder to ignore.

An AI system does not need to be malicious to expose sensitive data. It can create risk while doing exactly what it was designed to do: search faster, summarize better, connect ideas, infer meaning, and deliver answers in plain language.

If that system has access to over-permissioned data, poorly classified repositories, sensitive records, privileged documents, source code, regulated data, or ungoverned business information, it may surface information that was technically accessible but practically hidden.

That is the real AI data security problem.

AI turns buried exposure into usable answers.

Imagine a company deploying an internal AI assistant. The assistant connects to SharePoint, Google Drive, Slack, Jira, ServiceNow, email, CRM records, source code repositories, and a cloud data warehouse. The project is approved because the business case is obvious. Employees can find information faster. Support teams can resolve tickets more quickly. Sales can prepare for meetings. Engineering can search documentation. Executives can ask natural-language questions instead of waiting for reports.

Then an employee asks:

"Summarize all files related to the upcoming acquisition."

The AI assistant returns a detailed summary of deal documents, legal notes, financial models, board updates, and internal strategy.

No one hacked anything.

The AI did not bypass security controls. It simply retrieved information from locations where access was already too broad.

A set of permissions that had been ignored for years suddenly became a business-critical exposure.

That is why securing data for AI must start before the AI system is connected, trained, prompted, indexed, or deployed.

The foundation is not the model.

The foundation is the data.

Organizations cannot safely adopt AI if they do not know what data they have, where sensitive data lives, who owns it, who and what can access it, whether access is appropriate, whether the data is regulated, whether it can be used for AI, whether prompts and outputs are stored, whether vendors can train on it, and whether AI activity can be monitored and investigated.

AI security is not only about model behavior, hallucinations, prompt injection, or agentic workflows. Those risks matter, but they are only part of the story.

For most organizations, the larger and more immediate risk is data exposure through connected systems.

The question is not only:

Is the model safe?

The better question is:

Is the data environment safe enough for AI?

16.1 The Four AI Security Conversations That Often Get Blurred

AI security discussions often become confusing because people use the phrase "AI security" to describe several different problems.

A CISO, privacy officer, data leader, engineer, vendor manager, and board member may all be talking about AI risk but mean different things.

A strong program separates these conversations.

Area	Primary Question	Main Concern
AI Data Readiness	*Is the data estate safe enough for AI to use?*	Sensitive data discovery, classification, ownership, permissions, retention, minimization, and AI eligibility
AI System Security	*Is the AI application or model secure?*	Prompt injection, data poisoning, insecure output handling, model abuse, application security, red teaming, and monitoring
AI Governance	*Is AI being used in an approved, accountable, and controlled way?*	Policies, risk tiering, approvals, oversight, human review, documentation, metrics, and regulatory alignment
AI Vendor Risk	*Can the organization trust how vendors process, store, use, retain, and protect data?*	Contract terms, model training restrictions, subprocessors, residency, audit rights, deletion, and tenant isolation
AI Identity and Authorization	*Who or what can the AI access, act as, or act on behalf of?*	Agents, service accounts, OAuth grants, connectors, delegated access, privileges, and human approval

This chapter focuses primarily on **AI data readiness**.

The next chapter focuses on **operating controls for AI-connected data**, including AI system security, governance, vendor risk, identity, authorization, monitoring, response, and agentic controls.

This distinction matters because many organizations try to secure AI by starting with the model. That is incomplete. If the underlying data estate is overexposed, poorly governed, and full of sensitive data in the wrong places, even a well-designed AI system can create risk.

AI data readiness asks a simpler and more foundational question:

Before AI uses this data, should this data be cleaned up, restricted, excluded, minimized, or governed differently?

16.2 Why AI Magnifies Existing Data Risk

AI systems are powerful because they reduce friction. They make it easier for people to find, use, interpret, summarize, and act on information.

That same strength creates security challenges.

Before AI, sensitive information might have been technically accessible but difficult to find. A user might have needed to know the exact folder, file name, project code, database table, Jira ticket, Slack channel, or archive location. In many environments, poor data hygiene survived because the exposure was not obvious.

AI changes that.

A user no longer needs to know where the information lives. They can simply ask for it. The AI system can search, retrieve, summarize, correlate, and explain. It may combine information from multiple systems, identify patterns, infer relationships, and present the result in language that is easy to understand.

That makes AI useful.

It also makes it risky.

AI magnifies data risk in several ways:

AI Effect	Why It Matters
Expanded discoverability	Information that was hard to locate becomes easier to surface.
Accelerated access	Users can retrieve and summarize large volumes of information quickly.
Increased inference	Sensitive meaning can be derived from data that may not appear sensitive in isolation.
Context combination	Data from multiple systems can be joined into a more revealing answer.
New records	Prompts, outputs, embeddings, logs, summaries, and agent actions become part of the data environment.
New identities	Agents, service accounts, plug-ins, connectors, and API integrations may access systems on behalf of users or workflows.
Unclear accountability	It may be hard to determine whether a disclosure came from user behavior, retrieval logic, model behavior, vendor retention, or weak governance.

This is why AI adoption often reveals weaknesses that were already present. The organization may have had excessive permissions for years. It may have had unclassified regulated data sitting in collaboration tools. It may have had sensitive source code in shared repositories. It may have had customer records exported into spreadsheets. It may have had service accounts with broad access.

AI simply makes those weaknesses easier to exploit, misuse, or accidentally expose.

In that sense, AI is a force multiplier.

It multiplies productivity when data is governed well.

It multiplies exposure when data is unmanaged.

16.3 Real-World Lesson: Prompt Injection Revealed Hidden Instructions

The AI Incident Database includes an incident involving early Bing Chat testers who used prompt injection to reveal built-in initial instructions. The incident is useful because it shows that AI systems can expose information that developers or operators believed was internal to the system.

This is not only a model security issue. It is a data governance lesson.

System prompts, configuration instructions, hidden context, retrieval rules, tool instructions, and internal policy text may all become sensitive AI-adjacent data. If those artifacts are not treated as protected records, they may leak through unexpected model behavior, prompt injection, debugging, logging, or support workflows.

The lesson for DSPM is straightforward:

AI systems create new sensitive data.

Organizations should inventory and protect AI-specific artifacts, including system prompts, prompt templates, retrieved context, tool descriptions, agent instructions, embeddings, evaluation records, and policy rules.

If those artifacts shape system behavior, expose internal architecture, reveal control logic, or describe protected workflows, they deserve classification, ownership, access control, retention rules, and monitoring.

16.4 AI Data Readiness: The Pre-Deployment Question

AI data readiness is the process of determining whether data is appropriate, governed, and safe enough for AI use.

This should happen before the data is connected to a model, indexed into a vector database, made available to a copilot, exposed through an agent, sent to a vendor, or used for training or fine-tuning.

AI data readiness should answer:

- *What data is being considered for AI use?*
- *Who owns it?*
- *Why does the AI need it?*

- *Is the data classified?*
- *Is the data regulated?*
- *Is the data confidential or business-critical?*
- *Is the data accurate and current?*
- *Is the data under legal hold?*
- *Is the data past retention?*
- *Is the data overexposed?*
- *Is access appropriate?*
- *Is the data approved for AI use?*
- *Is the intended AI use consistent with privacy notices, contracts, and customer expectations?*
- *Can the data be minimized, masked, tokenized, anonymized, or excluded?*
- *Can the organization monitor how the data is used?*
- *Can the organization delete, restrict, or suppress AI-derived artifacts later?*

The goal is not to block AI.

The goal is to prevent the organization from connecting powerful AI capabilities to a messy, overexposed, and poorly governed data estate.

16.5 The AI Data Lifecycle

To secure data before AI uses it, organizations need to understand how data interacts with AI systems. AI data risk does not exist in one place. It appears throughout the lifecycle.

Training and Fine-Tuning

Training and fine-tuning involve using data to influence model behavior. This can include public data, licensed data, customer data, internal documents, source code, chat logs, support tickets, call transcripts, knowledge articles, or domain-specific records.

The primary question is:

Should this data be used to shape the model at all?

Sensitive, regulated, confidential, privileged, or proprietary data should not be included in training or fine-tuning unless there is clear business justification, legal approval, privacy review, contractual protection, and technical control.

Once data influences a model, it may be difficult to fully understand, extract, or remove that influence.

Key risks include sensitive data included in training sets, lack of consent or legal basis for data use, regulated data used without proper controls, proprietary data incorporated into third-party systems, poor dataset documentation, inability to delete or isolate training data, data poisoning or manipulation of training sources, and model behavior that reflects confidential or biased data.

Prompting

Prompting occurs when users or systems submit information to an AI model. In enterprise environments, prompts may include far more than casual questions. They may contain customer records, employee information, contracts, source code, security findings, architecture diagrams, vulnerability details, legal questions, financial forecasts, incident response notes, or intellectual property.

The primary question is:

What data are users sending to AI, and where does it go?

Prompts should be treated as business records. In some cases, they may also be regulated records, legal records, investigation records, or security logs. Organizations need to understand whether prompts are stored, retained, reviewed, used for model improvement, shared with vendors, or included in telemetry.

Key risks include employees pasting sensitive data into public AI tools, prompts retained longer than necessary, prompts used for model training without approval, credentials or secrets submitted to AI systems, regulated data included in prompts, lack of prompt monitoring, and lack of user awareness.

Retrieval-Augmented Generation

Retrieval-augmented generation, often called RAG, allows an AI application to retrieve information from enterprise data sources and use that information to generate an answer.

RAG is often presented as safer than training because the model is not permanently trained on the data. That is partially true, but it does not eliminate data risk.

RAG changes where the risk lives.

Instead of asking:

Did we train the model on sensitive data?

The organization must ask:

What sensitive data can the AI retrieve at the moment of use?

A RAG system is not just an AI feature. It is a privileged search and reasoning layer over enterprise data. If retrieval is not permission-aware, classification-aware, and monitored, the AI application can expose sensitive information at scale.

Key risks include AI retrieving documents a user should not access, over-permissioned repositories producing sensitive answers, sensitive information included in vector stores, embeddings revealing meaning even when raw text is not visible, retrieved content containing malicious instructions, lack of source attribution, lack of retrieval logs, and inconsistent access control between source systems and AI systems.

Output

AI output may include answers, summaries, recommendations, code, reports, emails, decisions, tickets, or workflow actions. Output can expose sensitive information directly, or it can reveal sensitive meaning indirectly.

The primary question is:

Could the AI output disclose something the user should not know or create a record that must be protected?

Organizations need to monitor outputs for sensitive data, confidential business information, regulated content, inaccurate statements, unsafe recommendations, or policy violations. Output controls are especially important when AI is used in customer support, healthcare, finance, legal, human resources, cybersecurity, or software development.

Key risks include AI revealing sensitive source material, generating summaries from restricted documents, producing regulated content in uncontrolled locations, disclosing trade secrets or customer information, generating insecure code or configuration guidance, creating inaccurate or unsupported business conclusions, and creating outputs that are copied into systems without review.

Memory and Agents

AI systems increasingly include memory, plug-ins, tools, and agentic capabilities. These systems may remember user preferences, retain conversation history, call APIs, open tickets, send email, update records, query databases, execute code, trigger workflows, or make recommendations that influence business decisions.

The primary question is:

What can the AI remember, access, change, approve, or send?

This is where AI becomes an identity and access management issue. An AI agent should be governed like a non-human identity. It should have a defined owner, limited permissions, scoped access, monitored behavior, and a lifecycle that includes provisioning, review, rotation, and decommissioning.

Key risks include AI agents using overly broad service accounts, shared credentials used by multiple agents, agents performing actions without approval, agents accessing systems outside their business purpose, agent memory storing sensitive data, lack of audit trails for AI-initiated actions, and difficulty attributing actions to a user, agent, or workflow.

Monitoring and Retention

AI creates new forms of telemetry: prompts, outputs, retrieved documents, model responses, user feedback, embeddings, tool calls, agent actions, error logs, policy decisions, and vendor support artifacts.

The primary question is:

Can the organization reconstruct what happened if AI exposes data or takes an unauthorized action?

Security, privacy, compliance, and legal teams need enough logging to investigate misuse, prove control effectiveness, support audits, and respond to incidents. At the same time, logs themselves may contain sensitive data and must be protected.

Key risks include no visibility into AI use, logs containing sensitive prompts or outputs, logs retained too long or not long enough, lack of integration with SIEM/SOAR/IAM/DLP/DSPM tools, no audit trail for retrieved data, and no incident response playbooks for AI-related data exposure.

16.6 AI Data Sovereignty and Residency

AI forces organizations to redefine data sovereignty.

In traditional cloud governance, sovereignty often focuses on storage location, residency, and transfer mechanisms. In AI systems, sovereignty must also account for processing location, retrieval scope, prompt retention, model provider terms, embeddings, logs, agent actions, vendor support, and derived outputs.

A data source may remain in the correct country or cloud region, while an AI workflow still creates sovereignty exposure by sending prompts to a vendor, storing embeddings in another region, allowing offshore support access, retaining prompt logs globally, or using enterprise content to improve a model.

For AI architecture reviews, the sovereignty question should be explicit:

Where does the data go, where is it processed, who can access it, what artifacts are created from it, how long are those artifacts retained, and can the organization delete or restrict them when required?

Sovereignty should not be treated as a storage-only issue. In AI systems, processing, retrieval, logging, support access, telemetry, and model improvement can all create data residency and transfer concerns.

16.7 Classifying Data for AI Eligibility

Data classification should not stop at "public," "internal," "confidential," and "restricted." AI use requires an additional question:

Is this data eligible for AI use?

A useful AI-aware classification model may include:

Classification	Description	AI Handling Guidance
Public	Approved for external release	Generally safe for AI use
Internal	Intended for employees or approved internal users	Allowed in approved tools with logging
Confidential	Business-sensitive information	Requires business justification and access controls
Restricted	Highly sensitive information	Use only with approved enterprise AI controls
Regulated	Data subject to legal or regulatory requirements	Requires privacy, legal, and compliance review
Secrets and Credentials	Passwords, keys, tokens, certificates, private keys	Never allowed in prompts, training data, vector stores, or AI logs
Privileged or Legal	Attorney-client, work product, litigation, investigation materials	Requires legal approval and strict handling
AI-Excluded	Data not approved for AI use	Block from training, prompting, retrieval, indexing, and vendor processing

Classification should also identify toxic combinations. A single data element may not be highly sensitive by itself, but when combined with other data, it may create regulated, confidential, or high-impact exposure.

AI is especially good at combining context, so toxic combinations matter.

For example, name plus diagnosis may become protected health information. Name plus account number may become financial exposure. Email plus location plus badge access logs may reveal employee behavior. Vendor name plus contract terms plus renewal date may reveal negotiation leverage. Source code plus vulnerability findings may reveal exploit paths.

Classification gives AI systems guardrails.

Without classification, the organization cannot reliably decide what AI may access, summarize, retain, or disclose.

16.8 Minimize Before Connecting

Data minimization is one of the most important AI security controls.

The more data an AI system can access, the more data it can expose, misuse, summarize, infer from, or retain.

Before connecting data to AI, organizations should reduce unnecessary exposure. This includes removing stale data, duplicate data, orphaned data, outdated exports, abandoned repositories, old project folders, unnecessary permissions, and data that no longer has a business purpose.

Minimization should apply to training datasets, fine-tuning datasets, RAG source repositories, vector databases, prompt inputs, output retention, AI logs, agent memory, and vendor data sharing.

The safest data for AI to process is the minimum data required to accomplish the approved business purpose.

Questions to ask include:

- *Does the AI system need full documents or only selected fields?*
- *Does the model need raw data or masked data?*
- *Does the agent need write access or only read access?*
- *Does the vendor need persistent storage or temporary processing?*
- *Do prompts need to be retained?*
- *Do outputs need to be stored?*
- *Can regulated data be excluded from the use case?*
- *Can synthetic, tokenized, redacted, or anonymized data meet the objective?*
- *Can stale repositories be cleaned before indexing?*
- *Can broad permissions be reduced before retrieval?*

Data minimization is not only a privacy principle.

It is an AI security strategy.

16.9 RAG Readiness: Do Not Connect AI to a Messy Repository

Retrieval-Augmented Generation deserves special attention because it is one of the most common ways organizations bring enterprise data into AI.

RAG allows an AI application to retrieve relevant content from internal sources and use that content to generate an answer. This can be extremely valuable. It allows organizations to use AI with current, business-specific information without necessarily training a model on all internal data.

However, RAG is not automatically safe.

A RAG system can become a new data access plane. It may sit above multiple repositories, search across systems, retrieve snippets, assemble context, and generate answers that are easier to consume than the source material.

That means RAG must be governed with the same seriousness as identity, search, data access, and application security.

Organizations often make several mistakes when deploying RAG.

First, they assume that if a user has access to a repository, AI access is automatically acceptable. This ignores the fact that AI changes the usability of access. A user who would never manually inspect thousands of files can ask an AI assistant to summarize them in seconds.

Second, they rely on folder-level permissions without understanding whether those permissions are appropriate. Many collaboration environments have years of accumulated access grants, shared links, inherited permissions, and stale groups.

Third, they index too much data too quickly. Teams often connect broad repositories to prove business value, then discover later that the index contains sensitive or regulated information.

Fourth, they overlook embeddings and metadata. Even if raw documents are protected, embeddings, chunks, metadata, and search results may reveal sensitive meaning.

Fifth, they fail to log retrieval. If an AI answer exposes sensitive information, the organization needs to know what documents were retrieved, what user asked the question, what permissions were evaluated, what answer was generated, and what policy decisions were made.

The most important principle is simple:

Do not connect AI to data that the organization would be embarrassed to discover is already overexposed.

AI is not the right place to discover that everyone has access to the legal folder.

16.10 DSPM's Role in AI Data Readiness

Data Security Posture Management is highly relevant to AI because AI depends on data visibility, classification, access control, exposure management, and continuous monitoring.

DSPM helps answer questions that AI governance cannot answer through policy alone:

- *Where does sensitive data live?*
- *Which repositories contain regulated data?*
- *Which users have excessive access?*
- *Which service accounts can reach sensitive data?*
- *Which cloud buckets, databases, or file shares are exposed?*
- *Which data stores are stale, orphaned, or unmanaged?*
- *Which sensitive files are accessible to too many people?*
- *Which data sources are connected to AI tools?*
- *Which AI use cases involve high-risk data?*
- *Which data should be excluded, masked, minimized, or reviewed before AI use?*

DSPM does not replace AI governance, IAM, DLP, privacy review, vendor risk, or application security. It strengthens them by giving the organization a clearer understanding of the data itself.

For AI, DSPM can support pre-AI data readiness assessments, sensitive data discovery, classification and labeling, access exposure analysis, over-permissioned data remediation, data owner identification, RAG source review, detection of secrets and credentials, monitoring of sensitive data movement, policy enforcement support, compliance reporting, and risk-based prioritization.

In practical terms, DSPM helps organizations avoid connecting AI to a messy, overexposed data estate.

That is the heart of AI data readiness.

16.11 Practical Checklist: Before Connecting Data to AI

Before connecting a data source to an AI system, organizations should answer the following questions.

Data Understanding

- *What data source is being connected?*
- *Who owns the data?*
- *What business purpose does the AI use case serve?*
- *What types of data are included?*
- *Is the data classified?*
- *Does the source contain regulated data?*
- *Does the source contain secrets, credentials, or keys?*
- *Does the source contain confidential business information?*
- *Is the data current, accurate, and appropriate for the use case?*
- *Is the data under legal hold?*
- *Is the data past retention?*
- *Is the data approved for AI use?*

Access and Permissions

- *Who can access the data today?*

- *Is current access appropriate?*
- *Are there stale users, groups, or service accounts?*
- *Are there shared links or inherited permissions?*
- *Will the AI enforce source-system permissions?*
- *Will retrieval be identity-aware?*
- *Will retrieval be classification-aware?*
- *Can users export AI outputs?*
- *Can the AI access more than the user can access directly?*
- *Can service accounts or connectors access more than intended?*

AI Processing

- *Will data be used for training?*
- *Will data be used for fine-tuning?*
- *Will data be indexed into a vector database?*
- *Will data be sent to a third-party model provider?*
- *Will prompts or outputs be retained?*
- *Will the vendor use data for model improvement?*
- *Can training be disabled?*
- *Can data be deleted?*
- *Can embeddings, chunks, logs, and derived artifacts be deleted?*

Security Controls

- *Is data encrypted in transit and at rest?*
- *Are prompts inspected for sensitive data?*
- *Are outputs inspected for sensitive data?*
- *Are retrieved sources logged?*
- *Are AI actions logged?*
- *Are high-risk actions approved by a human?*
- *Is there a kill switch for agents?*
- *Are logs protected?*
- *Is source attribution available?*
- *Are vector databases protected?*

Governance and Compliance

- *Has legal reviewed the use case?*
- *Has privacy reviewed the use case?*
- *Has security reviewed the architecture?*
- *Has compliance reviewed regulatory impact?*
- *Has procurement reviewed vendor terms?*
- *Has the data owner approved the use case?*
- *Is there an incident response plan?*
- *Is there an exception process?*
- *Is there a documented approved-use decision?*
- *Does the use create sale, sharing, monetization, or cross-border transfer concerns?*

Sovereignty and Residency

- *Where is the source data stored?*
- *Where is the data processed during AI use?*
- *Where are prompts, outputs, embeddings, chunks, logs, and telemetry stored?*
- *Can the AI vendor process or support the data from other countries?*
- *Are cross-border transfer mechanisms documented?*
- *Are region restrictions technically enforced?*
- *Can AI-derived artifacts be deleted, expired, or excluded from future retrieval?*
- *Are data residency, sovereignty, and vendor processing terms documented in the AI use-case approval?*

16.12 Common Opportunities for Improvement

Organizations often have immediate opportunities to reduce AI data risk before connecting data to AI.

Clean Up Over-Permissioned Collaboration Data

Collaboration platforms are often the easiest place to start. Shared drives, document libraries, channels, and folders frequently contain sensitive data with broad access.

Before connecting these platforms to AI, review access to legal, finance, HR, executive, product, engineering, customer, and security folders.

Identify Secrets in AI-Accessible Locations

Secrets, API keys, tokens, certificates, and private keys should not be available to AI systems. They should be detected, removed, rotated if exposed, and monitored going forward.

Review SaaS AI Features

Many SaaS vendors are adding AI capabilities. Organizations should determine which features are enabled, what data they process, whether users can opt in individually, and whether administrative controls exist.

Build a Safe AI Intake Process

Business teams need a clear path to request AI use cases. The intake process should be practical, not punitive. It should help teams move forward safely by identifying data, access, vendors, risks, and required controls.

Connect DSPM to AI Governance

DSPM findings should inform AI decisions. If a repository contains regulated data and excessive access, it should not be indexed into an AI assistant until the exposure is remediated or compensating controls are in place.

Train Employees with Real Examples

AI training should not be vague. Employees need concrete examples of what not to paste, which tools are approved, how to request new use cases, and what to do if they accidentally submit sensitive data.

16.13 What AI Data Readiness Is Not

AI data readiness is not simply buying an enterprise AI license.

Enterprise licensing may provide better contractual terms, administrative controls, privacy settings, or retention options, but it does not automatically fix overexposed data or weak governance.

AI data readiness is not simply blocking public chatbots.

Blocking unmanaged tools may reduce risk, but employees still need approved paths to do their work. If security only says no, the business will find a workaround.

AI data readiness is not only a privacy issue.

Privacy is important, but AI can also expose intellectual property, trade secrets, credentials, legal strategy, financial information, source code, security vulnerabilities, and business plans.

AI data readiness is not only a model problem.

The model matters, but so do the data sources, permissions, prompts, outputs, logs, vendors, agents, and workflows around it.

AI data readiness is not a one-time review.

AI systems change. Data changes. Users change. Vendors change. Risk changes. Controls must be monitored and improved continuously.

16.14 Actionable Recommendations

Organizations can take the following actions before connecting data to AI:

1. Build and maintain an inventory of AI tools, AI features, AI vendors, AI agents, and AI-connected data sources.
2. Identify sensitive, regulated, confidential, and business-critical data before connecting it to AI.
3. Classify data by sensitivity, regulation, business value, owner, retention, and AI eligibility.
4. Remove excessive permissions from repositories that may be used by AI.
5. Block secrets, credentials, payment data, health data, and other restricted information from unauthorized AI tools.
6. Require approved enterprise AI platforms for sensitive business use cases.
7. Disable training on enterprise prompts and data unless explicitly approved.
8. Apply permission-aware and classification-aware retrieval for RAG systems.
9. Secure vector databases, embeddings, chunks, and metadata.
10. Give AI agents dedicated identities and least-privilege access.
11. Require human approval for high-risk agent actions.
12. Monitor prompts, outputs, retrievals, and agent actions for sensitive data exposure.
13. Include AI features in vendor risk reviews and contract negotiations.
14. Red-team AI applications before production.

15. Create incident response playbooks for AI-related data exposure, prompt injection, data poisoning, and agent misuse.
16. Measure AI data security maturity using exposure, access, monitoring, and remediation metrics.
17. Reassess AI use cases regularly as data, users, vendors, and business needs change.

Key Takeaways

AI gives organizations a powerful new way to use information. It can help employees find answers, automate work, improve decisions, support customers, generate content, write code, and unlock value from data that was previously difficult to use.

But AI also changes the risk profile of data.

Sensitive information that was once buried in folders, tickets, chats, and databases can become instantly searchable. Over-permissioned files can become summarized answers. Poor classification can become policy failure. Shadow IT can become shadow AI. Service accounts can become autonomous agents. Logs can become sensitive records. Vendor features can become new data processing pathways.

Securing data for AI starts before deployment.

Organizations need to understand which data should be used, which data should be protected, which data should be excluded, and which controls must surround the entire AI lifecycle.

AI can help organizations move faster, but only if the data foundation is trustworthy.

The future of AI security starts with data readiness.

Chapter 17: Operating Controls for AI-Connected Data

Securing data before AI uses it is only the first step.

Once AI is connected to enterprise data, organizations need operational controls that can be enforced, monitored, measured, and improved. Policies are important, but AI risk moves too quickly for policy alone.

Chapter 16 focused on whether the data estate is ready for AI.

This chapter focuses on how to operate controls once AI systems, copilots, agents, vendors, and AI-enabled SaaS features begin interacting with enterprise data.

A practical AI-connected data security program should be built around five operating domains:

Domain	Focus
AI System Security	Securing AI applications, prompts, retrieval, outputs, models, agents, memory, and tool use
AI Governance	Defining approved use, risk tiers, oversight, accountability, documentation, and metrics
AI Vendor Risk	Governing third-party AI processing, retention, model training, subprocessors, deletion, and audit rights
AI Identity and Authorization	Controlling users, service accounts, agents, OAuth grants, delegated access, and non-human identities
AI Monitoring and Response	Detecting misuse, investigating exposure, responding to incidents, and improving controls

The goal is not to create a separate AI security empire.

The goal is to connect AI controls to existing security, privacy, identity, data governance, vendor risk, application security, and incident response programs.

17.1 Discover and Inventory AI Use

The first operating control is visibility.

Organizations need to know where AI is already in use and which data sources are connected to it.

Discovery should include approved AI tools, unapproved AI tools, AI features embedded in SaaS platforms, internal AI assistants, RAG applications, fine-tuned models, vector databases, AI agents, AI plug-ins, browser extensions, development tools, meeting assistants, security tools, analytics platforms, and vendors using AI on the organization's behalf.

A simple but powerful principle applies:

You cannot secure AI you do not know exists, and you cannot safely use data you have not discovered.

AI inventory should answer:

- *What AI tools are approved?*
- *What AI tools are being used without approval?*
- *Which AI features are embedded in existing SaaS platforms?*
- *Which vendors process enterprise data through AI?*
- *Which systems are connected to AI?*
- *Which data sources are indexed, retrieved, summarized, or analyzed?*
- *Which AI tools store prompts, outputs, embeddings, logs, or telemetry?*
- *Which AI systems can take action through APIs, plug-ins, or agents?*
- *Who owns each AI use case?*

Discovery also needs to include shadow AI. Employees may use public AI tools, browser plug-ins, personal productivity tools, unmanaged transcription tools, AI coding assistants, or SaaS AI features before security teams know they exist.

The point is not to shame users.

The point is to create a safe, visible path for AI adoption.

17.2 Govern AI Use Cases

AI governance defines who approves AI use, what data may be used, what tools are allowed, what reviews are required, and what controls must be in place.

AI governance should include security, privacy, legal, compliance, IT, data governance, procurement, architecture, records management, and business stakeholders.

The goal is not to slow the business down.

The goal is to create a repeatable path for safe adoption.

A practical AI governance process should include:

Governance Area	Operating Requirement
AI use-case intake	Capture purpose, owner, users, data sources, vendor, processing type, and expected business value
Risk tiering	Classify use cases by data sensitivity, autonomy, external impact, regulatory relevance, and business criticality
Data eligibility	Define what data may be used for prompting, retrieval, training, fine-tuning, logging, or agent actions
Approved-use review	Confirm whether the data may be used for the intended AI purpose
Human oversight	Define when human review or approval is required

Exception process	Document exceptions, compensating controls, owner, approval, and expiration date
Evidence	Preserve approvals, assessments, architecture reviews, vendor terms, and control decisions
Ongoing review	Reassess use cases when data, vendors, models, permissions, or business purpose changes

AI governance should avoid two extremes.

The first extreme is saying yes to everything because the business wants speed.

The second extreme is saying no to everything because the risk feels unfamiliar.

A mature program creates a governed yes.

17.3 Authorize AI Access

Authorization defines who and what may access data. In the AI era, authorization must apply to humans, applications, models, agents, plug-ins, APIs, service accounts, connectors, and vendors.

The goal is not simply to confirm that access exists.

The goal is to confirm that access is appropriate for the use case.

AI access should be based on least privilege, business purpose, identity context, data classification, and risk.

A user who can access a folder directly should not automatically be allowed to ask an AI assistant to summarize every sensitive document in that folder. AI can change the risk profile of access because it makes retrieval, summarization, and inference easier.

Authorization controls should include:

- Role-based access control
- Attribute-based access control where appropriate
- Just-in-time access for sensitive data
- Approval workflows for high-risk repositories
- Separate permissions for read, write, execute, approve, and export
- Service account governance
- Non-human identity management
- OAuth grant review
- AI connector review
- Regular access reviews
- Automatic removal of stale or excessive permissions
- Enforcement of source-system permissions in AI retrieval

For AI agents, the principle should be explicit:

Do not give an AI agent more access than you would give a new employee on their first day.

Each AI agent should have a dedicated identity, defined owner, documented purpose, scoped permissions, credential vaulting, rotation, monitoring, and a decommissioning process.

AI identity and authorization is one of the strongest bridges between DSPM and existing CISO priorities. Most organizations already fund IAM, IGA, PAM, and access review programs. AI makes those investments more important because overpermissioned identities can become overpermissioned AI retrieval and action paths.

17.4 Protect AI-Connected Data

Protection controls reduce the likelihood and impact of unauthorized access, misuse, leakage, or manipulation.

AI data protection should include familiar controls such as encryption, access control, DLP, masking, tokenization, secrets detection, key management, logging, and network security. It should also include AI-specific controls such as prompt filtering, retrieval filtering, output inspection, vector database protection, model access controls, and agent guardrails.

Protection should be applied at multiple layers:

Layer	Protection Examples
Source data	Encryption, access control, classification, retention, ownership
AI application	Authentication, authorization, prompt controls, output controls
Retrieval layer	Permission-aware retrieval, classification filters, source attribution
Vector database	Encryption, access control, segmentation, metadata protection
Model interface	API security, rate limiting, abuse detection, logging
Agent layer	Scoped permissions, approval gates, action limits, kill switch
Vendor layer	Contractual restrictions, tenant isolation, retention limits, audit rights

One of the most important protections for RAG is permission-aware retrieval. The AI system should only retrieve information the user is authorized to access, and it should apply classification-based restrictions before producing an answer.

Another important control is source attribution. Users should be able to see where an AI answer came from. Source attribution supports trust, validation, investigation, and compliance.

17.5 Secure RAG as a Data Access Plane

RAG deserves its own operating controls because it changes how users access enterprise data.

A secure RAG architecture should include:

- Source-system permission enforcement
- Identity-aware retrieval
- Classification-aware filtering

- Chunk-level access control where possible
- Sensitive data redaction or masking
- Secrets detection before indexing
- Exclusion of high-risk repositories by default
- Data owner approval before indexing
- Source attribution in answers
- Retrieval logs
- Output inspection
- Prompt injection detection
- Vector database encryption
- Access control for embeddings and metadata
- Index refresh and deletion processes
- Testing with adversarial prompts
- Review of overexposed source repositories before connection

RAG controls should be tested before production. The organization should confirm that the AI cannot retrieve documents outside the user's authorization, cannot surface restricted content through summaries, cannot leak sensitive metadata, and cannot be manipulated by malicious instructions hidden in retrieved content.

The most important principle is simple:

RAG is not only an AI pattern. It is an enterprise data access pattern.

Treat it that way.

17.6 Govern Prompts as Business Records

Many employees treat prompts as casual conversation. That is understandable. AI tools feel conversational by design.

But in enterprise environments, prompts can contain highly sensitive business information.

A prompt may include customer data, employee data, source code, contracts, legal strategy, M&A activity, credentials, security findings, architecture diagrams, incident details, financial forecasts, product plans, board materials, or regulated records.

Prompts should be governed like business records. Depending on the content, they may also be regulated records, legal records, audit evidence, or incident response artifacts.

Organizations should define prompt policies that answer:

- *What data may users submit to approved AI tools?*
- *What data may never be submitted?*
- *Are prompts stored?*
- *How long are prompts retained?*
- *Are prompts used for model training?*
- *Can prompts be reviewed by vendor personnel?*
- *Are prompts encrypted?*
- *Can prompts be exported for audit?*
- *Can users delete prompt history?*

- *Are prompts monitored for sensitive data?*
- *Are prompts subject to legal hold?*

The "Do Not Feed the Model" List

Organizations should clearly define data that may not be entered into public or unmanaged AI systems.

At minimum, this list should include passwords, API keys, tokens, private keys, certificates, protected health information, payment card data, Social Security numbers, government identifiers, customer contracts, legal strategy, M&A documents, unreleased financials, sensitive source code, incident response evidence, internal vulnerability findings, proprietary product designs, trade secrets, and confidential board materials.

For approved enterprise AI systems, some sensitive data may be permitted under strict controls, but the default should be caution.

The fact that a tool is approved does not mean all data is approved for all uses.

17.7 Real-World Lesson: AI Connectors Can Become Exfiltration Paths

The AI Incident Database includes reports involving AI connectors and indirect prompt injection. One report describes a scenario in which Copilot could be manipulated through malicious email content to offer sensitive data. Another report describes attacks against ChatGPT connectors where a seemingly harmless document uploaded to cloud storage could contain indirect prompt injection instructions intended to exfiltrate sensitive data such as API keys.

These incidents are directly relevant to DSPM.

The risk is not only that the model follows a bad instruction. The risk is that the AI system is connected to enterprise repositories, scans content before the user does, retrieves sensitive information through trusted connectors, and may act on malicious instructions embedded in data.

This changes how organizations should think about AI-connected data.

Documents, emails, tickets, web pages, and files are no longer just data. They can become instruction surfaces.

That means AI-connected repositories need stronger controls:

- Sensitive repositories should not be indexed until access is reviewed.
- Retrieved content should be treated as untrusted input.
- Prompt injection testing should include documents, emails, tickets, and web content.
- Connectors should be scoped narrowly.
- API keys, secrets, credentials, and sensitive tokens should be removed before indexing.
- Retrieval and tool calls should be logged.

- Output should be inspected before disclosure.
- Human approval should be required for high-impact actions.

This is one of the clearest examples of why AI data security cannot stop at policy.

The AI system must be designed to distrust the data it retrieves.

17.8 AI Agents as Non-Human Identities

AI agents are changing the security conversation because they can do more than answer questions.

They can perform tasks.

An AI agent may be able to search repositories, query databases, send emails, create tickets, update records, trigger workflows, open pull requests, execute scripts, generate reports, approve routine actions, or interact with other applications.

That means AI agents should be governed like non-human identities.

Every AI agent should have a documented business purpose, named business owner, technical owner, dedicated identity, scoped permissions, access limited to required systems, separate development/test/production permissions, credential vaulting, credential rotation, logging and monitoring, human approval for high-risk actions, transaction limits where appropriate, a kill switch, periodic access reviews, and decommissioning procedures.

Shared service accounts are especially risky. If multiple agents use the same account, accountability becomes difficult. If an agent behaves unexpectedly, the organization may not know which system acted, why it acted, or what data it accessed.

AI agents should not inherit broad administrative permissions because it is convenient.

Convenience is not a control.

A practical rule is:

Give AI agents the least access necessary, for the shortest time necessary, with the clearest accountability possible.

17.9 Securing Agentic AI Architectures

Agentic AI changes the risk model for enterprise AI. Earlier AI applications mostly generated text, summarized content, or assisted a human user. Newer agentic systems can plan, call tools, use credentials, retain memory, interact with APIs, delegate tasks to other agents, and complete multi-step workflows with limited human involvement.

That shift matters because the security question is no longer only:

What did the model say?

It becomes:

What did the agent do, with whose authority, using which tools, against which data, and with what lasting side effects?

An AI agent is not just a chatbot with better prompting. It is a system that can combine reasoning, tools, data access, and execution. For example, an enterprise agent may read an email, query a CRM, summarize a contract, create a ticket, update a record, notify a user, and trigger a workflow in another platform.

Each step may be legitimate on its own, but the combination can create unexpected risk.

The most important architectural difference is agency. Agency is the ability of the system to decide what action to take next. The more autonomy the agent has, the more important it becomes to constrain its permissions, validate its actions, monitor its behavior, and preserve human accountability.

A practical security principle for agentic systems is:

Grant agents the least agency required to complete the task safely.

This extends least privilege into the agentic AI era. The agent should have only the tools, data, credentials, workflow permissions, memory scope, and decision authority needed for its assigned purpose.

Key Agentic Risk Areas

Agentic Area	Risk	Control
Tool-calling interfaces	Model output becomes operational behavior	Tool allowlisting, schema validation, parameter constraints, approval gates
OAuth grants	Agents inherit broad delegated access	Narrow scopes, JIT authorization, token review, access monitoring
Plug-ins and extensions	Third-party tools expand the supply chain	Vendor review, approved plug-in inventory, permission review
Agent memory	Sensitive or poisoned context persists	Memory scoping, review, sanitization, retention limits
Autonomous workflows	Small mistakes cascade into downstream harm	Design-time controls, runtime controls, post-action review
Excessive agency	Agent can do more than its purpose requires	Narrow agents, limited tools, explicit goals, escalation paths
Multi-agent systems	One agent can mislead or influence another	Trust boundaries, signed messages, identity validation, communication controls

The better pattern is to create narrow agents with explicit goals, constrained tools, limited data access, and clear escalation paths.

17.10 Real-World Lesson: Prompt Manipulation Can Create Business Liability

The AI Incident Database includes an incident in which a Chevrolet dealer chatbot was manipulated into agreeing to sell a vehicle for one dollar. The incident is useful because it shows how AI systems connected to customer-facing workflows can be manipulated when goals, guardrails, and human oversight are weak.

The Air Canada chatbot incident provides another governance lesson. A Canadian tribunal ordered Air Canada to compensate a customer after its chatbot reportedly provided incorrect bereavement fare information. Air Canada argued the chatbot was responsible for its own actions, but the tribunal rejected that position and treated the chatbot as part of Air Canada's website and responsibility.

These incidents are not classic DSPM incidents, but they belong in an AI governance chapter because they show that AI output creates business accountability.

The lesson is not simply "chatbots hallucinate."

The lesson is that organizations remain accountable for AI-enabled workflows, especially when the AI system interacts with customers, gives advice, summarizes policy, performs actions, or influences decisions.

For enterprise data security, the same principle applies:

If an AI system uses enterprise data to generate an answer, recommendation, decision, or action, the organization needs governance over the data, the system, the output, and the accountability chain.

17.11 AI-Specific Threats to Data

Securing AI-connected data requires understanding how AI systems can be attacked or misused. Traditional threats still matter, but AI introduces new patterns.

Threat	Description	Example	Defensive Controls
Prompt injection	Malicious instructions manipulate model behavior	A document tells the AI to ignore policy and reveal hidden context	Input handling, retrieval filtering, prompt hardening, output inspection
Indirect prompt injection	Malicious instructions are hidden in retrieved content	A file, email, web page, or ticket instructs an AI agent to leak data	Treat retrieved content as untrusted, sanitize retrieval, log tool calls
Sensitive data disclosure	AI reveals confidential or regulated data	Assistant summarizes restricted HR documents	Permission-aware retrieval, classification, access reviews, monitoring
Data poisoning	Training or retrieval data is manipulated	False information is inserted into a knowledge base	Source integrity, change monitoring, approval workflows
Model inversion	Attacker infers sensitive training data	Repeated queries reveal private details	Avoid sensitive training data, privacy testing, rate limiting
Model theft	Proprietary model behavior or prompts are extracted	Attacker replicates system prompts or model logic	Access control, monitoring, rate limits, watermarking where appropriate
Excessive agency	AI agent performs unauthorized actions	Agent sends confidential report externally	Scoped permissions, approval gates, transaction limits, kill switch

Supply chain compromise	AI dependency, plug-in, or API is compromised	Malicious plug-in exfiltrates prompt data	Vendor review, dependency monitoring, software supply chain controls
Shadow AI	Employees use unapproved tools with sensitive data	Staff paste customer records into a public chatbot	Discovery, policy, training, DLP, CASB/SSE controls
Vector database exposure	Embeddings or chunks are accessed improperly	Search index leaks sensitive document meaning	Encryption, access control, segmentation, deletion workflows
Insecure output reliance	Users act on incorrect or unsafe AI output	AI recommends insecure configuration	Human review, confidence indicators, source attribution, testing

The purpose of this table is not to overwhelm the reader. It is to show that AI data security must include governance, architecture, identity, application security, vendor risk, monitoring, and incident response.

17.12 AI Vendor Risk Management

Many organizations will not build their own AI systems from scratch. They will consume AI through SaaS platforms, productivity suites, security tools, customer support systems, analytics platforms, development tools, and specialized vendors.

This means AI security is also vendor risk management.

A vendor that processes enterprise data through AI may act as a data processor, subprocessor, model provider, application provider, infrastructure provider, or analytics provider. Organizations need to understand those roles and the contractual, technical, and compliance implications.

AI vendor reviews should include questions such as:

- *What customer data is processed by the AI feature?*
- *Is customer data used for training, fine-tuning, evaluation, or improvement?*
- *Can training on customer data be disabled?*
- *Are prompts and outputs stored?*
- *How long are prompts and outputs retained?*
- *Where is data processed and stored?*
- *Are subprocessors used?*
- *Can data leave approved regions?*
- *Is customer data encrypted in transit and at rest?*
- *Is tenant isolation enforced?*
- *Are embeddings stored separately from customer data?*
- *Can customer data be deleted?*
- *Can logs be exported?*
- *Can customers audit AI activity?*
- *Does the vendor support role-based access control?*
- *Does the vendor support DLP integrations?*

- *Does the vendor allow administrative control over AI features?*
- *Are AI features enabled by default or opt-in?*
- *Has the AI system undergone security testing or red teaming?*
- *Does the vendor align to recognized frameworks such as NIST AI RMF, ISO/IEC 42001, ISO/IEC 27001, SOC 2, or the CSA AI Controls Matrix?*
- *Is the vendor certified in ISO/IEC 42001?*
- *What happens to customer data when the contract ends?*

Vendor risk teams should also evaluate whether AI features have changed the nature of an existing product. A SaaS platform that previously stored documents may now summarize, classify, translate, analyze, or recommend actions based on those documents.

That may require a new privacy review, security review, data protection impact assessment, or contractual amendment.

AI features should not quietly appear in production systems without governance.

17.13 Monitor AI Activity

Monitoring is how organizations detect when AI activity becomes risky.

AI monitoring should include more than model performance. Security teams need visibility into how AI interacts with data.

Monitoring should cover:

- Sensitive data in prompts
- Sensitive data in outputs
- Retrieval of high-risk documents
- Access to regulated repositories
- Unusual prompt volume
- Repeated policy bypass attempts
- Prompt injection attempts
- AI agent actions
- Changes to connected data sources
- New AI integrations
- New vector stores
- New plug-ins or API connections
- Model configuration changes
- Prompt template changes
- Data exported from AI tools
- Vendor-side processing events where available

Monitoring should be integrated with existing security operations. AI telemetry should feed into SIEM, SOAR, IAM, DSPM, DLP, CASB, SSE, ticketing, and incident response workflows where appropriate.

The goal is not to monitor every word out of curiosity.

The goal is to identify meaningful risk signals and create defensible accountability.

17.14 Respond to AI-Related Incidents

AI-related incidents require response plans. Organizations should not wait for an AI data exposure event to decide who owns the issue.

Incident response playbooks should cover:

- Sensitive data entered into an unauthorized AI tool
- AI output exposing confidential or regulated data
- RAG retrieving documents outside the user's authorization
- Prompt injection against an AI application
- Data poisoning of source content or training data
- AI agent taking unauthorized action
- Vendor AI feature processing data outside policy
- Credentials or secrets submitted to an AI system
- Vector database exposure
- Unauthorized model, plug-in, or API access
- AI-generated output creating legal, customer, or compliance exposure

Response plans should identify stakeholders from security, privacy, legal, compliance, IT, data governance, business operations, procurement, communications, and vendor management.

AI incidents can cross traditional ownership boundaries quickly. A prompt containing regulated data may require privacy review. An AI agent action may require IT investigation. A vendor retention issue may require legal review. A sensitive output may require compliance analysis. A prompt injection attack may require application security and engineering support.

Response should include containment, evidence preservation, access review, data impact analysis, notification assessment, vendor engagement, remediation, and lessons learned.

17.15 Regulatory and Framework Alignment

AI governance is becoming more formal. Organizations should expect regulators, auditors, customers, insurers, boards, and business partners to ask how AI systems are governed and how data is protected.

Several frameworks and standards can help structure an AI data security program.

NIST AI Risk Management Framework and Generative AI Profile

NIST's AI Risk Management Framework provides a structure for managing AI risks across governance, mapping, measurement, and management. The Generative AI Profile extends that thinking to generative AI risks. It is useful because it frames AI risk as a lifecycle problem, not a one-time technical assessment.

For data security, the most relevant lesson is that organizations need to understand context, intended use, data inputs, risks, controls, and monitoring before and after deployment.

NIST Secure Software Development Framework for Generative AI

NIST's guidance for secure development of generative AI systems extends secure software development practices into AI. This is especially important for organizations building internal AI applications, integrating models into products, or creating AI-enabled workflows.

The connection to data security is clear: secure AI development must include dataset handling, data provenance, testing, access control, logging, and protection of sensitive information throughout the development lifecycle.

OWASP Top 10 for Large Language Model Applications

OWASP's LLM guidance is practical for application security teams. It highlights risks such as prompt injection, sensitive information disclosure, insecure output handling, supply chain vulnerabilities, excessive agency, and overreliance.

This is helpful for security teams because it translates AI risk into application security language. It also reinforces the idea that AI applications are still applications. They need threat modeling, testing, monitoring, and controls.

OWASP Top 10 for Agentic Applications

Agentic AI introduces risks tied to autonomy, identity, memory, tool use, delegation, and runtime behavior. Agentic systems need special attention because they can reason, decide, and act across tools and workflows.

The central question for agentic security is not only whether the AI says something unsafe.

It is whether the AI can do something unsafe.

Cloud Security Alliance AI Controls Matrix

The CSA AI Controls Matrix provides control objectives across AI security domains and maps to other frameworks and standards. It can help organizations evaluate vendors, assess internal programs, and identify control gaps.

This is especially useful for organizations that need a structured questionnaire or control mapping for governance, audit, procurement, or risk management.

ISO/IEC 42001

ISO/IEC 42001 is an AI management system standard. It is useful for organizations that want a governance structure for policies, roles, responsibilities, risk management, monitoring, and continual improvement.

A key distinction is that organizations can pursue certification against ISO/IEC 42001. That makes it different from guidance frameworks that are useful but not certification standards.

EU AI Act

The EU AI Act shows where AI regulation is heading, especially for high-risk AI systems. While not every organization or use case will fall under the same requirements, the direction is clear: organizations will need stronger governance, transparency, risk management, data controls, documentation, logging, human oversight, and cybersecurity protections.

Even organizations outside the EU can learn from this approach because customers and partners may begin expecting similar levels of discipline.

17.16 Building an AI-Connected Data Security Program

A mature AI-connected data security program should not be built as a side project. It should connect to existing security, privacy, compliance, data governance, identity, architecture, procurement, and business processes.

The following phased approach can help organizations make progress without waiting for perfection.

Phase 1: Establish Visibility

Start by identifying where AI is already in use. Include approved tools, unapproved tools, embedded SaaS AI features, internal pilots, vendor-enabled AI, development tools, productivity tools, and business-led experiments.

At the same time, identify sensitive data repositories that could be used for AI. This includes collaboration tools, databases, data lakes, file shares, ticketing systems, CRM systems, code repositories, and cloud storage.

Deliverables for this phase include an AI use-case inventory, AI vendor inventory, data source inventory, list of AI-connected repositories, list of high-risk data repositories, and initial shadow AI findings.

Phase 2: Define Governance

Governance should define who approves AI use, what data may be used, what tools are allowed, what reviews are required, and what controls must be in place.

The goal is not to slow the business down. The goal is to create a repeatable path for safe adoption.

Deliverables for this phase include an AI acceptable use policy, AI data handling standard, AI vendor review checklist, AI use-case intake process, classification-based AI usage rules, approval workflow for sensitive AI use cases, and exception process.

Phase 3: Reduce Exposure

Before connecting AI to enterprise data, reduce unnecessary exposure. Review permissions, remove stale access, clean up abandoned repositories, identify sensitive data in inappropriate locations, and address critical misconfigurations.

This phase is where DSPM can provide immediate value.

Deliverables for this phase include a sensitive data exposure report, over-permissioned repository list, high-risk access findings, secrets and credentials findings, remediation tickets, data owner assignments, and risk-based remediation priorities.

Phase 4: Secure AI Architecture

AI architecture should include secure identity, access control, logging, monitoring, retrieval filtering, source attribution, vendor controls, and incident response integration.

For RAG systems, architecture reviews should evaluate how data is indexed, stored, retrieved, filtered, cited, logged, and deleted.

For agents, architecture reviews should evaluate identity, permissions, actions, approval gates, and kill switches.

Deliverables for this phase include an AI architecture review, RAG security design, agent permission model, vector database security requirements, logging and monitoring plan, data retention plan, and security testing plan.

Phase 5: Monitor and Improve

AI security is not complete at launch. Data changes, permissions change, vendors change, models change, users change, and business use cases evolve.

Organizations need continuous monitoring and periodic review.

Deliverables for this phase include an AI activity monitoring dashboard, prompt and output policy alerts, retrieval monitoring, agent action monitoring, vendor review cadence, access review cadence, AI incident response playbooks, and AI governance metrics.

17.17 Metrics for AI-Connected Data Security

Organizations should measure AI-connected data security in practical terms. Metrics should show whether risk is being reduced and whether governance is working.

Useful metrics include:

- Number of approved AI use cases
- Number of unapproved AI tools detected
- Percentage of AI use cases with completed data review
- Percentage of AI-connected data sources classified
- Number of sensitive repositories connected to AI
- Number of over-permissioned AI-connected repositories
- Number of secrets detected in AI-accessible data
- Percentage of AI agents with dedicated identities
- Percentage of AI agents reviewed in the last quarter
- Number of sensitive prompt violations
- Number of sensitive output violations
- Number of prompt injection attempts detected
- Mean time to remediate high-risk AI data exposure
- Number of AI vendor reviews completed
- Percentage of AI vendors with training restrictions documented
- Number of AI incidents or near misses

The best metrics connect technical findings to business risk.

For example:

500 sensitive files exposed is useful.

500 sensitive files related to pending litigation exposed to 1,200 users and indexed by an AI assistant is far more useful.

17.18 Tabletop Exercise: AI-Connected Data Exposure

Scenario

The organization deploys an internal AI assistant connected to collaboration platforms, ticketing systems, and a document repository. The assistant uses retrieval-augmented generation to answer employee questions.

A user asks for a summary of customer complaints related to a product defect. The assistant returns details from support tickets, legal review notes, draft customer communications, and privileged investigation documents. Some of the content came from folders the user could technically access, but had never used before. The AI answer is copied into a Teams channel and later forwarded to a vendor.

During the investigation, the team discovers that the AI assistant indexed stale legal folders, inherited broad permissions from a connector service account, and retained prompt and output logs in a region that had not been approved for this type of data.

Exercise Questions

1. *Which data sources were connected to the AI assistant?*
2. *Who approved those data sources for AI use?*
3. *Were the retrieved documents classified?*
4. *Did the user have legitimate need for the underlying documents?*
5. *Did the AI enforce source-system permissions?*
6. *Did the connector service account have excessive access?*
7. *Were privileged or legal documents included?*
8. *Were prompts and outputs retained?*
9. *Were logs stored in an approved region?*
10. *Did the vendor receive sensitive or privileged information?*
11. *Is notification, contractual notice, or legal action required?*
12. *What evidence must be preserved?*
13. *What controls failed?*
14. *What remediation is required before expanding AI access?*

Expected Learning

The exercise should show that AI-connected data risk is rarely caused by one failure. It usually combines weak classification, excessive access, unclear ownership, connector permissions, retention gaps, vendor terms, and insufficient monitoring.

17.19 Actionable Recommendations

Organizations can take the following actions to operate AI-connected data safely:

1. Maintain an inventory of AI tools, AI features, AI vendors, AI agents, and AI-connected data sources.
2. Define approved AI use cases and data eligibility rules.
3. Require data owner approval before indexing sensitive repositories.
4. Apply permission-aware and classification-aware retrieval for RAG systems.
5. Secure vector databases, embeddings, chunks, and metadata.

6. Govern prompts and outputs as business records.
7. Give AI agents dedicated identities and least-privilege access.
8. Review OAuth grants, service accounts, connectors, and plug-ins.
9. Require human approval for high-risk agent actions.
10. Monitor prompts, outputs, retrievals, tool calls, and agent actions.
11. Include AI features in vendor risk reviews and contract negotiations.
12. Red-team AI applications before production.
13. Use real-world incidents from resources such as the AI Incident Database to inform threat models and tabletop exercises.
14. Create incident response playbooks for AI-related data exposure, prompt injection, data poisoning, and agent misuse.
15. Measure AI data security maturity using exposure, access, monitoring, and remediation metrics.
16. Reassess AI use cases regularly as data, users, vendors, and business needs change.

Key Takeaways

AI-connected data requires operating controls, not just policy.

Once AI systems are connected to enterprise data, organizations must govern how data is accessed, retrieved, summarized, retained, logged, shared, and acted upon.

AI system security focuses on protecting the AI application, model interface, retrieval layer, outputs, agents, memory, and tool use.

AI governance focuses on approved use, accountability, risk tiering, oversight, evidence, human review, and continuous improvement.

AI vendor risk focuses on how third parties process, store, train on, retain, delete, and support customer data.

AI identity and authorization focuses on users, agents, service accounts, OAuth grants, connectors, delegated access, and non-human identities.

AI monitoring and response focus on detecting misuse, investigating exposure, preserving evidence, and improving controls.

Real-world incidents show that AI risk is not theoretical. Prompt injection can reveal hidden instructions. AI connectors can become exfiltration paths. Customer-facing chatbots can create business liability. Agentic workflows can turn bad data or bad instructions into real-world action.

The organizations that succeed with AI will not be the ones that connect every dataset as quickly as possible. They will be the ones that understand which data should be used, which data should be protected, which data should be excluded, and which controls must surround AI-connected workflows.

AI can help organizations move faster.

But only if the operating model can keep up.

Chapter 18: How to Build a 30, 60, 90+ Day Data Security Program

Most data security programs do not begin with a perfect strategy document. They begin with a question no one can answer confidently.

"Where is our sensitive data?"

Sometimes the question comes from an executive. Sometimes it comes from legal after a privacy request. Sometimes it comes from a customer security review, an auditor, a board member, or a security leader preparing for an AI initiative. However it arrives, the effect is usually the same. The room gets quiet.

Security may know about some systems. IT may know where infrastructure lives. Compliance may know which regulations apply. Business teams may know which data matters most to operations. But very few organizations have one complete view of their sensitive and business-critical data.

That is the real starting point for a data security program.

Not a tool.

Not a dashboard.

Not a policy.

The starting point is the moment an organization realizes it has more data than it can confidently govern.

A 30, 60, 90-day data security plan gives that organization a practical way forward. It creates enough structure to move from uncertainty to visibility, from visibility to ownership, and from ownership to measurable risk reduction. It does not solve every problem in three months. That would be unrealistic. What it does is create momentum, accountability, and a foundation for long-term maturity.

The first 90 days should help the organization answer five essential questions:

- *Where does our sensitive data live?*
- *Who owns it?*
- *Who has access to it?*
- *Where is it exposed?*
- *What are we going to do about it?*

These questions sound simple, but they are not. In modern environments, data moves constantly. It lives in cloud storage, SaaS platforms, databases, file shares, collaboration tools, development repositories, backups, data lakes, analytics platforms, and increasingly, AI workflows. It is copied, exported, shared, duplicated, retained, and forgotten.

A successful data security program has to account for that reality. It must follow the full data lifecycle: discover, classify, govern, protect, monitor, and eventually retire or destroy data that no longer needs to exist.

The first 90 days are where that discipline begins.

18.1 A Running Example: Sunny Health

To make this practical, let's follow a fictional healthcare organization called Sunny Health.

Sunny Health is a regional healthcare provider with several clinics, a growing telehealth practice, and a mix of on-premises and cloud systems. The organization uses Microsoft 365, Azure, a patient billing platform, a clinical records system, several SaaS applications, and a collection of shared drives that have grown over time.

The security team is small. IT is busy supporting clinic operations. Compliance is preparing for an audit. The business is beginning to explore AI-assisted patient support and analytics. Leadership wants to know whether the organization has control over protected health information, employee records, billing data, and other sensitive information.

The honest answer is: partially.

Some systems are well understood. Others are not. Sensitive data exists in expected places, such as clinical and billing systems, but it also appears in spreadsheets, shared folders, exported reports, support tickets, and old project archives.

This is a common situation. Sunny Health does not need to panic, but it does need a plan.

The next 90 days will not create a perfect data security program. They will create the first version of a sustainable one.

18.2 Before Day One: Define the Mission

Before the first scan is run or the first policy is drafted, the organization needs to define the purpose of the program.

This step is easy to skip because it feels abstract. It is not. A clear mission prevents the program from becoming a disconnected set of technical findings.

For Sunny Health, the mission might be:

Our data security program exists to identify, classify, govern, protect, monitor, and responsibly retire sensitive and business-critical data across the organization, while supporting patient care, regulatory compliance, secure innovation, and business trust.

That statement matters because it makes the program bigger than security operations. It connects the work to patient trust, compliance, business continuity, and responsible use of data.

This is also the moment to identify who needs to be involved. Data security cannot sit entirely inside the security team. Security can lead, guide, and operationalize much of the work, but it cannot make every decision alone.

At Sunny Health, the core group includes security, IT, compliance, privacy, legal, clinical operations, billing, HR, and a representative from the data analytics team. Each group sees a different part of the data landscape. Together, they can create a more complete picture.

This is one of the first lessons of a 30, 60, 90-day program: data security is a shared responsibility, but shared responsibility only works when ownership is explicit.

Someone must own the program. Someone must own the systems. Someone must own the data. Someone must approve risk decisions. Someone must remediate findings.

Without that clarity, the program will produce reports but not results.

18.3 Days 1 to 30: Stop Guessing

The first 30 days are about visibility.

At this stage, the organization should resist the temptation to solve everything immediately. That may sound counterintuitive, especially when early findings reveal sensitive data in risky places. But if the team jumps too quickly into isolated remediation, it may fix individual issues without understanding the broader pattern.

The first month is about building a baseline. The organization needs to understand where sensitive data lives, what types of data exist, who has access, and where exposure appears most significant.

For Sunny Health, this means starting with the systems most likely to contain sensitive or regulated data. The team begins with Microsoft 365, Azure storage, shared drives, the billing platform, and selected SaaS applications used by clinical and administrative teams.

The goal is not to scan every system in the enterprise by day 30. The goal is to choose a meaningful starting scope and document why it was chosen.

That distinction matters. A focused scope creates progress. An undefined scope creates confusion.

During this phase, the organization also needs to define what "sensitive data" means in its environment. For a healthcare provider, protected health information is obvious, but it is not the only concern. Employee records, financial data, contracts, credentials, insurance information, executive communications, and operational reports may also carry significant risk.

A practical classification model helps the organization make consistent decisions. Many organizations start with simple categories such as public, internal, confidential, and restricted. The labels themselves are less important than the shared understanding behind them.

The restricted category should be reserved for the data that would create the greatest harm if exposed, misused, or mishandled. In Sunny Health's case, that includes PHI, payment-related data, employee personal information, credentials, and certain legal or executive materials.

Once scope and classification are defined, discovery begins.

This is where Data Security Posture Management becomes valuable. A DSPM platform can help identify sensitive data across cloud, SaaS, and data environments. It can classify information, identify excessive access, detect public or external exposure, and show where sensitive data exists outside approved locations.

But the technology is not the entire story. Discovery results need interpretation. A platform may identify sensitive data in hundreds or thousands of locations, but the program team must determine which findings matter most.

At Sunny Health, the first scan produces several important discoveries. Some are expected. PHI appears in clinical and billing systems. Employee records appear in HR folders. Financial reports appear in finance repositories.

Other findings are more concerning. The team finds patient-related spreadsheets in shared folders with broad access. Several folders containing billing exports are shared externally. A few former employees still have access through old group memberships. Some sensitive reports have no clear business owner. The team also finds test data that appears to contain real patient information.

This is the moment when the program becomes real.

The purpose of the first 30 days is not to shame teams for where data ended up. In most organizations, data spreads because people are trying to get work done. Reports are exported to solve business problems. Files are shared to support operations. Data is copied into test environments because teams need realistic scenarios. These behaviors may create risk, but they usually come from business need rather than negligence.

That is why the program should approach early findings with curiosity before judgment.

The right question is not simply:

"Who did this?"

The better question is:

"What business process caused this data to land here, and how do we reduce the risk without breaking the work?"

By the end of the first 30 days, Sunny Health has not fixed everything. That is okay. It has something more important for this stage: a defensible baseline.

The team knows where the highest concentrations of sensitive data are located. It knows which systems have obvious exposure. It knows where ownership is unclear. It has identified several high-risk findings that require remediation. It has also created a risk register to track findings, owners, business impact, compliance relevance, and status.

The first month should end with a short executive summary. This summary does not need to include every technical detail. Leadership needs to understand what was reviewed, what was found, where risk is concentrated, and what decisions or support are needed next.

For Sunny Health, the message to leadership is clear:

The organization has sensitive data in expected and unexpected locations. Some of that data is overexposed. Ownership is inconsistent. The highest-risk issues are known and remediation is ready to begin. The next phase will focus on governance, ownership, and reducing the most urgent exposure.

That is meaningful progress.

18.4 Days 31 to 60: Turn Visibility into Governance

The second 30 days are where the program shifts from finding risk to managing risk.

This is an important transition. Many organizations get stuck after discovery. They produce dashboards, reports, and heat maps, but the findings do not translate into action. The reason is usually not a lack of concern. It is a lack of ownership and process.

Data security findings often sit between teams. Security sees the risk, but does not own the business process. IT owns the platform, but not the data. Compliance understands the obligation, but cannot remediate the system. The business owns the data, but may not know what action is required.

Governance closes that gap.

For Sunny Health, the second month begins by assigning ownership to the highest-risk repositories and data domains. IT may own the Microsoft 365 environment, but clinical operations owns certain patient workflows. Finance owns billing exports. HR owns employee records. Legal owns contract repositories. Analytics owns data used for reporting and AI exploration.

This distinction between system ownership and data ownership is critical.

A system owner can manage technical controls. A data owner can confirm business purpose, approve access, validate retention needs, and make risk decisions. Mature data security requires both.

Once ownership is assigned, the team begins drafting practical governance policies. The word "practical" matters here. A policy that no one can follow will not reduce risk. It will only create the appearance of control.

At this stage, Sunny Health focuses on a small set of policies that support immediate risk reduction: data classification, external sharing, access reviews, retention, and acceptable use of sensitive data in analytics or AI workflows.

The external sharing policy becomes especially important. The organization cannot simply ban all external sharing because some sharing is necessary for patient care, billing, legal review, and business operations. Instead, the policy defines when external sharing is allowed, what types of data require approval, how long access should remain active, and how shared data should be monitored.

This is what good governance does. It does not blindly say no. It defines the conditions for a safer yes.

During days 31 to 60, remediation also begins in earnest. Sunny Health removes anonymous access to folders containing patient information. Former employees are removed from groups that still had access to sensitive repositories. Broad access permissions are reduced for several shared folders. Billing exports are moved into approved locations with tighter controls. The team opens tickets for remaining issues and assigns each one to a technical owner and a business owner.

This is where the program starts to earn credibility. Discovery may get attention, but remediation builds trust.

The organization also begins access reviews for the most sensitive repositories. The first review is not perfect. Some managers are unsure who should have access. Some group memberships are confusing. A few service accounts have unclear purpose. This is normal.

The first access review often reveals how much inherited complexity exists beneath the surface. Groups were created years ago. Employees changed roles. Vendors came and went. Temporary access became permanent. Service accounts outlived their original projects.

The point of the review is not only to clean up access. It is to expose the process gaps that allowed access risk to accumulate.

Sunny Health also begins connecting findings to compliance obligations. PHI exposure has HIPAA implications. Payment-related data may affect PCI scope. Employee data may trigger privacy and retention obligations. Contracts may include confidentiality requirements. This mapping helps leadership understand that data security findings are not isolated technical issues. They represent business, legal, regulatory, and reputational risk.

By day 60, the program has become more structured. Findings are tracked. Owners are assigned. Policies are being drafted. High-risk exposures are being remediated. Metrics are beginning to show progress.

The metrics do not need to be sophisticated yet. At this stage, useful measures include how many sensitive repositories were identified, how many high-risk findings remain open, how many have been remediated, how many repositories still lack owners, and how long critical remediation is taking.

For Sunny Health, the 60-day executive update tells a stronger story than the 30-day summary. The first month answered, *"What do we have?"* The second month answers, *"What are we doing about it?"*

That movement matters.

18.5 Days 61 to 90: Make the Program Operational

The final 30 days are about sustainability.

By this point, the organization has visibility, ownership, early policies, remediation activity, and basic metrics. The danger now is treating the effort as a one-time project.

Data security cannot be handled as a quarterly cleanup exercise or an annual audit preparation activity. Data changes too quickly. New repositories are created. Employees join and leave. Vendors are added. Reports are exported. Developers create test environments. Business teams adopt SaaS tools. AI initiatives introduce new data flows. Access changes constantly.

The purpose of days 61 to 90 is to turn the program into an operating model.

For Sunny Health, this means defining what happens on a recurring basis. Sensitive data discovery will continue. High-risk findings will be reviewed weekly. Critical exposures will trigger tickets. Restricted data repositories will go through periodic access reviews. Policy exceptions will require approval and expiration dates. Executive reporting will occur monthly. Data retention reviews will begin with the highest-risk stale data.

This operating rhythm is what prevents the organization from sliding back into guesswork.

Automation also becomes more important in this phase. The team should look for repeatable work that can be made more consistent through workflow automation. For example, when restricted data is found in an externally shared folder, the system can create a ticket, notify the owner, assign a severity, recommend remediation, and track the issue to closure.

Automation should start carefully. In many organizations, it is better to begin with notification and approval workflows before moving into automatic enforcement. This allows teams to build trust in the process.

Over time, certain actions may become candidates for automatic remediation. For example, removing public access from a repository containing restricted data may be appropriate if the policy is clear and the business impact is understood. But automation should not be reckless. The goal is to reduce risk without disrupting essential work.

During this phase, Sunny Health also begins integrating the data security program with existing security and IT processes. Findings are routed through the ticketing system. Identity teams are involved in access cleanup. Compliance receives evidence for audit readiness. Incident response playbooks are updated to include sensitive data exposure scenarios. Cloud and SaaS administrators receive guidance on configuration standards.

This is where the program becomes part of the broader security ecosystem.

Data security should connect to identity, cloud security, SaaS governance, GRC, incident response, privacy, DevSecOps, backup and recovery, and vendor risk management. If it remains isolated, it will struggle to influence real behavior.

Monitoring and response also mature during days 61 to 90. Sunny Health defines response playbooks for several common scenarios: public exposure of restricted data, inappropriate external sharing, unusual access to sensitive repositories, sensitive data found in development environments, and possible PHI exposure.

A good playbook does not need to be long. It needs to be clear. It should explain how to validate the finding, who to notify, how to contain the exposure, how to review access logs, when to involve legal or privacy, how to document the response, and how to prevent recurrence.

The final part of the 90-day effort is often the most overlooked: retention and destruction.

Many organizations focus heavily on protecting data but spend far less time asking whether the data should still exist. Old exports, duplicate reports, former employee folders, outdated archives, and unmanaged backups all increase risk. If sensitive data no longer has business, legal, or regulatory value, retaining it may create unnecessary exposure.

Sunny Health begins with a targeted review of stale patient-related exports and old billing reports. The team does not delete anything casually. Legal, compliance, and business owners are involved. Retention requirements are reviewed. Where deletion is approved, evidence is retained.

This is an important maturity moment. Data security is not only about locking data down. It is also about reducing the amount of sensitive data that needs protection in the first place.

By day 90, Sunny Health performs a maturity assessment. The organization is not at the highest level of maturity, and that is expected. It has moved from scattered visibility and inconsistent ownership toward a defined and managed program.

The team identifies its current state as somewhere between Level 2 and Level 3. Basic processes now exist. Ownership is improving. Remediation is underway. Some workflows are becoming repeatable. The long-term target is Level 4 because healthcare is highly regulated and the organization has a low tolerance for patient data exposure.

The 90-day executive report does not claim victory. It shows progress, remaining risk, and the roadmap ahead.

That is exactly what it should do.

18.6 The 30, 60, 90-Day Program at a Glance

Timeframe	Primary Focus	What the Organization Should Accomplish
Days 1 to 30	Discovery and baseline	Define the mission, identify stakeholders, set scope, discover sensitive data, classify priority data, map exposure, identify ownership gaps, and create the initial risk register.
Days 31 to 60	Governance and remediation	Assign owners, draft practical policies, begin high-risk remediation, perform priority access reviews, connect findings to compliance obligations, and establish basic metrics.
Days 61 to 90	Operations and maturity	Build recurring workflows, automate where appropriate, integrate with IT and security processes, create response playbooks, begin retention reviews, assess maturity, and define the next roadmap.

18.7 What Good Looks Like After 90 Days

At the end of 90 days, the organization should not expect perfection. That is not the goal.

The goal is to be in a fundamentally better position than when the program began.

A healthy 90-day outcome means the organization can speak with more confidence about where sensitive data lives, who owns it, who has access, where the greatest exposures exist, what has already been remediated, and what still needs attention.

The organization should also have a working governance structure. That means data owners are identified, policies are taking shape, high-risk findings are tracked, access reviews have begun, and leadership has visibility into progress.

Most importantly, the program should have moved beyond discovery.

Discovery tells the organization what exists. Governance tells the organization who is accountable. Protection reduces the likelihood of misuse or exposure. Monitoring identifies when risk changes. Retention and destruction reduce the amount of sensitive data that can be exposed in the first place.

Together, these activities create a real data security program.

18.8 What to Stop Doing After 90 Days

At the end of the first 90 days, the organization should pause and deliberately stop behaviors that made sense during startup but will weaken the program if they continue.

The first 90 days are allowed to be imperfect. Teams are learning. Scopes are being refined. Findings are being validated. Owners are being identified. Early policies are being drafted. Some work may depend on manual effort because the operating model is still forming.

That cannot remain the normal state.

After 90 days, the organization should stop treating DSPM as a discovery project. Discovery is only the first stage. If the program continues to produce findings without assigning owners, tracking remediation, or reporting risk reduction, it will lose credibility.

The organization should also stop chasing every finding equally. Early enthusiasm can create a desire to fix everything at once, but that usually leads to fatigue. After 90 days, prioritization should be risk-based, tied to data sensitivity, exposure, identity risk, regulatory impact, business criticality, and AI readiness.

Teams should stop allowing undefined ownership. Every critical or high-risk finding should have a business owner, technical owner, remediation owner, and escalation path. "Security is looking into it" is not an ownership model.

The program should stop relying on manual spreadsheets as the primary system of record if workflow tooling is available. Spreadsheets may help during startup, but they do not scale well for evidence, accountability, SLA tracking, exception review, or executive reporting.

The organization should stop accepting permanent exceptions without review. Temporary access, external sharing exceptions, unresolved remediation, or suppressed alerts should have owners, justification, compensating controls, and expiration dates.

The team should stop reporting only activity. Metrics such as scans completed, files discovered, or alerts generated may show motion, but they do not prove risk reduction. After 90 days, reporting should increasingly show exposure reduced, owners assigned, access removed, stale data retired, exceptions reviewed, and critical findings closed.

Finally, the organization should stop pretending that data security is only a security team responsibility. By day 90, business, IT, privacy, legal, compliance, data governance, and application owners should understand their roles in the operating model.

Stop Doing / Start Doing

Stop Doing	Start Doing
Treating DSPM as a scan-and-report project	Treat DSPM as an operating model for data risk reduction
Reviewing all findings equally	Prioritize based on sensitivity, exposure, identity, business impact, and regulatory risk
Leaving findings with unclear ownership	Assign business, technical, and remediation owners

Managing everything in disconnected spreadsheets	Route findings through durable workflow and evidence systems
Allowing open-ended exceptions	Require owner, justification, compensating controls, and expiration
Reporting activity only	Report measurable risk reduction
Treating security as the sole owner	Make data security a shared business, technology, and governance responsibility
Expanding scope without operational capacity	Expand only when ownership, workflow, and remediation capacity exist

This is an important maturity checkpoint. The first 90 days prove the organization can see risk. The next stage proves the organization can manage it.

18.9 Common Traps That Slow the First 90 Days

Even with a good plan, organizations can lose momentum if they fall into predictable traps.

One common trap is trying to classify everything perfectly before acting. Classification matters, but perfection can become a delay tactic. Early classification needs to be accurate enough to support risk-based decisions. It can mature over time.

Another trap is treating the DSPM platform as the program. A tool can provide visibility and workflow support, but it cannot define risk appetite, assign business ownership, approve retention decisions, or build trust with stakeholders. The program must be bigger than the technology.

A third trap is focusing only on regulated data. Regulations are important, but business-critical data also deserves protection. Source code, contracts, pricing models, executive strategy, intellectual property, credentials, and operational data may not always fit neatly into a regulatory category, but exposure can still harm the organization.

Organizations also struggle when they create policies that do not reflect how people work. If a policy blocks necessary business activity without offering a safe path forward, users will route around it. Good governance should define safe operating conditions, not simply issue unrealistic restrictions.

Finally, many programs fail to connect findings to remediation. Dashboards can create awareness, but tickets, owners, deadlines, and escalation paths create action.

18.10 The Leadership Conversation

One of the most valuable outcomes of the first 90 days is a better leadership conversation.

Before the program, leadership may ask:

"Are we secure?"

That question is too broad to answer meaningfully.

After the first 90 days, the conversation can become more specific:

We found restricted data in 47 repositories. Twelve had excessive access. Five had external sharing exposure. Three critical issues have been remediated. Four require business owner approval. Two require policy decisions. Our next priority is automating detection and review for restricted data in Microsoft 365 and Azure.

That is a much better conversation.

It is specific. It is measurable. It shows progress. It identifies decisions. It connects technical findings to business risk.

This is how data security earns executive confidence. Not by claiming everything is fixed, but by showing that risk is known, owned, prioritized, and actively managed.

18.11 When to Expand Scope

Scope expansion is one of the most important decisions after the first 90 days.

A DSPM program should grow, but it should not expand blindly. Expanding too quickly can bury the team in findings, overwhelm business owners, create alert fatigue, and turn a promising program into another dashboard no one has time to manage.

The right question is not:

"Can we connect more systems?"

The better question is:

"Can we operationalize the risk we discover?"

An organization should consider expanding scope when the initial data sources are stable, connectors are healthy, high-risk findings are being routed to owners, remediation workflows are functioning, and the team has enough capacity to review and act on new findings.

Expansion is also appropriate when new business priorities require it. For example, a new AI initiative may require review of collaboration platforms, knowledge bases, code repositories, or data warehouses before those sources are indexed. A privacy initiative may require broader coverage of systems involved in DSAR or retention workflows. A merger or acquisition may require discovery across new environments. A regulatory exam may require evidence from additional data stores.

Healthy scope expansion should be intentional and tied to business outcomes.

Expand Scope When	Do Not Expand Yet When
Initial connectors are healthy and monitored	Existing connectors are failing or stale
High-risk findings have owners and workflows	Findings are visible but not assigned
Remediation SLAs are being met or improving	Critical findings are piling up without action
Business owners understand their role	Business units are not engaged
Reporting shows risk reduction	Reporting shows only scan activity

New scope supports AI, privacy, compliance, cloud, SaaS, or business priorities	New scope is being added only because the tool can connect to it
The team has capacity to interpret and act on findings	Analysts, owners, or remediation teams are already overloaded
Governance can handle exceptions and accepted risk	Exceptions are unmanaged or permanent

For Sunny Health, scope expansion might begin with Microsoft 365, Azure, billing exports, and clinical-adjacent shared drives. Once those workflows are stable, the organization may expand into additional SaaS platforms, analytics environments, data warehouses, endpoint locations, backup metadata, and AI-connected repositories.

Scope expansion should follow risk and readiness, not curiosity.

18.12 180 Days After Purchase: Operational Ownership and Ongoing Maintenance

By the 180-day mark, the DSPM program should be moving from initial deployment into steady-state operations. At this stage, the focus shifts from onboarding, discovery, and early remediation to long-term ownership, repeatable governance, measurable adoption, and continuous improvement.

This checkpoint defines the operating model that should be in place six months after purchase, including connector health checks, administrative roles, permission reviews, tuning cadence, platform ownership, renewal criteria, adoption metrics, and ongoing maintenance practices.

Objective of the 180-Day Review

The 180-day checkpoint is designed to answer one central question:

Has the platform become an operational part of the organization's data security program, or is it still functioning as a standalone tool?

At this point, the organization should be able to demonstrate that the DSPM platform is actively monitored, regularly tuned, and used by defined stakeholders across security, privacy, compliance, cloud, data, and application teams.

The review should validate whether connectors are healthy and complete, administrative ownership is clearly assigned, access and permissions are being reviewed, policies and alerts have been tuned to reduce noise, business units are engaging with findings, adoption can be measured, and renewal criteria are understood before the renewal cycle begins.

Connector Health Checks

Connector health is one of the most important maintenance areas after initial deployment. A DSPM platform is only as useful as the visibility it maintains across cloud environments, SaaS platforms, data stores, identity providers, and collaboration tools.

At the 180-day mark, connector health checks should become part of a formal operating rhythm.

Connector reviews should confirm that all originally scoped connectors remain active, authentication tokens, service accounts, and API permissions are still valid, data ingestion is current and not delayed, newly added cloud accounts, SaaS tenants, storage buckets, databases, or repositories have been onboarded, connector errors are assigned to an owner, retired systems have been removed or marked inactive, and coverage gaps are documented and tracked.

A common issue at this stage is connector drift. This happens when new systems are added to the environment but are not added to the DSPM platform. To prevent this, connector reviews should be tied to cloud account creation, SaaS onboarding, data platform provisioning, and vendor management workflows.

Recommended cadence: Connector health should be reviewed weekly for critical production environments and at least monthly for lower-risk or stable environments.

Admin Roles and Platform Access

Administrative access should be reviewed and tightened by the 180-day milestone. During early deployment, broader access is often granted to speed up configuration, testing, and troubleshooting. That access should not remain unchanged once the platform is operational.

The organization should define clear roles for platform owner, security administrator, compliance or privacy reviewer, data owner or business unit reviewer, read-only executive or audit viewer, integration or automation administrator, and support or vendor access where applicable.

Each role should align to least privilege. Not every user needs the ability to modify connectors, change policies, suppress alerts, export sensitive findings, or invite additional users.

The 180-day review should confirm that named administrators are still appropriate, former project users have been removed, role-based access is being used where available, privileged actions are limited to approved users, vendor or third-party access is time-bound and reviewed, and administrative activity is logged and monitored.

This is also the right time to document who can make platform-level decisions, such as changing classification logic, adjusting severity scoring, approving suppressions, or modifying integrations with ticketing and SIEM platforms.

Permission Reviews

DSPM findings often uncover excessive access, stale permissions, public exposure, inherited privileges, and sensitive data shared with the wrong audience. By 180 days, the organization should have a repeatable process for reviewing and acting on these findings.

Permission reviews should focus on publicly exposed sensitive data, external sharing of regulated or confidential data, over-permissioned users, groups, roles, and service accounts, dormant users with access to sensitive repositories, excessive administrative access, cross-tenant or cross-account access paths, and sensitive data accessible by broad groups such as Everyone, All Employees, or Domain Users.

The goal is not to review every permission finding manually. Instead, the organization should prioritize access risks based on data sensitivity, exposure level, business context, and likelihood of misuse.

A practical model is to separate permission findings into three categories:

Category	Meaning
Immediate action	Public exposure, external sharing of highly sensitive data, or access that violates policy.
Owner review	Business-unit access that may be excessive but requires validation before removal.
Accepted or monitored risk	Access that is understood, justified, documented, and periodically reviewed.

Permission reviews should include security, data owners, application owners, and compliance teams. Security may identify the issue, but the business owner usually needs to confirm whether access is appropriate.

Tuning Cadence

By the 180-day point, default policies and alerts should no longer be treated as final. Every environment has different data types, business processes, regulatory requirements, and risk tolerance. Tuning is required to make the platform useful and trusted.

Tuning should address classification accuracy, false positives and false negatives, severity levels, alert thresholds, suppression rules, business context, data owner mapping, ticket routing, policy exceptions, and integration behavior.

Poor tuning can create alert fatigue and reduce confidence in the platform. Over-tuning can hide meaningful risk. The right balance is to reduce unnecessary noise while preserving visibility into material data security issues.

Recommended cadence:

Timeframe	Tuning Cadence
First 90 days	Weekly tuning
Days 90 to 180	Biweekly tuning
After day 180	Monthly tuning
Major environment change, new regulation, new data source, or incident lesson learned	Immediate tuning

Tuning decisions should be documented. This is especially important when alerts are suppressed, severity is lowered, or certain repositories are excluded from monitoring.

Platform Ownership

A DSPM platform needs a named owner after deployment. Without ownership, the platform can quickly become shelfware, even if it was technically implemented correctly.

The platform owner is accountable for ensuring the tool remains operational, relevant, and aligned to business risk. This person does not need to perform every task personally, but they are responsible for coordinating the operating model.

Platform ownership should include responsibility for connector health and coverage, user and role management, policy and classification tuning, remediation workflow oversight, reporting and adoption metrics, stakeholder engagement, vendor relationship management, renewal preparation, roadmap alignment, and escalation of unresolved risks.

In many organizations, ownership sits within data security, cloud security, security architecture, or governance, risk, and compliance. The exact team matters less than having clear accountability.

A strong ownership model also includes a backup owner. DSPM platforms often depend on integrations, credentials, and operational knowledge that should not be tied to one individual.

18.13 12-Month Maturity Target

The first 90 days create the foundation. The 180-day review proves whether the platform has become operational. The 12-month mark should show whether the organization has a sustainable data security program.

By month 12, the organization should be able to demonstrate that DSPM is not only deployed, but embedded into the way the business manages sensitive data risk.

A realistic 12-month maturity target should include:

Maturity Area	12-Month Target
Coverage	Critical data sources are connected, prioritized, and monitored. Known gaps are documented with owners and timelines.
Ownership	High-risk sensitive repositories have assigned data owners and technical owners. Orphaned ownership is tracked and escalated.
Classification	Classification has moved beyond default rules into tuned, business-relevant sensitivity, regulatory, and AI-readiness categories.
Access Governance	Excessive access findings are reviewed through a repeatable process involving data owners, supervisors, IT, and security where appropriate.
Remediation	Critical and high-risk findings have defined SLAs, assigned owners, tracked status, and evidence of closure.
Exception Management	Exceptions and suppressions have business justification, owner, compensating controls, expiration, and recurring review.
Integrations	DSPM is integrated with ticketing and at least one broader workflow such as SIEM, SOAR, GRC, IAM, DLP, privacy, or cloud security.
Reporting	Executive reporting shows risk trends, exposure reduction, remediation progress, ownership gaps, and open decisions.

AI Readiness	AI-connected or AI-candidate repositories are reviewed for sensitive data, excessive access, classification, ownership, and approved use.
Retention and Destruction	At least one targeted stale or expired sensitive data cleanup effort has been completed with evidence.
Operating Cadence	Connector health, tuning, permission reviews, exception reviews, and reporting occur on a defined schedule.
Business Adoption	Business units are participating in ownership, remediation, access review, and exception decisions.

The 12-month target should not be perfection. It should be evidence of operational maturity.

A strong 12-month program can answer:

- *What sensitive data is covered?*
- *What sensitive data is not yet covered?*
- *Which risks were reduced?*
- *Which risks remain open?*
- *Who owns those risks?*
- *What decisions does leadership need to make?*
- *What data security work is now repeatable?*
- *What still depends on heroic effort?*

For Sunny Health, the 12-month maturity target is not to scan every byte of data everywhere. The target is to maintain reliable coverage of the most critical PHI, billing, HR, legal, analytics, and AI-candidate repositories; prove that critical exposures are remediated faster; show that owners are engaged; and demonstrate that data risk is trending down.

That is the difference between a tool deployment and a program.

18.14 When Not to Renew

Renewal planning should not begin 30 days before the contract expires. By the 180-day mark, the organization should already know how value will be measured. By the 12-month mark, the organization should know whether the platform is earning its place in the operating model.

Renewal criteria should be agreed upon by the platform owner, executive sponsor, procurement, and key stakeholders. These criteria should connect the platform to measurable business outcomes rather than technical activity alone.

Renewal criteria may include:

- Percentage of critical data sources connected
- Reduction in publicly exposed sensitive data
- Reduction in excessive access to sensitive data
- Number of high-risk findings remediated
- Improvement in data owner engagement
- Reduction in time to identify sensitive data exposure
- Integration with ticketing, SIEM, SOAR, GRC, IAM, DLP, or privacy workflows

- Support for compliance reporting
- Evidence of regular usage by security and business teams
- Alignment to privacy, cloud security, AI governance, or zero trust initiatives
- Reduction in stale or orphaned sensitive repositories
- Reduction in unmanaged sensitive data in collaboration platforms
- Evidence that DSPM findings influenced executive or board-level decisions

Renewal should also consider operational friction. If the platform requires too much manual effort, produces too many low-value alerts, lacks stakeholder adoption, or cannot integrate into existing workflows, those issues should be addressed well before renewal discussions.

A useful CISO renewal test is:

If the platform disappeared tomorrow, which operational decisions would become harder, slower, or less defensible?

That question is powerful because it forces the organization to identify whether the platform has become operationally necessary.

If no one can answer clearly, the platform may not yet be embedded into the program.

If the answer is specific, renewal value becomes easier to defend.

For example:

- It would be harder to identify where PHI exists outside clinical systems.
- It would take longer to validate whether a repository contains regulated data during an incident.
- Access reviews would be less defensible because they would lack sensitivity context.
- Privacy teams would lose evidence for DSAR and retention scoping.
- AI governance teams would struggle to determine which repositories are safe to index.
- Executive reporting would lose visibility into whether data exposure is improving.

The strongest renewal argument is not that the platform was purchased.

It is that the organization now depends on it to make better, faster, and more defensible data risk decisions.

When Not to Renew

Not every platform should be renewed.

A renewal decision should be honest. Continuing a platform that is not operationalized can waste money, distract teams, and create false confidence. The fact that a tool found risk once does not mean it deserves renewal forever.

The organization should consider not renewing, renegotiating, replacing, or pausing expansion when the platform has not become part of the operating model.

Warning signs include:

Warning Sign	What It May Indicate
Connectors are unhealthy or incomplete	The organization is not maintaining visibility.
Findings are not assigned to owners	The tool is producing awareness without accountability.
Critical findings remain open without escalation	The program lacks authority or operational follow-through.
Business owners are not engaged	Data risk remains security-owned instead of business-owned.
Alerts are noisy and untuned	The platform may be creating fatigue instead of focus.
Exceptions and suppressions are unmanaged	Risk is being hidden rather than governed.
Reports show activity but not risk reduction	Leadership cannot tell whether the investment matters.
The tool does not integrate with workflow systems	Findings may remain trapped in the dashboard.
Licensing or support costs outweigh demonstrated value	The business case is weak.
The platform cannot support critical environments	Coverage gaps may limit usefulness.
The vendor cannot meet data residency, privacy, or support requirements	The platform may introduce governance risk.
The platform is used only during audits or renewal season	It has become shelfware.

Not renewing does not mean the data security program failed. It may mean the organization learned what it needs and should change approach.

Before deciding not to renew, leaders should ask whether the issue is the platform, the implementation, the operating model, the staffing model, or the ownership model. A good platform can fail under weak governance. A weak platform can look acceptable during a pilot but fail under real operational demand.

The renewal decision should be based on evidence.

If the platform does not improve visibility, prioritization, remediation, governance, reporting, audit readiness, AI readiness, privacy operations, or business decision-making, renewal should be challenged.

A CISO should never renew a DSPM platform only because it exists.

It should be renewed because it helps the organization reduce risk in ways that are measurable, repeatable, and defensible.

18.15 Adoption Metrics

Adoption metrics show whether the platform is being used as intended. They also help identify where additional enablement, integrations, or executive support may be needed.

Useful adoption metrics include:

- Number of active users by role
- Frequency of platform logins
- Number of connected data sources
- Percentage of scoped environments covered
- Number of findings reviewed
- Number of findings assigned to owners
- Number of findings remediated
- Average time to remediation
- Number of accepted risks documented
- Number of recurring reports generated
- Number of business units participating
- Number of tickets created and closed
- Number of policy tuning changes completed
- Reduction in repeat findings over time

Adoption should be measured by meaningful usage, not just access. A large number of users does not prove adoption if findings are not reviewed, tickets are not closed, and data owners are not engaged.

The best adoption metrics connect usage to outcomes. For example, "75 percent of critical findings assigned to owners within seven days" is more meaningful than "25 users logged in this month."

18.16 Ongoing Maintenance

Ongoing maintenance keeps the DSPM program accurate, trusted, and aligned to the changing environment. This work should be documented as a recurring operational process.

Maintenance activities should include reviewing connector health, validating data source coverage, reviewing admin access, performing permission reviews, tuning policies and classification rules, reviewing open findings, validating ticket routing, confirming data owner mappings, reviewing suppressions and exceptions, updating reports and dashboards, reviewing vendor updates and new features, preparing executive and compliance reporting, and tracking adoption and remediation metrics.

Maintenance should also account for organizational change. Mergers, new cloud accounts, SaaS adoption, new business units, workforce changes, AI initiatives, and regulatory changes can all affect DSPM coverage and priorities.

A mature program treats DSPM maintenance as part of the broader security operating model, not as a one-time implementation task.

18.17 Recommended Operating Cadence

The following cadence can be used as a baseline:

Activity	Recommended Frequency	Primary Owner
Connector health review	Weekly or monthly	Platform owner / security admin
Admin role review	Monthly	Platform owner
Permission risk review	Monthly	Security and data owners
Policy and alert tuning	Monthly	Security admin / platform owner
High-risk finding review	Weekly	Security operations / data security
Adoption metrics review	Monthly	Platform owner
Executive reporting	Quarterly	Executive sponsor / platform owner
Renewal value review	Quarterly after 180 days	Platform owner / procurement / sponsor
Suppression and exception review	Quarterly	Security governance
Data source coverage review	Quarterly	Platform owner / cloud and data teams
Scope expansion review	Quarterly or tied to business initiatives	Platform owner / executive sponsor
12-month maturity review	Annually	Executive sponsor / platform owner

18.18 Common Gaps at the 180-Day Mark

Organizations often miss the same areas after initial deployment:

- Connectors were configured once but are not actively monitored.
- New data sources are not being onboarded.
- Too many users still have administrative access.
- Alerts have not been tuned.
- Findings are visible but not assigned to owners.
- Business units do not understand their role.
- Sensitive data exposure is reported but not remediated.
- Metrics focus on activity instead of outcomes.
- Renewal value is not being tracked early enough.
- Exceptions and suppressions are not reviewed.
- Scope expansion happens before the operating model can support it.
- AI-connected repositories are not prioritized for review.
- Retention and destruction remain disconnected from discovery.

These gaps do not mean the program has failed. They are normal signs that the organization needs to mature from implementation mode to operational mode.

18.19 Actionable Recommendations

At 180 days and beyond, the organization should take the following actions:

1. Assign a named platform owner and backup owner.
2. Review all connectors and document coverage gaps.
3. Remove unnecessary administrative access.
4. Establish a monthly permission review process.
5. Tune policies based on actual findings and business context.
6. Define adoption metrics and review them monthly.
7. Map critical findings to remediation owners.
8. Document accepted risks and review them quarterly.
9. Align DSPM reporting to compliance and executive priorities.
10. Define renewal success criteria before the renewal cycle begins.
11. Establish a 12-month maturity target tied to coverage, ownership, remediation, exception management, reporting, AI readiness, and business adoption.
12. Identify what the organization will stop doing after 90 days so startup habits do not become permanent operating weaknesses.
13. Define when scope should expand and when it should pause.
14. Use the CISO renewal test: If the platform disappeared tomorrow, *which operational decisions would become harder, slower, or less defensible?*
15. Challenge renewal if the platform is not producing measurable, repeatable, and defensible risk reduction.

Key Takeaways

DSPM success is not achieved by deploying a platform alone. It is achieved when visibility becomes operational.

For Sunny Health, the first 90 days established the foundation by identifying sensitive data risk, assigning ownership, remediating urgent exposures, creating practical policies, and building a roadmap for continued improvement.

After 90 days, the organization must stop treating DSPM as a discovery project and start treating it as an operating model. That means no more unmanaged exceptions, unclear ownership, activity-only metrics, or dashboards without remediation.

By the 180-day mark, success becomes measurable through healthy connectors, reviewed permissions, tuned alerts, adoption, governance alignment, and demonstrated risk reduction.

By the 12-month mark, the program should show sustainable maturity. Critical data sources should be covered. Owners should be engaged. Findings should move through repeatable workflows. Exceptions should be governed. Reporting should show risk trends. AI-connected data should be reviewed before use. Retention and destruction should begin reducing unnecessary exposure.

Scope should expand only when the organization can operationalize what it finds. More connectors do not automatically mean more maturity. Expansion should follow risk, readiness, and business need.

Renewal should be based on evidence, not inertia. The best CISO renewal question is: ***If the platform disappeared tomorrow, which operational decisions would become harder, slower, or less defensible?***

If the answer is specific, the platform is becoming part of the operating model.

If the answer is unclear, value realization needs attention.

The goal is not perfection. It is sustained progress, stronger trust, greater resilience, and a data security program built on clarity instead of assumptions.

Chapter 19: How to Measure Progress and Report It to Executives

Executives do not need every detail of a data security program. They need to know whether risk is going down, whether the organization is becoming more resilient, whether investments are producing results, and where leadership decisions are still needed.

A strong DSPM program should not report activity for activity's sake. It should show progress against business risk.

That means moving beyond statements like:

"We scanned 100 repositories this month."

And toward statements like:

"We reduced public exposure of sensitive data by 42%, closed 87% of critical access findings within SLA, and identified three business units where unresolved data ownership gaps are slowing remediation."

The first statement shows effort.

The second shows impact.

This chapter explains how to measure DSPM maturity, define meaningful metrics, build an executive reporting model, connect data security progress to cost and risk, report residual risk clearly, and tell a story that helps leaders understand what is known, what is improving, what remains risky, and what decisions are needed.

19.1 Why Measurement Matters

DSPM programs often begin with a visibility problem.

Organizations do not know:

- *Where sensitive data lives*
- *Who has access to it*
- *Whether it is properly protected*
- *Which repositories are exposed or misconfigured*
- *Whether data is being retained longer than necessary*
- *Whether controls are improving over time*
- *Whether AI systems can access sensitive or poorly governed data*

Discovery and classification create the baseline. Governance turns that baseline into a plan. Protection, monitoring, remediation, and destruction reduce risk.

Measurement proves whether the plan is working.

Without measurement, the organization is left with assumptions. With measurement, security leaders can show progress, justify investment, prioritize remediation, and hold teams accountable.

Measurement also helps avoid a common failure pattern: treating DSPM as a one-time tool deployment instead of an operating model.

A mature DSPM program should answer three executive-level questions:

1. *Are we reducing data risk?*
2. *Are we improving operational maturity?*
3. *Where do we need leadership support?*

A CISO also needs a fourth question:

What risk remains, and who has accepted it?

That question matters because no data security program eliminates all risk. Executive reporting should show not only progress, but also the residual risk the organization is choosing to tolerate, fund, defer, or escalate.

19.2 Start With the Baseline

You cannot measure progress until you know where you started.

The baseline should capture the current state of the data environment, including sensitive data locations, exposure points, access risks, policy violations, ownership gaps, and remediation maturity.

A useful DSPM baseline usually includes:

Area	Baseline Question
Sensitive data inventory	*Where does sensitive, regulated, or business-critical data reside?*
Data classification	*How much data is classified, and how accurate is the classification?*
Exposure	*Which sensitive data stores are public, externally accessible, misconfigured, or overly permissive?*
Access	*Who and what has access to sensitive data? Is access appropriate?*
Ownership	*Does each sensitive data store have a business owner and technical owner?*
Remediation	*Are issues assigned, tracked, and resolved within SLA?*
Governance	*Are policies defined, enforced, and monitored consistently?*
Monitoring	*Are risky changes, access anomalies, and violations detected continuously?*
Retention	*Is stale, duplicate, or unnecessary sensitive data being reduced?*
AI readiness	*Which repositories are safe for AI use, which require cleanup, and which should be excluded?*

The first baseline does not need to be perfect. In fact, it rarely will be. Early DSPM measurement often exposes how much the organization does not yet know.

That is not failure.

That is the starting point.

19.3 Measure Maturity, Not Just Findings

A DSPM program should measure both risk reduction and maturity improvement.

Risk metrics show what has changed in the environment. Maturity metrics show whether the organization is becoming more capable of managing data risk over time.

For example, reducing public storage buckets is a risk reduction metric. Integrating DSPM findings into ServiceNow with ownership and SLA tracking is a maturity improvement metric.

Both matter.

The DSPM maturity model can be reported across five levels:

Level	Description	Executive Meaning
Level 1: Initial / Ad Hoc	Reactive, inconsistent, little ownership or automation	High risk, limited visibility
Level 2: Defined	Basic policies and scheduled processes exist	Foundational controls emerging
Level 3: Managed	Standardized workflows, ownership, and risk-based remediation	Repeatable program with accountability
Level 4: Quantitatively Managed	KPIs, dashboards, automation, and continuous measurement	Data-driven program management
Level 5: Optimizing	Predictive, adaptive, self-improving governance	Proactive and business-aligned resilience

Executives do not need a technical lecture on every level. They need to understand where the organization is now, where it is trying to go, and what is required to get there.

A simple statement works well:

We are currently operating at Level 2 for data governance and Level 3 for discovery and classification. Our target over the next two quarters is to reach Level 3 across governance, access remediation, and executive reporting by standardizing ownership, SLA tracking, and recurring risk reviews.

That gives leadership a clear picture of current maturity, target maturity, and next steps.

19.4 Choose Metrics That Executives Actually Care About

Not all metrics belong in an executive report.

Technical teams may need hundreds of data points. Executives need a smaller set of indicators that show whether risk is improving, whether the program is maturing, and whether decisions are needed.

Good executive metrics are:

- Easy to understand
- Tied to business risk
- Tracked consistently over time

- Actionable
- Comparable against targets
- Clear about ownership and accountability
- Connected to cost, risk, resilience, compliance, or business enablement

Avoid vanity metrics.

For example, "number of scans completed" is less useful than "percentage of critical sensitive data stores scanned continuously." "Number of findings" is less useful than "critical findings older than SLA."

The best metrics connect technical facts to business meaning.

19.5 Bad Metrics vs. Good Metrics

A common executive reporting mistake is using metrics that describe activity without explaining value. Activity matters, but only when it connects to outcomes.

The table below shows how to convert weak metrics into stronger ones.

Bad Metric	Why It Falls Short	Better Metric	Why It Works
Number of scans completed	Shows effort, not coverage or risk reduction	Percentage of critical data sources under continuous discovery	Shows visibility over the data that matters most
Total findings generated	More findings may mean more noise, not more risk	Critical findings by risk theme, age, owner, and SLA status	Shows what requires action
Number of files classified	Does not prove classification accuracy or usefulness	Percentage of high-risk repositories accurately classified and mapped to policy	Shows whether classification supports decisions
Number of alerts	Can reward noise	Percentage of high-confidence alerts routed to accountable owners	Shows operational effectiveness
Number of tickets opened	Does not show closure or risk reduction	Percentage of critical findings closed within SLA	Shows remediation performance
Number of users with platform access	Does not prove adoption	Number of active business owners reviewing and resolving findings	Shows cross-functional engagement
Number of dashboards created	Does not prove leadership value	Executive scorecard showing trends, residual risk, and decisions needed	Shows decision support
Total volume of sensitive data found	Can be overwhelming without context	Sensitive data in overexposed, stale, unowned, or AI-accessible locations	Shows where risk is concentrated
Number of exceptions	Does not show whether exceptions are governed	Percentage of exceptions with owner, business justification, compensating controls, and expiration	Shows risk acceptance discipline

Storage volume reduced	Useful, but incomplete by itself	Stale sensitive data reduced, exposure lowered, and storage cost avoided	Connects security, privacy, and cost

The reporting question should always be:

What does this metric help leadership understand or decide?

If the answer is unclear, the metric probably belongs in an operational dashboard, not an executive report.

19.6 Cost and Risk Framing

DSPM reporting becomes more powerful when it connects security progress to cost and business risk.

Executives and boards do not fund dashboards. They fund risk reduction, operational resilience, audit readiness, regulatory confidence, business enablement, and cost control.

A strong DSPM report should explain how data security work affects the business in financial and risk terms.

Cost and risk framing may include:

Business Concern	DSPM Reporting Connection
Breach impact	Less sensitive data exposed, fewer overprivileged users, fewer public repositories, and reduced blast radius
Regulatory exposure	Better visibility into regulated data, policy violations, retention gaps, and evidence of remediation
Legal and privacy risk	Reduced stale data, better DSAR scoping, clearer retention decisions, and documented exceptions
Audit cost	Stronger evidence, fewer manual searches, clearer control ownership, and faster response to auditors
Storage and data management cost	Reduced stale, duplicate, and unnecessary sensitive data
Cyber insurance and customer trust	Stronger evidence of control maturity, monitoring, and remediation discipline
AI readiness	Safer data environments for copilots, agents, analytics, and AI-enabled workflows
Incident response efficiency	Faster data impact analysis during investigations
Operational efficiency	Automated discovery, classification, ticket routing, and reporting
Business continuity	Better understanding of critical data locations, owners, and dependencies

The goal is not to claim unrealistic savings or inflated return on investment. The goal is to show credible linkage between DSPM work and business outcomes.

For example:

This quarter, the program reduced stale sensitive data by 22 TB, lowering unnecessary exposure and reducing storage burden. More importantly, the cleanup removed outdated customer exports from unmanaged repositories, reducing privacy and breach impact risk.

That sentence is stronger than:

We deleted 22 TB of data.

The first version explains why it matters.

The second only describes the action.

Practical Cost/Risk Language

A CISO can use language like:

The DSPM program is reducing risk in three ways: decreasing the amount of sensitive data exposed, reducing the number of identities that can access high-risk data, and improving the evidence we can provide during audits, incidents, and AI governance reviews.

Or:

The value of the program is not limited to breach prevention. It also improves audit readiness, reduces manual investigation time, supports privacy operations, lowers unnecessary storage exposure, and helps determine which data is safe for AI use.

Cost framing should be careful and defensible. Avoid promising exact savings unless the organization has validated the numbers. It is safer to report directional value, known cost avoidance, measurable cleanup, reduced manual effort, and improved decision speed.

19.7 Core DSPM Metrics

1. Sensitive Data Coverage

This measures how much of the known environment is covered by DSPM discovery and classification.

Example metrics:

Metric	What It Shows
Percentage of cloud data stores scanned	Visibility across cloud environments
Percentage of SaaS repositories scanned	Coverage of collaboration and SaaS platforms
Percentage of databases classified	Classification progress
Percentage of business-critical applications mapped to data stores	Connection between business services and data risk
Number of unclassified repositories containing likely sensitive data	Unknown or unmanaged risk
Percentage of AI-candidate repositories reviewed	Readiness for safe AI adoption

Executive framing:

DSPM coverage increased from 48% to 76% this quarter, with the largest gap remaining in SaaS repositories managed outside central IT.

This tells leadership that visibility is improving, while also identifying where support may be needed.

2. Sensitive Data Exposure

Exposure metrics show where sensitive data is unnecessarily accessible, public, misconfigured, or over-permissioned.

Example metrics:

Metric	What It Shows
Number of public data stores containing sensitive data	Direct exposure risk
Number of externally accessible repositories with regulated data	Compliance and breach risk
Percentage reduction in critical exposure findings	Risk reduction over time
Sensitive data stores without encryption	Control gaps
Sensitive data shared with external users	Third-party and collaboration risk
High-risk findings by business unit	Accountability and prioritization
Sensitive data indexed or accessible by AI tools	AI exposure and governance readiness

Executive framing:

Critical sensitive data exposure findings decreased by 38% this quarter. Remaining risk is concentrated in two business units with legacy file shares and unclear ownership.

This is far more useful than listing every misconfigured repository.

3. Access Risk

Access risk metrics show whether users, groups, service accounts, applications, and third parties have appropriate access to sensitive data.

Example metrics:

Metric	What It Shows
Number of overprivileged users with access to sensitive data	Least privilege gaps
Number of dormant accounts with sensitive data access	Identity hygiene risk
Number of external collaborators with sensitive data access	Third-party exposure
Privileged accounts accessing regulated data	High-impact risk
Sensitive repositories with broad group access	Access governance weakness
Percentage of excessive access findings remediated	Program effectiveness
AI agents or connectors with broad access to sensitive data	AI identity and authorization risk

Executive framing:

We removed excessive access for 1,240 users across sensitive repositories, including 312 dormant accounts. However, service account ownership remains a gap and requires application team participation.

This tells a story of progress and clearly identifies the blocker.

4. Remediation Performance

Remediation metrics show whether the organization is acting on DSPM findings.

Example metrics:

Metric	What It Shows
Mean time to remediate critical findings	Speed of risk reduction
Percentage of findings closed within SLA	Operational discipline
Open critical findings older than SLA	Persistent risk
Findings without assigned owner	Governance gaps
Remediation backlog by severity	Workload and prioritization
Repeat findings	Process or control weakness
Remediation blocked by business decision	Leadership action needed

Executive framing:

Critical findings are now being remediated in an average of 11 days, down from 27 days last quarter. The largest delay is findings without a confirmed business data owner.

This helps executives understand both improvement and friction.

5. Governance and Ownership

Governance metrics show whether the organization has clear accountability for data risk.

Example metrics:

Metric	What It Shows
Percentage of sensitive data stores with assigned owner	Accountability
Percentage of policies mapped to regulatory requirements	Compliance readiness
Number of policy exceptions approved and reviewed	Risk acceptance discipline
Percentage of business units participating in data risk review	Cross-functional maturity
Number of unresolved ownership conflicts	Executive decision points
Frequency of governance review meetings	Operating rhythm
Percentage of high-risk repositories with approved-use determination	Privacy and AI governance maturity

Executive framing:

Ownership is now assigned for 69% of high-risk sensitive data stores, up from 31%. The remaining 31% requires executive sponsorship because ownership crosses business and application boundaries.

This connects governance maturity to leadership action.

6. Compliance Alignment

Compliance metrics show whether data risk is being managed in relation to legal, regulatory, and contractual requirements.

Example metrics:

Metric	What It Shows
Sensitive data mapped to applicable regulations	Regulatory visibility
Data stores containing PCI, PHI, PII, or financial data	Compliance scope
Policy violations by regulation	Audit readiness
Retention violations	Legal and privacy risk
Encryption gaps for regulated data	Control maturity
Access violations involving regulated data	Compliance exposure
AI use cases involving regulated data without completed review	Emerging compliance and governance risk

Executive framing:

We identified 18 repositories containing regulated data outside approved storage locations. Twelve have been remediated, four are in progress, and two require business-approved exceptions.

This is the kind of summary executives can act on.

7. Data Retention and Reduction

DSPM should not only protect data. It should help reduce unnecessary data risk.

Example metrics:

Metric	What It Shows
Volume of stale sensitive data	Retention risk
Duplicate sensitive data stores	Data sprawl
Sensitive data past retention period	Legal and privacy exposure
Percentage of stale sensitive data deleted or archived	Risk reduction
Number of repositories retired	Attack surface reduction
Storage cost reduction from cleanup	Business value
AI-derived artifacts reviewed for retention	AI lifecycle maturity

Executive framing:

The program reduced stale sensitive data by 22 terabytes this quarter, lowering both exposure risk and storage costs.

This is a powerful executive message because it connects security, privacy, and cost.

19.8 Use Leading and Lagging Indicators

Executives often understand lagging indicators, such as number of incidents or unresolved critical findings. But mature reporting should also include leading indicators.

Lagging indicators show what already happened.

Leading indicators show whether the organization is becoming more or less likely to experience future risk.

Examples:

Leading Indicator	Why It Matters
Percentage of sensitive repositories with assigned owners	Predicts remediation effectiveness
Percentage of critical findings with SLA	Predicts operational discipline
Reduction in excessive access	Predicts lower breach impact
Increase in continuous scanning coverage	Predicts stronger visibility

Number of unresolved policy exceptions	Predicts compliance and audit risk
Growth in stale sensitive data	Predicts future exposure
Number of AI-candidate repositories not yet reviewed	Predicts AI readiness risk
Number of service accounts with sensitive data access and no owner	Predicts identity-driven data exposure

A good executive report includes both.

For example:

No data security incidents occurred this quarter, but stale sensitive data increased by 19% in unmanaged SaaS repositories. This is a leading indicator of rising exposure risk.

That is a mature message.

It does not wait for failure before asking for action.

19.9 Build an Executive Scorecard

An executive scorecard should fit on one page.

It should not be a data dump. It should show the current state, trend, target, and business meaning.

A practical scorecard might include:

Category	Current	Target	Trend	Executive Message
DSPM coverage	76%	90%	Improving	Cloud coverage strong; SaaS still incomplete
Critical exposure findings	24	<10	Improving	Public exposure reduced, legacy shares remain
Critical findings within SLA	81%	95%	Improving	Ownership gaps slowing closure
Sensitive stores with owner	69%	90%	Improving	Business owner assignment needed
Excessive access findings	410	<150	Improving	Dormant account cleanup successful
Stale sensitive data	38 TB	<20 TB	Worsening	Retention enforcement needed
Policy exceptions overdue	7	0	Worsening	Requires governance review
AI-candidate repositories reviewed	42%	85%	Improving	Review needed before AI expansion

Each row should answer: ***So what?***

Executives should not have to interpret the dashboard themselves. The report should explain the story.

19.10 Tell the Story in Three Layers

The best executive reporting uses three layers.

1. What changed?

This is the factual update.

Example:

Critical exposure findings decreased from 39 to 24.

2. Why does it matter?

This connects the metric to business risk.

Example:

This reduces the likelihood of sensitive data being exposed through public or misconfigured repositories.

3. What action is needed?

This tells leadership what decision, support, or accountability is required.

Example:

The remaining findings are tied to legacy repositories without clear ownership. We need business unit leaders to assign accountable owners by the end of the month.

That is the reporting pattern:

What changed?

Why does it matter?

What action is needed?

This pattern keeps reports clear, business-focused, and useful.

19.11 Report by Risk Theme, Not Tool Finding

Executives do not need to know every tool finding. They need to know the major risk themes.

Instead of reporting:

The DSPM platform generated 4,382 findings.

Report:

The top three data risk themes are excessive access to regulated data, stale sensitive data in unmanaged repositories, and inconsistent ownership for high-risk data stores.

Then summarize each theme:

Risk Theme	Business Impact	Current Status	Needed Action
Excessive access	Increases breach impact	Improving	Continue access cleanup
Stale sensitive data	Raises legal and privacy exposure	Worsening	Approve retention enforcement

Ownership gaps	Slows remediation	Improving but incomplete	Assign business owners
AI-accessible sensitive repositories	Increases risk of unauthorized retrieval or summarization	Emerging	Require review before AI expansion

This prevents the conversation from becoming too technical and keeps executives focused on decisions.

19.12 Show Progress Over Time

A single report is useful. A trend is better.

Executives need to see whether the organization is improving, stalled, or getting worse.

Trend reporting should show movement across quarters or months.

Examples:

Metric	Q1	Q2	Q3	Direction
DSPM coverage	42%	61%	76%	Improving
Critical exposure findings	57	39	24	Improving
Findings closed within SLA	48%	67%	81%	Improving
Sensitive stores with owner	22%	44%	69%	Improving
Stale sensitive data	24 TB	31 TB	38 TB	Worsening
AI-candidate repositories reviewed	10%	24%	42%	Improving

This kind of view makes the story obvious.

The program is improving in discovery, exposure reduction, remediation, ownership, and AI readiness. But retention risk is getting worse.

That leads to a clear executive message:

The DSPM program is reducing immediate exposure risk, but data retention risk is increasing. The next maturity step is to enforce retention policies and reduce stale sensitive data.

19.13 Connect Metrics to Business Outcomes

Executive reporting should connect DSPM progress to outcomes leadership already cares about.

Those outcomes may include:

Business Outcome	DSPM Connection
Reduced breach impact	Less sensitive data exposed and fewer users with unnecessary access
Audit readiness	Better evidence of controls, ownership, and remediation
Regulatory compliance	Visibility into regulated data and policy violations

Operational efficiency	Automated discovery, classification, and ticketing
Cost reduction	Reduced stale and duplicate data
Business trust	Stronger protection of customer, patient, employee, and partner data
AI readiness	Better understanding of what data can safely be used
Faster incident response	Faster data impact analysis during investigations
Better risk acceptance decisions	Clearer visibility into residual risk, owner, and compensating controls

This is especially important when reporting to non-security executives.

A CFO may care about cost and risk reduction. A general counsel may care about regulatory exposure and retention. A CIO may care about operational maturity and integration. A CISO may care about attack surface reduction and control effectiveness. A business leader may care about speed, trust, and avoiding disruption.

The same DSPM metrics can be framed differently depending on the audience.

19.14 Residual Risk Reporting

No executive report should imply that all data risk can be eliminated.

A mature DSPM program should show what has been fixed, what is improving, and what risk remains after remediation, compensating controls, or business decisions.

Residual risk is the risk that remains after controls have been applied or after the organization has chosen not to fully remediate a condition.

Residual risk reporting matters because it prevents three common problems:

1. Risk disappears into exceptions.
2. Security owns risk that belongs to the business.
3. Leadership receives positive trend reports without understanding what remains unresolved.

A residual risk report should answer:

- *What risk remains?*
- *Why does it remain?*
- *Who owns it?*
- *What compensating controls are in place?*
- *What is the potential business impact?*
- *Is the risk accepted, deferred, transferred, mitigated, or escalated?*
- *When will it be reviewed again?*
- *What decision is needed from leadership?*

Residual Risk Categories

Residual Risk Category	Example	Reporting Message
Accepted risk	Business owner approves temporary external sharing for a regulated workflow	Accepted by named owner with expiration and compensating controls
Deferred remediation	Legacy system cannot support access changes until migration	Risk remains until migration milestone; requires timeline visibility
Compensating control	Data cannot be moved yet, but access is restricted and monitored	Risk reduced but not eliminated
Ownership unresolved	Sensitive repository lacks clear business owner	Requires executive assignment decision
Policy exception	DLP exception approved for business workflow	Exception must have owner, reason, scope, and expiration
Technical constraint	Platform lacks required control	Requires roadmap, vendor escalation, or alternative control
Cost or staffing constraint	Remediation requires funding or dedicated resources	Requires leadership decision
AI readiness gap	Sensitive repository is needed for AI use but access is still overbroad	AI use should remain blocked until remediation or acceptance

Residual Risk Example

Remaining risk is concentrated in legacy collaboration repositories containing regulated data. Public exposure has been removed, but broad internal access remains. Remediation is delayed because ownership crosses three business units. Security has applied monitoring and disabled external sharing as compensating controls. Leadership decision needed: assign a single accountable data owner or approve continued residual risk through Q4.

That kind of statement is useful because it is clear, honest, and decision-oriented.

Residual risk reporting should not sound like failure. It should sound like governance.

The goal is to ensure risk is visible, owned, reviewed, and acted on.

19.15 Example Executive Summary

Executive reporting is where the DSPM program becomes visible to leadership. The goal is not to overwhelm executives with every discovered data issue. The goal is to clearly communicate whether data risk is improving, where material exposure remains, what progress has been made, and what decisions are needed to reduce residual risk.

A strong DSPM executive summary should connect operational findings to business impact. It should explain what changed, why it matters, what still needs attention, and where leadership support is required.

The following examples can be adapted for quarterly reporting, steering committee updates, executive briefings, or board-level communication.

Example One-Page DSPM Executive Summary

DSPM Executive Summary
Reporting Period: Q3
Overall Status: Improving, with retention and ownership requiring leadership attention

During Q3, the DSPM program expanded coverage from 61% to 76% of known data repositories. Critical exposure findings decreased by 38%, and remediation performance improved, with 81% of critical findings now closed within SLA.

The strongest progress was in cloud storage visibility, public exposure remediation, and dormant account cleanup. These improvements reduce the likelihood and potential impact of sensitive data exposure.

Two areas require executive attention. First, stale sensitive data increased from 31 TB to 38 TB, primarily in unmanaged SaaS repositories and legacy file shares. Second, 31% of high-risk sensitive data stores still do not have assigned business owners, which slows remediation, policy enforcement, and risk acceptance decisions.

Top Wins

Win	Impact
Reduced critical exposure findings by 38%	Lower breach and compliance risk
Removed excessive access for 1,240 users	Improved least privilege and reduced insider risk
Increased DSPM coverage to 76%	Better visibility and control across sensitive data environments
Assigned ownership for 69% of high-risk sensitive stores	Stronger accountability and faster remediation

Top Risks

Risk	Business Impact	Action Needed
Stale sensitive data increased by 7 TB	Higher privacy, legal, regulatory, and breach exposure	Approve retention cleanup plan
31% of high-risk stores lack an assigned owner	Slower remediation and unclear accountability	Require business units to assign owners
SaaS coverage remains incomplete	Continued blind spots outside central IT	Expand DSPM integrations next quarter
AI-candidate repositories not fully reviewed	AI use may expose overpermissioned or unapproved data	Require AI data readiness review before expansion

Recommended Executive Decisions

1. Approve retention enforcement for stale sensitive data in unmanaged repositories.
2. Require business units to assign owners for all high-risk sensitive data stores.
3. Expand DSPM coverage to priority SaaS platforms next quarter.

4. Require AI data readiness review before connecting sensitive repositories to AI tools.

Overall Message

The DSPM program is reducing immediate exposure risk and improving operational maturity. The next phase should focus on retention enforcement, business ownership, broader SaaS visibility, and AI-ready data governance.

19.16 One-Page Board Report Example

A board-level DSPM update should be shorter, more outcome-focused, and less operational than a standard executive summary. The board does not need every technical detail. It needs to understand whether material data risk is increasing or decreasing, where the organization remains exposed, and what decisions require leadership approval.

Board Data Security Posture Update

Reporting Period: Q3
Overall Direction: Improving
Primary Concern: Residual risk remains in legacy collaboration platforms, stale sensitive data, and unreviewed AI-accessible repositories.

Current Risk Posture

The organization's data security posture improved this quarter. DSPM coverage expanded across cloud storage, SaaS platforms, and priority data repositories. Critical exposure findings decreased, remediation timelines improved, and business ownership was assigned to a greater percentage of high-risk data stores.

Residual risk remains elevated in legacy collaboration platforms, unmanaged SaaS repositories, excessive access to regulated data, and repositories that may be accessible to AI-enabled tools without sufficient review.

Material Changes This Quarter

Area	Change	Board Meaning
DSPM coverage	Increased from 61% to 76%	Visibility is improving, but SaaS and warehouse gaps remain
Critical exposure findings	Reduced by 38%	Immediate exposure risk is decreasing
Critical remediation	12 of 15 critical findings closed	Program is moving from discovery to action
Business ownership	74% of Tier 1 data stores assigned owners	Accountability is improving
Stale sensitive data	Increased from 31 TB to 38 TB	Retention risk is worsening
AI readiness	42% of AI-candidate repositories reviewed	AI expansion should remain gated by data readiness

Top Three Data Risk Themes

Theme	Board-Level Concern	Current Direction
Legacy collaboration platforms	Sensitive data remains in older repositories with inconsistent access controls and retention enforcement	Mixed
Excessive access to regulated data	Users, groups, service accounts, or AI connectors may have broader access than required	Improving
Unreviewed AI-accessible repositories	Sensitive data may be available to AI-enabled workflows before ownership, classification, and access controls are validated	Emerging

Residual Risk

Remaining risk is concentrated in legacy collaboration platforms, excessive access to regulated data, stale sensitive data, and unreviewed AI-accessible repositories.

Immediate exposure risk has been reduced, but continued progress depends on expanding DSPM visibility, assigning data ownership, enforcing retention decisions, and reviewing AI-accessible repositories before broader AI adoption.

Decisions Requested

Management is requesting approval to:

1. Expand DSPM coverage to the remaining priority SaaS and data warehouse environments.
2. Enforce retention cleanup for stale sensitive data in unmanaged repositories.
3. Require each business unit to assign accountable owners for Tier 1 and high-risk sensitive data stores.
4. Require AI data readiness review before expanding internal AI use cases.

Cost and Risk Framing

The program is reducing breach and regulatory risk by removing public exposure, reducing excessive access, and improving ownership. Retention cleanup may also reduce storage burden and legal exposure by removing stale sensitive data that no longer has a business or regulatory purpose.

The next investment priority is not simply more tooling. It is operational expansion: broader SaaS coverage, ownership enforcement, retention execution, and AI readiness review.

Suggested Board Message

This quarter, the organization reduced externally exposed restricted data repositories by 38%, assigned business ownership to 74% of Tier 1 data stores, and remediated 12 of 15 critical exposure findings. Remaining risk is concentrated in legacy collaboration platforms, excessive access to regulated data, stale sensitive data, and unreviewed AI-accessible repositories. Management is requesting approval to expand DSPM coverage to the remaining priority SaaS and data warehouse environments, enforce retention cleanup, and require AI data readiness reviews before additional AI-connected repositories are approved.

The overall direction is positive. The organization is reducing immediate exposure risk and improving data security maturity. The next phase requires leadership support to expand visibility, enforce ownership, clean up stale sensitive data, and prepare data environments for safe AI adoption.

19.17 Example Board-Level DSPM Update

A more narrative board-level update may be useful when the board prefers brief written commentary instead of a table-heavy report.

Current Risk Posture

The organization's data security posture improved this quarter. DSPM coverage expanded across cloud storage, SaaS platforms, and priority data repositories. Critical exposure findings decreased, remediation timelines improved, and business ownership was assigned to a greater percentage of high-risk data stores.

However, residual risk remains elevated in legacy collaboration platforms, unmanaged SaaS repositories, excessive access to regulated data, stale sensitive data, and repositories that may be accessible to AI-enabled tools without sufficient review.

Material Changes This Quarter

This quarter, the organization reduced externally exposed restricted data repositories by 38%, assigned business ownership to 74% of Tier 1 data stores, and remediated 12 of 15 critical exposure findings.

These improvements reduce the organization's exposure to unauthorized access, data leakage, regulatory findings, and incident response complexity.

Top Three Data Risk Themes

Theme	Board-Level Concern
Legacy collaboration platforms	Sensitive data remains in older repositories with inconsistent access controls and retention enforcement
Excessive access to regulated data	Users, groups, service accounts, or AI connectors may have broader access than required for their role
Unreviewed AI-accessible repositories	Sensitive data may be available to AI-enabled workflows before ownership, classification, and access controls are validated

Remediation Progress

Remediation performance improved during the quarter. The organization closed most critical exposure findings, reduced public or external exposure, and removed excessive access for a significant number of users.

Progress was strongest where business ownership was clear and remediation workflows were already defined. Remediation slowed in areas where data ownership was unclear, repositories were unmanaged, or retention decisions required business approval.

Open Decisions Needed

Management is requesting approval to:

1. Expand DSPM coverage to the remaining SaaS and data warehouse environments.
2. Enforce retention cleanup for stale sensitive data in unmanaged repositories.
3. Require each business unit to assign accountable owners for Tier 1 and high-risk sensitive data stores.
4. Review AI-accessible data repositories before expanding internal AI use cases.

Residual Risk

Remaining risk is concentrated in legacy collaboration platforms, excessive access to regulated data, stale sensitive data, and unreviewed AI-accessible repositories.

The organization has reduced immediate exposure risk, but continued progress depends on expanding DSPM visibility, enforcing ownership, and making retention decisions that may require business and legal approval.

AI/Data Readiness Impact

DSPM is becoming a foundational control for AI readiness. Before sensitive data is used by AI tools, copilots, automation platforms, or analytics workflows, the organization must understand where that data lives, who owns it, who can access it, whether it is properly classified, and whether it should be available to AI-enabled systems.

The current DSPM program improves AI readiness by identifying sensitive data, mapping ownership, reducing excessive access, and flagging repositories that require review before AI enablement.

Next-Quarter Priorities

Next quarter, the DSPM program should focus on expanding SaaS and data warehouse coverage, completing ownership assignment for Tier 1 data stores, enforcing retention decisions for stale sensitive data, and reviewing AI-accessible repositories before broader AI adoption.

Suggested Board Message

This quarter, the organization reduced externally exposed restricted data repositories by 38%, assigned business ownership to 74% of Tier 1 data stores, and remediated 12 of 15 critical exposure findings. Remaining risk is concentrated in legacy collaboration platforms, excessive access to regulated data, stale sensitive data, and unreviewed AI-accessible repositories. Management is requesting approval to expand DSPM coverage to the remaining SaaS and data warehouse environments.

The overall direction is positive. The organization is reducing immediate exposure risk and improving data security maturity. The next phase requires leadership support to expand visibility, enforce ownership, clean up stale sensitive data, and prepare data environments for safe AI adoption.

19.18 Avoid Common Reporting Mistakes

Mistake 1: Reporting Too Much Detail

Executives should not receive every finding. They should receive risk themes, trends, and decisions needed.

Too much detail creates noise.

Mistake 2: Reporting Activity Instead of Outcomes

Activity metrics show work. Outcome metrics show value.

Instead of:

We classified 10 million files.

Say:

We identified 4,200 files containing regulated data in unmanaged repositories and remediated 73% of high-risk exposure.

Mistake 3: Hiding Bad News

Executive reporting should be honest. If a risk is worsening, say so clearly.

A mature program does not pretend everything is green. It explains where risk is increasing and what action is needed.

Mistake 4: Using Security Language Without Business Translation

Terms like "misconfigured ACLs," "orphaned service principals," or "toxic permission combinations" may be accurate, but they need translation.

For executives, explain the business meaning:

These access issues could allow users or applications to reach sensitive data they do not need, increasing breach impact and compliance exposure.

Mistake 5: Reporting Without Asking for Decisions

Executive reports should not only inform. They should help leaders act.

Every report should make clear whether leadership needs to approve funding, assign ownership, accept risk, enforce policy, or remove blockers.

Mistake 6: Reporting Only What Improved

Improvement matters, but executives also need to know what remains risky.

A report that only shows progress can accidentally hide residual risk. Strong reporting shows both:

- What improved
- What remains exposed
- What risk is accepted
- What decision is needed

Mistake 7: Reporting Cost Without Risk, or Risk Without Cost

A storage cleanup metric without risk context sounds like an IT efficiency project. A risk metric without cost context may sound like an endless security request.

The strongest reports connect both.

Example:

Retention cleanup reduced stale sensitive data by 22 TB, lowering unnecessary exposure while also reducing storage and eDiscovery burden.

19.19 Practical Reporting Cadence

DSPM reporting should happen at multiple levels.

Audience	Cadence	Focus
Technical teams	Weekly or biweekly	Findings, remediation, ownership, SLAs
Security leadership	Monthly	Risk trends, blockers, control performance
Governance committee	Monthly or quarterly	Policy adherence, exceptions, ownership
Executives / board	Quarterly	Business risk, maturity, major decisions
Audit / compliance	As needed	Evidence, control mapping, remediation history

The executive report should be concise, but it should be supported by detailed evidence for teams that need it.

19.20 What Good Looks Like

A mature DSPM reporting program has these characteristics:

- Clear baseline
- Defined target maturity
- Consistent metrics
- Trend reporting over time
- Business-aligned risk themes
- Cost and risk framing
- Ownership and SLA tracking
- Integration with remediation workflows
- Residual risk visibility
- Honest reporting of blockers
- Executive-level decision requests
- Evidence available for audit and compliance

The goal is not to make every metric green.

The goal is to make risk visible, measurable, owned, and manageable.

Key Takeaways

DSPM measurement should prove that the organization is reducing data risk and improving maturity.

Executives need reporting that is clear, honest, and tied to business outcomes. The most effective reports show what changed, why it matters, what action is needed, and what risk remains.

Strong DSPM reporting should include coverage, exposure, access risk, remediation performance, governance, compliance alignment, retention, AI readiness, cost/risk framing, and residual risk. These should be shown as trends over time, not isolated snapshots.

A good executive report does not overwhelm leadership with technical findings. It tells a business risk story and makes decisions easier.

CISOs need to show what is known, what is improving, what remains risky, and what decisions are needed. That means reporting progress without hiding residual risk.

The best metrics connect security activity to business impact. They show whether exposure is decreasing, ownership is improving, remediation is getting faster, stale sensitive data is being reduced, AI readiness is improving, and leadership decisions are being made.

The real value of measurement is not the dashboard.

It is the conversation it enables.

When done well, DSPM reporting helps executives understand where the organization is exposed, where it is improving, where it is stuck, which risks remain, and how leadership can help move the program forward.

Conclusion: Trusted AI Begins With Trusted Data

Data security has changed because the business use of data has changed.

For years, security programs were built around protecting systems, networks, endpoints, applications, identities, cloud environments, and infrastructure. Those controls still matter. They remain essential. But they are no longer enough on their own. Data no longer stays neatly inside the systems we designed to hold it. It moves through cloud platforms, SaaS applications, collaboration tools, databases, data lakes, warehouses, endpoints, backups, developer environments, third-party services, analytics pipelines, automation workflows, and AI-enabled platforms.

The question for modern leaders is no longer simply whether their systems are secure. The better question is whether the organization understands its data well enough to govern it, protect it, use it responsibly, and prove that risk is being reduced. That question sits at the center of this book.

Data Security Posture Management is not just a product category. It is not a scanner, dashboard, or vendor platform that can be dropped into an environment and expected to create accountability. DSPM is a discipline. At its best, it brings visibility, ownership, context, prioritization, remediation, governance, and measurement together around the data itself. It gives organizations a way to understand where sensitive and business-critical data lives, who and what can access it, how it is exposed, whether its use is appropriate, and what must happen next.

A tool can help discover sensitive data. It can classify information, map exposure, identify excessive access, detect risky patterns, and reveal risks that were previously hidden. But a tool cannot decide what the business values most. It cannot define risk appetite, assign true ownership, resolve conflicts between legal and operational needs, or determine whether a business process is appropriate. It cannot build trust with executives, customers, regulators, auditors, users, or the board.

The organization must do that work.

That is why strong DSPM programs are built before the purchase, not after it. They begin with business objectives, stakeholder alignment, critical data definitions, ownership models, severity rules, remediation workflows, exception processes, metrics, and executive reporting. Technology supports the program, but it should not define the program.

I have seen this firsthand working with early adopters of DSPM tools. The organizations that struggled often treated DSPM as a technology rollout. They scanned broadly, produced findings, and expected the business to respond simply because the tool identified risk. The few that succeeded took a different path. They slowed down long enough to think through the role of AI in the business. They asked which data should be available to AI, which data should be excluded, which repositories needed cleanup, which users and systems required access, and which decisions needed to be made before the tool created findings no one was ready to own.

Those successful organizations also built a real program plan. They did not leave data security sitting only with the security team. They created buy-in with the board, executive leadership, departments, data owners, legal, privacy, IT, and users. They understood that DSPM introduces new policies, new workflows, new accountability, and sometimes uncomfortable conversations about how data has been handled for years. They treated adoption as a leadership challenge, not just a technical one.

That is where storytelling becomes a critical skill.

People rarely change behavior because a tool tells them they are wrong. They change when they understand the risk, see how it affects the mission, believe the process is fair, and know what action to take. A strong data security leader must be able to explain why the policy exists, what problem it solves, what could happen if the organization ignores it, and how users can comply without feeling punished for how work has always been done. Storytelling helps turn findings into understanding, understanding into adoption, and adoption into measurable risk reduction.

AI has made this work urgent. Artificial intelligence does not create every data security problem. It exposes the problems that were already there. Over-permissioned folders, unmanaged repositories, stale exports, duplicate data, unclear ownership, excessive service account access, forgotten contractor permissions, shadow SaaS, weak retention practices, and poorly governed collaboration spaces were already risks. AI makes those risks easier to search, summarize, combine, infer from, automate, and expose.

That is the uncomfortable truth of AI-era security. Many of the biggest AI risks do not begin with a malicious actor. They begin with approved users, approved tools, approved integrations, and approved workflows accessing data that was never properly governed for that purpose.

Trusted AI depends on more than model safety. It depends on data control. Organizations must know what data they have, where it lives, where it is processed, who can access it, which AI systems can use it, what outputs and artifacts are created from it, and whether those artifacts remain within the organization's legal, contractual, regulatory, and operational control.

In that sense, data sovereignty has become part of AI strategy. If the enterprise cannot govern the data boundary, it cannot fully govern the AI boundary. That is why AI readiness begins with data readiness.

An organization should not connect AI to data it cannot find, classify, govern, or defend. It should not allow AI systems to index repositories that no one owns. It should not give agents broad access through shared service accounts. It should not allow sensitive prompts, outputs, embeddings, logs, or agent actions to become unmanaged records. It should not treat enterprise AI licensing as a substitute for data governance.

AI can help the business move faster, but only when the data foundation is trustworthy.

This book has returned to one idea again and again: visibility is only the beginning. Discovery matters, but discovery without ownership creates noise. Classification matters, but classification without context creates confusion. Dashboards matter, but dashboards without remediation create frustration. Automation matters, but automation without governance creates risk. Reporting matters, but reporting without business impact becomes activity tracking.

The goal is not to find every possible issue and overwhelm the organization. The goal is to reduce meaningful data risk in a measurable, repeatable, and defensible way.

That requires practical prioritization. Sensitive data must be evaluated in context. Leaders need to understand where the data lives, who can access it, how it is exposed, whether it is regulated, whether it is business critical, whether it is stale or duplicated, whether it is used by AI, whether compensating controls exist, and whether someone is accountable for the decision. Without that context, organizations may generate findings, but they will struggle to reduce risk in a way the business understands.

It also requires connection across disciplines. Identity, privacy, DLP, retention, legal, compliance, data governance, IT, security, engineering, and AI governance cannot operate as separate islands. Identity determines who and what can reach sensitive data. Privacy determines whether data use is appropriate, disclosed, minimized, retained, or deleted. DLP helps enforce rules at key points of movement. Retention and destruction reduce the amount of data that can be exposed in the first place. Legal and compliance define obligations, evidence needs, privilege concerns, and defensibility. Data governance brings ownership, stewardship, metadata, quality, and business meaning. AI governance determines whether data can safely be used by copilots, agents, models, retrieval systems, analytics workflows, and automated decisions.

Each discipline sees part of the picture. DSPM helps connect the picture.

When these functions work together, organizations can move from isolated controls to a living data security operating model. They can answer not only where sensitive data exists, but whether it is owned, protected, necessary, appropriately used, and trending toward lower risk.

Risk reduction must be measurable. A mature program does not settle for saying, "We scanned more data," or "We found more issues." It shows whether exposure is decreasing, whether excessive access is being removed, whether critical findings are closing within SLA, whether ownership is improving, whether stale sensitive data is being retired, whether exceptions are governed, whether AI-connected repositories have been reviewed, and whether residual risk is visible to the right leaders.

That is how data security becomes defensible.

It also requires humility. No organization has a perfect data environment. Data security is messy because business is messy. People export reports. Teams share folders. Developers copy data for testing. Business units adopt SaaS tools. Employees create workarounds. Managers ask for speed. AI tools appear inside workflows before governance is ready. Old data remains long after its purpose is gone.

Most data risk is not created by bad intent. It is created by speed, complexity, unclear ownership, workflow friction, leadership pressure, and years of accumulated decisions. A mature data security program does not shame the business for that reality. It makes risk visible and gives people a practical path to fix it.

The human layer matters. Users need guidance at the moment of risk, not only annual training. Administrators need clear remediation playbooks. Data owners need context they can understand. Managers need to reinforce secure behavior and validate business need. Executives need reporting tied to outcomes, and they must model the behavior they expect from the rest of the organization.

Leadership behavior shapes user behavior. If leaders demand speed while ignoring governance, users will often interpret that pressure as permission to work around controls. If leaders reward secure delivery, fund usable workflows, assign ownership, and treat data security as a business responsibility, the organization has a much better chance of turning policy into practice.

Modern data security is a team sport. It is also a lifecycle discipline.

Organizations must discover data, classify it, govern it, protect it, monitor it, respond to misuse, and eventually retire or destroy data that no longer has a valid purpose. Keeping unnecessary sensitive data is not neutral. It creates liability. It increases breach impact. It complicates privacy requests, legal holds, audits, investigations, discovery, and AI governance.

Sometimes the best security control is not stronger protection. Sometimes it is safely letting the data go.

That is the full arc of a mature data security program: from visibility to action, from action to evidence, and from evidence to trust.

For leaders, the most important question is not whether the organization has purchased a DSPM tool. The more important question is whether the organization can explain where its critical data lives, who owns it, who and what can access it, whether that access is appropriate, whether the use of that data is approved, where data is exposed or duplicated, which risks matter most, how those risks are remediated, and whether the organization can prove that risk is going down.

Those questions define the next era of data security.

The future will not reward organizations that simply collect the most data or connect the most repositories to AI. It will reward organizations that understand their data, govern it well, protect it intelligently, use it responsibly, and measure whether risk is actually decreasing.

Data is no longer hidden in the background of the business. It is in plain sight. It fuels operations, decisions, customer trust, regulatory obligations, innovation, automation, and AI.

The work ahead is not easy, but it is clear.

Organizations must find the data, understand it, assign ownership, protect it, use it wisely, retire it when its purpose is gone, measure progress, and tell the truth. That is how organizations move from data exposure to data trust.

And in the AI era, data trust is business trust.

This book is not only about finding sensitive data. It is about helping leaders make better decisions with it. The future of AI, privacy, security, and trust depends on whether organizations can govern data with enough clarity, humility, and discipline to use it safely.

Trusted AI does not begin with the model.

It begins with the data.

Research and Standards Referenced

The following sources informed the research, standards alignment, regulatory discussion, incident examples, product context, and practical guidance throughout this book. They are included for transparency, validation, and further reading. This bibliography supports the book, but it does not replace local endnotes, chapter-level citations, or source notes where specific statistics, legal requirements, regulatory expectations, public incidents, enforcement actions, framework language, vendor capabilities, product descriptions, or official terminology are discussed.

This book uses external sources in four ways:

1. Factual support: statistics, regulatory requirements, incident facts, public enforcement history, and named reports.
2. Framework alignment: official terminology, control categories, lifecycle concepts, maturity concepts, and risk-management structures from recognized standards, laws, regulations, and frameworks.
3. Product and market context: vendor documentation, analyst research, and public product descriptions used to understand capabilities that may change over time.
4. Author analysis: field observations, operating models, templates, examples, maturity guidance, decision tables, and recommendations created from the author's professional experience and adapted for this book unless a specific external source is cited.

This bibliography is not legal, regulatory, compliance, cybersecurity, privacy, or technical advice. Readers should confirm current requirements with qualified counsel, auditors, regulators, vendors, and authoritative source materials before making decisions based on any framework, law, standard, control requirement, or technology capability.

When this book uses official terms, framework names, regulatory language, vendor terminology, or standard-defined concepts, those terms belong to their respective source frameworks, laws, standards, vendors, or organizations. The surrounding interpretation, field application, practical guidance, and data security lessons are the author's analysis unless otherwise stated.

Unless otherwise noted, references were reviewed for publication context and source integrity on June 23, 2026. Cybersecurity, privacy, artificial intelligence, regulatory expectations, vendor capabilities, and technical standards change frequently. Readers should validate current versions, effective dates, licensing terms, and applicability before relying on any source in an operational, legal, compliance, audit, or purchasing decision.

Cybersecurity and Data Breach Research

IBM Security. Cost of a Data Breach Report 2025. IBM, 2025.

Used to support discussions of breach cost, AI governance gaps, shadow AI, incident impact, data discovery, classification, access control, encryption, and executive risk reporting.

https://www.ibm.com/reports/data-breach

Verizon. 2025 Data Breach Investigations Report. Verizon Business, 2025.

Used to support discussion of ransomware, third-party involvement, credential abuse, vulnerability exploitation, and the broader breach landscape affecting data security programs. Specific statistics from this report should be cited locally in the chapter where they appear.

https://www.verizon.com/business/resources/reports/2025-dbir-data-breach-investigations-report.pdf

World Economic Forum. Global Cybersecurity Outlook 2025. World Economic Forum, 2025.

Used to support discussion of global cyber-risk trends, executive cybersecurity concerns, AI-related risk expansion, cyber resilience, supply chain dependency, and the changing threat landscape.

https://www.weforum.org/publications/global-cybersecurity-outlook-2025/

World Economic Forum. Artificial Intelligence and Cybersecurity: Balancing Risks and Rewards. World Economic Forum, 2025.

Used to support discussion of AI's effect on cybersecurity, the expanding attack surface, AI-enabled defense, AI-enabled adversary activity, governance needs, and organizational risk tradeoffs.

https://reports.weforum.org/docs/WEF_Artificial_Intelligence_and_Cybersecurity_Balancing_Risks_and_Rewards_2025.pdf

Artificial Intelligence Risk, Governance, and Security

National Institute of Standards and Technology. Artificial Intelligence Risk Management Framework, AI RMF 1.0. NIST, 2023.

Used to support discussion of AI risk governance, AI lifecycle management, trustworthy AI, measurement, accountability, and risk-based oversight.

https://www.nist.gov/itl/ai-risk-management-framework

National Institute of Standards and Technology. Artificial Intelligence Risk Management Framework: Generative Artificial Intelligence Profile, NIST AI 600-1. NIST, 2024.

Used to support discussion of generative AI risks, prompt security, synthetic content, data exposure, model misuse, model evaluation, and governance practices specific to generative AI systems.

https://www.nist.gov/publications/artificial-intelligence-risk-management-framework-generative-artificial-intelligence

National Institute of Standards and Technology. SP 800-218A, Secure Software Development Practices for Generative AI and Dual-Use Foundation Models: An SSDF Community Profile. NIST, 2024.

Used to support discussion of secure AI development, AI supply chain risk, model development practices, testing, deployment, acquisition, and lifecycle security. The final publication was released in July 2024.

https://csrc.nist.gov/pubs/sp/800/218/a/final

Open Worldwide Application Security Project. OWASP Top 10 for Large Language Model Applications, 2025. OWASP, 2025.

Used to support discussion of prompt injection, sensitive information disclosure, insecure output handling, training data poisoning, supply chain vulnerabilities, excessive agency, model/application abuse, and other LLM application risks.

https://owasp.org/www-project-top-10-for-large-language-model-applications/

Open Worldwide Application Security Project. OWASP Top 10 for Agentic Applications, 2026. OWASP, 2025.

Used to support discussion of agentic AI risks, autonomous workflows, tool use, excessive agency, identity misuse, data exposure, and control expectations for AI agents. If a chapter references an earlier draft or pre-release version, preserve that version in the local citation.

https://genai.owasp.org/resource/owasp-top-10-for-agentic-applications-for-2026/

Cloud Security Alliance. AI Controls Matrix. Cloud Security Alliance, 2025.

Used to support discussion of AI control objectives, AI assurance, cloud AI governance, control mapping, audit readiness, and alignment with broader security and governance programs.

https://cloudsecurityalliance.org/artifacts/ai-controls-matrix

Cloud Security Alliance. Cloud Controls Matrix. Cloud Security Alliance.

Used as supporting context for cloud security controls, cloud governance, shared responsibility, and the relationship between cloud security posture and AI/data security posture.

https://cloudsecurityalliance.org/research/cloud-controls-matrix

International Organization for Standardization. ISO/IEC 42001: Artificial Intelligence Management System. ISO, 2023.

Used to support discussion of AI management systems, AI governance, policy ownership, risk management, accountability, lifecycle controls, management review, and continuous improvement.

https://www.iso.org/standard/81230.html

MITRE. MITRE ATLAS: Adversarial Threat Landscape for Artificial-Intelligence Systems. MITRE.

Used as supporting context for AI threat modeling, adversary techniques, model/system abuse patterns, and AI-specific security testing considerations.

https://atlas.mitre.org/

Data Strategy, Governance, and Program Foundations

U.S. Department of Defense. DoD Data Strategy. Department of Defense, 2020.

Used to support discussion of data as a strategic asset, data-centric organizations, and DoD's VAULTIS goals: Visible, Accessible, Understandable, Linked, Trustworthy, Interoperable, and Secure. VAULTIS should be treated as DoD terminology, not author-created terminology.

https://media.defense.gov/2020/Oct/08/2002514180/-1/-1/0/dod-data-strategy.pdf

National Institute of Standards and Technology. Cybersecurity Framework 2.0. NIST, 2024.

Used as supporting context for governance, identify, protect, detect, respond, and recover functions across cybersecurity and data security programs. The CSF 2.0 "Govern" function should be cited locally when its wording or structure is discussed.

https://www.nist.gov/cyberframework

Cyera. Pete Chronis, Building a Modern Data Security Program. Cyera, December 2, 2024.

Used only as an example of public market framing around data security program development and lifecycle thinking. The program model, templates, operating model, and practical guidance in this book are the author's field-derived structure unless a specific source is cited.

https://www.cyera.com/blog/building-a-modern-data-security-program

Gartner. Market Guide and Research on Data Security Posture Management. Gartner.

Used as supporting context for DSPM category definition, mandatory capabilities, vendor evaluation, discovery, classification, posture management, and data risk prioritization. Gartner materials are proprietary and should be cited according to the version, publication date, and licensed report used.

Privacy, Data Protection, and Regulatory Sources

European Union. General Data Protection Regulation, Regulation (EU) 2016/679. European Union, 2016.

Used to support discussion of data protection by design and default, security of processing, right to erasure, minimization, retention, deletion, privacy operations, data subject rights, and cross-border data governance. Exact legal rights and article references should be cited locally where discussed.

https://gdpr-info.eu

European Union. Artificial Intelligence Act, Regulation (EU) 2024/1689. European Union, 2024.

Used to support discussion of high-risk AI systems, AI data governance, cybersecurity, transparency, technical documentation, human oversight, robustness, and lifecycle accountability.

https://digital-strategy.ec.europa.eu/en/policies/regulatory-framework-ai

European Union Agency for Cybersecurity and EU AI Office. Cybersecurity and the EU AI Act Guidance. ENISA and EU AI Office.

Used to support discussion of AI cybersecurity, regulatory readiness, trustworthy AI, lifecycle risk, security obligations, and implementation considerations under the EU AI Act.

California Privacy Protection Agency. California Consumer Privacy Act and California Privacy Rights Act Guidance and Frequently Asked Questions. CPPA.

Used to support discussion of consumer privacy rights, deletion, data minimization, retention, sharing, and privacy program obligations.

https://cppa.ca.gov/faq.html

California Office of the Attorney General. California Consumer Privacy Act. California DOJ.

Used as an official state source for CCPA rights, business obligations, enforcement context, and consumer privacy explanations.

https://oag.ca.gov/privacy/ccpa

California Privacy Protection Agency. Enforcement Advisory No. 2024-01: Applying Data Minimization to Consumer Requests. CPPA, 2024.

Used to support discussion of data minimization as a practical privacy and data security control, especially in AI-enabled data environments. This replaces secondary commentary links where an official CPPA source is available.

https://cppa.ca.gov/pdf/enfadvisory202401.pdf

U.S. Department of Health and Human Services. HIPAA Privacy, Security, and Breach Notification Rules. HHS.

Used to support discussion of electronic protected health information, administrative safeguards, physical safeguards, technical safeguards, confidentiality, integrity, availability, access controls, audit controls, and healthcare data protection.

https://www.hhs.gov/hipaa/index.html

Federal Trade Commission. Standards for Safeguarding Customer Information, Gramm-Leach-Bliley Act Safeguards Rule. FTC.

Used to support discussion of customer information protection, written information security programs, access controls, encryption, disposal, monitoring, testing, service provider oversight, and board reporting.

https://www.ftc.gov/business-guidance/resources/ftc-safeguards-rule-what-your-business-needs-know

Electronic Code of Federal Regulations. 16 CFR Part 314, Standards for Safeguarding Customer Information. eCFR.

Used as the authoritative rule text for the FTC Safeguards Rule where rule wording, scope, or obligations are discussed.

https://www.ecfr.gov/current/title-16/chapter-I/subchapter-C/part-314

Federal Trade Commission. Health Breach Notification Rule and GLBA Safeguards Rule Breach Notification Materials. FTC.

Used to support discussion of breach notification, customer information exposure, unauthorized acquisition, and regulatory consequences of weak data security.

https://www.ftc.gov/legal-library/browse/rules/health-breach-notification-rule

https://www.ftc.gov/business-guidance/blog/2024/05/safeguards-rule-notification-requirement-now-effect

U.S. Securities and Exchange Commission. Cybersecurity Risk Management, Strategy, Governance, and Incident Disclosure Final Rule. SEC, 2023.

Used to support discussion of material cybersecurity incident disclosure, governance, risk management, strategy, board oversight, and executive accountability.

https://www.sec.gov/rules-regulations/2023/07/s7-09-22

New York State Department of Financial Services. 23 NYCRR Part 500, Cybersecurity Requirements for Financial Services Companies. NYDFS.

Used to support discussion of cybersecurity programs, encryption, nonpublic information, asset inventory, secure disposal, third-party service provider risk, monitoring, training, incident response, business continuity, and disaster recovery.

https://www.dfs.ny.gov/industry_guidance/cybersecurity

Data Lifecycle, Retention, and Destruction

National Institute of Standards and Technology. SP 800-88 Revision 2, Guidelines for Media Sanitization. NIST, 2025.

Used to support discussion of media sanitization, clear, purge, destroy, verification, disposal workflows, sanitization programs, and evidence of destruction. Rev. 2 is the current final publication and supersedes Rev. 1. If exact NIST definition language is used in the book, quote it and cite it locally.

https://csrc.nist.gov/pubs/sp/800/88/r2/final

National Institute of Standards and Technology. SP 800-88 Revision 1, Guidelines for Media Sanitization. NIST, 2014.

Historical reference only. Rev. 1 was withdrawn on September 26, 2025 and superseded by SP 800-88 Rev. 2. Retain this reference only if the book discusses historical sanitization guidance or earlier program materials.

https://csrc.nist.gov/pubs/sp/800/88/r1/final

National Institute of Standards and Technology. SP 800-53, Security and Privacy Controls for Information Systems and Organizations. NIST.

Used as supporting context for access control, audit and accountability, configuration management, incident response, risk assessment, system and information integrity, privacy controls, and security program governance.

https://csrc.nist.gov/publications/detail/sp/800-53/rev-5/final

National Institute of Standards and Technology. SP 800-61, Computer Security Incident Handling Guide. NIST.

Used as supporting context for incident response planning, preparation, detection, analysis, containment, eradication, recovery, and post-incident improvement.

https://csrc.nist.gov/publications/detail/sp/800-61/rev-2/final

Data Security, DLP, Identity, and Cloud Security

Microsoft. Microsoft Purview Documentation. Microsoft.

Used as supporting context for data classification, sensitivity labels, information protection, DLP, retention, eDiscovery, insider risk, Microsoft 365 data governance, and platform-native controls.

https://learn.microsoft.com/en-us/purview/

Microsoft. Learn about Data Loss Prevention. Microsoft Purview Documentation.

Used as supporting context for Microsoft Purview DLP concepts, policy design, locations, monitoring, and enforcement behavior.

https://learn.microsoft.com/en-us/purview/dlp-learn-about-dlp

Google. Google Workspace Admin Help: Data Loss Prevention and Data Protection Documentation. Google.

Used as supporting context for SaaS data controls, collaboration security, DLP policies, file sharing governance, and cloud productivity platform data protection.

https://support.google.com/a/topic/7556687

Box. Box Governance, Shield, and Data Protection Documentation. Box.

Used as supporting context for collaboration data security, content governance, retention, legal hold, classification, threat detection, and data protection in SaaS repositories.

https://support.box.com/hc/en-us/categories/360004526374-Box-Governance

https://support.box.com/hc/en-us/categories/360004526394-Box-Shield

Snowflake. Security, Access Control, and Data Governance Documentation. Snowflake.

Used as supporting context for cloud data warehouse access control, role-based access, data governance, logging, masking, tagging, and data-sharing risk.

https://docs.snowflake.com/en/user-guide/security

https://docs.snowflake.com/en/user-guide/security-access-control-overview

Google Cloud Mandiant. UNC5537 Targets Snowflake Customer Instances for Data Theft and Extortion. Google Cloud/Mandiant, 2024.

Used to support discussion of valid credential abuse, cloud data warehouse exfiltration, MFA gaps, access monitoring, and the limits of traditional SaaS and cloud controls. Incident facts should be cited locally when summarized.

https://cloud.google.com/blog/topics/threat-intelligence/unc5537-snowflake-data-theft-extortion

Incident and Enforcement References

Office of the Privacy Commissioner of Canada. Investigation into Desjardins Data Breach. OPC.

Used to support discussion of insider risk, partial DLP deployment, excessive access, monitoring limitations, and long-running data exfiltration.

https://www.priv.gc.ca/en/opc-actions-and-decisions/investigations/investigations-into-businesses/2020/pipeda-2020-005/

U.S. Government Accountability Office. Equifax Data Breach Report. GAO.

Used to support discussion of vulnerability management, data governance, database segmentation, detection, and failure to protect large volumes of sensitive personal information.

https://www.gao.gov/products/gao-18-559

Federal Trade Commission. Marriott and Starwood Data Security Enforcement Materials. FTC.

Used to support discussion of long-running compromise, encryption gaps, access controls, segmentation, monitoring, MFA, and protection of customer records.

https://www.ftc.gov/legal-library/browse/cases-proceedings/marriott-international-inc-starwood-hotels-resorts-worldwide-llc

Office of the Comptroller of the Currency. Capital One Enforcement Action and Cloud Risk Management Findings. OCC.

Used to support discussion of cloud security, risk assessment, DLP gaps, alerting, configuration weakness, and cloud data exposure.

https://www.occ.gov/news-issuances/news-releases/2020/nr-occ-2020-101.html

AI Incident Database. Incident 473: Bing Chat's Initial Prompts Revealed by Early Testers Through Prompt Injection. AI Incident Database.

Used to support discussion of prompt injection, hidden system instructions, and the governance lesson that AI systems may expose operational instructions or sensitive context if prompt and output controls are weak.

https://incidentdatabase.ai/cite/473/

AI Incident Database. Incident 622: Chevrolet Dealer Chatbot Agrees to Sell Tahoe for $1. AI Incident Database.

Used to support discussion of prompt manipulation, customer-facing chatbot risk, brand risk, and the need for guardrails and human oversight. The book should avoid stating that the vehicle was actually sold unless supported by a primary source.

https://incidentdatabase.ai/cite/622/

Moffatt v. Air Canada, 2024 BCCRT 149, and related legal analysis.

Used to support discussion of chatbot representations, customer reliance, and business liability for inaccurate AI-generated customer-facing information. Legal summaries should use measured wording and avoid overstating the holding.

https://www.mccarthy.ca/en/insights/blogs/techlex/moffatt-v-air-canada-misrepresentation-ai-chatbot

https://www.americanbar.org/groups/business_law/resources/business-law-today/2024-february/bc-tribunal-confirms-companies-remain-liable-information-provided-ai-chatbot/

Open-Source, Governance, and Data Cataloging References

Apache Software Foundation. Apache Atlas Documentation.

Used as supporting context for open-source metadata management, data cataloging, lineage, classification, and governance foundations.

https://atlas.apache.org/

OpenMetadata. OpenMetadata Documentation.

Used as supporting context for open-source data discovery, metadata management, data lineage, collaboration, and governance foundations.

https://docs.open-metadata.org/

DataHub Project. DataHub Documentation.

Used as supporting context for metadata platforms, data cataloging, lineage, ownership, discovery, and governance workflows.

https://datahubproject.io/docs/

OpenDLP Project. OpenDLP Documentation and Historical Materials.

Used as historical context for open-source data discovery and legacy DLP/classification approaches.

https://code.google.com/archive/p/opendlp/

Vendor and Product Documentation Used for Context

Vendor and product documentation may have been used for contextual understanding of tool capabilities, but references to products in this book are informational only and do not imply endorsement. Product features, licensing, integrations, branding, technical capabilities, and availability change frequently, so readers should validate current functionality directly with the vendor.

Relevant vendor categories include:

- DSPM platforms
- DLP platforms
- CNAPP platforms
- CASB and SSE platforms
- Data catalogs
- Privacy operations platforms
- Identity governance platforms
- Backup and cyber recovery platforms
- SaaS collaboration security tools
- AI-native data security platforms
- Cloud provider native security and governance tools

For adversarial source hygiene, vendor capability tables should be worded as evaluation areas rather than definitive product claims unless the statement is supported by a current vendor source. A safe phrasing pattern is: "Capability areas commonly evaluated include..." or "As of the publication date, vendor documentation described support for...".

Author's Professional Experience

This book also draws from the author's professional experience in cybersecurity architecture, penetration testing brokerage, data security health assessments, DSPM program design, incident response planning, risk advisory work, identity and access governance, DLP modernization, privacy/security collaboration, and executive security communication.

Vocabulary

Term	Explanation
ABAC	Attribute-Based Access Control. Access decisions use attributes such as department, location, device, data sensitivity, time, or risk level. Useful for more dynamic, data-centric access control.
Access governance	The process of reviewing, approving, certifying, and removing access to data and systems. DSPM strengthens access governance by showing which access matters most based on data sensitivity and exposure.
Access review	A formal process for checking whether users, groups, service accounts, applications, or third parties still need access to specific systems or data.
Agentic AI	AI systems that can take actions, call tools, interact with APIs, use memory, complete tasks, or orchestrate workflows with some level of autonomy. Agentic AI increases data risk because it may not only retrieve information, but also move, modify, send, approve, or act on it.
Aggregation	Combining individual-level data into group-level summaries so trends can be analyzed without exposing specific people or records.
AI connector	An integration that allows an AI system, copilot, agent, or assistant to access enterprise data from repositories, SaaS platforms, databases, APIs, or collaboration tools.
AI data risk	Risk created when sensitive, proprietary, or regulated data is used in AI tools, prompts, embeddings, training sets, or model workflows. DSPM helps identify where AI-relevant sensitive data exists and how it is exposed.
AI inherited permissions	Permissions an AI tool, copilot, connector, agent, or automation workflow receives from a user, service account, OAuth grant, SaaS role, or application identity. This matters because AI can expose, summarize, or act on data that was already overpermissioned before AI was introduced.
AI readiness	The state of data, access, ownership, classification, retention, and governance being mature enough to safely connect data to AI systems.
Alert fatigue	A condition where too many alerts, findings, or low-value notifications cause teams to miss or ignore meaningful risk.
Anonymization	Privacy technique where identifying information is removed or changed so the data can no longer be reasonably linked back to a specific person. Removes or transforms identity so it should not be reasonably recoverable.
API	Application Programming Interface. A way for systems, applications, services, or AI tools to exchange data or trigger actions.
Approved use	A formally allowed business purpose for collecting, accessing, processing, sharing, retaining, or using data. Approved use is different from technical access. A person or system may be able to access data, but that does not automatically mean the data may be used for a new purpose, AI workflow, analytics model, vendor process, or monetization activity.
Attack surface	All the places an attacker could exploit to gain access to systems, identities, applications, or data.
Audit evidence	Documentation, logs, reports, approvals, screenshots, tickets, or records used to prove that a control operated or a decision was made.

Blast radius	The potential scope of damage if a user, account, system, or repository is compromised. DSPM helps estimate breach impact by showing how much sensitive data could be reached.
Business context	Information about why data matters, who owns it, what process it supports, and how damaging exposure would be. DSPM findings are stronger when technical risk is tied to business impact.
CASB	Cloud Access Security Broker. A security control category used to monitor, govern, and protect the use of cloud and SaaS applications.
CIEM	Cloud Infrastructure Entitlement Management. Analyzes cloud identities, permissions, roles, privilege paths, and excessive access. DSPM adds data sensitivity context to entitlement risk.
Cloud data risk	Risk tied to sensitive data stored in cloud services such as object storage, databases, data lakes, warehouses, snapshots, and backups.
CNAPP	Cloud Native Application Protection Platform. Broad cloud security category covering cloud posture, workloads, identities, containers, IaC, vulnerabilities, and runtime risk. DSPM adds data sensitivity and exposure context.
Compensating control	An alternate control used to reduce risk when the preferred or required control cannot be implemented immediately.
Consent	Permission from an individual to collect, use, share, or process their personal data for a specific purpose. Consent requirements vary by law and context.
Credentials	Information used to authenticate a user, system, or service, such as passwords, API keys, tokens, certificates, or secrets.
Crown jewel data	The most valuable or mission-critical data in the organization. This may include customer data, financial records, regulated data, intellectual property, or operational data.
CSPM	Cloud Security Posture Management. Identifies cloud misconfigurations, insecure storage, exposed services, weak network settings, and risky cloud configurations. DSPM adds whether sensitive data is involved.
DAM	Database Activity Monitoring. Monitors database activity, queries, privileged access, and suspicious database behavior. DAM is database-specific, while DSPM looks across broader data stores.
Dark data	Data the organization stores but does not actively use, understand, classify, or manage. Dark data increases risk and cost while offering little business value.
Data asset	Any meaningful collection of data, such as a database, table, bucket, file share, SaaS repository, data lake, warehouse, or folder.
Data attack surface	All locations, access paths, identities, exposures, misconfigurations, and workflows through which sensitive data could be accessed or misused.
Data catalog	A business and analytics inventory of data assets, often including metadata, lineage, owners, glossary terms, schemas, and usage context. DSPM focuses more on sensitivity, access, exposure, and risk.
Data classification	The process of identifying data type, sensitivity, business value, regulatory relevance, and handling requirements. Foundational to DSPM.
Data custodian	The IT or technical team responsible for storing, operating, backing up, and securing data systems. Custodians often execute DSPM remediation tasks.
Data flow	The movement of data between systems, applications, users, SaaS platforms, cloud environments, APIs, and third parties.

Data governance	Policies, roles, ownership, stewardship, quality rules, lifecycle decisions, and accountability model for data. Governance defines the rules; DSPM helps validate and operationalize them.
Data inventory	A structured record of data assets, locations, repositories, owners, sensitivity, business purpose, and related governance information.
Data labeling	Applying labels or tags such as Public, Internal, Confidential, Restricted, PII, PHI, PCI, or Legal Hold. Labels can drive access, DLP, retention, and governance workflows.
Data lineage	A record of where data came from, how it moved, how it changed, and where it is consumed. Useful for understanding downstream risk and business impact.
Data minimization	Collecting, storing, and retaining only the data needed for a legitimate business purpose. A strong way to reduce data risk.
Data owner	The business person accountable for a dataset's purpose, acceptable use, access decisions, and lifecycle.
Data posture	The current security state of data based on sensitivity, location, access, exposure, encryption, ownership, retention, and policy compliance.
Data processor	A party that processes personal data on behalf of another organization according to instructions, contracts, or applicable legal requirements.
Data protection by design	The practice of building privacy and security controls into systems, workflows, and data processes from the beginning instead of adding them after deployment.
Data repository	A location where data is stored, such as S3, Azure Blob, Google Cloud Storage, Snowflake, Databricks, SharePoint, Google Drive, OneDrive, databases, or file shares.
Data risk score	A calculated risk rating based on sensitivity, exposure, access, business criticality, compliance relevance, and threat context.
Data sovereignty	The legal, regulatory, contractual, and operational requirements that govern where data is stored, processed, accessed, transferred, indexed, logged, or used. In the AI era, sovereignty applies not only to primary data storage, but also to prompts, outputs, embeddings, vector stores, AI logs, telemetry, support access, and vendor processing locations.
Data steward	A person responsible for day-to-day data quality, metadata, classification, and proper handling. Stewards can help validate DSPM findings.
Data subject	The person whose personal data is being collected, stored, processed, shared, protected, or deleted.
Database security	Controls for protecting databases, including access control, encryption, masking, auditing, patching, monitoring, backup, and activity analysis.
DDR	Data Detection and Response. The monitoring and response layer of data security focused on detecting risky data behavior, unusual access, suspicious movement, misuse, exposure, or potential exfiltration, and helping teams respond quickly.
De-identification	A broad privacy technique used to reduce or remove the ability to connect data back to a specific person. De-identification may include anonymization, pseudonymization, masking, aggregation, suppression, or generalization.
Derived data	New information created from existing data, such as summaries, embeddings, analytics outputs, AI-generated content, classifications, inferences, or transformed datasets.
DLP	Data Loss Prevention. Enforces policies that block, alert, quarantine, encrypt, or restrict risky data movement through email, endpoint, web, cloud, or SaaS channels.
DPIA	Data Protection Impact Assessment. A privacy risk assessment for processing activities that may create higher risk to individuals. DSPM can provide evidence about sensitivity, access, and exposure.

DSPM	Data Security Posture Management. A set of capabilities and practices used to discover where sensitive data lives, classify it, map access and exposure, identify risky posture, and prioritize remediation across cloud, SaaS, databases, data stores, and AI-connected environments.
Effective access	The access an identity actually has after direct permissions, inherited permissions, nested groups, shared links, SaaS roles, service accounts, OAuth grants, privileged roles, and AI inherited permissions are resolved. Effective access is more useful than simply asking who appears to have direct access.
Embeddings	Mathematical representations of data used by AI systems to compare meaning, similarity, and context. Embeddings may not look like the original record, but they can still carry sensitive meaning, support inference, or enable retrieval of protected information.
Encryption	Protecting data by converting it into unreadable form unless the right key is available. Important, but it does not solve excessive access or public exposure by itself.
Excessive access	Access that is broader than necessary, outdated, inherited, unused, or inconsistent with job function. One of the most common DSPM risks.
False positive	A finding that appears to indicate risk but, after validation, does not represent an actual issue or does not require remediation.
GRC	Governance, Risk, and Compliance. A category of processes and tools used to manage policies, risks, controls, evidence, audits, and compliance obligations.
IAM	Identity and Access Management. Controls authentication, authorization, roles, policies, groups, and permissions. DSPM evaluates whether access creates data risk.
IGA	Identity Governance and Administration. Manages identity lifecycle, access requests, access reviews, certifications, and segregation of duties. DSPM adds data sensitivity context.
Inference	A conclusion, prediction, or assumption generated from data, even when the original data did not directly state that conclusion.
Intellectual property	Business-sensitive information such as source code, formulas, designs, strategies, research, product plans, and trade secrets.
Lawful basis	The legal reason an organization relies on to process personal data. Examples may include consent, contract, legal obligation, legitimate interest, or other recognized bases depending on the applicable law.
Least privilege	Giving users, groups, applications, and service accounts only the access required to perform their job. A core DSPM remediation theme.
Legal hold	A requirement to preserve specific data because of litigation, investigation, audit, or regulatory need. DSPM remediation must account for legal hold before deletion or archival.
Masking	Hiding or obfuscating sensitive data, often in non-production, analytics, support, or testing environments.
Metadata	Data about data, such as file name, owner, location, creation date, schema, tags, classification, lineage, usage, or retention status.
Model output	Content produced by an AI model, such as text, code, summaries, classifications, recommendations, images, or decisions.
Non-human identity, or NHI	An identity used by machines, applications, workloads, services, APIs, automations, or AI agents rather than by a human user.
Non-production data risk	Sensitive production data copied into development, testing, staging, training, or analytics environments. Often overlooked and over-permissioned.

OAuth app grant	Permission given to an application to access data or perform actions on behalf of a user or organization. OAuth grants can create risk when they are broad, stale, or poorly reviewed.
Orphaned data	Data with no clear owner, abandoned project, disabled user, legacy system, or unclear business purpose.
Overexposed data	Sensitive data that too many users, identities, groups, public links, third parties, or services can access.
PCI / CHD	Payment Card Industry / Cardholder Data. Data such as primary account numbers, cardholder names, expiration dates, and security codes.
Personal data	Information that relates to an identified or identifiable person, either directly or when combined with other information.
PHI	Protected Health Information. Health-related identifiable information protected under healthcare privacy and security rules.
PII	Personally Identifiable Information. Data that can identify, contact, locate, or distinguish a person, either alone or combined with other data.
Policy enforcement	Applying rules that control who can access data, where it can live, how long it can be retained, and how it can move.
Privacy platform	Tooling for privacy operations such as RoPA, DSAR, consent, DPIA, retention, lawful basis, and regulatory privacy workflows.
Privileged access	Elevated access that allows a user, administrator, service account, or system to perform sensitive actions or access high-value data.
Prompt injection	An attack or misuse pattern where instructions are crafted to manipulate an AI system into ignoring rules, revealing sensitive information, using unauthorized tools, or performing unintended actions. Prompt injection can be direct, through user input, or indirect, through retrieved documents, emails, web pages, tickets, or other content.
Prompt logs	Records of prompts, responses, metadata, user activity, and system interactions created when people or systems use AI tools. Prompt logs may contain sensitive or regulated data.
Pseudonymization	Privacy technique where identifying information is replaced with a substitute value, such as a code, token, or alias, so the data can no longer be directly tied to a person without additional information. Identity is masked but can be restored with additional information.
Public exposure	Data accessible from the internet, through public buckets, anonymous links, open shares, or misconfigured permissions.
Purpose limitation	A privacy principle that data should only be collected, used, shared, or retained for specific, approved, and legitimate purposes.
RAG	Retrieval-Augmented Generation. An AI architecture pattern where a system retrieves relevant information from enterprise or external data sources and uses that context to generate an answer. RAG can improve accuracy and business relevance, but it also creates risk if retrieval is not permission-aware, classification-aware, logged, and governed.
RBAC	Role-Based Access Control. Access is assigned based on roles such as HR Manager, DBA, Analyst, or Developer. Useful, but risky when roles become too broad or outdated.
Redaction	The removal or obscuring of sensitive information from a document, record, image, or dataset before it is shared, retained, published, or used for another purpose.
Regulated data	Data protected by legal, contractual, or industry rules such as HIPAA, GDPR, CCPA/CPRA, PCI DSS, GLBA, SOX, or state breach laws.

Re-identification	The process of linking de-identified, anonymized, or pseudonymized data back to a specific person, often by combining it with other data sources.
Remediation	The action taken to reduce risk, such as removing public access, deleting ROT data, changing permissions, encrypting data, assigning ownership, or opening a ticket.
Residual risk	The risk that remains after controls, remediation, compensating measures, or governance decisions have been applied. Residual risk should be visible, owned, reviewed, and either accepted, mitigated, transferred, deferred, or escalated.
Retention	Rules defining how long data should be kept before deletion, archival, or legal hold. Poor retention creates ROT, dark data, and unnecessary breach exposure.
Right to know / DSAR	Privacy workflows where individuals request access to, deletion of, or details about their personal data. Accurate discovery helps privacy teams respond confidently.
Risk acceptance	A documented decision to accept a known risk instead of remediating it immediately, usually with a business owner, reason, timeframe, and review date.
RoPA	Record of Processing Activities. A privacy inventory documenting how personal data is collected, used, shared, retained, and protected.
ROT data	Redundant, Obsolete, or Trivial data. Data that no longer has clear business value but still creates cost, exposure, compliance, and breach risk.
SaaS data risk	Risk created by sensitive data stored in platforms such as Microsoft 365, Google Workspace, Salesforce, ServiceNow, Slack, Box, GitHub, or similar SaaS tools.
Secrets	Credentials or authentication material such as API keys, tokens, passwords, certificates, private keys, and service account credentials.
Semi-structured data	Data with some organization but not a rigid table structure, such as JSON, XML, logs, and NoSQL records.
Sensitive data	Data that could create harm if exposed, misused, altered, or accessed by the wrong person. Examples include PII, PHI, PCI data, credentials, IP, legal records, and financial data.
Service account	A non-person account used by an application, system, integration, script, automation, or service to access data or perform tasks.
Shadow AI	The use of AI tools, copilots, browser-based assistants, plugins, or automation services without formal approval, governance, or security review.
Shadow data	Data that exists outside approved, documented, or governed systems. Dangerous because security teams often do not know it exists.
SIEM	Security Information and Event Management. A platform used to collect, correlate, analyze, and alert on security logs and events.
SOAR	Security Orchestration, Automation, and Response. Technology used to automate security workflows, enrichment, ticketing, and response actions.
SSE	Security Service Edge. A cloud-delivered security architecture that commonly includes secure web gateway, CASB, zero trust access, and data protection capabilities.
Stale data	Data that has not been accessed, updated, or used for a long period of time. Stale sensitive data is a strong candidate for archival, deletion, or access reduction.
Structured data	Data organized in rows, columns, schemas, or tables, commonly found in relational databases and warehouses.
Subprocessor	A third party used by a data processor to help process personal data. Subprocessors can create additional privacy, contractual, and security oversight requirements.
Third-party data exposure	Sensitive data shared with vendors, partners, contractors, processors, or external collaborators.

Tokenization	Replacing sensitive values with non-sensitive tokens that can be mapped back under controlled conditions.
Toxic combination	A high-risk combination of conditions that becomes more dangerous together than each condition would be alone. Examples include sensitive data plus public exposure, regulated data plus excessive access, stale data plus no owner, or confidential data plus AI inherited permissions.
Training data	Data used to train, fine-tune, evaluate, or improve an AI model. Training data can create privacy, security, ownership, and retention risk if not governed properly.
Unstructured data	Data without a fixed schema, such as documents, PDFs, spreadsheets, images, presentations, chats, and emails. Often messy, duplicated, overexposed, and hard to govern.
VAR	Value Added Reseller. A partner that helps customers evaluate, purchase, implement, integrate, or support technology solutions.
Vector database	A database designed to store and search vector embeddings. Vector databases are commonly used in AI and RAG systems to retrieve semantically similar content. They should be protected because embeddings, chunks, metadata, and retrieval results may reveal sensitive or regulated information.

Index

Key terms and primary references. Page numbers refer to the printed pagination in this formatted edition. Cross-references are included for common acronyms, alternate terms, and related concepts.

About the Author

Heather Case-Hall is a cybersecurity strategist, Army veteran, former CISO, speaker, mentor, builder, and self-described "cybersecurity therapist" with nearly three decades of experience helping organizations protect what matters most: their data, their people, and their ability to keep going when things get hard.

Her career did not begin in a polished corporate security program. It began in the practical, messy, high-stakes world of military communications and IT operations. Heather shipped to basic training just days after her eighteenth birthday, eventually serving on active duty and later in the Nevada Army National Guard. What started as a path to the GI Bill became the foundation for a lifelong career in technology, leadership, and security.

In the Army, Heather learned early that communications are only valuable when they are reliable, protected, and understood under pressure. She served across signal, communications, information assurance, and cyber defense roles, eventually retiring as a Chief Warrant Officer 3 and leader of the Nevada Army National Guard Computer Network Defense Team. She worked across secure communications, incident response, forensics, vulnerability management, identity, SIEM, and cyber operations long before many of those areas became boardroom topics.

Heather's transition into cybersecurity was anything but traditional. While serving in the military, she was sent to a CISSP course on only a few days' notice. She passed, and that moment changed the direction of her career. She became one of the early Army-trained cybersecurity specialists and one of the first women in the National Guard to pass the required Army cyber certifications on her first attempt. That experience shaped how she still approaches security today: prepare quickly, learn deeply, adapt constantly, and never underestimate the person who was not supposed to be in the room.

Outside the military, Heather built her career from the ground up. She started in casino IT, printing checks, fixing systems, supporting executives, and learning how technology behaves when real people depend on it. She later held roles as a computer specialist, programmer, information assurance manager, database administrator, senior system administrator, SIEM programmer, director of operations, director of IT and security, information security program manager, CISO, demand and delivery leader, and senior cybersecurity solutions architect.

That range matters. Heather has not only advised security programs from the outside. She has lived inside them. She has owned the pager, managed the incident, handled the audit, built the team, trained the users, fought for the budget, explained risk to executives, and carried the weight of decisions that had real business consequences.

As a former CISO, Heather led security, compliance, awareness, and data protection work in an environment where uptime, trust, regulation, and human behavior all collided. She later advised Fortune 100 and enterprise clients through roles at organizations including a private wealth family, Koch, EMPLOYERS, Optiv, and Myriad360. Her work has spanned military, government, hospitality, gaming, insurance, consulting, and technology services environments.

Today, Heather serves as a Senior Cybersecurity Solutions Architect at Myriad360, where she works at the intersection of security strategy, client advisory, data protection, penetration testing, AI enablement, and practical risk reduction. She created Penetration Testing 360, a brokerage model designed to help organizations move beyond checkbox penetration testing and toward a more strategic, risk-informed offensive security capability. She also helped build the Data Security Health Assessment program, focused on helping organizations understand where sensitive data lives, who can access it, how it is exposed, and what should be fixed first.

Heather is known for translating complex cyber risk into language people can actually use. She has a gift for taking a messy security problem, untangling the technical, emotional, operational, and political pieces, and helping people make better decisions without making them feel small. That is where the "cybersecurity therapist" label comes from. Not because security is soft, but because the hardest moments in cybersecurity require trust, calm, honesty, and the ability to help people think clearly when everything feels urgent.

She is also a mentor and speaker who cares deeply about helping others find their place in cybersecurity, especially those who did not follow a traditional path. Heather speaks with the kind of honesty that makes people lean in. She talks about technical risk, career resilience, leadership, imposter syndrome, burnout, mentorship, and what it means to stay human in an industry that often rewards jargon more than judgment.

Heather is also the owner and creator of Gloria's Pottery Barn, a creative business that reflects another side of who she is: an artist, maker, storyteller, and builder of things that feel personal and lasting. For Heather, creativity and cybersecurity are not opposites. Both require patience, curiosity, pattern recognition, problem-solving, and the willingness to shape something useful from uncertainty.

Most importantly, Heather is a mother of three: a son and identical twin daughters. Motherhood has shaped her leadership, resilience, humor, and sense of purpose as much as any title or certification ever could. It has taught her how to manage chaos, listen closely, advocate fiercely, and keep showing up even when the work is hard. Those lessons show up in the way she leads, mentors, writes, and helps organizations through difficult security decisions.

Heather holds a master's degree in Cybersecurity and Information Assurance, a Bachelor of Science in Information Technology, and a long list of industry certifications, including CISSP, GCFA, GCIA, GCIH, GPEN, GSEC, GCSA, CHFI, CNDA, ITIL 4, and others. Her background includes work across ISO 27001, PCI-DSS, FedRAMP, CMMC, cloud security, incident response, governance, risk, compliance, identity, vulnerability management, disaster recovery, DLP, DSPM, and AI-era data security.

At her core, Heather is a builder. She builds programs, frameworks, teams, relationships, language, confidence, and community. She helps organizations see security not as a pile of tools, but as a living system of people, data, decisions, behavior, and trust.

And in a field that can sometimes feel cold, abstract, and unforgiving, Heather brings something rare: technical credibility, emotional intelligence, humor, courage, creativity, and a deep human voice.

www.ingramcontent.com/pod-product-compliance
Ingram Content Group UK Ltd.
Pitfield, Milton Keynes, MK11 3LW, UK
UKHW051117290926
15471UKWH00010B/1725

9 798996 263806